POLICY DEVELOPMENT AND NEGOTIATIONS IN INTERNATIONAL TRADE

A Practical Guide to Effective Commercial Diplomacy

GEZA FEKETEKUTY, ED.

Institute for Trade and Commercial Diplomacy

ISBN: 1477502564
ISBN-13: 9781477502563

CONTENTS

PREFACE

This textbook covers the skills required by practicing professionals involved in the development of government policies affecting trade and the negotiation of international trade agreements. The range of activities involved in the development of policies affecting trade and the negotiation of trade agreements can be encompassed by the term Commercial Diplomacy. Effective Commercial Diplomacy requires a unique set of skills and knowledge not normally taught on an integrated basis by traditional educational institutions, hence the need for a book such as this. It requires basic analytical skills in micro and macro economics, politics, domestic and international law, public relations, and a wide range of domestic policies. It also requires effective oral and written communication and negotiation skills.

Practicing professionals in Commercial Diplomacy include not only the government officials involved in the development of trade policies and the negotiation of trade agreements, but also the representatives of businesses and nonprofit organizations that seek to influence the development of trade policies and negotiation of trade agreements. Any organization affected by the trade policy actions or negotiations of its own government or by foreign governments has to be able to interact effectively with the governments involved, and to do that effectively it needs professionals that have the same set of skills and knowledge as the government officials involved. An effective professional in this field has to have the ability to analyze the commercial, macroeconomic, policy-related, political, and legal aspects of any trade or investment issue, and to communicate and negotiate effectively with domestic and foreign stakeholders and governments.

This book leads readers through the steps an accomplished professional in Commercial Diplomacy must follow in advancing the interests of the organization he/she represents in trade policy decisions, trade negotiations, and the settlement of trade disputes. It covers:

- ▸ The analytical skills and research methods required for an in-depth understanding of policy issues that affect international business and investment;

- ▶ The communication and consensus-building skills required for influencing national trade policy decisions and negotiating positions; and

- ▶ The negotiating and dispute settlement skills required for the development of international agreements and the resolution of international disputes.

The book is organized into five sections:

- ▶ **Section I** covers the basic elements of Commercial Diplomacy.

- ▶ **Section II** covers the basic analytical tools required for understanding the policy implications of a particular trade issue, the range of options available to policy makers and negotiators, and the political process leading to a decision on the issue by the policy makers involved. The chapters are designed to give the practitioner a basic grasp of the analytical tools and methods involved, but not to substitute for the more in-depth training required of a professional economist, lawyer, or political analyst. Practitioners of Commercial Diplomacy need to be able to carry out some rudimentary analysis of their own and to understand the results of more in-depth analysis carried out by professionals in the requisite field, but will inevitably have to consult with more fully trained professionals for a more in-depth professional analysis.

- ▶ **Section III** covers three forms of communication that a Commercial Diplomat typically uses to persuade others in the process of building consensus at home or in negotiating with foreign governments. The chapters offer skills for effective writing, speaking, and data presentation, all of which are necessary for a Commercial Diplomat to convey the essence of the most important factors driving an issue.

- ▶ **Section IV** covers the consensus-building skills required for influencing stakeholders and decision makers and managing the policy development process.

- ▶ **Section V** covers the negotiating skills required for the development of agreements with governments and between governments.

Many individuals have contributed to the content of this book. Each of the chapters is based on individual training manuals that were coauthored by a number of different experts in the field. They are Laura Anderson, Eve Connell, Fernando De Paolis, Jane Earley, Leslie Eliason, Sara Givens, Robert McCleery, William Monning, Colleen Morton, Andrew Procassini, Moyara Ruehsen, Jill Stoffers, and Irving Williamson. Their individual contributions are acknowledged in the footnotes of each chapter. I want to thank them profoundly for their contributions. In addition to these coauthors, a number of other individuals contributed to this book In particular I want to thank Suzi Slomback for her contributions in editing and formatting the text, and doing much of the fact checking. I also want to thank Alan Wolff, the Chairman and Cofounder of ITCD, who supported this effort by helping to found the Institute and by his helpful comments on the text, in particular the Legal chapter. Finally, I want to thank all my former colleagues in the US and foreign trade policy community who gave me the insights into the trade policy and trade negotiating craft reflected in my contributions to this book

SECTION I

UNDERSTANDING COMMERCIAL DIPLOMACY

Chapter 1

INTRODUCTION TO COMMERCIAL DIPLOMACY

By: Geza Feketekuty[1]

WHAT IS COMMERCIAL DIPLOMACY?

Commercial Diplomacy (CD) is diplomacy with a commercial twist – diplomacy designed to influence foreign government policy and regulatory decisions that affect global trade and investment.

Commercial Diplomacy involves the application of advocacy tools to government policies that affect international commerce. Since government policy is the province of government officials and international commerce is the province of business managers, the dialogue between the two is at the heart of Commercial Diplomacy. Sound management of the relationship between government and business is crucial to good trade policy.

In recent years there has been a growing awareness that trade decisions also affect broader interests of society in areas such as health, the environment, and labor standards. This noneconomic dimension of trade policy has grown progressively as the trade agenda has expanded from barriers at the border, such as tariffs and quotas, to domestic regulatory measures, such as environmental and health measures. These broader interests of society are often represented by public interest groups that have increasingly demanded a role in the trade policy decision making process in their own countries, as well as globally. Beyond government and business, Commercial Diplomacy therefore involves nongovernmental organizations (NGOs) that represent the interests of citizens as workers, as consumers, and as supporters of social objectives such as a clean environment and a safe community.

---

1 The content of this chapter is substantially taken from the original training manual entitled *Professionalizing Training in Commercial Diplomacy and Building an Institutional Training Capacity in Disadvantaged Countries* authored by Geza Feketekuty, which is available on the ITCD website, www.commercialdiplomacy.org.

A study of Commercial Diplomacy focuses on how these three groups (government, business, and NGOs) in society can manage their relationships with each other as part of the trade policy decision-making process, and how Commercial Diplomats working for any government, business, or public interest group can seek to influence the attitudes, objectives, and actions of decision makers in all three sectors and thereby achieve desired policy outcomes. A key to effective management of the relationships involved is a basic understanding of the different roles, values, motivations, and objectives of actors in each of the three sectors. Effective advocacy has to be based on a sound understanding of potential partners or opponents. Achieving such an understanding is particularly challenging when it involves actors whose role and frame of reference is different than one's own.

There are considerable differences in how countries around the world organize their government, their economic enterprises, and civil society. These differences affect how much independence business and public interest groups have from the government, and conversely how much political influence either business or public interest groups can exert in trade policy decisions. Notwithstanding these differences, there are many similarities in the fundamental roles of business, government, and public interest groups in most countries, regardless of their economic and political organization. This similarity arises from the distinct roles played by each of these three social actors, which defines their basic objectives, motivations, and values.

THE COMMERCIAL DIPLOMAT

The Commercial Diplomat is a professional skilled in advancing the interests of an organization on international trade and investment-related policy issues, in developing agreements on international commercial issues, and in resolving policy conflicts among nations over commercial issues. Commercial diplomats can act as representatives of business, government, or civil society. Practitioners of many professions— lawyers, economists, political analysts, accountants— become involved in some aspects of Commercial Diplomacy, but what distinguishes the practice of Commercial Diplomacy is the integration of knowledge and skills from many different professional disciplines to address policy issues that affect international commerce.

Although Commercial Diplomacy activity has existed from the earliest time of trade, only in the last ten years has it been recognized that this field requires professionals who have received education and training specific to the field. Prior to this time, Commercial Diplomats received training in many different academic disciplines and acquired the knowledge and skills required for the effective practice of Commercial Diplomacy on the job. Today, however, professional training focused on the requirements of Commercial Diplomacy is finally being developed. In fact, the policy process works best when all three sectors deploy representatives into the field with good Commercial Diplomacy skills.

In the highly interdependent world we live in today, the policy issues subject to trade negotiations are often very complex and touch on a myriad of domestic policy issues, legal provisions, institutional issues, and political interests. The first step for the Commercial Diplomat is to undertake an in-depth analysis of all the issues that could be raised during the policy decision-making process at home and abroad. It requires an in-depth analysis of all the dimensions of an issue:

- The commercial interests at stake,

- The macro-economic impact of alternative policy options,

- The objectives of all possible stakeholders and their ability to exert political influence,

- The domestic policy issues entwined with the trade issue,

- The applicable domestic and international legal provisions, and

- The impact of media coverage on public opinion.

The Commercial Diplomat deals with political decision making; therefore, Commercial Diplomacy is all about exercising political influence. In fact, issues related to the access of foreigners to domestic markets, their right to buy domestic assets such as land and businesses, and their qualification to provide a wide range of services are often even more political than purely domestic regulation by governments. Commercial Diplomacy thus usually requires a heavy dose of domestic political activity, both at home and in the foreign country – including the active use of a wide range of advocacy and coalition-building tools.

At home, the Commercial Diplomat must utilize the full range of political advocacy tools and techniques to assure support of the home government for desired outcomes abroad, or to obtain favorable policy actions by the home government in areas such as taxation, export credits, and export controls. To obtain governmental decisions favorable to the stakeholders he/she represents, the Commercial Diplomat must be able to make effective use of advocacy tools such as letters, testimony, white papers, speeches, op-ed pieces in newspapers, phone calls, and personal visits to key stakeholders and decision makers. The Commercial Diplomat must also be successful in building coalitions within the organization he/she represents – within the government, industry or interest group, and among stakeholders with similar interests – thus increasing the political influence that is brought to bear in support of the desired outcome. The international phase of Commercial Diplomacy involves the same advocacy and coalition-building steps required at home, as part of a process of building support for negotiations or the settlement of a dispute.

What Does the Commercial Diplomat Need to Know?

Commercial Diplomacy requires all the finesse and knowledge of traditional diplomacy. In addition, it requires a familiarity with commercial and macroeconomic analysis, the analysis of policy issues ranging from health and the environment to the prudential supervision of insurance, the politics of trade and foreign investment, national trade laws and global trade rules, and the role of the media in forming public opinion.

A Commercial Diplomat must learn how to analyze all the factors that have a bearing on the policy decision-making process at home and abroad, including an in-depth analysis of:

▶ The commercial interests at stake,

▶ The macro-economic impact of alternative policy options,

▶ The political influence of all the stakeholders with commercial, policy-oriented, or institutional interests,

▶ The domestic policy issues that may be entwined with the foreign trade issue,

▶ The applicable domestic and international legal provisions, and

▶ The state of public opinion, including the impact of media coverage.

Most issues addressed by Commercial Diplomacy today are political since they concern issues that are the subject of domestic political debate and they affect the interests of many stakeholders who are capable of influencing the outcome through a political process. A stakeholder is anyone who has an interest or stake in the outcome of a trade policy decision and who can exercise political influence of one kind or another to shape the outcome. Stakeholders in trade policy decisions can include:

▶ Officials of any government department or regulatory agency with a policy interest or a bureaucratic stake;

▶ Any firm, union, or industry association with a commercial stake;

▶ Any nongovernmental organization with a policy or organizational stake in the outcome; and

▶ Individual citizens as voters.

The increased focus on domestic regulatory issues in trade negotiations has substantially increased the potential pool of stakeholders and thus expanded the role of domestic politics in Commercial Diplomacy.

Commercial Diplomacy increasingly requires the use of a wide range of advocacy and coalition-building tools in pursuit of favorable decisions at home and abroad. To obtain the support of the home government in trade disputes with other countries, or to gain favorable decisions from the home government on trade-related issues, the Commercial Diplomat must use a range of advocacy tools. Advocacy tools include advocacy letters, testimony, white papers, speeches, op-ed pieces in newspapers, phone calls, and personal visits to key stakeholders and decision makers. The Commercial Diplomat must also build coalitions — within the government, industry, or interest group — to exert political influence in support of desired outcomes. Internationally, Commercial Diplomats must apply the same advocacy and coalition building tools in building support among key stakeholders in all the countries involved in a negotiation or the resolution of an international trade or investment issue.

Who Needs Training in Commercial Diplomacy?

The most obvious candidates for training in Commercial Diplomacy are the officials responsible for developing their country's international trade and investment policies and for negotiating international trade and investment agreements with other countries. What is less obvious is that all other stakeholders involved in the trade policy development and advocacy processes need the same training. Trade officials are only the most visible Commercial Diplomats. They usually are outnumbered by officials with trade-related responsibilities in many other government departments and ministries — officials from departments or ministries responsible for foreign affairs, finance, agriculture, industry, labor, health, the environment, the regulation of banks, telecommunications, air transportation, or the licensing of professionals.

Others who need instruction in Commercial Diplomacy include managers in the international departments of industry associations, corporations, unions, and nongovernmental organizations that have a stake in the outcome of trade policy decisions. In order to play an effective role in the domestic and global political advocacy and coalition-building process that precedes negotiations, these stakeholders need most of the same Commercial Diplomacy skills as government trade negotiators. Skill in Commercial Diplomacy is also required of corporate managers posted in foreign countries, who often must interact with the host government on a broad range of regulatory issues.

Another group that requires training in Commercial Diplomacy is the secretariat staff of international organizations that deal with global trade, investment, and trade-related regulatory issues. While such officials as a rule play less of a direct role in the political management of trade issues, they can most effectively do their job if they understand the politics of trade.

KEY RELATIONSHIPS IN COMMERCIAL DIPLOMACY

The Role of Government, Business, and Public Interest Groups

The key to understanding the challenge in managing the relationship between government and business on one hand, and between government and public interest groups on the other hand, is a profound appreciation of the differences in the respective roles, objectives, motivations, and values of actors in these three sets of actors. Therefore, we will focus initially on the unique mission of each and how that affects their frame of reference.

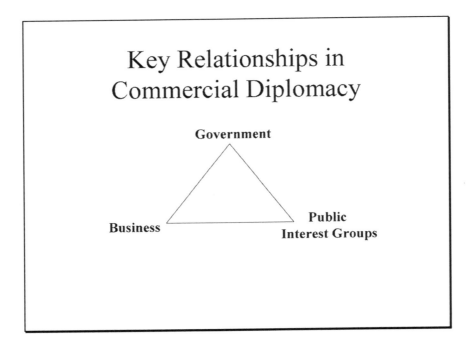

Figure 1.1

Business: The role of business (i.e., economic enterprises) is to efficiently organize production. In free market economies, which in different degrees now encompass most of the world, competition among competing producers is expected to result in the most efficient production of the goods and services that consumers wish to purchase. Within this framework, business managers have the responsibility to make decisions on the allocation of scarce resources for the production of goods and services that maximize their own profits.

In making production decisions, managers are required to obey the laws and regulations of the cities, counties, states, provinces, and countries in which they live. They may also choose to consider ethical aspects of their decisions over and above the laws they are required to obey. They may do so for moral reasons or because they believe that basic ethical values will shape the attitudes of employees, customers, the community, and government toward the firm. For the same reason, firms may choose to make financial contributions to charities or the arts in the communities in which they operate.

Government: It is the responsibility of the government to establish laws and regulations that will encourage or mandate socially desirable actions and discourage or prohibit socially undesirable behavior by enterprises. It is thus the responsibility of government to identify public policy goals in areas such as the environment or human health that are impacted by decisions made by enterprises and to pursue the achievement of such public policy goals through the promulgation and enforcement of appropriate laws and regulations. Similarly, it is the responsibility of government to identify public goods, such as education, police protection, defense, or medical care for the elderly, that society does not wish to allocate on the basis of an ability to pay, and to provide for the production and distribution of those public goods.

Public Interest Groups: Public interest groups help to crystallize public policy goals. They bring together private actors united by a common public policy goal. They give individual citizens the opportunity to exert a greater collective political influence on the public debate over a particular policy issue than they could achieve by acting individually. Public interest groups thus help to focus public policy issues for public debate and speak on behalf of members who share certain values or policy objectives.

Mission, Objectives, Motivations, and Values

Leaders in all institutional settings also have many things in common. They tend to value power, both as measured by the number of people or the amount of money under their stewardship, and by the impact of their decisions on society. Bureaucratic turf is a fairly standard measure of status in organizations.

The implication of the link between organizational mission and private motivations and values is that successful advocacy in Commercial Diplomacy depends on a sound understanding of the different missions, objectives, motivations, and values of the different actors.

> ▶ In order to persuade a business leader on a course of action, one needs to emphasize how the desired action will enhance economic opportunities for the enterprise or industry (or minimize the economic losses that are likely to be incurred by the enterprise or industry).

> ▶ In order to persuade a government leader on a course of action, one needs to emphasize how the desired action will strengthen political support for a policy outcome favored by the leader involved.

> ▶ In order to persuade a public interest advocate on a course of action, it is necessary to emphasize how the desired policy action will lead to increased public awareness and/or support for the desired cause.

As summarized below, business, government, and public interest groups are necessary for the smooth functioning of society. Both private and public goods and services are necessary for society to function and to achieve the well being of its members. All three groups often play a role in the trade policy decision-making process. Commercial Diplomats must be able to understand the contrasting missions, objectives, motivations, and values of leaders in government, business, and public interest groups.

Business: In the private market economies, the success of a business is measured in terms of its profits and/or its growth. It follows that the performance of individual business managers is measured in terms of their contribution to profits and/or growth. Business managers, therefore, are likely to support policies that advance their ability to generate higher profits or growth. It is also inevitable that in such an environment, where success is equated with economic performance, economic criteria will tend to feature prominently in the value system of business managers. In state-run economies, success is measured in terms of achievement of the production targets set by the state. Their managers will tend to support policies that will facilitate and enhance their ability to achieve these targets.

Government: In the government, success is measured in terms of the successful development, implementation, or enforcement of a government policy or program, all of which requires the consent and cooperation of a large number of officials, legislators, and ultimately voters. In other words, the performance of government leaders is most often measured in terms of success in building a political consensus in support of desirable policy goals. Government leaders, therefore, are likely to support policy actions that will help them to achieve this goal. It is inevitable that dedication to public policy goals and political skill will feature prominently in the value system of government leaders.

Public Interest Groups: In public interest groups, success is measured in terms of achieving public attention on a public policy issue and/or success in achieving a political consensus in support of such a goal. An organization's ability to accomplish these goals is a function of the number of its supporters/members and/or the size of the financial contribution made by its supporters/members. The performance of public interest advocates, therefore, is usually measured by the members and money they can attract, which in turn is a function of success in attracting attention to an issue or bringing about desired policy outcomes. Like government officials, public interest advocates live in an environment that values public policy and social goals, and these ideals are likely to feature prominently in their value systems.

The Political Marketplace

By its very nature, policy actions by governments are the result of a political process in which actors in all three spheres of society (business, government, and public interest groups) seek to shape the outcome. There is no way other than politics by which the government can make decisions on policy goals and government programs. This is true regardless of the political philosophy and the political organization of a country. Even dictators need bureaucracies to administer the government, and all decisions within such bureaucracies involve politics.

In any political process, all actors impacted by a government decision will seek to influence the outcome through persuasion and the exercise of political influence. Some have likened the process to a political marketplace within which advocates for alternative public policy goals and public goods compete for political support among the relevant decision makers. Everyone who wants to influence the outcome of a policy decision or the procurement of a public good has to allocate political capital to that

8

objective, and policy goals or public goods that receive the most political capital are adopted by the government.

The advocacy tools used by Commercial Diplomats to advance a particular organization or country's interests can be seen as the means for participating in the political marketplace for policies and programs. Effective management of the relationships among government, business, and public interest groups is essential for Commercial Diplomacy, in as much as it is essential for achieving success in the political marketplace for decisions on government policies and programs that affect trade.

Commercial Diplomacy and Managing Relationships

Commercial Diplomacy involves the application of the tools of diplomacy to policy issues that affect international trade and investment, or to policy conflicts created by international trade and investment. The tools of Commercial Diplomacy include operational documents such as briefing memos, advocacy letters, policy white papers, press releases, and public testimony. Other tools include oral means of persuasion such as consultations, negotiations, public speaking, and oral briefings. Commercial Diplomacy requires analytical skills in economics, politics, law, public policy, and public relations.

Commercial Diplomacy targets all policy measures that affect the flow of goods, services, information, people, and capital across national and regional borders. Policy measures addressed by Commercial Diplomacy include not only measures at the border such as tariffs, quotas, and visas, but also internal regulatory measures such as labor standards, environmental regulations, health and safety rules, and competition policy. Today's trade conflicts thus focus not only on disputes over tariffs and quotas, but also differences over subsidies, industrial policies, industry standards, and intellectual property laws. These regulatory issues often go to the heart of a country's public policy goals in sectors such as telecommunications, transportation, pharmaceuticals, and medical equipment. The modern day treatment of trade policy thus goes far beyond the landing dock for imported goods and well into the heart of the institutional, regulatory machinery of nations.

In today's rapidly converging world economy, Commercial Diplomacy is an essential catalyst for the smooth functioning of economic activity and cordial relationships among nations. International trade accounts for well over 40% of the world's gross domestic product, and the sales of the foreign affiliates of corporations have exceeded that of world exports by 90%. In light of this high degree of economic interdependence, trade conflicts could prove highly disruptive. By the same token, achievement of desired public policy goals requires an increasing degree of cooperation among countries on social issues such as the environment and health.

Commercial Diplomacy makes an important contribution to continued improvements in international trade, foreign direct investment, and solutions to international nonmarket conflicts. These improvements are contributing to the achievement of world economic development.

Chapter 2

THE POLICY PROCESS

By: Leslie Eliason and Geza Feketekuty[2]

HOW DO TRADE-RELATED POLICY ISSUES BECOME THE SUBJECT OF COMMERCIAL DIPLOMACY?

Before exploring the analytical questions a Commercial Diplomat must answer, how does a policy issue becomes the target of Commercial Diplomacy? In other words, we are interested in knowing how the issue got onto the public policy agenda. The initial impetus often comes from an enterprise or industry directly affected by a policy action or government regulation. Private interests can make a policy the focus of Commercial Diplomacy by raising it as a trade-related policy issue with political decision makers at home or abroad or by enlisting the support of lobbyists, politicians, legislators, or home government officials who will advocate change. Not all issues raised by enterprises, such as trade-related policy issues, are accepted by either the home government or a foreign government as legitimate concerns for government-to-government trade discussions or negotiations.

In order to persuade trade officials to involve themselves in any effort to address a trade-related issue, Commercial Diplomats representing an enterprise that is seeking help from its own government in removing a foreign trade barrier must be able to demonstrate that:

> ► The commercial problem they have identified is caused by an identifiable policy action;

---

2 The content of this chapter is substantially taken from the original training manual entitled *Policy Analysis for Trade* co-authored by Leslie Eliason and Geza Feketekuty, which is available on the ITCD website, but has been further edited for the purposes of this textbook by Geza Feketekuty. The original manual can be found at www. commercialdiplomacy.org.

► The impact of the measure on international commerce is substantial; and

► The policy action constitutes a violation of an international trade provision, or at a minimum, that the government could achieve its desired social objective through alternative measures that create less of a burden on international commerce.

Consider the report below in which U.S. farmers and biotechnology corporations associated with the use of genetically modified crops or organisms (GMOs) have identified decisions by the European Union (EU) as adversely affecting their ability to enter European markets. As the article points out, U.S. trade representatives have filed a complaint with the WTO.

Trade or investment problems identified by businesses as trade-related policy issues sometimes turn out to be nothing more than a commercial issue (e.g., poor sales performance due to inadequate marketing or product design, a low level of demand by consumers, poor management, or noncompetitive pricing). In order to persuade government officials to treat a commercial problem such as low export sales as a policy issue, the business or industry seeking the change in policy needs to demonstrate that the low sales are the result of a policy action such as a burdensome regulation, rather than the result of commercial factors such as poor product design. Where a regulation is restricting trade, the enterprise seeking the elimination of the measure must also demonstrate that the measure is either a violation of an international agreement or, at a minimum, that less trade restrictive measures are available to achieve legitimate social objectives. **The Commercial Diplomat, therefore, must be able to discern whether the concern is a legitimate focus for policy action.** In the following example, what is the policy concern? Is it a legitimate focus for trade policy action?

STUDY SAYS EU RULES TO COST U.S. FARMERS

BRUSSELS – U.S. farmers could be forced to spend hundreds of millions of dollars to comply with new European rules governing biotech food, changing how they plant and transport their crops, a study conducted by the University of Missouri showed.

The study was funded by Croplife International, a trade organization that represents the plant-science industry, and the Illinois-Missouri Biotechnology Alliance. The alliance, which is a joint program run by the Universities of Illinois and Missouri that receives much of its funding from the U.S. Department of Agriculture, is dedicated to funding biotech research.

The report released in Brussels is one of the first attempts to quantify the financial cost of U.S. farmers of European biotech-food rules. It showed that farmers of maize seeds might have to spend between $250 to $350 million to change how they grow and store their crops in order to comply with the rules.

Next month, the European Parliament is due to vote on rules requiring products made with even tiny amounts of genetically modified organisms, or GMOs, to carry warning labels. The legislation would end a de facto moratorium on approving new genetically modified crops in Europe, now the subject of a complaint the U.S. has filed with the World Trade Organization.

The European Commission declined to comment on the report.

(Source: The Wall Street Journal Europe (June 6-8, 2003), p. A2.)

Even when a policy measure can be identified as the source of a problem, the commercial impact may be too small or insignificant to warrant policy advocacy or policy action by officials. Taking time out to investigate an issue, to advocate policy changes, and to build the consensus necessary to implement changes can be costly in human resources. Therefore, someone from the private sector who wants to persuade officials to take time out from their busy schedules to investigate a policy issue and, if necessary, to become an advocate for policy change needs to demonstrate why the issue is important enough to warrant a commitment of time and political effort. Is the issue of GMO restrictions in the EU sufficiently significant to be the focus of trade policy action by U.S. officials?

A current policy may be shown to have a significant undesirable impact on international commerce, but without a clear rationale for change, policy action may not be warranted. This involves demonstrating the political and legal basis for change. What is the rationale for changing the EU's policy on GMOs?

The proposed policy action might be fully consistent with international rules, but policy actors need a viable alternative to achieve legitimate domestic social goals. The trade policy analyst can assist trade policymakers by identifying the range of viable alternatives for achieving legitimate social objectives. Ultimately, decision makers must choose from alternative policy options. What alternative policies might accomplish the desired objectives of the EU's current (or proposed) restrictions?

The impetus for addressing a policy issue through channels of Commercial Diplomacy can also come from issue-oriented NGOs that believe a trade-related action adversely affects other social objectives. In order to persuade trade officials to engage an issue, NGO representatives must make the case that the trade measure has an identifiable, adverse impact on a legitimate public concern. In other cases, the NGO will need to persuade trade officials that a trade action, such as the imposition of an import ban on certain goods and services, is necessary. Which NGOs might be interested in this policy? Why? How great is their influence? What resources might they bring to bear on this policy?

The push for change in a trade-related policy can also emanate from either a foreign government or the home government itself. A government may pursue an initiative to negotiate a reduction of foreign trade barriers as part of an effort to stimulate growth through increased exports. Another government may initiate a reduction of its own import barriers to reduce consumer prices or to improve the economic efficiency of its domestic producers.

Officials responsible for negotiating trade-related regulatory reform initiatives need to make the case that:

- ▶ Proposed changes in the policy measures at issue are necessary to achieve desired trade policy objectives,

- ▶ The proposed changes will not undermine important social objectives, and

► A change in the policy may also be justified in terms of good governance or the more effective pursuit of the relevant nontrade objectives.

One of the central tasks of the effective Commercial Diplomat is to analyze trade-related policy initiatives, to provide a thorough and informed assessment of the policymaker's options, and to indicate how a recommended option will enable the decision maker to achieve an acceptable, and wherever possible, superior outcome.

COMMERCIAL DIPLOMACY AND THE POLICY PROCESS

Commercial Diplomacy encompasses the formulation, negotiation, adoption, and implementation of trade policy. In this sense, Commercial Diplomacy and trade policy are important and increasingly salient aspects of public policy. Public policy is developed through the interactions among those who demand change, those who make decisions, and those who are affected by the policy in question. In the field of trade policy, demands or pressures for change may come from private commercial interests such as businesses and industry associations, from public interest groups, from legislators or politicians, or from officials within the government. A significant part of analyzing a trade policy issue, therefore, involves collecting information about the positions and demands of key actors and interest groups engaged in the policy process. Key actors are often referred to in policy analysis as *stakeholders.* The analysis of stakeholders' interests is, as we shall see, an important aspect of policy analysis. These actors seek to exercise political influence in the course of the policy-making process. We can conceptualize the policy process using the model presented here.

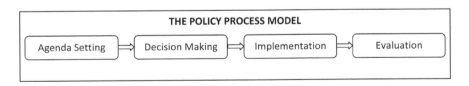

Figure 2.1

We use the term "policy process" to refer to the sequence of events that lead to policy action. Usually analysts refer to at least four stages of the policy process:

► **Agenda setting** involves policy advocacy by key actors, and is the recognition of problems to be resolved and often the identification of a range of alternative approaches to addressing the problem.

► **Decision-making** includes the choice of a preferred alternative by public officials with the responsibility to exercise public authority.

▶ **Implementation** involves actively executing a plan.

▶ **Evaluation** involves assessing the impact of the decision and the implementation strategy.

Note: While implementation and evaluation is not discussed explicitly in this chapter, the Commercial Diplomat is often involved in an ongoing assessment of how well trade-related policy is serving the targeted economic goals. The focus of this chapter is principally on agenda setting and decision aspects of the policy process.

SECTION II

THE ANALYTICAL TOOLS

Chapter 3

THE ANALYTICAL FRAMEWORK

By: Geza Feketekuty[3]

This chapter provides an overview of the steps involved in developing a comprehensive analysis of a trade policy or negotiating issue. In making decisions on policies and agreements affecting foreign trade or investment, government decision makers have to take into account of a wide range of factors:

- ▶ The impact of the potential action on particular industries and on the economy as a whole;

- ▶ The impact of the potential action or agreement on a variety of domestic social objectives and foreign policy considerations;

- ▶ The existing local, national and international regulations, laws, and rules that apply to the proposed action or agreement;

- ▶ The views of the various stakeholders and their ability to influence the final decision through the political process; or

- ▶ Public opinion and the role of the media in shaping public opinion.

A professional involved in the policy-making and negotiation process has to understand how the proposed action affects all of these factors, whether the professional involved is responsible for briefing and making a recommendation to the decision maker, or seeking to influence the decision maker through the political process. Stakeholders inside or outside of the government are likely to be far more successful in influencing decision makers if they can address the factors to consider in making a decision.

---

3 The content of this chapter is substantially taken from the original training manual entitled *A Commercial Diplomat's Brief Guide to Analyzing a Trade Issue* authored by Geza Feketekuty, which is available on the ITCD website, www.commercialdiplomacy.org.

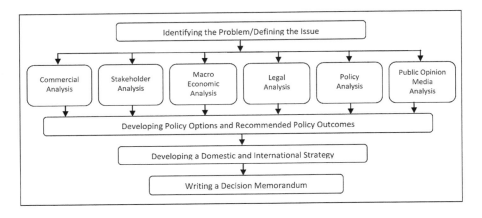

Figure 3.1

The analytical framework provides a basic template for carrying out a comprehensive analysis of all the factors involved and preparing a recommendation for the decision maker. The schematic above provides a graphical overview of the process.

CLEARLY DEFINING THE ISSUE

A clear definition of the problem is the essential foundation of all efforts in Commercial Diplomacy. It provides the basis for a clear and well-focused analysis of the issues that need to be addressed in solving the problem. It also provides the basis for effective communication of the issue with superiors, decision makers, other stakeholders, and potential allies. As you learn more about the subject and the issues involved you will need to update the statement of the issue/definition of the problem. A need for a change in the definition of the issue may arise as you find out more about the nature of the policy action and the social issues the policy is intended to address, the domestic laws and international rules that apply to the case, or the issues raised by other stakeholders or by foreign governments. Updating your statement of the issue regularly will help you to maintain a clear direction for your analytical and advocacy efforts and for clear communication of the issue to others.

A statement of the issue needs to describe succinctly

► The policy measure that is being challenged,

► The nature and magnitude of the impact on international commerce that creates the desire for a change in the policy (or the nature and magnitude of the impact on any social objectives outside of the trade arena that is creating the desire for a change in a trade measure), and

► The rationale and justification for the desired change in the policy.

Such a statement of the issue constitutes a definition of the problem that is to be addressed through Commercial Diplomacy. It should be short and to the point (i.e., no more than a paragraph of few sentences).

ANALYZING THE ISSUE IN DEPTH

Having defined the issue, the trade policy practitioner has to analyze the issue in depth. There are many aspects to such an analysis:

► **An analysis of the commercial issue** has to establish the impact of a policy change on the commercial interests of the key stakeholders at home and abroad.

► **A policy analysis of the targeted policy measure** has to establish the social policy objectives served by the policy measure and the alternative policy tools available for achieving the desired objectives.

► **A political analysis of interested stakeholders** has to lead to an identification of the key stakeholder and their political means for influencing the decision-making process at home and abroad.

► **A legal analysis** has to identify the relevant domestic and international legal provisions, how these legal provisions can be applied to the issue that has been identified, and any legal issues of interpretation that may affect the application of these legal provisions to the specific case.

► **A macro-economic analysis** has to provide an estimate of the economic impact of a policy change on the national economy.

► **A public relations analysis** determines whether the press and public opinion are likely to affect the decisions-making process, and if so, to what extent they would most likely do so.

Commercial Analysis

International commercial transactions are at the heart of Commercial Diplomacy. The whole purpose of Commercial Diplomacy is to facilitate exports, imports, and foreign investment activities by making sure that government policies directed at a wide range of social objectives do not impede these transactions more than is necessary to achieve the desired social goals. We thus have two key focal points for an analysis of a trade related policy issue that is a candidate for Commercial Diplomacy, namely the commercial aspects of the issue and the policy aspects of the issue.

Since the commercial rationale drives the need for Commercial Diplomacy, the Commercial Diplomat must develop an in-depth understanding of the commercial impact of alternative policy decisions. The commercial impact needs to be estimated in terms of changes in exports and imports, investments, total sales revenue, market share, growth prospects, costs, employment, and wages. In order to make these estimates, the Commercial Diplomat needs to be able to know enough accounting to be able to read the income statements and balance sheets of individual enterprises, and thereby gain a good understanding of the current condition of the firms or industry impacted by the policy decisions at issue. The Commercial Diplomat also needs to know enough economics to be able to estimate the impact of various policy decisions on future economic activity. The Commercial Diplomat does not need to be a professional accountant or economist; however, he/she does need to have a basic grounding in these subjects.

Commercial Analysis: Questions to Ask

- ► Who are the stakeholders with a commercial interest?
- ► What is their commercial stake in the outcome?
- ► How does the issue or a solution to the issue affect them?
- ► What is the impact on their exports and imports? On domestic sales? Overall revenues? Costs? Profits? Market share? Future growth prospects?

Policy Analysis

Traditionally, trade policy use to be about tariffs and quotas, and these policy instruments remain an important, although much less dominant, aspect of Commercial Diplomacy. Increasingly, however, government policies that are the subject of Commercial Diplomacy today are aimed at a wide range of domestic social objectives such as health, safety, environment, consumer protection, stability of infrastructure networks, and so on. The policy issues that arise with respect to tariffs and quotas are relatively simple compared to the policy issues that arise with respect to complex domestic regulations. The policy issues with respect to tariff and quota decisions usually come down to a trade-off between the protection of certain domestic economic activities from international competition and the economic efficiencies and new growth opportunities that can be derived from increased trade. It also involves a redistribution of domestic income between shareholders and workers in protected industries on one hand and consumers as a whole and producers in export-related industries on the other hand.

The policy analysis challenge is much greater when the policy issues involve domestic regulations. The challenge for the Commercial Diplomat in such cases is to identify alternative policy actions that will achieve the same social benefits as the existing policy instruments, while reducing or eliminating the adverse impact on international commerce. In order to arrive at this outcome, the Commercial Diplomat first needs to identify the social objectives served by the targeted policy action and how the policy action achieves the desired objective. Identifying the desired social objectives may require extensive legal analysis as well as an interactive dialogue with regulators. We need to know what legislators had in mind when drafting the laws underlying the regulations involved, and we need to know how the perception of the social objectives may have evolved over time. Understanding how the regulation in question achieves the social objective, and how alternative policy actions could be crafted to meet the desired objective, may require the collection of a considerable amount of scientific knowledge about the biology, chemistry, or physics underlying the regulatory issue.

Policy Analysis: Questions to Ask

▶ What policy areas would be affected by any actions to solve the trade problem? What specific objectives would be impacted?

▶ How do policy objectives relate to trade rules?

▶ What are the objective performance measures?

▶ What alternative policy measures are available to achieve the desired policy objectives?

▶ What combination of measures would solve the trade problem and preserve other legitimate policy objectives?

Political Stakeholder Analysis

The political challenge for a Commercial Diplomat is to build consensus in support of a particular outcome in trade-related policy disputes. Decisions on trade-related policy issues get made in a highly political environment. To build a viable political coalition in support of a desired outcome, the Commercial Diplomat has to identify the stakeholders. A stakeholder is any person or organized group that is affected by a policy decision or has vested interest in the policy and is able to influence the outcome through political action. In order to shape the outcome of the decision-making process, the Commercial Diplomat not only needs to identify all stakeholders who can influence the outcome, but their interests, their views, and objectives regarding the policy issue as well as their means of exercising political influence to affect the outcome.

The purpose of the political analysis is build the information necessary for building a coalition of stakeholders dedicated to the common purpose of achieving the desired policy reform. In order to make this coalition powerful enough to overcome opposition to the desired reform, the Commercial Diplomat must not only bring together stakeholders who are aware of the issue and ready to use their influence, but also stakeholders who are potential supporters. It may only be necessary to bring the issue to their attention or to adjust the desired policy outcome to accommodate their interests. The successful Commercial Diplomat also seeks to weaken opposition to the desired policy outcome. In order to weaken the opposition, the Commercial Diplomat may need to accommodate some of their interests or to persuade them that they stand more to lose by opposition.

Political analysis thus serves to provide the information necessary for successful political strategy. Information about personal relationships between stakeholders and key decision makers, and the ability of particular groups to mobilize voters or to raise campaign contributions for legislative elections, all provide the basis for assessing the potential political influence of supporters and opponents. Information about interests and positions provides the basis for shaping the message and the desired policy outcome to make it as attractive as possible to potential supporters and to weaken the opposition.

Political Analysis: Questions to Ask

▶ What stakeholders are affected by the trade problem or an effort to solve the trade problem?

▶ What are their interests? Positions on the problem or possible solutions? Options? Political influence?

▶ In what way is each stakeholder likely to use political influence to affect the outcome on the issue?

Legal Analysis

Domestic laws and regulations as well as international trade agreements govern most policy actions that affect trade. Legal analysis of trade-related issues can determine whether the trade-related problem arises from an administrative decision or from the text of the underlying regulation, law, or constitutional provision. Legal analysis can help us determine whether we can solve the problem by persuading an official to change the way a regulation is applied or whether we need to seek a change in the regulation or the underlying law. To accomplish this, we have to identify and analyze the relevant legal provisions, examine the legislative and regulatory history, and review past judicial interpretations. To put it another way, the objective of domestic legal analysis of trade-related policy issues is to identify permissible interpretations of applicable laws and regulations and the extent to which such alternative interpretations would enable us to reduce or eliminate the trade problem.

In applying their policy measures, national and lower governments are bound by the provisions of international trade agreements. The second purpose of legal analysis in Commercial Diplomacy is to determine whether the targeted policy measures are consistent with all relevant provisions of international trade agreements, or whether they could be challenged. International rules, like domestic laws and regulations, are subject to interpretation, and we may, therefore, have to identify both the most and the least favorable interpretations. We may also need to investigate how the international rules may constrain possible actions we might take to solve the problem directly.

Legal Analysis: Questions to Ask

▶ How does the trade problem relate to applicable domestic laws?

▶ Is the problem created by a failure to implement domestic laws?

▶ Is the problem created by an interpretation/implementation of a domestic law?

▶ Is the problem created by an arbitrary decision by an official or by a decision that could be altered in a manner consistent with domestic law?

▶ How does the trade problem relate to applicable provisions of international trade agreements?

▶ Is the problem created by a domestic law, regulation, or policy action that is inconsistent with international trade rules?

▶ What domestic laws and international agreements can be invoked to solve the trade problem?

▶ What domestic laws and international rules do we take as given and which do we seek to change as part of our effort to solve the trade-related problem?

ECONOMIC ANALYSIS

Commercial Diplomacy touches not only the commercial interests of individual firms and industries, but also the economic interests of the country as a whole. Countries trade with each other and invest in each other's economies to improve the economic performance of the economy, and thereby increase the standard of living of a country's citizens. Trade allows a country's citizens to concentrate on tasks they are best qualified to perform and to produce the goods and services in which the country enjoys a comparative advantage. By increasing competition, trade also stimulates a country's producers to seek out more efficient production methods and to improve the quality of the goods and services they produce. This, in turn, increases the productivity and growth of the economy, which then translates into higher wages for many workers, lower prices, and a higher standard of living.

Any policy change, however, will affect the distribution of income within the country, leaving some better off and some worse off. This is because trade increases the demand for some goods and services and by extension the wages of workers employed in those industries. Trade also reduces the demand for other goods and services and by extension the wages earned by workers in those industries.

National decision makers, therefore, want to know how a particular trade policy-related action would affect the performance of the economy and the distribution of income between different groups in society. For that reason, the Commercial Diplomat has to estimate the impact of trade policy decisions on trade flows, national economic output, productivity and growth, jobs and wages, consumer prices, industry profits, and income distribution. A basic knowledge of economics and key concepts like price elasticity as well as a familiarity with rule-of-thumb estimating techniques, should allow a trade analyst to approximate some of these values, although state-of-the-art estimates will require the assistance of a professionally trained economist.

Economic Analysis: Questions to Ask

▶ How does the problem affect the economy as a whole, including prices of the traded and non-traded good or service?

- How will it affect trade flows? Production? Productivity? Wage incomes? Consumer welfare?

Analyzing Public Opinion and the Media Treatment of the Issue

Many decisions involving Commercial Diplomacy are of concern only to groups in society most directly involved in the issue. In the past, these decisions often were discussed behind the scenes without much public awareness and received little treatment in the popular press. Issues of concern to particular groups typically were covered in periodicals focused on the particular industry or policy interest group that was most concerned about the issue. Only issues or decisions of broad concern were covered in mass media such as newspapers, TV broadcasts, and radio shows.

Over the past decade the internet has created multiple options for people to access information – through dedicated websites, social media, and blogs. For instance, social media sites such as Facebook connect people to other like-minded individuals or introduce them to similar organizations involved in the issue. Also blogs offer user-friendly options to individuals/groups who would like to share information, news, and views on issues. As a matter of fact, social media and blogs have become one of the most effective ways to pass on information – and it is inexpensive and relatively accessible for the collection and distribution of information.

Public opinion, and by extension the media, can have a major impact on policy outcomes. In these cases, the Commercial Diplomat needs to understand the concerns that drive public opinion and to address these concerns by shaping both the proposed policy action and the advocacy message. The Commercial Diplomat must also analyze the views disseminated by the media, either indirectly through the treatment of the issue in press reports, news broadcasts, and internet/social media, or directly through editorials, in order to shape the further evolution of the story in the press through press releases, interviews, speeches, and other channels.

Media/Public Opinion Analysis: Questions to Ask

- Does public opinion play a role in the problem or any attempts to solve the problem?

- Has either the popular media or the specialized media covered the problem?

- Is the press likely to cover efforts to address the problem?

- What public information initiatives are available to shape public opinion?

DEVELOPING THE RESEARCH STRATEGY

The multi-disciplinary analysis that underlies Commercial Diplomacy requires the collection of a great deal of information, and the application of a variety of analytical tools. As was mentioned earlier, the Commercial Diplomat needs to have a command of the basic analytical tools in a variety of disciplines in order to get a comprehensive grasp of the issues that need to be addressed in developing a successful strategy for obtaining a desired outcome on a trade-related policy issue. Few Commercial Diplomats can develop a professional level of knowledge in all the required disciplines, and part of the analytical process is the identification of professional experts and professional studies that can fill in any gaps in professional skills and areas of knowledge.

The amount of information a trade policy analyst may need to collect to prepare a policy issue for decision by superiors is quite large. In order to accomplish this task efficiently, the analyst will need to map out a well-organized research strategy. The first step is to list all the questions that need to be answered and the most likely sources of information from the Internet to libraries, professional or industry associations, think tanks, NGO's, or individual knowledgeable experts. The analyst will also need to identify the analytical tools that will need to be applied to data, and the extent to which the analyst's own professional skills and knowledge in individual disciplines and areas of knowledge will need to be augmented by professional colleagues with greater professional training in the area.

Research Strategy: Questions to Ask

► What information will I need to analyze all the issues I have mapped out both at home and abroad?

► What sources of information are available?

► What professional skills/expertise will I need to analyze all the issues?

► What professional experts can I consult to fill gaps in my own knowledge and skills?

Analyzing the Factual Data

Having compiled voluminous data and information on all the issues during the research phase, the trade analyst has the challenge of organizing and analyzing the data. Analysis is a process of extracting the implications of the factual data for the trade problem or opportunity we were asked to address, including:

► Interpreting how various laws and regulations apply to the policy issues we have identified,

► Analyzing how alternative policy actions will affect the commercial interest of the key stakeholders,

► Evaluating how various policy options will affect the various policy objectives that will concern various stakeholder groups and decision makers,

► Estimating the overall macroeconomic impact of alternative policy measures on the national economy, and

▶ Assessing how variations in policy options will affect the support or opposition of various stakeholder groups and the relative political influence of these groups.

The analytical phase is where the analyst adds value to the data collected through research. Obviously, experience generally enhances the value that an individual analyst can provide. Inexperienced analysts frequently confuse prodigious research and the compilation of a large volume of facts as analysis. However, research per se and the compilation of facts, even if it is voluminous, does not constitute analysis. In order to draw meaning from data we must interpret the data, examine its relevance for the case hand, examine the impact of alternative policy outcomes on policy objectives and on the interests of different stakeholder groups, and weigh the relative importance of different factors. Analysis helps us to understand the relevance of the data collected for the decision that has to be made on the desired policy outcome and on the different aspects of the strategy for getting there.

Analyzing Factual Data: Questions to Ask

▶ Is the collected data from credible sources?

▶ Does historical data reflect present/future scenarios?

▶ Is the data relevant to the analysis of the identified issue/problem?

▶ Does the data support or undermine identified policy goals?

DEVELOPING POLICY OPTIONS AND A RECOMMENDED POLICY OUTCOME

As the Commercial Diplomat learns more and more about an issue, the nature of the problem to be solved or the nature of the challenge to be pursued evolves. What may have started out as a fairly simple issue may become increasingly complex, and the fairly straightforward policy solution that seemed to provide the answer to the organization's problem turns out not to provide a viable solution to the problem. The reasons may be manifold: The scientific facts may turn out to be more ambiguous or complicated; research may reveal the existence of an obscure law and regulation; or the policy debate could inject a new stakeholder into the picture with strong political connections. For all these reasons, it is wise to periodically review the statement of the issue and the implied solution to the organization's problem.

Having researched and analyzed all aspects of the policy issue, and having updated the statement of the issue, the trade policy analyst is in a position to identify alternative policy options for addressing the issue, to weigh the advantages and disadvantages of each option, and to recommend a preferred policy solution. Some superiors will ask for a recommended solution for approval and an explanation why they should support it; others will ask for a set of options with the pros and cons of each option. Similarly, some superiors will ask for a strategy for implementing your recommendation before approving it. As a general matter, you should think through how you intend to implement a recommended option before committing yourself to a specific option.

The recommended policy option and accompanying strategy for implementing it has to take account of all the various aspects of the issue that may have surfaced during the course of your research and analysis:

▶ The commercial interests of the key commercial stakeholders,

▶ The policy issues that have been raised by politically influential stakeholders,

▶ The domestic and international legal requirements, and

▶ The national economic interest, institutional bottlenecks, and the bureaucratic interests of various committees and departments, and public opinion.

Not every trade-related policy issue raises a critical legal or economic issue or is a matter of concern to the general public and the media, but a serious problem in any one of the functional areas could kill a desired policy outcome, even if all other issues have been satisfactorily addressed. A policy proposal that meets all the requisite commercial, political, policy, and macroeconomic criteria may nevertheless fail if it violates an obscure legal provision. Similarly, a trade-related policy measure that supports important policy objectives, has many economic benefits, satisfies all legal requirements, and is supported by powerful political groups may nevertheless fail if public opinion is strongly opposed to the measure.

While a critical problem in any of the functional areas – whether in the commercial, political, policy, economic, legal, or public relations area - can kill a proposal, a strong case in one area can offset a weak case in another area. A policy proposal that has a strong policy rationale, a strong economic case, and strong political support could be adopted even if the law is not clear on the issue.

The Commercial Diplomat must weigh all the factors in proposing a recommended policy solution to a trade-related policy issue. Being able to assess the relative importance of different factors is a matter of experience. The foundation for an informed decision, however, is solid research and analysis. Gaps in the research and analysis can lead to flawed policy recommendations.

Developing a Domestic and International Strategy

You should be prepared to support any policy recommendation you make with a well-developed strategy for obtaining a favorable decision by the domestic and/or foreign officials that will have to agree. Such a strategy should identify potential coalition partners and the message that will win their support, the answers to questions that may be raised by opponents or the media, the legal case and the economic arguments, and a plan for getting the message out to key stakeholders and the public.

If the desired policy action involves an action by a foreign government, and you seek to involve the home government in a negotiation with the foreign government, you will first need a strategy for persuading the home government to add the issue to its negotiating agenda with the country (or countries) involved, and secondly a successful negotiating strategy with the foreign government. In other words, when the issue calls for government-to-government negotiations, you need both a domestic political strategy and an international negotiating strategy. A successful strategy builds synergies and positive feedback loops among supporters and among the different issue areas, while blunting the arguments and the message of opponents.

PUTTING TOGETHER THE DECISION MEMORANDUM

The Commercial Diplomat usually acts on behalf of an organization – a government department, ministry or regulatory agency, an industry association or enterprise, or a nongovernmental organization. Therefore, before adopting a course of action on a particular policy issue, the Commercial Diplomat must seek the approval of superiors and other stakeholders with a role in the decision-making process. The approval process usually involves the submission of a decision memorandum to everyone who will be participating in the decision.

The senior manager empowered to make a decision for an organization is usually an extremely busy individual who does not have the time to read through a thick document and sort through voluminous data and information. A decision memorandum, therefore, has to be relatively short, to the point, and well organized. A somewhat longer paper may be attached to the decision memorandum to give the decision maker's staff additional details. The writer of a decision memorandum has to be highly selective in the choice of background information and analysis that is included in the memorandum. Such a memorandum should typically not exceed a few pages, and may need to be as short as one page. While the attachment can be longer, it should include only information that is necessary for making a well-informed decision on the issue. The attachment itself should be in a format that makes it easy to read, with tables and backup documents relegated to separate appendixes at the back of the paper. Typically, an analyst will collect several times as much data as should be included in the complete document, and the decision-making memorandum itself should include only a small fraction of that data, which includes the most critical information.

A good decision memorandum above all needs a concisely written introductory paragraph that describes the problem or opportunity from the point of view of the organization, why the issue is important to the organization, the key hurdles that need to be addressed in obtaining a desirable outcome, and the recommended course of action. The introductory issue section should be followed by:

► **The Background section** that provides the most relevant background information;

► **The Analytical section** that provides the writer's own interpretation of the background data and analysis of the issues that is likely to have a significant bearing on the decision;

► **The Option and Recommendation section** that describes available options (if desired by the decision maker) and a recommended policy outcome, including the rationale for the recommended choice; and

► **The Strategy section** that recommends a course of action for implementing the desired outcome.

Each of these sections should be subdivided into key topics. Subheadings should provide an outline of the topics addressed, thus presenting the reader with a quick overview of the main lines of the argument and allowing the reader to decide which paragraphs to read when time is limited.

Both the background section and the analytical section should cover the commercial and policy issues, the politics, the national economic effects, the relevant legal provisions, and the public relations aspects of the issue. All factual material, including numerical data, information about stakeholders and their interests and views, applicable laws and international rules, actions by policymakers, news articles, and opinion polls belong in the analytical section. This section should cover the writer's own interpretation and analysis of the data and information presented in the background section. Where we are dealing with a policy issue that involves a foreign government, the information and analysis presented in these sections will need to cover both the situation in the home country and abroad.

Each successive section of the decision memorandum should establish a solid foundation for the next section. Thus, the background section should provide all the background information needed to support the analysis provided in the analytical section. The analytical section needs to provide support for the recommended policy outcome and every element of the proposed strategy for obtaining a favorable decision. Background information that does not support an element of the analysis presented in the analytical section can probably be left out of the memorandum without reducing its effectiveness. In fact, leaving unessential information out of the memorandum is likely to enhance its effectiveness. Similarly, analytical observations that do not directly relate to the policy options, the recommended policy outcome, or the recommended strategy should also be left out.

On the other hand, elements of a recommendation unsupported by analysis, or analysis unsupported by key facts, may call for additions to the paper. Recommendations not backed by analysis are unlikely to impress decision makers unless you are the world's greatest authority on a subject.

Writing a Decision Memorandum: Questions to Ask

► What factual background does the decision maker need to make an informed decision?

► What analysis can I add to support the recommended course of action?

► What are the elements of my recommended course of action? How will that solve the trade problem and satisfy other policy requirements?

► What is my strategy for developing the necessary consensus among domestic and foreign stakeholders? For making the legal case? For managing institutional issues? For building broader public support?

Appendix: Template for Analytical Framework

ANALYTICAL FRAMEWORK	
Identifying the Problem	
What is the problem?	
What policy measures are at issue?	
How does the problem relate to trade?	
How important is the trade problem? Is it worth our time?	
Analyzing the Commercial Issues at HOME and ABROAD	
Which industries and firms are complaining about the problem?	
What industries or firms are affected by the problem, or would be affected by available solutions to the problem?	
How does the problem affect the commercial interests of industries or firms abroad?	
How does the problem affect the revenues, costs, profits, wages, and employment and growth prospects of the industries and firms above?	At Home
	Abroad
Analyzing the National Macroeconomic Impact	
Analyzing the Domestic Policy Issues at Home and Abroad	
• What domestic policy issues does the problem touch upon? • What policy areas would be affected by any actions to solve the trade problem?	At Home
• What specific policy objectives would be impacted? • What alternative policy measures are available to achieve these objectives?	Abroad

Analyzing the Role of Public Opinion and the Media	
• What does the public think about this problem? • Does public opinion play a role in the problem or any attempts to solve the problem? • Has the media covered the problem? • Is the press likely to cover efforts to solve the problem?	At Home
	Abroad
Analyzing the Domestic Politics at Home and Abroad	
Who are the domestic stakeholders, both private and governmental?	At Home
	Abroad
How much political influence can the various stakeholders exert, and how would they seek to influence the outcome?	At Home
	Abroad
How does public opinion influence the politics?	At Home
	Abroad
Analyzing the Legal Issues	
What domestic regulations or laws are at the root of the problem at home or abroad and which laws and regulations can be invoked to solve the problem?	At Home
	Abroad
What regulations, laws or constitutional provisions do we take as given, and which can we realistically challenge?	At Home
	Abroad
What provisions in international trade agreements or other international legal instruments can we apply to the issue, and what dispute settlement arrangements can we invoke?	
Assessing Our Information Needs	
Overall, what information are we missing in order to better analyze the problem and look towards a solution?	

Chapter 4

ESTIMATING THE IMPACT ON
INDUSTRIES AND THE ECONOMY

By: Fernando De Paolis, Geza Feketekuty, Robert McCleery, and Moyara Ruehsen[4]

The reason we engage in international trade is because such trade will improve our national economic well-being by increasing the economic efficiency and productivity of our economy and giving consumers a greater choice of goods and services. Therefore, when governments consider policy measures or negotiations with the aim of increasing trade, the first question that comes to mind is how much the measure or negotiation under consideration will improve the nation's economic well-being through greater job opportunities, reduced costs of production, greater productivity, and lower prices.

At the same time, while trade may increase the economic welfare of the country as a whole, it may reduce the incomes of some workers and businesses whose products are replaced by imports. On the other hand, it may provide larger-than-average gains for some other workers and businesses who gain from increased exports. When considering trade policy decisions or trade negotiation, the second set of questions that comes to mind are, who will gain or lose and how much.

The first step in carrying out a thorough analysis of a trade policy decision or negating proposal, therefore, is to estimate the economic gains and losses. While some basic training in economics is necessary to make such calculations or even to understand the estimates prepared by professional economists, for most day-to-day activities in trade policy a trade policy practitioner does not need a PhD in economics.

---

4 The content of this chapter is substantially taken from the original training manual entitled *Using Economic Data in Commercial Diplomacy: Making Rule of Thumb Calculations on the Economic Effects of Trade Policy Decisions* co-authored by Geza Feketekuty, Robert McCleery, Moyara Ruehsen, and Fernando De Paolis, which is available on the ITCD website, but has been further edited for the purposes of this textbook by Geza Feketekuty. The original manual can be found at www.commercialdiplomacy.org.

This chapter is broken down into two parts. Part A provides an overview of the use of economic analysis in trade policy and is largely designed to help someone without a background in economics or an understanding of how economic estimates are made. Part B is a more technical treatment of the use of economic analysis in trade policy decisions. This section covers most of the same analytical tools as in Part A but in much greater technical depth. Based on your level of comfort with economic analysis, for those who have basic economic training, proceed to Part B. If you do not have basic training in economics you may want to focus on Part A and go to Part B for a more in-depth analysis at a later time. Therefore, as a result of the way this chapter is designed, some of the information from Part A will be repeated for emphasis in Part B. While Part B provides a more technical treatment of the subject, it should be accessible for readers with basic training in economics and does not require a PhD to make the recommended rule-of-thumb calculations.

Part A
Introduction to the Use of Commercial and Economic Data in Commercial Diplomacy

Commercial Diplomacy is all about persuasion, and economic data play an extremely important role in persuasion. The Commercial Diplomat must be able to support arguments in favor of policy positions with data highlighting the economic impact of policy decisions on key stakeholders and on the country as a whole. Learning how to use commercial and economic data effectively is, therefore, one of the critical skills in Commercial Diplomacy.

The economic impacts of trade policy actions, of course, are not the only policy impacts that matter. Policy decisions that affect global trade and investment flows inevitably affect such other policy dimensions as health, safety, environment, foreign policy, or national security. Estimating these other policy impacts largely requires other policy tools that are treated elsewhere. The sections that follow are designed to give the practitioner and the student an insight into the questions that need to be asked by Commercial Diplomats about the commercial and economic impact of trade policy decisions and the approaches and tools used by economists to answer them.

Estimating the Economic Magnitude of Trade Policy Actions

To understand the impact of trade policy actions, we need to review the foundation on which trade theory rests. This foundation is based on the work of David Ricardo in the early 1800s. The crucial concept is *comparative advantage*, which motivates gains from trade among countries that are able to produce similar products.

In this section we will consider how to obtain an initial assessment of the relative economic importance of a decision and whom it will affect. This section describes how an analyst can quickly assemble readily available data on the policy measure and on the affected industries.

A country has a comparative advantage in production of a certain product if it can produce that product at a lower *opportunity cost*. Opportunity cost is the amount of another product that cannot be produced as a result of the decision to produce the first product. In other words, if Ireland can produce 20 more computers by not producing one car, while Germany can produce one more car at the expense of 12 computers, then Ireland has a lower opportunity cost in producing computers and Germany has a lower opportunity cost in producing cars. Thus, there are gains from bilateral trade, with Ireland exporting computers and importing German cars, and freer trade between the two countries will lead to an expansion in Ireland's computer industry and contraction in its auto industry.

What is a "Trade Policy" Issue?

One might think the boundaries of trade policy would be self-evident. However, trade policy analysts must think in broad terms about a wide range of policy issues that affect trade flows. From EU directives to U.S. tax laws to state of California rulings on gasoline additives, virtually any policy action that will have a differential impact on domestic and foreign firms can be a WTO case.

This modern-day reality has two main implications. First, the Commercial Diplomat must be a quick study, as it is impossible to keep current with every single aspect of policy that may result in a trade dispute. Secondly, the toolbox of techniques a Commercial Diplomat must command is expanding. While understanding the basics of tariffs, quotas, and other traditional trade restrictions is still necessary, it is insufficient for the wide range of issues that arise during one's professional career.

All of these trade-related issues, broadly defined, have certain characteristics in common. Stakeholders must be identified, data collected, and analysis performed to generate rough estimates of the likely impacts on domestic stakeholders.

Who are the Stakeholders?

Commercial Diplomacy affects the economic interests of a variety of stakeholders.

▶ Stakeholders are those producers, importers, exporters, consumers, workers, government (and indirectly the taxpayers), and other interested parties who are directly affected by the policy action.

For sound trade policy advocacy, trade policy making, and trade negotiating decisions, it is important to understand stakeholders' economic interests. The number of industries likely affected by an issue or policy action, the volume of production affected, the trade, and jobs accounted for by such industries are of economic importance to potential stakeholders. It is also vital information for politicians and politically inclined decision makers.

Getting the attention of a busy decision maker is often the first challenge for a Commercial Diplomat, and data on the size of affected sectors is an avenue for getting that attention. Even before that, in the absence of guidance from superiors, such data can indicate whether it is worth probing deeper into the issue and the relevant economic data.

The amount of trade "covered" by liberalizing or protectionist action, or the amount of jobs directly affected by a trade action, is often described as "coverage." In situations where data is unavailable or the complexity of an issue makes it impossible to develop a defensible quantitative estimate of the policy impact, coverage can become a rough measuring rod for policy decisions. Thus, trade negotiators and politicians often discuss the amount of trade "covered" by liberalizing or protectionist actions as a proxy for the importance of the issue.

Estimating the trade or industry coverage of a policy issue or action involves two simple steps:

(1) Deciding which industries or industry sub-sectors are likely affected and then finding sources of data, and

(2) Making qualitative judgments specific to each case. This second step of data collection is more of a challenge.

Creating Initial Rough Estimates

When information about the nature and magnitude of the policy action is combined with information about the amount of trade or production affected by the policy action, it is possible to convey a good idea of the likely economic impact. In some cases, policymakers want to hear whether a particular issue is sufficiently important to deserve analysis; in others, the answer is obvious.

You may be asked to make those initial estimates yourself. Let us take the example of a "foreign country," which we will call Xenia. Xenia proposes to cut its 10% duty on car imports in half to 5%. Our "home country" now exports cars worth $10 billion to Xenia out of total exports of $200 billion. Assume the total size of the "home" economy $1 trillion. With this information we are in a fairly good position to conclude that the impact will be significant. How do we know this?

Let us assume that the overall output and employment of the auto industry is $50 billion and 300,000 respectively (information that can be obtained fairly easily). One option is for producers to capture the extra $500 million ($10 billion * 5%) as additional profits. Another option, more likely in a highly competitive market, is to cut the price by 5% and increase output to gain market share. It is an open question whether exporters will choose to cut their delivered price by 5%, increase their profit margin by 5%, or some combination of the two.

Where the proposed policy action does not take the form of a tariff cut or increase, it is useful to translate that policy's impacts into an equivalent tariff or subsidy. The first thing to discover is whether the proposed policy action changes incentives for producers. If not, it is just a matter of calculating the direct impact. Such measures are called by economists *lump-sum* taxes or subsidies.

If incentives change, we need to estimate the actual response by producers. This is done by calculating how the proposed policy action will affect incentives such as costs and prices and then translating that into an equivalent tariff cut or increase (or an equivalent change in a subsidy). Thus, if we know that the proposed policy action will reduce the costs of exports by $5 million, and the total exports by the industry amount to $100 million, we can say that the proposed policy action has an effect equivalent to eliminating a 5% tariff.

ESTIMATING THE IMPACT OF TRADE POLICY CHANGES ON THE PRICE OF IMPORTED PRODUCTS AND ON TRADE IN SUCH PRODUCTS

One of the most frequently raised questions on policy actions covered by Commercial Diplomacy is the impact on trade flows. Understanding and communicating the impact of trade policy on trade, and ultimately on revenues, costs, profits, wages, and jobs is the foundation of Commercial Diplomacy. While economists tend to emphasize the economic efficiency and consumer benefits of trade, the political debate over trade is dominated by arguments over the benefit of increased exports to producers in export industries and the loss generated by increased imports for producers in import-competing industries. In other words, economists see imports as good, because they allow consumption of goods produced using another country's resources and exports as necessary to finance imports. Policy makers, however, often see imports as a threat to domestic producers and interest groups and exports as a source of new wealth, increased national output, employment, profits, and tax revenues. These policy perceptions are reinforced politically by producers being better organized politically than consumers. Consumer organizations are often co-opted by producer interests. This can result in a *mercantilist* tilt to trade policy.

Mercantilists of the eighteenth century believed that exports were good and imports were bad. Therefore, the role of trade policy was to create a trade surplus that would result in an inflow of gold and stimulate the domestic economy. Adam Smith's *Wealth of Nations* explains the fallacy of the mercantilist argument, but the political strength of producer interests has preserved the mercantilist element in trade policy. In view of these political realities, proponents of trade liberalization usually focus on new export opportunities created by reducing foreign trade barriers, while opponents of trade liberalization focus on the displacement of domestic production through increased imports.

In this section we review the steps necessary to calculate the impact of trade policy on trade flows, and in subsequent sections we will review the steps necessary to calculate the impact on revenues, costs, profits, wages, and jobs. Calculating the impact of a policy measure on trade is generally a two-step process. First, the analyst must calculate the effect of the policy action on the price at which the good or service could be sold in the import market. Second, the analyst must calculate the impact of the change in price on the quantity consumers wish to purchase. Our starting point is small countries that can buy as much as they wish at a constant world price.

For a large country like the United States, a third step is necessary. The analyst must determine if the change in import demand for a product is sufficient to alter the world price of that product. For economists, the definition of a "large" or "small" country is product specific and rests on whether a policy change in that producing or consuming country has a noticeable impact on world price. Thus Kuwait, despite its small land area and low population, may be a large country in the oil market, while India may be considered small in many manufactured goods markets like autos and aircraft. In general, the analysis of trade effects is complicated by any departure from the assumption of *perfect competition* built into most economic models.

▶ Perfect competition is the assumption that the market is composed of many small producers and consumers acting independently, freely entering and exiting the market as profitability dictates, with all producers making identical products. Therefore, no market participant can manipulate prices.

Calculating the Price Impact of a Policy Action

Tariffs: We focus here on the case of a small county in a competitive market. Calculating the impact of the policy action on price is a fairly straightforward calculation in the case of changes to *ad valorem tariffs* or fees on imported products that vary in proportion to the price.

As the above sentence indicates, **ad valorem tariffs** are those imposed in proportion to the price of an item. Hence a 10% tariff imposed on imports of books would require payment of $1 in duties for a $10 book, $5 on a $50 book, etc. The other main type of tariff is a **specific tariff**, which is a set dollar amount of duty imposed per unit of imports. A specific tariff of $2 per book, in the above example would raise $4 in duties on the two books.

Provided both the importers and domestic retailers are operating under competitive market conditions, we can assume that the increase or reduction of the tariff is passed on to the consumer. Thus, a 50% reduction of an 80% duty translates into a 22% percent reduction of the consumer price in the import market. Here is an example: assuming the world price is $1, a 50% cut in the 80% tariff translates into a price reduction of $0.40 from $1.80 to $1.40.[5] Note, however, that a 50% reduction of a 10% duty translates into only a 4 ½% cut in the retail price of the import (assuming again that the import price is $1, a 50% cut in the 10% duty translates into a 5-cent cut from $1.10).

Quotas: Another common policy action is the reduction or increase of an import quota. Translating a change in the quota to a price change is complicated, but in most cases not necessary for calculating an impact on trade as long as the changed quota continues to restrict trade. In such a case we can assume that trade is increased (reduced) by the full increase (reduction) in the quota. Where the quota that emerges from the change in policy does not bind trade, as happens frequently in the case of textile quotas allocated to highly specific apparel items, you must resort to estimates based on a survey of practitioners or an examination of historical data.

---

5 Prior to the tariff change, domestic consumers paid $1.80 for the imported product, $1 to the foreign producer and $0.80 to the government. The tariff reduction halves the payment to the government to $0.40. In percentage terms, this is can be expressed as about a 22% reduction in price.

When a particular regulation overshadows all other import-related regulations, an initial approach to estimating the price effect of removing the regulation is to examine the difference in the price at which the product is sold in the export and import market and to deduct from that price difference all other known costs such as shipping, tariffs, fees, insurance, etc. Since a single regulation seldom is the only cost element that cannot be clearly identified, and differences in retailing costs also play an important role, there is usually a great deal of controversy around such estimates. They nevertheless provide a useful starting point for a more detailed analysis.

Estimating How a Change in the Price of Imported Products Impacts Trade

Estimating the impact of a change in the price of an imported product on trade in that product involves another two-step process. Economists call the factor used to calculate the direct impact the price elasticity of demand.

▶ *The price elasticity of demand (PED)* measures consumer response to price changes and varies from commodity to commodity, from country to country, and from common items of daily consumption to luxury goods.

When a percentage reduction in the price leads to a less-than-proportional increase in quantity demanded, economists say that the demand is inelastic, and when quantity demanded changes more than the change in price, economists say the demand is elastic. Economists estimate a numeric value for this elasticity. A value of 1 means that demand changes in equal proportion to changes in price. Inelastic demand is defined as a value of less than 1, and elastic demand is a value of greater than 1. An elasticity of 0.5 means that quantity demanded changes only half as much proportionally as the price, while an elasticity of 1.5 means that demand changes 50% more proportionally than the price. The price elasticity of demand for various products can be measured by examining historical data. Economists have studied and published price elasticities for various commodities in different countries.

Generally, demand for luxury goods and essential food products is relatively price inelastic. People who can afford to pay for luxury goods are not very sensitive to the price when few close substitutes exist (quality gemstones, pleasure craft, etc.). The demand for essential foodstuffs is also usually inelastic since people generally buy them even if the price goes up. In contrast, many consumer goods have a high elasticity since people can easily find substitutes or do without them.

Consider another intuitive way to think about price elasticities of demand. Suppose you spend 10% of your income on a certain product. If the price of this product falls, you buy more, but do you buy so much more that the fraction of your total income spent on the product increases, or just a little bit more, so that the fraction of income spent on that product falls under 10 percent? In the first case, demand would be elastic, in the second, inelastic. Clearly in the case of food, the "savings" from a fall in the price of food would not be spent only on additional food, with the exception of those consumers well below the poverty line. Lower airfares, however, might cause a business traveler to take the whole family on a future business trip, increasing the fraction of income devoted to airfare.

For trade policy purposes we want to measure the impact of a change in the price of an imported product on the demand for that product. The response of consumers to a change in the price of an imported product is affected by a number of things, including the overall desire of consumers to buy more of a particular type of product when its price falls, the extent to which consumers are willing to substitute imported goods or services for domestically produced substitutes, and the willingness and ability of domestic producers to change their prices. The import price elasticity of demand captures the responsiveness of consumers, while holding all other factors constant, including the response of domestic producers, the income of consumers, and the prices of substitutes and complements.

To summarize, the impact of a policy on trade can be measured by estimating first the impact of that measure on the price of the imported product in the import market, then multiplying that percentage change in price by a price elasticity, which measures the consumer response to a change in price. One can estimate the impact of a change in foreign trade barriers on domestic exports in the same way, with the additional step of assuming (unless clearly inappropriate) that the share of the increased imports captured by domestic exporters is the same as their current market share.

ESTIMATING THE IMPACT OF POLICY ACTIONS AFFECTING TRADE ON INDUSTRY REVENUES, COSTS, AND PROFITS

In the last section we explored how policy actions change trade flows by affecting the cost and price of traded goods or influence prices by changing trade flows directly. Information on the impact on trade flows still does not tell us, however, how the economic interests of stakeholders are affected. The focus of this section is the subset of stakeholders participating in the profits of firms producing goods and services domestically. To estimate these effects, we must calculate how a change in prices and trade flows translates into changes in the domestic production of goods and services and thus on industry revenues, costs and profits.[6]

An increase in exports will increase domestic production by an equal amount, provided the industry has unutilized production capacity or large inventories of final goods.[7] In some cases, we assume that the industry has the capacity to increase output. We want to estimate the change in domestic output in the industry after pro-

---

6 An import surge decreases demand, price, profits, and employment for domestically produced *substitutes*, but could actually increase demand, price, profits, and employment for domestically produced *complements* (goods used along with the imported goods, such as Pentium processors and cheap Korean memory chips), or *service* contracts on Mexican-assembled color TV sets, transportation services associated with international trade, and sales people in Toyota dealerships.

7 While varying by industry, manufacturing firms in the large industrialized economies generally run at 80-85% capacity in normal times, rising close to 100% after several years of strong economic growth (see the 2001 California energy situation) and falling as low as 60% in a sharp recession. Thus, U.S. firms may easily provide 10% more exports due to a trade agreement, but a Mexican or Central American producer might have to divert products from the domestic market to increase significantly exports to the U.S. (at least during a transition period in which new investments are made to expand production capacity), increasing both the domestic and export price to meet new demand in the U.S. unless imports are freely available.

ducers have adjusted their output to accommodate the increased export demand. We can simply add the projected increase in exports to the projected level of domestic consumption (abstracting from imports) to obtain the new, higher level of output. The argument in policy debates can be simplified still more. It is not unreasonable to de-link foreign and domestic demand and say that the increase in output attributable to a trade policy that increases exports is simply the increase in exports. Remember that our goal is generally not to predict future sales and profits but to isolate the impact of a proposed trade policy on sales and profits. Economists sometimes express these numbers as changes from a "baseline" or "status quo" scenario.

To calculate the impact on growth in the industry, we divide the increase in exports by the current level of output. The result tells us how much additional growth has been or will be created by the trade policy action. We can also measure the significance of the trade policy action by calculating how the growth generated by the increase in exports compares to the current growth in domestic demand or the underlying growth trend in exports.

We need to also consider the effect of time. In the very short term, producers may not be able to increase production because they do not have sufficient parts or raw materials on hand. Or they may not want to increase production because they first want to reduce inventory of finished products before paying overtime, hiring new workers, or installing new machines, particularly if they feel that the increase in demand may be temporary. An increase in sales satisfied through a reduction in inventories increases revenues and profits but does not increase the level of output (and employment).

At some later stage producers may adjust the supply chain with inventories fallen enough to demand replenishing. At this stage the increased demand for products is translated into increased production, up to a level that can be accommodated by the production capacity. We will explore next what happens when producers reach full capacity utilization. Given enough time they can increase production capacity through more investment in plants and equipment. New firms may enter the industry, adding to total production. Over time, we should witness a sequence of three events:

- ▶ In the very short run a reduction in inventories;

- ▶ In the intermediate run an increase in output (by using existing capital and labor more intensively); and

- ▶ In the long run an increase in production capacity (through new capital investment, hiring and training at existing firms, and new firms entering the market).[8]

To provide a quick overview, changes in trade flows can affect domestic industry in different ways, depending on:

---

8 A more complete discussion of trade and employment is postponed to Part B of this chapter, but note that the stage at which employment increases in the three-stage process depends on the country and industry we consider. Generally employment increases in stage two, and may increase further in stage three, but in economies with flexible labor markets and industries that do not require major training efforts, the employment increase comes earlier.

▶ **Capacity utilization in domestic industry:** At high rates of capacity utilization, additional demand is likely met by price increases, while lower demand may be met by production cuts. At low rates of capacity utilization, the reverse is likely.

▶ **Degree of substitutability between foreign and domestic products:** For extremely close substitutes, a fall in the price of imports will force domestic producers to match the lower price, lowering profits, and production levels. For less close substitutes, we would expect the same changes but of lesser magnitude. Demand for complementary products will increase when the price of imports falls.

▶ **Production technologies (increasing returns, constant returns, or decreasing returns):** In increasing returns industries, firms are more likely to expand production than to raise prices, and more likely to cut prices than contract production.

▶ **Corporate culture:** U.S. firms are considered more sensitive to quarterly profits, while Japanese firms are considered more concerned with market share and long-term growth. The price versus quantity adjustments above may reflect these different concerns.

▶ **Time frame:** Are we are considering the short run, when economic decision makers are in the process of adjusting to changes, or the long run, when everyone makes the necessary adjustments?

▶ **Industry competitiveness:** Is the industry competitive, or does a single firm or group of firms have the power to set prices? Does a change in domestic trade policy (making the domestic market more or less open to imports) affect the degree of competitiveness in the market?

ESTIMATING THE IMPACT OF TRADE POLICY ON JOBS AND WAGES

The impact of trade policy decisions on jobs and wages is often the central focus of political debate. Most economists are uncomfortable with this focus because they consider macroeconomic policy the proper economic tool for achieving full employment.

The three main areas of macroeconomic policy making are fiscal policy, monetary policy, and exchange rate policy:

▶ Fiscal policy covers the manipulation of government spending and tax rates.

▶ Monetary policy covers the manipulation of interest rates and the money supply.

▶ Exchange rate policies cover the manipulation of exchange rates.

Most economists consider the reduction of consumer prices, the increase in competition, and the creation of more productive, higher-paying jobs the proper focus of trade policy. Whatever the merits from the point of view of economic theory, the political pull toward a focus on jobs is usually so strong that economists and practitioners of Commercial Diplomacy are drawn into the debate on those terms. However, the standard trade calculations introduced in the previous section are not appropriate for this debate, since they deal with the direct impact on affected industries, not the overall impact on the economy.

With a few exceptions, trade leads to increased production and jobs that are characterized by higher levels of worker productivity. In a competitive labor market, such higher-productivity jobs bring higher wage rates. Trade, however, also leads to the elimination of jobs in less competitive industries, whose workers typically have fewer or more narrowly specialized skills and frequently do not have the option of moving into the new jobs being created in the more competitive industries without substantial retraining. All too often these workers end up in lower paying jobs, and some may remain unemployed, hoping in vain that their previous job will return.

One of the key concerns over trade policy decisions, therefore, is the distributional effect: workers with the necessary training, experience, and skills gain, while workers without the necessary training, experience, and skills lose. Consequently, in a full-employment economy, the debate over jobs is often a proxy for the real issue, which is the impact on low-skilled workers.[9] A second problem is that openness to trade both accentuates and speeds up the economy's adjustment to new technologies, which has a similar impact on income distribution and unemployment.

Estimating Direct Job Creation in Export Industries

One way to estimate the number of new jobs created in export industries from increased production is by multiplying the increased output by the ratio of output to workers in the economy, in the sector, or in the industry. In the United States, this ratio is normally calculated as the number of jobs created by each $1 billion in output. Since the number of workers required to generate $1 billion in output differs between services and manufacturing, and differs among industries, estimates based on industry data are likely to be more accurate than estimates based on broader sectoral or economy-wide data. All that is required to calculate these ratios is to divide the number of workers employed in the industry by the value of the output in the industry. The primary benefit of this method is its simplicity. It is an appropriate method for most trade analysis purposes, but you should be aware of several weaknesses.

When a policy action affects many different industries, however, quick back-of-the-envelope calculations tend to be based on sector or economy-wide output per worker ratios. Based on estimates from around the year 2000, the number widely (and wrongly) used for manufactured exports in the United States was 20,000 jobs per $1 billion of output, despite the ratio having declined to just 14,000 jobs per

---

9 The term "full employment" does not literally mean that anyone who wants to work can find a job. It means that an additional policy stimulus to create jobs would have a more detrimental impact on inflation than it would be worth in job creation.

$1 billion in output by the mid-1990s due to rapid productivity growth. The appropriate number to use for quick, economy-wide calculations of the U.S. job effects today would, therefore, be about 12,500 jobs per $1 billion in output after five more years of rapid growth in labor.

Rule of Thumb for Calculating Indirect Job Creation

In addition to the direct employment effects of an increase in production in export industries, we must consider the indirect employment effects in industries that supply inputs or in industries that distribute the output.

A commonly used rule of thumb is that each new job created in export industries ultimately leads to the creation of two additional jobs in downstream and upstream industries.

In today's globalized economy, it is worth considering how many of these additional jobs will be filled by domestic workers. Do U.S. firms have the in-house capabilities to localize products to the Japanese market, or will the associated marketing, service, transportation, and other service jobs be created in Japan? Will the additional demand for components and raw materials be met by affiliates in Malaysia and Mexico? These are important issues to policymakers, and applying rules of thumb without at least cursory study of the industry in question can lead to embarrassing mistakes.

The Difference Between a New Job in an Industry and a New Job in the Economy

There is obviously a difference between an increase of jobs in a particular industry or industries and in the economy as a whole. If there is full employment in the economy, the total number of jobs can increase only through a net increase in immigration or through an increase in the labor force participation of women, retired people, students, or other underemployed groups. In calendar year 2000, for example, the United States had many unfilled positions in software programming and engineering, and one of the major policy issues revolved around increased immigration quotas. Thus, one could argue that a fair assessment of the impact of trade on jobs would not focus on jobs lost or created, but on jobs moved from one sector of the economy to another. Acute, long-term labor shortages in export industries can be addressed by investments in labor-saving technologies that raise productivity and pay for existing workers. Alternatively, labor shortages can be addressed by outsourcing portions of the production or support process in addition to efforts to train domestic workers and bring in foreign workers with needed skills. Which methods a particular company uses depends on relative costs and corporate strategies. We can see all of these strategies at work in the information technology sector.

Direct Employment Effects of an Increase in Imports

On the other end of the spectrum, an increase in imports can lead to a decline of production and jobs in domestic industries competing with the imports. However, the relationship is not one-to-one for several reasons. First, some imported products are treated by consumers as distinct products, rather than as substitutes for equivalent domestically produced goods or services. In such cases, the imports constitute primarily an increase in total demand in that industry, rather than the substitution of an imported product for a domestically produced product. Second, as we saw above, an increase in imports of inputs may be essential to support increased domestic production in downstream industries. Third, in a full-employment economy, imports can satisfy domestic demand that cannot be filled by domestic producers. In other words, a strong increase in domestic demand due to rising incomes can increase imports even as it stimulates additional domestic production. Fourth, an increase in imports from one country as a result of a trade agreement (from Mexico under NAFTA, for instance) may displace imports from other countries (Southeast Asia and South America), leaving net imports and the impact on domestic production roughly unchanged.

In light of these complexities, how do we calculate job losses due to increased imports? There is no simple way. We would like a method more accurate than reducing the one-to-one ratio by a judgmental factor, but less difficult than empirically measuring past relationships between increased imports and job losses in particular industries using multiple regression analysis to isolate the impact of increased imports from all other factors that influence employment, such as changes in the business cycle. Rather than making those estimates yourself, you can look for economists' estimates.

Impact of Trade on Labor Productivity and Wages

When political pressure does not dictate a jobs-oriented debate, supporters of trade liberalization are likely to run into fewer analytical problems by focusing on the increase in labor productivity and wages associated with increased trade. Increased trade adds to the number of relatively high-productivity, high-wage jobs and reduces the number of low-productivity, low-wage jobs. This can readily be measured by identifying the productivity and wage differential between the industries experiencing export gains on one hand and the industries experiencing an increase in imports and a relative decline in domestic production on the other hand. This difference was calculated for U.S. trade overall in the 1990s, and later data shows a 4-5% differential. Keep in mind other cases in other countries may produce different results in magnitude or even in sign.

Just as proponents of trade liberalization are on more solid analytical ground focusing on the productivity/wage equation than the jobs equation, opponents of trade liberalization are on more solid analytical ground by focusing on the adjustment costs and distributional consequences associated with increased trade. An analysis that includes treatment of adjustment costs and distributional effects has the added virtue of pointing to appropriate remedies when the economic advantages of increased trade are believed to outweigh the costs. It might also indicate accompanying policies to improve the economy's ability to utilize the potential gains from trade expansion in the long run.

One can view the impact of trade policies on jobs in two ways. Trade policies, like technological progress, can increase labor productivity, raising wages, but lowering the amount of workers needed to produce the same amount of output. But the second impact of trade is to expand the potential market for your product, increasing demand so that more workers are needed even at the higher level of productivity.

Summary for Rule-of-Thumb Calculations

▶ **Step 1**: Estimate the production changes in domestic industries as a result of trade policy changes.

▶ **Step 2**: Once we have these estimates, we can use one of two rules of thumb, in the absence of detailed information about the industry.

  o We can apply an appropriate jobs multiplier to the production increase (e.g., 12,500 jobs per billion dollars of production, times $4.5 billion production rise equals 56,250 jobs).

  o We can apply the percentage increase in output to total industry employment (e.g., 3% growth in production implies a 3% increase in employment from a base of 2 million, or 60,000 jobs).

▶ **Step 3:** (if applicable): We can further estimate indirect job impacts as a multiple of direct jobs. A commonly used multiple is 2, thus 112,500 indirect jobs in addition to the 56,250 direct jobs in the above example. (Be sure that those indirect jobs are filled by domestic citizens/residents before using that number in domestic policy debates!)

Note: Increased demand for labor in a full-employment economy or changes in the demand for labor where employment is inflexible will generally result in wage changes rather than changes in employment levels. Empirically (in the United States in the 1990s), wages in export-related industries were higher on average than wages in import-competing industries, which is evidence to economists that reducing trade restrictions increases employment opportunities in higher-productivity, higher-wage jobs.

ESTIMATING THE COST OF PROTECTION TO CONSUMERS

One of the most direct benefits of trade is to lower the cost, increase the quality, or expand the variety of goods and services available to consumers. Since consumer groups are usually not as well organized as producer groups, consumer benefits or costs are not given the same prominence in narrow political decisions in trade as producer losses or gains, particularly where the issue focuses on highly specific goods or services. Nevertheless, in the context of a public debate over the national interest at stake in broad trade policy decisions, consumer benefits and costs often assume considerable importance. Publicizing the costs of protection to consumers is an effective weapon in swaying both public opinion and the views of policy makers.

Calculating Consumer Benefits and Costs When Price Effects are Known

Of the various consumer benefits of expanded trade, reduction in price is the easiest to calculate. Consumer costs are lowered in two ways. First, virtually all imported goods and services that face protection in the domestic market cost less in their country of origin than the competing domestic products (even after considering transportation costs). Second, increased competition from imports puts downward pressure on the price of competing domestic products.

Goods and services imported in large quantities usually find a market because they cost less or are of superior quality to domestic products. In developing countries, particularly those with an uneven distribution of income, imports of final goods often serve a high-value market of people willing to pay more for the greater variety or higher quality represented by imports. This segment of the market is usually quite limited since the proportion of the population who can afford to pay substantially more for the products they consume is small.

Conversely, a reduction of trade as a result of higher trade barriers increases the price paid by consumers for both imported and domestically produced goods and services. The cost of imported goods or services in such cases rises, either because the consumer is charged for the tariff imposed by the government or the consumer is charged a premium price that reflects the artificial scarcity created by an import quota or regulatory barrier.

The total benefit to consumers is the total money saved as a result of the reduction of an import barrier. By the same token, the total loss to consumers is the total money lost as a result of the increase of an import barrier. If we have the price data, we can calculate a rough approximation of the total benefit by multiplying the price reduction by the quantity purchased, and conversely we can calculate a rough approximation of the total cost of an import barrier to consumers by multiplying the increase in price by the quantity consumed. This estimate is more precise when considering small changes in quantity from a large base, as would be the case for a very inelastic demanded product.

In making this consumer benefit or cost calculation we must be cognizant that consumers generally buy more of a product at a lower price and less of a product at a higher price. Therefore, we need to multiply the change in price not by the quantity consumed in the past, but by the average of the old quantity and the expected future quantity when the price increase has taken effect. We can calculate the impact of the reduction or increase in price on consumer demand by multiplying the price change by the price elasticity of demand (PED), the factor that measures the relationship between changes in price and changes in the quantity consumed.

Estimating the Price Effects of Trade Policy Actions

In discussing the calculation of the consumer benefits of a reduction in import barriers, we have assumed that we know how much consumer prices will fall as a result of such trade liberalizing actions. When trade liberalization takes the form of a tariff cut and importers are free to compete openly once they have paid the tariff, we can assume that importers will pass on the full tariff cut to consumers. The percentage price reduction is calculated by dividing the percentage point cut in the tariff by the *landed cost* of the product plus the original tariff. Thus, if the tariff on imported tomatoes was cut by five percentage points from 10% to 5%, the expected price reduction will be 5 divided by 110, which is approximately 4.5%.

In basic economics courses, you learn the concept of price, but in the real world there are many different prices. **Factory-gate or farm-gate** price refers to the cost of production only, abstracting from any transport costs to market and markups through a distribution system. **Landed cost** (or landed price) is the production cost, plus all transport, warehousing, and distribution costs to place that product in a bonded warehouse in the importing country. All trade barriers, inspection requirements, etc., are then assessed when the product leaves that bonded area. **Retail price** is the price paid by consumers, whether they are households, businesses, or government agencies.

As noted earlier, a trade policy action will affect not only the prices charged for imported products but will also affect the prices of competing domestic goods. In a fully competitive economy, a fall or rise in the price of imported products will cause an equal fall or rise in the prices of equivalent domestic products. In cases where domestic competition is restricted or where domestic products are not full substitutes, the price changes in similar domestic products will be less than the price changes for imports.

We calculate consumer benefits and costs of the changes in the prices of domestic products in the same way we calculated the consumer benefits and costs of the changes in import prices. For a rough estimate, we multiply the change in price times the initial consumption level. A more precise estimate would be the change in price times the average of the pre- and post-adjustment consumption levels.

ESTIMATING THE ECONOMIC EFFICIENCY GAINS OF TRADE

Individuals engaged in trade are concerned with making money, but in the vast majority of cases, guided by Adam Smith's "invisible hand," the process of making money tends to improve economic efficiency and enhance welfare for the participant countries. Trade allows a country to concentrate more of its resources on goods and services it produces more efficiently, relative to other products and countries. This follows from the concept of comparative advantage. It involves so-called allocative or static efficiency gains. In some sectors of the economy, expanding the scale of production to serve the regional or global market leads to further cost savings and efficiency. Trade also stimulates domestic producers to adopt more efficient production methods and to develop new products that better meet consumer tastes. These two factors contribute to what economists call dynamic gains from trade.

It is generally easier to estimate the potential gains from trade liberalization for a single product, what economists call a *partial equilibrium* estimate. Here, the focus is not on the greater value of production possible if resources are transferred to another sector of the economy, but on three aspects of protection in that protected sector. The first is the additional cost of making a product at home, compared to the cost of importing the product. The second cost is the consumer surplus lost at the higher domestic price due to lower consumption. The third aspect is the change in government revenues. In the following section, we compare the gains to producers and the increase in government revenues (in the case of tariff protection) to consumer losses to calculate a net national impact of protection. The same exercise in reverse shows the net national impact of trade liberalization.

STUDIES OF THE IMPACT OF TRADE POLICIES ON NATIONAL WELFARE

Numerous economic studies attempt to measure the net impact of trade policies on national welfare. We can put such studies into several subcategories:

- ▶ Specific trade policies (NAFTA, EU, etc.) or free trade with the world.

- ▶ Static efficiency only or static and dynamic efficiency.

- ▶ Competitive markets or noncompetitive markets.

- ▶ Trade only or investment changes as well.

Not surprisingly, the largest impacts on national welfare are from studies that examine global free trade, dynamic efficiency, noncompetitive markets, and foreign investment. Such studies yield estimates of potential gains as high as 8-12% of national income for such medium-sized countries with moderate trade barriers as Canada and Mexico.[10]

Estimates of the potential gains from trade for the huge U.S. economy tend to be much smaller. Without dynamic gains or investment effects, these estimates are around one-half of 1%.[11] One study indicates that the elimination of all U.S. tariffs would *reduce* national welfare by 0.6%! [12] The elimination of quotas and other quantitative restrictions would raise national welfare by 1.3%, for a net benefit of free trade.

Another way to highlight the benefits of trade liberalization is to look at global gains rather than national gains. An Australian study placed the global gains from cutting all trade barriers in half at $400 billion (U.S.).[13] A rule of thumb to remember is that, due to the nature of deadweight social loss triangles, a 50% reduction in trade barriers captures about three-fourths of the potential gains from liberalization.

---

10 Adams, Alanis and del Rio, "The Mexico-U.S. Free Trade and Investment Area Proposal," Journal of Policy Modeling, 14(1), pp. 99-119; Young and Romero, "A Dynamic Dual Model of the North American Free Trade Agreement," and Sobrazo, "The Gains for Mexico from a North American Free Trade Agreement," both in Modeling Trade Policy, Francois and Shiells, eds., (NY: Cambridge U. Press, 1994) (for Mexico). Cox and Harris, 1984, for global free trade for Canada.

11 But even one-half of 1% of the U.S. economy is nearly $40 billion dollars, much more than the total amount of U.S. aid to developing countries.

12 Goulder, 1992. The implication is that the U.S. is such a large consumer of many products that its tariffs force world price down in many cases, creating national gains at the expense of foreign exporters.

13 Financial Times, May 26, 1999.

Part B
Technical Appendix on Economic Estimating Techniques

We see two gaps in the skills that many entry-level professionals bring to the practice of Commercial Diplomacy.

► The first gap is in understanding the impacts of commercial policy changes on private sector actors. How will firms adapt their production, ordering, hiring, and other decisions? What will be the impact on their bottom line? If there are commercial policy options to accomplish a certain goal, will those options have similar or very different impacts on workers, firms, suppliers, etc.?

► The second gap is in understanding the big picture of international commerce. How are international movements of goods related to international financial flows, movements of labor, and technology transfer? More simply, how does the economic health of an economy relate to international transactions in the long run?

Part B of this chapter seeks to enable students and practitioners who may not have much mathematical or economics background to understand quantitative assessments provided by professional economists and to make basic rule-of-thumb calculations when a professional economist is not available. The concepts covered are intended to help Commercial Diplomats become more knowledgeable of both the details and the big picture, thus reducing their dependence on specialists. Part B, therefore, serves three separate objectives:

► Help trade policy practitioners and students of Commercial Diplomacy who lack extensive training in economics and data analysis to make rule-of-thumb calculations of the economic impact of trade policy decisions;

► Give both the practitioner and the student a handy reference guide to other pedagogical resources; and

► Provide background to instructors for seminars and courses.

INTRODUCTION TO THE USE OF ECONOMIC DATA IN TRADE POLICY

Why is the Effective Use of Economic Data So Important?

The trade policy practitioner must be able to support arguments in favor of policy positions with data highlighting the economic impact of policy decisions on key stakeholders and on the country as a whole. Learning how to use economic data effectively is, therefore, one of the critical skills in Commercial Diplomacy.

For Whom and for What Areas of Trade and Investment is this Relevant?

In the past Commercial Diplomacy was concerned largely with negotiations over tariffs and quotas on imports. In today's more interdependent world, trade negotiations cover a much wider range of government regulations and actions that affect international commerce. These include:

- ▶ Standards for health, safety, environment, and consumer protection;

- ▶ Regulations covering services such as banking, telecommunications, and accounting;

- ▶ Competition policy;

- ▶ Laws concerning bribery and corruption;

- ▶ Agricultural support programs;

- ▶ Industrial subsidies;

- ▶ Policies affecting foreign investment and foreign exchange controls; and

- ▶ Historically "domestic" policy issues, such as taxation and immigration policies.

The primary practitioners of Commercial Diplomacy are trade officials who are charged with solving trade problems created by government policy actions and negotiating international trade and investment agreements. Commercial Diplomacy skills are also required of officials in many other government departments and ministries with trade-related responsibilities covering foreign affairs, finance, agriculture, industry, labor, health, the environment, regulation of banks, telecommunications, air transportation, or the licensing of professionals.

The same skills are also required of managers in international government relations departments of industry associations, corporations, unions, and nongovernmental organizations. These organizations frequently have a stake in the outcome of trade policy decisions and can play a role in the domestic and global political advocacy and coalition-building process that usually precedes government-to- government negotiations on international trade and investment issues. Skills in Commercial Diplomacy are required of corporate managers posted in foreign countries who must interact extensively with the host government on a broad range of regulatory issues, and officials in international organizations dealing with global trade, investment, and trade-related regulatory issues.

How Does Effective Use of Data Fit into the Policy Process?

There are three main stages to the policy process, and data and data analysis play an important role in all of them:

- ▶ **Stage 1**: Collecting relevant data on current and proposed policies, trade flows, production, employment levels in the industry, and linkages to other industries.

▶ **Stage 2**: Seeking guidance from supervisors on a proposed course of action and seeking to develop consensus among participants who share the same interests. The Commercial Diplomat must be able to identify the most important economic impacts from the point of view of all relevant decision makers.

▶ **Stage 3**: Summarizing the issue by finding and highlighting the key economic issue(s) that will persuade stakeholders that their interests are best served by a particular course of action.

Interfacing with Economists

The objective of this section is not to make trade policy practitioners into PhD economists. That task is too difficult and not necessary. Instead, it is to make the trade policy practitioner both less dependent on economists and more knowledgeable and critical of the work of economists.

There is an expression, that "A little bit of knowledge is a dangerous thing." We intend, both to raise the level of your economics awareness and effectiveness, and to show the limitation of some of the back-of-the-envelope tools presented here. We hope the result will increase the respect economists have for Commercial Diplomats, and vice versa.

> *"The Commercial Diplomat is the international economist's worst nightmare: an advocate on behalf of trade policy 'stakeholders' armed with just enough economics to be convincing to policymakers but not enough to be encumbered by the truth."*

The statement above, by an international economist active in the trade arena, portrays the current situation at its worst. That person says that an ideal would be "to help Commercial Diplomats understand and communicate with economists in the interest of bringing about better, or at least better informed, trade policy decisions."

How to Use this Material

Part B serves three separate objectives. First and foremost, it is designed to equip trade policy practitioners with the analytical tools to understand and make quick "back-of-the-envelope" calculations on the economic impact of policy decisions affecting international trade and investment. The Commercial Diplomat must understand the impact on the constituency he/she represents, the impact on other key stakeholders, and the impact on the country at large. We will also offer detailed guidelines and some simple rules of thumb, while also alerting readers to caveats and potential pitfalls in such calculations. Each subsection is organized around the calculations of a specific impact or group of impacts. These include the impacts of trade policies on prices, trade flows, industry revenues, costs, profits, jobs, wages, economic efficiency, the cost to taxpayers and the broader national interest, as well as the impacts of monetary and fiscal policy on trade.

Often the determination of each impact involves a chain of calculations. After providing background discussion on each issue, this section aims to provide basic "recipe" guidelines for each series of calculations. For example, suppose we wish to determine the impact of a proposed trade policy on the profits of producers. This seemingly simple calculation still involves at least five steps.[14]

1. Determine how the policy action affects costs for relevant producers, importers, and exporters.
2. Determine how those changes in costs will affect the retail prices of the goods offered for sale in the home market and/or the foreign market.
3. Calculate how the changes in prices will affect the demand for exports in the foreign market and the demand for imports and import substitutes in the home market.
4. Calculate how suppliers will respond to the changes in demand.
5. Calculate how the change in the costs and revenues of producers translates into changes in profits.

If we wish to take this a step further and calculate the impact of this same policy decision on workers, we would need to add three additional steps.

1. Calculate how changes in production obtained from the above calculations translate into changes in the number of jobs available in the industry.
2. Estimate how changes in the industry's conditions affect productivity of workers and the wages they can earn as a result.
3. Estimate, using elements of the seven steps above, the impact of the policy on *related* industries.

Going through each of the steps outlined above is not merely a simple mechanical process. First, we must assemble considerable data on current production, trade, costs, prices, employment, and wages. We also must acquire reliable information on historical relationships between price changes in the industry and changes in the amount of a product consumers wish to buy or producers wish to sell at those prices. Each of these tasks is handled in individual subsections, with tips to streamline the process as much as possible without compromising the final results.

The economic impacts of trade policy actions, of course, are not the only policy impacts that matter. Policy decisions that affect global trade and investment flows inevitably affect such other policy dimensions as health, safety, environment, foreign policy, or national security. Estimating these policy impacts largely requires other policy tools that are treated elsewhere. Exclusion of this information is not meant to signal that they are not important or less important.

The treatment of economic analysis here is designed to give the practitioner and the student tools to estimate the economic effects of trade policy decisions and tools to test

---

14 In this example we have omitted the additional consideration necessary in analyzing the case of intermediate goods and their impact on corresponding final products. An additional real-world complexity is the degree to which manufacturers control retail prices or large retailers affect wholesale prices.

and present results of earlier calculations. It shows them how to apply and to interpret basic economic tools, how to use simple mathematical calculations, how to read graphs and economic diagrams, and when and how to use them to illustrate a point most effectively.

Estimating the Economic Magnitude of Trade Policy Actions

To understand the impact of trade policy actions, we need to review the foundation on which trade theory rests. This foundation is based on the work of David Ricardo in the early 1800s. The crucial concept is *comparative advantage*, which motivates gains from trade among countries that are able to produce similar products.

A country has a comparative advantage in production of a certain product if it can produce that product at a lower *opportunity cost*. Opportunity cost is the amount of another product that cannot be produced as a result of the decision to produce the first product. In other words, if Ireland can produce 20 more computers by not producing one car, while Germany can produce one more car at the expense of 12 computers, then Ireland has a lower opportunity cost in producing computers and Germany has a lower opportunity cost in producing cars. Thus, there are gains from bilateral trade, with Ireland exporting computers and importing German cars, and freer trade between the two countries will lead to an expansion in Ireland's computer industry and contraction in its auto industry.

We will consider how to obtain an initial assessment of the relative economic importance of a decision and whom it will affect. We will describe how an analyst can quickly assemble readily available data on the policy measure and on the affected industries.

For sound trade policy advocacy, trade policy making, and trade negotiating decisions, it is important to understand stakeholders' economic interests. The number of industries likely affected by an issue or policy action, the volume of production affected, and the trade and jobs accounted for by such industries are of economic importance to potential stakeholders. It is also vital information for politicians and politically inclined decision makers. Getting the attention of a busy decision maker is often the first challenge for a Commercial Diplomat, and data on the size of affected sectors is an avenue for getting that attention. Even before that, in the absence of guidance from superiors, such data can indicate whether it is worth probing deeper into the issue and the relevant economic data.

The amount of trade "covered" by liberalizing or protectionist action, or the amount of jobs directly affected by a trade action, is often described as "coverage." In situations where data is unavailable or the complexity of an issue makes it impossible to develop a defensible quantitative estimate of the policy impact, coverage can become a rough measuring rod for policy decisions. Thus, trade negotiators and politicians often discuss the amount of trade "covered" by liberalizing or protectionist actions as a proxy for the importance of the issue.

Estimating the trade or industry coverage of a policy issue or action involves two simple steps:

(1)   Deciding which industries or industry sub-sectors are likely affected and then finding sources of data, and

(2)   Making qualitative judgments specific to each case. This second step of data collection is more of a challenge.

Creating Initial Rough Estimates

When information about the nature and magnitude of the policy action is combined with information about the amount of trade or production affected by the policy action, it is possible in many cases to convey a good idea of the likely economic impact. In some cases, policymakers want to hear whether a particular issue is sufficiently important to deserve analysis. In some cases, the answer is obvious. For instance, in the case of the Foreign Service Corporation (FCS) dispute in 2000, the magnitude of the estimated benefits to U.S. exporters ($4.2 billion by one estimate and $4.8 billion by another) and the magnitude of the WTO sanction ($4 billion) made it clear that the issues were important to the United States (http://trade.ec.europa.eu/doclib/docs/2003/november/tradoc_114503.pdf). When several sources or several methods concur on a rough magnitude of the expected effect, we can be more certain of the importance of the issue we are studying.

In some cases, you will be asked to make those initial estimates yourself. Let us take the example of a "foreign country," which we will call Xenia. Xenia proposes to cut its 10% duty on car imports in half to 5%. Our "home country" now exports cars worth $10 billion to Xenia, out of total exports of $200 billion. Assume the total size of the "home" economy $1 trillion. With this information we are in a fairly good position to conclude that the impact will be significant. How do we know this?

Let us assume that the overall output and employment of the auto industry is $50 billion and 300,000 respectively (information that can be obtained fairly easily). One option is for producers to capture the extra $500 million ($10 billion * 5%) as additional profits. Another option, more likely in a highly competitive market, is to cut the price by 5% and increase output to gain market share. It is an open question whether exporters will choose to cut their delivered price by 5%, increase their profit margin by 5%, or some combination of the two.

Where the proposed policy action does not take the form of a tariff cut or increase, it is useful to translate that policy's impacts into an equivalent tariff or subsidy. The first thing to discover is whether the proposed policy action changes incentives for producers. If not, it is just a matter of calculating the direct impact. Such measures are called by economists *lump-sum* taxes or subsidies.

If incentives change, we need to estimate the actual response by producers. This is done by calculating how the proposed policy action will affect incentives such as costs and prices and then translating that into an equivalent tariff cut or increase (or an equivalent change in a subsidy). Thus, if we know that the proposed policy action will reduce the costs of exports by $5 million, and the total exports by the industry amount to $100 million, we can say that the proposed policy action has an effect equivalent to eliminating a 5% tariff.

ESTIMATING THE IMPACT OF TRADE POLICY CHANGES ON THE PRICE OF IMPORTED PRODUCTS AND ON TRADE IN SUCH PRODUCTS

One of the most frequently raised questions on policy actions covered by Commercial Diplomacy is the impact on trade flows. Understanding and communicating the impact of trade policy on trade, and ultimately on revenues, costs, profits, wages, and jobs is the foundation of Commercial Diplomacy. While economists tend to emphasize the economic efficiency and consumer benefits of trade, the political debate over trade is dominated by arguments over the benefit of increased exports to producers in export industries and the loss generated by increased imports for producers in import-competing industries. In other words, economists see imports as good, because they allow consumption of goods produced using another country's resources and exports as necessary to finance imports. Policy makers, however, often see imports as a threat to domestic producers and interest groups and exports as a source of new wealth, increased national output, employment, profits, and tax revenues. These policy perceptions are reinforced politically by producers being better organized politically than consumers. Consumer organizations are often co-opted by producer interests. This can result in a *mercantilist* tilt to trade policy.

Mercantilists of the eighteenth century believed that exports were good and imports were bad. Therefore, the role of trade policy was to create a trade surplus that would result in an inflow of gold and stimulate the domestic economy. Adam Smith's *Wealth of Nations* explains the fallacy of the mercantilist argument, but the political strength of producer interests has preserved the mercantilist element in trade policy. In view of these political realities, proponents of trade liberalization usually focus on new export opportunities created by reducing foreign trade barriers, while opponents of trade liberalization focus on the displacement of domestic production through increased imports.

In this section we review the steps necessary to calculate the impact of trade policy on trade flows, and in subsequent sections we will review the steps necessary to calculate the impact on revenues, costs, profits, wages, and jobs. Calculating the impact of a policy measure on trade is generally a two-step process. First, the analyst must calculate the effect of the policy action on the price at which the good or service could be sold in the import market. Second, the analyst must calculate the impact of the change in price on the quantity consumers wish to purchase. Our starting point is small countries that can buy as much as they wish at a constant world price.

For a large country like the United States, a third step is necessary. The analyst must determine if the change in import demand for a product is sufficient to alter the world price of that product. For economists, the definition of a "large" or "small" country is product specific and rests on whether a policy change in that producing or consuming country has a noticeable impact on world price. Thus, Kuwait, despite its small land area and low population, may be a large country in the oil market, while India may be considered small in many manufactured goods markets like autos and aircraft. In general, the analysis of trade effects is complicated by any departure from the assumption of *perfect competition* built into most economic models.

► <u>Perfect competition</u> is the assumption that the market is composed of many small producers and consumers acting independently, freely entering and exiting the market as profitability dictates, with all producers making identical products. Therefore, no market participant can manipulate prices.

Calculating the Price Impact of a Policy Action

Tariffs: We focus here on the case of a small county in a competitive market. Calculating the impact of the policy action on price is a fairly straightforward calculation in the case of changes to *ad valorem tariffs* or fees on imported products that vary in proportion to the price.

As the above sentence indicates, **ad valorem tariffs** are those imposed in proportion to the price of an item. Hence a 10% tariff imposed on imports of books would require payment of $1 in duties for a $10 book, $5 on a $50 book, etc. The other main type of tariff is a **specific tariff**, which is a set dollar amount of duty imposed per unit of imports. A specific tariff of $2 per book, in the above example would raise $4 in duties on the two books.

Provided both the importers and domestic retailers are operating under competitive market conditions, we can assume that the increase or reduction of the tariff is passed on to the consumer. Thus, a 50% reduction of an 80% duty translates into a 22% percent reduction of the consumer price in the import market. Here is an example: assuming the world price is $1, a 50% cut in the 80% tariff translates into a price reduction of $0.40 from $1.80 to $1.40.[15] Note, however, that a 50% reduction of a 10% duty translates into only a 4 ½% cut in the retail price of the import (assuming again that the import price is $1, a 50% cut in the 10% duty translates into a 5-cent cut from $1.10). The general formula for calculating the change in price is the change in the tariff divided by one plus the original tariff rate. The same calculation can be applied to any fee on an imported product in proportion to its price.

$$\%\Delta Price = (\text{New Tariff} - \text{Old Tariff})/ (1 + \text{Old Tariff})$$

Quotas: Another common policy action is the reduction or increase of an import quota. Translating a change in the quota to a price change is complicated, but in most cases not necessary for calculating an impact on trade as long as the changed quota continues to restrict trade. In such a case we can assume that trade is increased (reduced) by the full increase (reduction) in the quota. Where the quota that emerges from the change in policy does not bind trade, as happens frequently in the case of textile

---

15 Prior to the tariff change, domestic consumers paid $1.80 for the imported product, $1 to the foreign producer and $0.80 to the government. The tariff reduction halves the payment to the government to $0.40. In percentage terms, this can be expressed as about a 22% reduction in price.

quotas allocated to highly specific apparel items, you must resort to estimates based on a survey of practitioners or an examination of historical data.

When a particular regulation overshadows all other import-related regulations, an initial approach to estimating the price effect of removing the regulation is to examine the difference in the price at which the product is sold in the export and import market and to deduct from that price difference all other known costs such as shipping, tariffs, fees, insurance, etc. Since a single regulation seldom is the only cost element that cannot be clearly identified, and differences in retailing costs also play an important role, there is usually a great deal of controversy around such estimates. They nevertheless provide a useful starting point for a more detailed analysis.

Estimating How a Change in the Price of Imported Products Impacts Trade

Estimating the impact of a change in the price of an imported product on trade in that product involves another two-step process. Economists call the factor used to calculate the direct impact the price elasticity of demand.

> ▶ *The price elasticity of demand (PED)* measures consumer response to price changes and varies from commodity to commodity, from country to country, and from common items of daily consumption to luxury goods.

When a percentage reduction in the price leads to a less-than-proportional increase in quantity demanded, economists say that the demand is inelastic, and when quantity demanded changes more than the change in price, economists say the demand is elastic. Economists estimate a numeric value for this elasticity. A value of 1 means that demand changes in equal proportion to changes in price. Inelastic demand is defined as a value of less than 1, and elastic demand is a value of greater than 1. An elasticity of 0.5 means that quantity demanded changes only half as much proportionally as the price, while an elasticity of 1.5 means that demand changes 50% more proportionally than the price. The price elasticity of demand for various products can be measured by examining historical data. Economists have studied and published price elasticities for various commodities in different countries. Generally, demand for luxury goods and essential food products is relatively price inelastic. People who can afford to pay for luxury goods are not very sensitive to the price when few close substitutes exist (quality gemstones, pleasure craft, etc.). The demand for essential foodstuffs is also usually inelastic since people generally buy them even if the price goes up. In contrast, many consumer goods have a high elasticity since people can easily find substitutes or do without them.

Consider another intuitive way to think about price elasticities of demand. Suppose you spend 10% of your income on a certain product. If the price of this product falls, you buy more, but do you buy so much more that the fraction of your total income spent on the product increases, or just a little bit more, so that the fraction of income spent on that product falls under 10 percent? In the first case, demand would be elastic, in the second, inelastic. Clearly in the case of food, the "savings" from a fall in the price of food would not be spent only on additional food, with the exception of those consumers well below the poverty line. Lower airfares, however, might cause a business traveler to take the whole family on a future business trip, increasing the fraction of income devoted to airfare.

For trade policy purposes we want to measure the impact of a change in the price of an imported product on the demand for that product. The response of consumers to a change in the price of an imported product is affected by a number of things, including the overall desire of consumers to buy more of a particular type of product when its price falls, the extent to which consumers are willing to substitute imported goods or services for domestically produced substitutes, and the willingness and ability of domestic producers to change their prices. The import price elasticity of demand captures the responsiveness of consumers, while holding all other factors constant, including the response of domestic producers, the income of consumers, and the prices of substitutes and complements.

Typical estimates of such import price elasticities are found in the table below, based on a survey by Robert Stern, an international economist, in 1976. These estimates were derived by scouring the published work of economists across a broad range of countries. Industry definitions used for this purpose are from the Standard International Trade Classification system, which is widely used internationally. Stern published values for all the major countries in his book *Price Elasticities in International Trade*.

Table 4A

Typical Import Price Elasticities		
Industry Category	**Range**	**Median**
SITC 0 & 1 (Food, beverages, and tobacco)	−0.09 to −1.59	−0.78
SITC 2 & 4 (Crude materials, oils & fats)	−0.17 to −1.15	−0.50
SITCS 3 (Mineral fuels)	−0.01 to −2.78	−0.96
SITC 5 – 9 (Manufactured goods)	−0.74 to −2.64	−1.34
SITC 0 – 9 (Total imports)	−0.42 to −1.37	−1.06

To summarize, the impact of a policy on trade can be measured by estimating first the impact of that measure on the price of the imported product in the import market, then multiplying that percentage change in price by a price elasticity, which measures the consumer response to a change in price. One can estimate the impact of a change in foreign trade barriers on domestic exports in the same way, with the additional step of assuming (unless clearly inappropriate) that the share of the increased imports captured by domestic exporters is the same as their current market share.

The Stern elasticities, however, are for commodity groups so large as to make them of limited use to policymakers. For example, the extreme range for mineral fuels (from 0.01 to 2.78) runs from extremely inelastic to quite elastic. Using the median of 0.96 would be a large mistake either way.

The next section provides a more technical treatment of elasticities for those familiar and comfortable with basic economic terminology.

ESTIMATING THE IMPACT OF POLICY ACTIONS AFFECTING TRADE ON INDUSTRY REVENUES, COSTS, AND PROFITS

In the last section we explored how policy actions change trade flows by affecting the cost and price of traded goods or influence prices by changing trade flows directly. Information on the impact on trade flows still does not tell us, however, how the economic interests of stakeholders are affected. The focus of this section is the subset of stakeholders participating in the profits of firms producing goods and services domestically. To estimate these effects, we must calculate how a change in prices and trade flows translates into changes in the domestic production of goods and services and thus on industry revenues, costs and profits.[16]

An increase in exports will increase domestic production by an equal amount, provided the industry has unutilized production capacity or large inventories of final goods.[17] In some cases, we assume that the industry has the capacity to increase output. We want to estimate the change in domestic output in the industry after producers have adjusted their output to accommodate the increased export demand. We can simply add the projected increase in exports to the projected level of domestic consumption (abstracting from imports) to obtain the new, higher level of output. The argument in policy debates can be simplified still more. It is not unreasonable to de-link foreign and domestic demand and say that the increase in output attributable to a trade policy that increases exports is simply the increase in exports. Remember that our goal is generally not to predict future sales and profits but to isolate the impact of a proposed trade policy on sales and profits. Economists sometimes express these numbers as changes from a "baseline" or "status quo" scenario.

To calculate the impact on growth in the industry, we divide the increase in exports by the current level of output. The result tells us how much additional growth

---

16 An import surge decreases demand, price, profits, and employment for domestically produced *substitutes*, but could actually increase demand, price, profits, and employment for domestically produced *complements* (goods used along with the imported goods, such as Pentium processors and cheap Korean memory chips), or *service* contracts on Mexican-assembled color TV sets, transportation services associated with international trade, and sales people in Toyota dealerships.

17 While varying by industry, manufacturing firms in the large industrialized economies generally run at 80-85% capacity in normal times, rising close to 100% after several years of strong economic growth (see the 2001 California energy situation) and falling as low as 60% in a sharp recession. Thus, U.S. firms may easily provide 10% more exports due to a trade agreement, but a Mexican or Central American producer might have to divert products from the domestic market to increase significantly exports to the U.S. (at least during a transition period in which new investments are made to expand production capacity), increasing both the domestic and export price to meet new demand in the U.S. unless imports are freely available.

has been or will be created by the trade policy action. We can also measure the significance of the trade policy action by calculating how the growth generated by the increase in exports compares to the current growth in domestic demand or the underlying growth trend in exports.

We need to also consider the effect of time. In the very short term, producers may not be able to increase production because they do not have sufficient parts or raw materials on hand. Or they may not want to increase production because they first want to reduce inventory of finished products before paying overtime, hiring new workers, or installing new machines, particularly if they feel that the increase in demand may be temporary. An increase in sales satisfied through a reduction in inventories increases revenues and profits but does not increase the level of output (and employment).

At some later stage producers may adjust the supply chain with inventories fallen enough to demand replenishing. At this stage the increased demand for products is translated into increased production, up to a level that can be accommodated by the production capacity. We will explore next what happens when producers reach full capacity utilization. Given enough time they can increase production capacity through more investment in plants and equipment. New firms may enter the industry, adding to total production. Over time, we should witness a sequence of three events:

- ▶ In the very short run a reduction in inventories;

- ▶ In the intermediate run an increase in output (by using existing capital and labor more intensively); and

- ▶ In the long run an increase in production capacity (through new capital investment, hiring, and training at existing firms, and new firms entering the market).[18]

Calculating Changes in Production and Profits

The remainder of this chapter introduces the standard graphic methodology for analyzing the impact of trade policy changes on producers. The same methodology also allows us to see and calculate the benefits and costs to consumers and the government. The benefits of this methodology are that it is well known and generally accepted by economists and relatively simple to learn and use.

This methodology has several drawbacks, however, making it unsuitable for some trade policy analysis questions. The underlying assumption is that domestic and foreign products in this market are perfect substitutes. Consumers will purchase the cheaper product, without regard for its national origins. Thus, there can be no real or perceived quality difference between products. The model is perfectly appropriate for homogeneous goods, like commodities (appropriately categorized by quality, such

---

18 A more complete discussion of trade and employment is postponed to the next section, but note that the stage at which employment increases in the three-stage process depends on the country and industry we consider. Generally employment increases in stage two, and may increase further in stage three, but in economies with flexible labor markets and industries that do not require major training efforts, the employment increase comes earlier.

as "light, sweet Brent crude" instead of just oil, Durum wheat, Arabica coffee, etc.).[19] A second problem with this methodology is that it does not lend itself to generalizations about the overall impact on the country (what we call "the national welfare"), since it focuses on a single industry. We would expect there to be "upstream" and "downstream" effects on industries that sell and buy with the industry in question.

As indicated above, we must know both the change in output and the change in price before estimating a change in profits for the industry. We also must know the change in output before we can estimate the likely change in employment, which we will cover in subsequent subsections. What we typically know with respect to our exports is how much the cost of our product will change in the foreign market(s) as a result of a policy action. We then use the estimated change in trade flows as a first guess for the long-run increase in production of the export.

Capacity Utilization

If capacity in the industry is limited, however, we must modify our estimate. If capacity utilization is high in the export industry, and the additional production for export would push it near or over 100%, prices and profits will rise, and output will rise less than our first guess would indicate. A rule of thumb is to use an 85–90% capacity utilization level as the turning point, with increases in demand below that level translating primarily into increased production and increases above that level resulting in higher prices.[20] In the language of economists, we can say that elasticities of supply, like those of demand, change as one moves along the supply curve. Once again, we must be careful in applying a single price elasticity to a large change in price and clearly state the time frame of the analysis.

Table 4B

Capacity Utilization in Different Sectors					
Year	Durable	Nondurable	Primary Processing	Advanced Processing	Utilities
1982	68.0%	77.5%	68.4%	74.0%	79.3%
1989	82.0%	85.7%	85.3%	82.7%	86.3%

19 One function of advertising is differentiating your product, making other products poorer substitutes. The makers or retailers of "Kona", Colombian, or Jamaican coffee have created a premium for their varieties through advertising. Hence the wording "no real or perceived" difference between products, with a subtle emphasis on perceived.

20 To get an idea of typical capacity utilization rates, the two lines of Table 4.1 show rates for broad categories of U.S. industry in recession (1982) and boom (1989). There is more variation at the product level.

Let us now turn to what happens to the output of domestic producers when the price of a competing imported product falls. We must consider how a fall in the price of imports will affect the price of the competing domestic products and consequently the demand for the domestic product. One might initially expect that an increase in imports would lead to a reduction in the price of competing domestic products, as domestic producers seek to preserve sales. However, an increase in imports is less likely to be met by a cut in the price of the domestic substitute if domestic capacity utilization rates are high than if substantial excess capacity already exists. Consider also the possibility of domestic complements, which face increased demand as the price of imports falls.

Producer Surplus for Export Industries

Thus, we see the complexity of decomposing a given change in projected trade flows into a price and production impact for domestic producers. But once we have those estimates, with just a few more assumptions we can calculate changes in profits. The supply curve shown in Figure 4.1 provides a graphic illustration of the impact of increased foreign demand for a country's exports on the profits of the export industry. The diagram shows the impact of the mutual elimination of tariffs between the United States and Costa Rica on export opportunities for Costa Rican garment producers. In Figure 4.1, increased demand results in both higher prices and greater output.

To estimate the potential impact of an action on profits, we must address what economists call *producer surplus*.

> ► *Producer surplus* is the difference between the minimum price a producer must receive to supply that product to the market and the price actually received for that product. When the minimum price, based on the supply curve, fully reflects the marginal cost of production (additional labor, electricity, etc.) then changes in producer surplus correspond to changes in gross operating profits (before depreciation charges, interest expenses, overhead, and taxes).

The shaded triangle in Figure 4.1 represents producer surplus prior to the trade agreement.

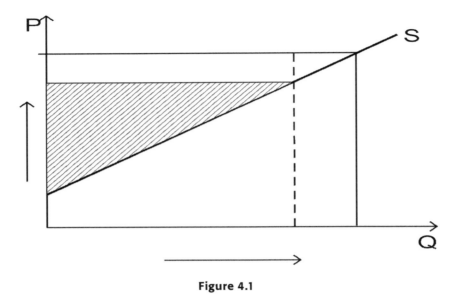

Figure 4.1

Producer Surplus Resulting from the Elimination of Foreign Tariffs

Producer surplus clearly increases for the Costa Rican exporter, and with numbers for the Qs and Ps, we can calculate the increase. Suppose Q increases from 6,000 to 8,000 units, and P increases from $15 to $20 per unit. In this simple model, production costs increase only for the increased output. Since the exporter can charge a higher price for *all* goods sold, profits will rise by the price increase times the old quantity of sales [$5 * 6,000] plus the triangular area of profits on new sales [1/2 * $5 * 2,000], or $35,000.[21] Total revenues increase from $15 * 6,000 = $90,000 to $20 * 8,000 = $160,000. The "other" $35,000 (the difference between the increase in revenues and the increase in profits) represents increases in costs of production (wages, electricity, etc.).

The simplifying assumptions in this calculation are repeated here to emphasize their importance:

► Decreasing returns to scale (new production is more costly than average).

► Industry output can be aggregated (added together) because products produced by different firms in the industry are nearly identical.

► An appropriate price elasticity of supply separates the impact on the domestic industry into output and price components.

► The market is competitive, with many sellers and many buyers.

---

21 In the real world, supply and demand curves are not likely to be straight lines, thus the triangular area calculated here is an approximation.

Effect on Imports in the Domestic Industry

Consider now the case of an increase in imports. Suppose a 10% fall in the price of imports results in a 10% increase in the demand for imports. What happens to the production of domestic substitutes?

Case I: Perfect substitutes

> It depends. Are the domestic and imported products close substitutes? Even in the case of perfect substitutes, domestic production will not fall by as much as the increased demand for imports, since total demand increases at the lower price. If the two products are perfect substitutes, then domestic producers must lower their prices to match the lower import price. At this lower price, there is greater demand for both the domestic and the imported product. The domestic producer loses from the price cut but gains from the increased domestic demand.

Case II: Imperfect substitutes

> If the products are imperfect substitutes, we use the cross-price elasticity of demand to find the impact of the fall in import prices on demand for the domestic product, all else being equal. In this case, we assume domestic producers make some reductions in price, but do not fully match the cut in import prices. Now some of the increased demand for imports comes at the expense of domestic producers, but the rest is new demand generated by lower consumer prices. The exact split depends on the elasticities of supply and demand. Profits will fall, but there is convincing evidence that competition encourages cost-cutting measures by firms in the long run, mitigating the fall.

Once you estimate the new price and quantity for the domestic product, you can calculate the change in profits as above. Suppose a U.S. garment producer lowers price from $25 to $24 and lowers production from 50 million to 48 million units, as a result of increased competition from all CBI (Caribbean Basin Initiative) and NAFTA countries combined. How might profits change?

In the short run, we can repeat the calculations above. Profits fall by one dollar per unit on the 48 million units still viable at the $24 price, plus the smaller margin on the higher-cost production that was phased out. The total area of profits lost is thus $49 million [$1 * 48 million + ½ * $1 * 2 million].

To summarize, changes in trade flows can affect domestic industry in different ways, depending on:

> ► **Capacity utilization in domestic industry:** At high rates of capacity utilization, additional demand is likely met by price increases, while lower demand may be met by production cuts. At low rates of capacity utilization, the reverse is likely.

► **Degree of substitutability between foreign and domestic products:** For extremely close substitutes, a fall in the price of imports will force domestic producers to match the lower price, lowering profits, and production levels. For less close substitutes, we would expect the same changes but of lesser magnitude. Demand for complementary products will increase when the price of imports falls.

► **Production technologies (increasing returns, constant returns, or decreasing returns):** In increasing returns industries, firms are more likely to expand production than to raise prices, and more likely to cut prices than contract production.

► **Corporate culture:** U.S. firms are considered more sensitive to quarterly profits, while Japanese firms are considered more concerned with market share and long-term growth. The price versus quantity adjustments above may reflect these different concerns.

► **Time frame:** Are we are considering the short run, when economic decision makers are in the process of adjusting to changes, or the long run, when everyone makes the necessary adjustments?

► **Industry competitiveness:** Is the industry competitive, or does a single firm or group of firms have the power to set prices? Does a change in domestic trade policy (making the domestic market more or less open to imports) affect the degree of competitiveness in the market?

ESTIMATING THE IMPACT OF TRADE POLICY ON JOBS AND WAGES

The impact of trade policy decisions on jobs and wages is often the central focus of political debate. Most economists are uncomfortable with this focus because they consider macroeconomic policy the proper economic tool for achieving full employment.

The three main areas of macroeconomic policy making are fiscal policy, monetary policy, and exchange rate policy:

► Fiscal policy covers the manipulation of government spending and tax rates.

► Monetary policy covers the manipulation of interest rates and the money supply.

► Exchange rate policies cover the manipulation of exchange rates.

Most economists consider the reduction of consumer prices, the increase in competition, and the creation of more productive, higher-paying jobs the proper focus of trade policy. Whatever the merits from the point of view of economic theory, the political pull toward a focus on jobs is usually so strong that economists and practitioners of Commercial Diplomacy are drawn into the debate on those terms. However, the standard trade calculations introduced in the previous section are not appropriate for this debate, since they deal with the direct impact on affected industries, not the overall impact on the economy.

With a few exceptions, trade leads to increased production and jobs that are characterized by higher levels of worker productivity. In a competitive labor market, such higher productivity jobs bring higher wage rates. Trade, however, also leads to the elimination of jobs in less competitive industries, whose workers typically have fewer or more narrowly specialized skills and frequently do not have the option of moving into the new jobs being created in the more competitive industries without substantial retraining. All too often these workers end up in lower paying jobs, and some may remain unemployed, hoping in vain that their previous job will return.

One of the key concerns over trade policy decisions, therefore, is the distributional effect: workers with the necessary training, experience, and skills gain, while workers without the necessary training, experience, and skills lose. Consequently, in a full-employment economy, the debate over jobs is often a proxy for the real issue, which is the impact on low-skilled workers.[22] A second problem is that openness to trade both accentuates and speeds up the economy's adjustment to new technologies, which has a similar impact on income distribution and unemployment.

Estimating Direct Job Creation in Export Industries

One way to estimate the number of new jobs created in export industries from increased production is by multiplying the increased output by the ratio of output to workers in the economy, in the sector, or in the industry. In the United States, this ratio is normally calculated as the number of jobs created by each $1 billion in output. Since the number of workers required to generate $1 billion in output differs between services and manufacturing, and differs among industries, estimates based on industry data are likely to be more accurate than estimates based on broader sectoral or economy-wide data. All that is required to calculate these ratios is to divide the number of workers employed in the industry by the value of the output in the industry. The primary benefit of this method is its simplicity. It is an appropriate method for most trade analysis purposes, but you should be aware of several weaknesses.

When a policy action affects many different industries, however, quick back-of-the-envelope calculations tend to be based on sector or economy-wide output per worker ratios. Based on estimates from around the year 2000, the number widely (and wrongly) used for manufactured exports in the United States was 20,000 jobs per $1 billion of output, despite the ratio having declined to just 14,000 jobs per $1 billion in output by the mid-1990s due to rapid productivity growth. The appropriate number to use for quick, economy-wide calculations of the U.S. job effects today

22 The term "full employment" does not literally mean that anyone who wants to work can find a job. It means that an additional policy stimulus to create jobs would have a more detrimental impact on inflation than it would be worth in job creation.

would, therefore, be about 12,500 jobs per $1 billion in output after five more years of rapid growth in labor.

Rule of Thumb for Calculating Indirect Job Creation

In addition to the direct employment effects of an increase in production in export industries, we must consider the indirect employment effects in industries that supply inputs or in industries that distribute the output.

A commonly used rule of thumb is that each new job created in export industries ultimately leads to the creation of two additional jobs in downstream and upstream industries.

In today's globalized economy, it is worth considering how many of these additional jobs will be filled by domestic workers. Do U.S. firms have the in-house capabilities to localize products to the Japanese market, or will the associated marketing, service, transportation, and other service jobs be created in Japan? Will the additional demand for components and raw materials be met by affiliates in Malaysia and Mexico? These are important issues to policymakers, and applying rules of thumb without at least cursory study of the industry in question can lead to embarrassing mistakes.

The Difference Between a New Job in an Industry and a New Job in the Economy

There is obviously a difference between an increase of jobs in a particular industry or industries and in the economy as a whole. If there is full employment in the economy, the total number of jobs can increase only through a net increase in immigration or through an increase in the labor force participation of women, retired people, students, or other underemployed groups. In calendar year 2000, for example, the United States had many unfilled positions in software programming and engineering, and one of the major policy issues revolved around increased immigration quotas. Thus, one could argue that a fair assessment of the impact of trade on jobs would not focus on jobs lost or created, but on jobs moved from one sector of the economy to another. Acute, long-term labor shortages in export industries can be addressed by investments in labor-saving technologies that raise productivity and pay for existing workers. Alternatively, labor shortages can be addressed by outsourcing portions of the production or support process in addition to efforts to train domestic workers and bring in foreign workers with needed skills. Which methods a particular company uses depends on relative costs and corporate strategies. We can see all of these strategies at work in the information technology sector.

Direct Employment Effects of an Increase in Imports

On the other end of the spectrum, an increase in imports can lead to a decline of production and jobs in domestic industries competing with the imports. However, the relationship is not one-to-one for several reasons. First, some imported products are treated by consumers as distinct products, rather than as substitutes for equivalent domestically produced goods or services. In such cases, the imports constitute primarily an increase in total demand in that industry, rather than the substitution of an imported product for a domestically produced product. Second, as we saw above, an increase in imports of inputs may be essential to support increased domestic production in downstream industries. Third, in a full-employment economy, imports can satisfy domestic demand that cannot be filled by domestic producers. In other words, a strong increase in domestic demand due to rising incomes can increase imports even as it stimulates additional domestic production. Fourth, an increase in imports from one country as a result of a trade agreement (from Mexico under NAFTA, for instance) may displace imports from other countries (Southeast Asia and South America), leaving net imports and the impact on domestic production roughly unchanged.

In light of these complexities, how do we calculate job losses due to increased imports? There is no simple way. We would like a method more accurate than reducing the one-to-one ratio by a judgmental factor, but less difficult than empirically measuring past relationships between increased imports and job losses in particular industries using multiple regression analysis to isolate the impact of increased imports from all other factors that influence employment, such as changes in the business cycle. Rather than making those estimates yourself, you can look for economists' estimates of the cross-price elasticities between imports and domestic products. Once you have such a cross-price elasticity, you multiply it by the percent change in the price of the import to get an estimate of how much demand for the domestic substitute will shift. By multiplying the change in production by the average number of direct and indirect jobs supported by a billion dollars in output you can arrive at a quick general estimate of the jobs created or lost as a result of a policy action. This will overestimate the impact, but the more elastic the demand and the less elastic the supply of this good, the better this rough estimate will be.

Impact of Trade on Labor Productivity and Wages

When political pressure does not dictate a jobs-oriented debate, supporters of trade liberalization are likely to run into fewer analytical problems by focusing on the increase in labor productivity and wages associated with increased trade. Increased trade adds to the number of relatively high-productivity, high-wage jobs and reduces the number of low-productivity, low-wage jobs. This can readily be measured by identifying the productivity and wage differential between the industries experiencing export gains on one hand and the industries experiencing an increase in imports and a relative decline in domestic production on the other hand. This difference was calculated for U.S. trade overall in the 1990s, and later data shows a 4-5% differential. Keep in mind other cases in other countries may produce different results in magnitude or even in sign.

Just as proponents of trade liberalization are on more solid analytical ground focusing on the productivity/wage equation than the jobs equation, opponents of trade liberalization are on more solid analytical ground by focusing on the adjustment costs and distributional consequences associated with increased trade. An analysis that includes treatment of adjustment costs and distributional effects has the added virtue of pointing to appropriate remedies when the economic advantages of increased trade are believed to outweigh the costs. It might also indicate accompanying policies to improve the economy's ability to utilize the potential gains from trade expansion in the long run.

One can view the impact of trade policies on jobs in two ways. Trade policies, like technological progress, can increase labor productivity, raising wages, but lowering the amount of workers needed to produce the same amount of output. But the second impact of trade is to expand the potential market for your product, increasing demand so that more workers are needed even at the higher level of productivity.

Indirect Impacts of Trade Policies on Jobs

What other impacts result from new trade agreements? Lower trade barriers in foreign markets may encourage domestic firms to move production facilities abroad, to serve either the home market through imports or regional markets abroad. The "giant sucking sound" of NAFTA, as predicted by Ross Perot, involved an anticipated movement of U.S. firms to Mexico to capitalize on cheap labor and lower environmental standards, while producing for the U.S. market. A substantial flow of U.S. investment to Mexico did occur as a result of NAFTA, but there was no corresponding decline in U.S. jobs. Why?

The single most important reason for this apparent paradox is that foreign direct investment (FDI) and portfolio investment to the United States surged far more than U.S. investment in Mexico. However, far from being an implication of NAFTA, it reflects the U.S. productivity boom of the 1990s in contrast to economic struggles abroad. If a country has an open capital market, investment opportunities will be gobbled up by someone. Other reasons include:

- ► **Complementary employment creation in the United States**. While assembly and parts operations thrived in Mexico, total production, and thus demand for other parts produced in the United States – services (transport, marketing, sales, legal, financial, etc.), headquarters facilities, etc. – increased.

- ► **Investment diversion from other regions**. Some new investments in Mexico were diverted from Southeast Asia or elsewhere in Latin America. These investments were more closely interlinked to U.S. supply chains, thus creating more U.S. jobs than similar investments further afield.

- ► **Cost savings in Mexico are not as great as they appear**. Better infrastructure, more skilled and productive employees, and lower transportation costs to market make the United States the preferred location for most producers. Large U.S. multinationals cannot afford to exploit local labor and environmental laws (actually, in the case of Mexico, poor enforcement of environmental laws), or they will face a public relations nightmare and consumer boycotts. Thus, most U.S. producers in Mexico use pollution control technologies (purchased from U.S. suppliers) similar to those used at home.

▶ **FDI targeting the Mexican market declines.** While new investments in service sectors (banking, telecom, tourism) rose, lower tariffs in Mexico meant less incentive to produce goods in Mexico for the protected Mexican market. Rather than move production facilities to Mexico, some companies now serve the Mexican market more cheaply from existing production facilities in the United States.

The points considered above can be generalized more or less to other trade policy changes and other countries. Thus, while trade agreements often do promote complementary investments, the net effect of these investments on job losses and adjustment costs is uncertain and unlikely to be large.

Summary for Rule-of-Thumb Calculations

▶ **Step 1**: Estimate the production changes in domestic industries as a result of trade policy changes.

▶ **Step 2**: Once we have these estimates, we can use one of two rules of thumb, in the absence of detailed information about the industry.

   o   We can apply an appropriate jobs multiplier to the production increase (e.g., 12,500 jobs per billion dollars of production, times $4.5 billion production rise equals 56,250 jobs).

   o   We can apply the percentage increase in output to total industry employment (e.g., 3% growth in production implies a 3% increase in employment from a base of 2 million, or 60,000 jobs).

▶ **Step 3:** (if applicable): We can further estimate indirect job impacts as a multiple of direct jobs. A commonly used multiple is 2, thus 112,500 indirect jobs in addition to the 56,250 direct jobs in the above example. (Be sure that those indirect jobs are filled by domestic citizens/residents before using that number in domestic policy debates!)

Note: Increased demand for labor in a full-employment economy or changes in the demand for labor where employment is inflexible will generally result in wage changes rather than changes in employment levels. Empirically (in the United States in the 1990s), wages in export-related industries were higher on average than wages in import-competing industries, which is evidence to economists that reducing trade restrictions increases employment opportunities in higher-productivity, higher-wage jobs.

ESTIMATING THE COST OF PROTECTION TO CONSUMERS

One of the most direct benefits of trade is to lower the cost, increase the quality, or expand the variety of goods and services available to consumers. Since consumer groups are usually not as well organized as producer groups, consumer benefits or costs are not given the same prominence in narrow political decisions in trade as producer losses or gains, particularly where the issue focuses on highly specific goods or services. Nevertheless, in the context of a public debate over the national interest at stake in broad trade policy decisions, consumer benefits and costs often assume considerable importance. Publicizing the costs of protection to consumers is an effective weapon in swaying both public opinion and the views of policy makers.

Calculating Consumer Benefits and Costs When Price Effects are Known

Of the various consumer benefits of expanded trade, reduction in price is the easiest to calculate. Consumer costs are lowered in two ways. First, virtually all imported goods and services that face protection in the domestic market cost less in their country of origin than the competing domestic products (even after considering transportation costs). Second, increased competition from imports puts downward pressure on the price of competing domestic products.

Goods and services imported in large quantities usually find a market because they cost less or are of superior quality to domestic products. In developing countries, particularly those with an uneven distribution of income, imports of final goods often serve a high-value market of people willing to pay more for the greater variety or higher quality represented by imports. This segment of the market is usually quite limited since the proportion of the population who can afford to pay substantially more for the products they consume is small.

Conversely, a reduction of trade as a result of higher trade barriers increases the price paid by consumers for both imported and domestically produced goods and services. The cost of imported goods or services in such cases rises, either because the consumer is charged for the tariff imposed by the government or the consumer is charged a premium price that reflects the artificial scarcity created by an import quota or regulatory barrier.

The total benefit to consumers is the total money saved as a result of the reduction of an import barrier. By the same token, the total loss to consumers is the total money lost as a result of the increase of an import barrier. If we have the price data, we can calculate a rough approximation of the total benefit by multiplying the price reduction by the quantity purchased, and conversely we can calculate a rough approximation of the total cost of an import barrier to consumers by multiplying the increase in price by the quantity consumed. This estimate is more precise when considering small changes in quantity from a large base, as would be the case for a very inelastic demanded product.

In making this consumer benefit or cost calculation we must be cognizant that consumers generally buy more of a product at a lower price and less of a product at a higher price. Therefore, we need to multiply the change in price not by the quantity consumed in the past, but by the average of the old quantity and the expected future quantity when the price increase has taken effect. We can calculate the impact of the reduction or increase in price on consumer demand by multiplying the price change by the price elasticity of demand (PED), the factor that measures the relationship between changes in price and changes in the quantity consumed.

Estimating the Price Effects of Trade Policy Actions

In discussing the calculation of the consumer benefits of a reduction in import barriers, we have assumed that we know how much consumer prices will fall as a result of such trade liberalizing actions. When trade liberalization takes the form of a tariff cut and importers are free to compete openly once they have paid the tariff, we can assume that importers will pass on the full tariff cut to consumers. The percentage price reduction is calculated by dividing the percentage point cut in the tariff by the *landed cost* of the product plus the original tariff. Thus, if the tariff on imported tomatoes was cut by five percentage points from 10% to 5%, the expected price reduction will be 5 divided by 110, which is approximately 4.5%.

In basic economics courses, you learn the concept of price, but in the real world there are many different prices. **Factory-gate or farm-gate** price refers to the cost of production only, abstracting from any transport costs to market and markups through a distribution system. **Landed cost** (or landed price) is the production cost, plus all transport, warehousing, and distribution costs to place that product in a bonded warehouse in the importing country. All trade barriers, inspection requirements, etc., are then assessed when the product leaves that bonded area. **Retail price** is the price paid by consumers, whether they are households, businesses, or government agencies. Thus, if the tariff on imported tomatoes was cut by five percentage points from 10% to 5%, the expected price reduction will be 5 divided by 110, which is approximately 4.5%.

What if the trade liberalization action involves a larger quota or the removal of a regulatory barrier? How can we calculate the cut in the price of imported products in this case? We can devise a fairly good estimate if we know by how much imports will increase as a result of the policy measure and we have an estimate of the price elasticity of demand. In effect, what we would be calculating is how much prices must drop to convince consumers to purchase the increased imports. In other words, we would be working backwards. We calculate the implied price change by multiplying the percentage increase of imports by 1 divided by the price elasticity of demand for the imported product. If the price elasticity of demand for tomatoes is 1.5 and the elimination of a quota will increase consumption by 12%, then the implied price cut is 12% divided by 1.5, which is 8%.[23] Of course, if we do not know how much imports will increase when we eliminate a quota, we have to make the best estimate possible on the basis of available data.[24]

Calculating the likely price increase that will result from a quota or other quantitative restriction on imports involves the same calculation as above. We divide the

---

23 The elasticity is equal to the percent change in quality divided by the percentage change in price. So in this example PED for imports = %Change in quantity demanded / %Change in import price. If PDE=1.5 and %Change in quantity demanded is 12%, then we solve for %Change in price. So, if the PED for tomatoes is 1.5 and the elimination of a quota will increase consumption by 12%, then the implied price cut is 12%/1.5, or 8%.

24 *Tariffication*, the process of replacing quotas with equivalent tariffs is an excellent example. The Uruguay round agreement required tariffication in agriculture. Policy makers faced exactly this question: how much would prices fall and domestic production decline if our quotas are eliminated, and what degree of tariff protection would exactly replace the quota? Policy makers were in the unenviable position of risking the wrath of domestic farmers of admitting the true extent of protection in agriculture to the international trading community. Most elected to replace quotas with tariffs, with Japan instituting a rice tariff of 780% to replace its quota restrictions!

percentage cut in imports created by the quota by the price elasticity of demand for the imported product.

As noted earlier, a trade policy action will affect not only the prices charged for imported products but will also affect the prices of competing domestic goods. In a fully competitive economy, a fall or rise in the price of imported products will cause an equal fall or rise in the prices of equivalent domestic products. In cases where domestic competition is restricted or where domestic products are not full substitutes, the price changes in similar domestic products will be less than the price changes for imports.

We calculate consumer benefits and costs of the changes in the prices of domestic products in the same way we calculated the consumer benefits and costs of the changes in import prices. For a rough estimate, we multiply the change in price times the initial consumption level. A more precise estimate would be the change in price times the average of the pre- and post-adjustment consumption levels.

ESTIMATING THE ECONOMIC EFFICIENCY GAINS OF TRADE

Individuals engaged in trade are concerned with making money, but in the vast majority of cases, guided by Adam Smith's "invisible hand," the process of making money tends to improve economic efficiency and enhance welfare for the participant countries. Trade allows a country to concentrate more of its resources on goods and services it produces more efficiently, relative to other products and countries. This follows from the concept of comparative advantage. It involves so-called allocative or static efficiency gains. In some sectors of the economy, expanding the scale of production to serve the regional or global market leads to further cost savings and efficiency. Trade also stimulates domestic producers to adopt more efficient production methods and to develop new products that better meet consumer tastes. These two factors contribute to what economists call dynamic gains from trade.

It is generally easier to estimate the potential gains from trade liberalization for a single product, what economists call a *partial equilibrium* estimate. Here, the focus is not on the greater value of production possible if resources are transferred to another sector of the economy, but on three aspects of protection in that protected sector. The first is the additional cost of making a product at home, compared to the cost of importing the product. The second cost is the consumer surplus lost at the higher domestic price due to lower consumption. The third aspect is the change in government revenues. In the following section, we compare the gains to producers and the increase in government revenues (in the case of tariff protection) to consumer losses to calculate a net national impact of protection. The same exercise in reverse shows the net national impact of trade liberalization.

Partial Equilibrium Measures of the Cost of Protection

Before beginning this section, we need to make two points. First, and most importantly, this simple model examines only static gains from trade. Some economic studies indicate that dynamic gains may be several times larger. Secondly, trade policy changes typically affect many sectors of the economy. A partial equilibrium model gives you just a partial picture of the impact on the entire economy. Nevertheless, such partial equilibrium studies are an important first step toward understanding the costs of protection, and they are widely used in policy debates.

Figure 4.2
Partial Equilibrium Competitive Model /Small Country

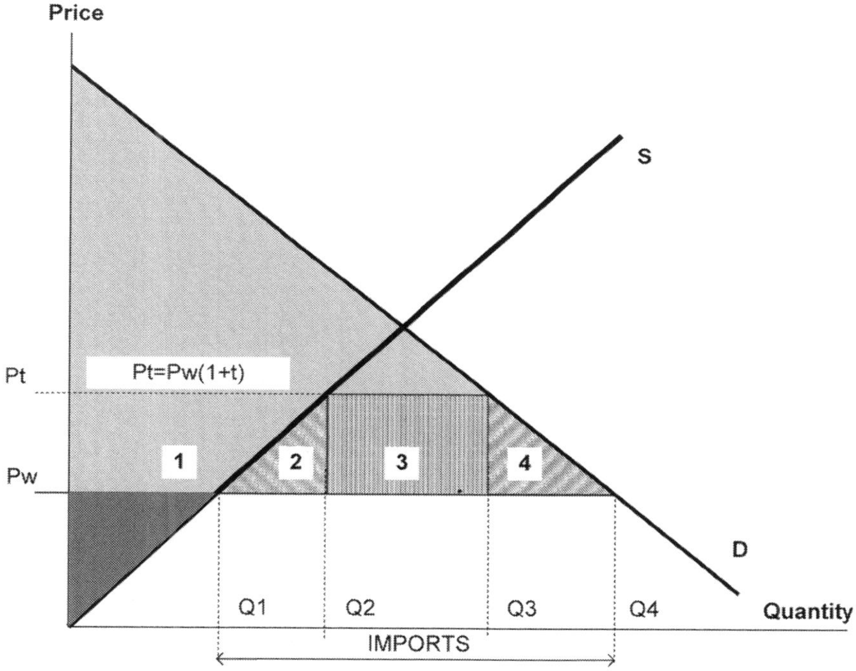

Explanation:
In this example shown in Figure 4.2 above, a tariff has raised the domestic price (or the price domestic consumers must pay) from Pw (the world price) to Pt (the domestic price, including the tariff). At a higher price, producers can increase their output. Firms that would have been inefficient at the lower world price can now enter the market because their marginal costs of production are between Pw and Pt. Notice how total producer surplus has increased from the small dark triangle to the small dark triangle + Area 1, but consumers now pay more for both domestic production and imports.

Before the tariff was imposed, consumers paid Pw for Q4; now they pay Pt for the smaller Q3. The additional amount they are paying corresponds to Areas 1, 2, and 3 in the figure. Area 1 becomes additional producer surplus and, therefore, represents a transfer from consumers to producers. But what happens to Area 2? Area 2 represents the additional production costs of the less-efficient producers. It is a loss due to inefficiency and represents what economists call a *dead-weight loss* due to domestic production that costs more to produce than the cost of imports at the world price.

- ► *Dead weight loss* in this case is the cost associated with overproduction and under-consumption. Overproduction occurs because the additional production in response to the higher domestic price is more costly than importing the good. Hence, even though the trade restriction has made additional production privately profitable, the production is inefficient by international standards. Under-consumption is the result of some consumers being priced out of the market, despite their utility from consuming more of the good exceeding the cost of importing it.

Area 3 is the tariff revenue collected by customs on all incoming imports of this product. It is important to remember that the tariff or import tax is only collected for imported goods, not domestically produced goods. Thus, Area 3 is a rectangle whose base is the amount of imports entering the country under the tariff, and the height is the rise in price due to the tariff. This area is transferred from consumers to the government. Foreign suppliers still supply their goods to the importing country at the world price, but after the tariff is added consumers must pay Pw * (1 + tariff), or Pt.[25] It is also worth noting that while the foreign suppliers may still receive the world price for their goods, they sell less of those goods (Q2Q3 instead of Q1Q4), so their revenue shrinks.

Let us consider consumers. Because the domestic price level has risen, consumer surplus has shrunk, both due to the higher product price but also due to the reduction in consumption at that higher price. Recall that consumer surplus is the area below the demand curve and above the price line. Now that the price line has been raised, consumer surplus has shrunk by Areas 1 + 2 + 3 + 4. Area 1 was transferred to producers in the form of producer surplus. Area 2 was a deadweight loss from inefficient production. Area 3 was transferred to the government in the form of tariff revenue. And Area 4, like Area 2, does not get transferred to anyone. Area 4 is another deadweight loss. Why? Consumers are paying more and getting less, and Area 4 represents part of this loss. Consumption that would benefit individuals is not taking place due to the higher domestic price.

To sum up, Areas 1 and 3 are transferred from consumers to producers and the government. The total net loss to national welfare from imposing the tariff equals Areas 2 and 4. To measure this net loss in financial terms, we sum the areas of the two triangles. (Recall that the area of a triangle = ½ * base * height.) Often the area of the two triangles can be calculated together, since the combined base is the change in imports and the height is the change in domestic price.

---

25 For an ad valorem tariff, $P_t = PW * (1 + t)$, as shown. For a specific tariff, $P_t = PW + t$.

With a *large country*, some new complications are introduced.

► *A large country is one that imports a significant portion of total world exports.* Thus its trade policies impact world prices. For instance, while no single European country affects the world price of wheat, EU trade policies indeed affect world prices.

Figure 4.2
Partial Equilibrium Competitive Model/Large Country

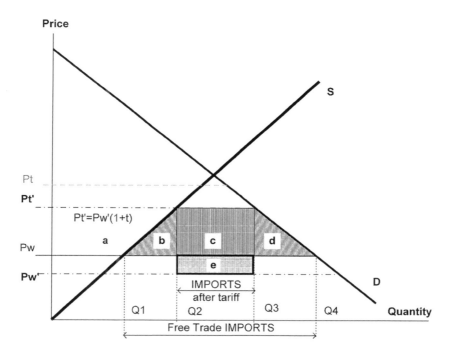

If such a country were to restrict its imports (e.g., by imposing a tariff), this would result in a sufficient dip in total world demand to lower world prices. In the diagram below, the world price falls from Pw to Pw'. What are the implications in terms of producer surplus, consumer surplus, deadweight losses and tariff revenue? Using the same logic of the previous example, consumer surplus shrinks by the amounts represented by Areas a + b + c + d. Producer surplus increases by Area a, and the deadweight losses equal Areas b + d. It is important to note that consumer surplus, producer surplus and the deadweight losses are based on the change in the domestic price since they are "before" and "after" comparisons of options available to domestic consumers.

Government tariff revenue, on the other hand, is calculated differently. Tariff revenue is equal to the new quantity of imports multiplied by the amount of the tariff (or import tax). In this example the import tax is equal to the difference between Pt' and Pw'. So tariff revenue is equal to Areas c + e. Area c is transferred from consumers (part of the lost consumer surplus) to the government, but where does Area e come from? Area e is a gain to national welfare, at the expense of foreign exporters. Not only do foreign exporters lose revenue because of the reduced import demand, but they also lose from lower world prices. Area e represents the difference between the old, higher world price and the new, lower world price on post-tariff imports.

Therefore, in order to determine the overall impact on national welfare for a large country, one needs to consider both the gain from lower world prices (Area e) and the deadweight losses (Areas b + d). The so-called optimal tariff is a tariff that maximizes the positive difference between Area e and Areas b + d. However, even an optimal tariff may result in a decline in national welfare if it induces a country's trading partners to place their own optimal tariffs on its export products in which they are large importers.

Figure 4.3 presents a numerical example with the various areas and totals calculated. We see that the United States benefit from the largess of its market. Sugar protection creates national gains at the expense of foreign exporters (including poor developing countries in Latin America, Asia, and Sub-Saharan Africa). U.S. sugar policies are actually much more complex than indicated in this simple example.

Figure 4.3
Partial Equilibrium Competitive Model Large Country, Example

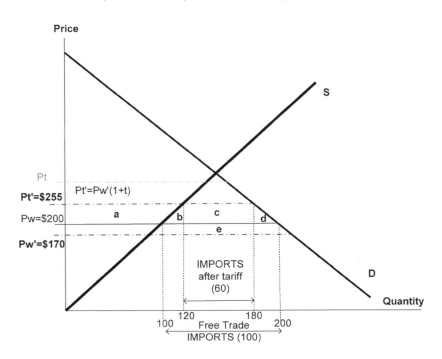

In this example, imposing a 50% tariff on U.S. sugar imports lowers the world price of sugar from \$200/ton to \$170/ton. Thus, the new domestic price rises by less than 50% to \$170/ton * 1.5 = \$255/ton. Suppose U.S. sugar production rises from 100 to 120 tons and consumption falls from 200 to 180 tons. Then, the deadweight social loss (b + d) is: ½*(\$255 - \$200)*[(200 - 180) + (120 - 100)] = \$1,100. Area e is (\$200 - \$170) * (180 - 120) = \$1,800. The change in national welfare is: e - (b + d) = \$1,800 -\$1,100 = \$700.

STUDIES OF THE IMPACT OF TRADE POLICIES ON NATIONAL WELFARE

Numerous economic studies attempt to measure the net impact of trade policies on national welfare. We can put such studies into several subcategories:

► Specific trade policies (NAFTA, EU, etc.) or free trade with the world.

► Static efficiency only or static and dynamic efficiency.

► Competitive markets or noncompetitive markets.

► Trade only or investment changes as well.

Not surprisingly, the largest impacts on national welfare are from studies that examine global free trade, dynamic efficiency, noncompetitive markets, and foreign investment. Such studies yield estimates of potential gains as high as 8-12% of national income for such medium-sized countries with moderate trade barriers as Canada and Mexico.[26]

Estimates of the potential gains from trade for the huge U.S. economy tend to be much smaller. Without dynamic gains or investment effects, these estimates are around one-half of 1%.[27] One study indicates that the elimination of all U.S. tariffs would *reduce* national welfare by 0.6%! [28] The elimination of quotas and other quantitative restrictions would raise national welfare by 1.3%, for a net benefit of free trade.

Another way to highlight the benefits of trade liberalization is to look at global gains rather than national gains. An Australian study placed the global gains from cutting all trade barriers in half at \$400 billion (U.S.).[29] A rule of thumb to remember is that, due to the nature of deadweight social loss triangles, a 50% reduction in trade barriers captures about three-fourths of the potential gains from liberalization.

---

26 Adams, Alanis and del Rio, "The Mexico-U.S. Free Trade and Investment Area Proposal," Journal of Policy Modeling, 14(1), pp. 99-119; Young and Romero, "A Dynamic Dual Model of the North American Free Trade Agreement," and Sobrazo, "The Gains for Mexico from a North American Free Trade Agreement," both in Modeling Trade Policy, Francois and Shiells, eds., (NY: Cambridge U. Press, 1994) (for Mexico). Cox and Harris, 1984, for global free trade for Canada.

27 But even one-half of 1% of the U.S. economy is nearly \$40 billion dollars, much more than the total amount of U.S. aid to developing countries.

28 Goulder, 1992. The implication is that the U.S. is such a large consumer of many products that its tariffs force world price down in many cases, creating national gains at the expense of foreign exporters.

29 Financial Times, May 26, 1999.

Chapter 5

ANALYZING DOMESTIC POLICIES AFFECTING TRADE

By: Leslie Eliason and Geza Feketekuty[30]

C ommercial Diplomacy focuses on the resolution of trade-related policy issues. Any policy or government action can become a trade-related policy issue if it affects international commerce (i.e., international trade and investment in goods and services). As a result of the globalization of economic activity, the range of issues that can become the subject of attention by trade policy makers and trade negotiators is quite broad, ranging from traditional trade policy tools such as tariffs and quotas to principally domestic policies such as health and environmental standards, agricultural support policies, banking regulations, and laws on bribery and corruption.

Traditionally, trade policy was all about tariffs and quotas, and these policy instruments remain an important, although much less dominant, aspect of Commercial Diplomacy. Increasingly, however, the government policies that are the subject of Commercial Diplomacy today are aimed at a wide range of domestic social objectives such as health, safety, environment, consumer protection, stability of infrastructure networks, and so on. The policy issues that arise with respect to tariffs and quotas are relatively simple compared to the policy issues that arise with respect to complex domestic regulations. The policy issue with respect to tariff and quota decisions usually comes down to a trade-off between the protection of certain domestic economic activities from international competition and the economic efficiencies and new growth opportunities that can be derived from increased trade. It also involves a redistribution of domestic income between shareholders and workers in protected

---

30 The content of this chapter is substantially taken from the original manual entitled *Policy Analysis* co-authored by Leslie Eliason and Geza Feketekuty, which is on the ITCD website, but has been further edited for the purposes of this textbook by Geza Feketekuty. The original manual can be found at www.commercialdiplomacy.org.

industries on one hand and consumers as a whole and producers in export-related industries on the other hand.

Governments make policies affecting so many areas of social and economic life that interactions among these policies are common and, therefore, difficult to antici-pate fully. Just a brief perusal of any country's government agency chart makes it clear that it is virtually impossible to coordinate fully any particular policy action with all the other areas potentially affected. Analyzing the wide range of regulations, direc-tives, and policies developed within so many different agencies presents a Herculean task. The "crowded policy space" of modern public decision-making means that many policies overlap or impinge on each other so that action in one area of public concern will often have consequences for policy action in other areas. Consequently, solving one policy problem may create new problems in other areas. Designing and imple-menting coherent trade policy requires the trade policy analyst to try to anticipate the more important effects the policy is likely to have in other areas of government activity or public concern.

Trade policy makers and trade negotiators have to resolve these issues through analysis, advocacy, political action, international negotiation, and dispute settlement. Trade policy generally involves state-to-state or government-to-government bargain-ing and negotiation. Domestic policy actors and institutions play important roles in the policy process affecting trade relations, too. The purpose of this chapter is to provide a rigorous analytical framework for analyzing the issues that become the focus of Commercial Diplomacy. A thorough analysis of the social objectives served by trade-related policies gives trade policy analysts a solid basis for developing a strategy to successfully address the issue.

Domestic Policy Issues: Questions to Ask

► What policy areas would be affected by any actions to solve the trade problem?

► What specific policy objectives would be impacted?

► How do policy objectives relate to trade rules?

► What are objective performance measures?

► What alternative policy measures are available to achieve the desired policy objectives?

► What combination of measures would solve the trade problem and preserve other legitimate policy objectives?

When trade-related domestic policy issues at stake involve domestic regulations, the trade policy professional's challenge is to identify alternative policy actions that will achieve the same social benefits as existing policy instruments, while reducing or eliminating adverse effects on international commerce. This can be accomplished by identifying the social objectives served by the targeted regulation and describing how policy action might achieve the same objective without impeding trade.

Identifying the desired social objectives may require extensive legal analysis as well as an interactive dialogue with regulators. We need to know what legislators had in mind when drafting the laws underlying the regulations involved, and we need to know how the perception of the social objectives may have evolved over time. Understanding how the regulation in question achieves the desired social objectives, and how alternative policy actions could be crafted to meet the desired objective, may require the collection of a considerable amount of technical or scientific knowledge. For example, a range of issues in trade policy involving food and agriculture fall into the area of phytosanitary standards or environmental regulation. The trade analyst may need to draw on expertise related to biology, chemistry, or physics in order to analyze the factors underlying a regulatory issue.

The key challenge in analyzing trade-related domestic policy issues involves identifying other potential policy options that might achieve the same policy objectives through other means. The policy analyst's job is to identify a range of possible (and feasible) alternatives and then to assess the impacts each is likely to have on other policies.

Trade policy analysts may also need to understand how other international organizations are attempting to address key issues on their agendas. For example, anti-corruption measures have become a key issue on the international policy agenda even though the problem of corruption in the public sector is as old as "civilized society itself."[31] Fighting corrupt activities by public authorities also helps promote trade by helping to reduce or eliminate rent-seeking behavior by public officials. Bribing customs officers, for example, is costly not only for those firms that pay out but also for those who refuse to do so. Two broad forces are at work to propel anti-corruption concerns onto the agenda of many international organizations including the IMF, the World Bank, the WTO, OECD, and others. "Internally, the forces of political accountability are demanding that governments take responsibility for illicit practices, while externally, the forces of globalization are pressing for reforms to remove the barriers that corruption places in the way of global trade and investment. These forces have transformed the corruption issue from one primarily of ethics and human behavior to one that, at its core, relates to international economic development, the effective operation of markets, good governance, and competitiveness."[32]

Transparency and accountability have become not only buzzwords fashionable within the international policy discourse, they are important policy objectives that now constitute major policy goals that condition foreign aid and development assistance programs. Globalization has helped stimulate further integration of policy objectives on the international agenda. Lack of accountability and transparency impede overall economic growth and distort development trajectories in many less developed nations. While this linkage is not fully understood, there is general agreement that without simultaneous attention to improving accountability and transparency, efforts to increase market access may fail to achieve significant improvements in economic

---

31 R.M. Gadbaw and T.J. Richards, "Anticorruption as an International Policy Issue: Its Origins and Implications," chapter 12 in G. Feketekuty with B. Stokes, *Trade Strategies for a New Era: Ensuring U.S. Leadership in a Global Economy* (New York: Council on Foreign Relations, 1998), pp. 223-42.

32 Ibid, p. 224.

efficiency and competitiveness. Both domestic and foreign interests, therefore, have a stake in reducing corruption.

To summarize, officials responsible for implementing the initiative need to make the case that

- ► The proposed changes in the policy measures at issue are necessary to achieve the desired trade policy objective,

- ► The proposed changes will not undermine an important social objective of the government, and

- ► A change in the policy can also be justified in terms of good governance and the more effective pursuit of the relevant nontrade objectives.

All of these factors suggest that one of the central tasks of the effective Commercial Diplomat is to analyze trade-related policy initiatives and provide a thorough and informed assessment of the policy maker's options and what will be necessary to achieve his/her desired objectives for any recommended alternative. This is the heart of policy analysis.

Trade-related Policy Areas: Questions to Ask

- ► What policy areas would be affected by any actions to solve the trade problem?

- ► What specific policy objectives would be affected?

- ► How do policy objectives relate to trade rules?

- ► What are objective performance measures?

- ► What alternative policy measures are available to achieve the desired policy objective?

- ► What combination of measures would solve the trade problem and preserve other legitimate policy objectives?

Chapter 6

ANALYZING THE POLITICS OF TRADE

By: Geza Feketekuty and Colleen Morton[33]

This chapter is designed to help educators, students, and practitioners of Commercial Diplomacy (i.e., representatives of government, business, NGOs, and associations) with understanding, preparing, and implementing a successful strategy for managing the political forces that affect decisions and negotiating positions on policy measures that affect international trade and investment. In particular, the objective of this chapter is to improve the practice of Commercial Diplomacy, by which we mean the creation and execution of strategies designed to promote the commercial interests of a specific political entity, be it a corporation, NGO, government department, or some other organization with international commercial interests.

The Political Marketplace

By its very nature, policy actions by governments are the result of a political process in which actors in all three spheres of society – business, government, and public interest groups – seek to shape the outcome. There is no way other than politics by which the government can make decisions on policy goals and government programs. This is true regardless of the political philosophy and the political organization of a country. Even dictators need bureaucracies to administer the government, and all decisions within such bureaucracies involve politics.

In any political process, all actors impacted by a government decision will seek to influence the outcome through persuasion and the exercise of political influence.

---

33 The content of this chapter is substantially taken from the original training manual entitled *Analyzing and Managing the Politics of Trade* co-authored by Colleen Morton and Geza Feketekuty, which is available on the ITCD website, but has been further edited for the purposes of this textbook by Geza Feketekuty. The original manual can be found at www.commercialdiplomacy.org.

Some have likened the process to a political marketplace, within which advocates for alternative public policy goals and public goods compete for political support among the relevant decision makers. Everyone who wants to influence the outcome of a policy decision or the procurement of a public good has to allocate political capital to that objective, and the government adopts policy goals or public goods that receive the most political capital.

The advocacy tools used by Commercial Diplomats to advance a particular organization or country's interests can be seen as the means for participating in the political marketplace for policies and programs. This chapter demonstrates how the effective management of the relationships among government, business, and public interest groups can contribute to success in the political marketplace for government policies and programs.

THE POLITICAL CHALLENGE OF COMMERCIAL DIPLOMACY IN AN INTERDEPENDENT WORLD

Trade policy today covers a wide range of domestic policies, not just tariffs. Increasingly, the formulation of trade policy affects policies in areas such as the regulation of banking or accounting; domestic subsidies benefiting farmers; health, safety and environmental standards; competition policy; and intellectual property laws. This has led to the involvement of a much broader and diverse range of interest groups in trade policy decisions. Decisions in these areas are often highly contested in domestic politics, and as they have become the focus of trade negotiations, trade policy itself has become more political.

Trade officials must understand both their own domestic politics and the politics that influence trade decisions and negotiating postures in other countries. Learning to navigate the diverse political and governmental systems in foreign countries is critical to the success of a Commercial Diplomat.

The Implications of Wide Policy Coverage for the Politics of Trade

The politics of negotiating tariff reductions was never easy, but was limited to relatively few national players and to only a few key ministries within the executive branches of these countries. In the world up to, and including the Kennedy Round of multilateral trade negotiations in the early 1960s, decisions on tariff levels were made by a relatively small number of officials in Trade, Finance, Commerce, and Foreign Ministries. Regulators and other domestic agencies and institutions were seldom involved. Moreover, only a small number of business organizations and labor unions paid much attention to the negotiations and sought to influence decisions through political activity.

This began to change with the expansion of the trade agenda in the 1970s to include standards and domestic subsidies, and in the 80s with addition of services, agricultural policies, and intellectual property. International trade negotiations now involve a larger number of more diverse players, and the politics of trade and politics of domestic policy have become more entangled and interdependent. As negotiations range beyond tariffs, countries increasingly find themselves with conflicted policies within their own administrations. Actors within the domestic sphere that now contribute to the formulation of trade policy include labor ministries, environmental departments, central banks, finance ministries, legislatures, sub-national levels of government, regulatory and standard-setting bodies; and, of course, the public through the intervention of a multitude of interest groups, advocacy groups, NGOs, experts, pundits, the media, and Internet newsgroups. Governments must simultaneously negotiate trade agreements domestically (internally) and externally: internally with other government departments and with private entities such as corporations, industry associations, issue-oriented public advocacy organizations, and externally with nations and groups of nations. If anything, the domestic negotiation has become the more difficult and sensitive —and most important of the two negotiations.

In this chapter we attempt to clarify the parameters of the political process, focusing on four main groups of players: trade negotiators and officials; legislators; business people; and NGOs. We could have included many other players, such as the media, regulators, and sub-national government officials, and, indeed, we mention these. We also divide the political process into a domestic and an international process. Since trade by definition involves economic activity with a foreign entity of some sort, trade actors must be prepared to deal with both domestic and foreign publics and decision makers. Finally, we distinguish between formal state-to-state trade relations, and the more informal (but still highly organized) processes of brokering, influencing, and shaping trade policy. This chapter treats state-to-state trade relations as the end product of a series of interactions among domestic and foreign, executive and legislative, and official and unofficial actors.

The Implications of Wide Dispersion of Responsibility for Policies Covered by Trade

As trade officials are viewed as having the main role in international trade negotiations, they are expected to take the lead not only on traditional trade issues, such as tariffs and customs, but to also co-manage the politics of domestic policies with other government departments and agencies (e.g., agriculture, bank regulators, intellectual property enforcement agencies, standards making bodies). This is doubly difficult, because trade officials have to become involved in political arenas in which they are less familiar, and they must lead negotiations in areas where they do not have the domestic decision-making power.

The Political Challenge for the Commercial Diplomat

The political challenge for a Commercial Diplomat is to build political support for policy decisions that will advance the interests of the organization he/she represents. Decisions on trade-related policy measures get made in a political environment where everyone affected by policy decisions seeks to influence the outcome through advocacy, coalition building, and other political activity. To obtain a desired policy decision, a Commercial Diplomat must build a winning coalition among all individuals and groups in society capable of influencing desired policy decisions or negotiating positions. This is constituency politics built around commercial and group interests, which most of the time needs to be viewed independently of party politics. There are times, of course, where decisions come down to party politics and political ideology, but more often than not constituency politics brings together politicians with different political and ideological views.

THE ROLE OF POLITICAL ANALYSIS

The purpose of political analysis is to obtain the information needed to influence the political decision-making process. In order to obtain a desired policy decision or negotiating outcome, the Commercial Diplomats must identify all individuals and groups in society who may have an interest and capacity to influence decisions. The Commercial Diplomat must also acquire information about their views and positions on the issues involved, their underlying interests and concerns, the policy outcomes they are pursuing, and their means to influence the actions of decision-makers. In order to create a political coalition powerful enough to overcome opposition to the desired policy decisions, the Commercial Diplomat must bring together not only groups and individuals actively involved in seeking to influence a decision, but also those who have a potential interest and could help influence the outcome. It may only be necessary to bring the issue to their attention, or to adjust the desired policy out-come to accommodate their interests. The successful Commercial Diplomat also seeks to weaken the opposition of those opposed to the desired policy outcome. In order to weaken the opposition, the Commercial Diplomat may need to accommodate some of their interests or to persuade them that they stand more to lose by opposition than by obtaining concessions in other areas.

Political analysis thus serves to provide the information necessary for successful political strategy. Political intelligence about personal relationships between stake-holders and key decision makers, or the ability of particular groups to mobilize voters or to raise campaign contributions for legislative elections, provides the basis for assessing the potential political influence of supporters and opponents. Information about interests and positions provides the basis for shaping the message and for fine-tuning the details of a policy decision or negotiating position to make it as attractive as possible to potential supporters and/or to opponents who might be persuaded to reduce their opposition.

WHO ARE ALL THE STAKEHOLDERS THAT CAN INFLUENCE POLICY OUTCOMES?

For purposes of political analysis it is useful to think of all individuals and groups in society whose interests are affected by trade policy decisions and trade negotiations who have the ability to influence such decisions as stakeholders. Stakeholders may include:

► Government departments at the national or sub-national level;

► Elected and appointed government officials and politicians;

► Government bureaucrats representing governmental entities at the local, state, regional, or national level;

► Industry and professional associations, unions, NGOs;

► Enterprises including small to large businesses, corporations, and multinational corporations;

► The media (print and electronic/private and public), including the Internet;

► Academic experts, think tanks, research labs, and institutes;

► The public, including voters, constituents, consumers, etc.

Not all of these stakeholders will be present or active in every trade negotiation or trade matter, nor will they be equally visible in every country. Nevertheless, a smart Commercial Diplomat will never discount the possibility of suddenly having to deal with one or more of these groups, particularly in this age of instantaneous information (or misinformation) delivery.

A good example of this is when the negotiators of the Canada-United States Free Trade Agreement (CFTA) were taken by surprise by a group of Canadian women who felt that the CFTA might jeopardize their health benefits and, in particular, their freedom to choose abortion, in light of the anti-abortion movement that was growing in the United States back in the 1980s. These women, urged on by an increasing number of anti-trade and anti-globalization activists, forced Canadian politicians and trade negotiators to spend an inordinate amount of time explaining why the CFTA would not affect Canadian health benefits in any way, shape, or form, including the right to choose.

The relative influence that each of these stakeholder groups can wield varies enormously depending on the political and economic context in which the trade negotiation or trade matter is being handled. In a rapidly growing, healthy economic environment, labor groups and unions will have much less leverage on negotiations than in a depressed, slow-growth period. Likewise, environmentalists will have more leverage in negotiations between a country with high standards and a country with low standards, than between two countries with equivalent, if different, standards. The political and ideological coloration of the administration in power will also tend to support or weaken the standing of specific groups.

Political Stakeholder Analysis: Questions to Ask

► Who are the active and the potential stakeholders, whose interests could be affected by the policy decisions or negotiating positions we are seeking?

► What are their views and publicly stated positions on the problem or possible solutions?

► What are their underlying interests and concerns?

► What is their ability to influence decisions?

► How will they seek to influence the decisions?

► What are their options?

UNDERSTANDING THE POSITIONS, OBJECTIVES, INTERESTS, AND MOTIVATIONS OF STAKEHOLDERS

If a trade official or Commercial Diplomat is going to try to understand, predict, influence, neutralize, or otherwise affect the politics of trade, then he/she must spend some time becoming familiar with the goals, motivations, interests, and strategies utilized by the other stakeholders. They should concentrate on those that seem to have the most impact on issues that are of primary concern to the official's country.

Most stakeholders who are actively involved in seeking to influence particular policy decisions or negotiating positions of their government have publicly announced positions on the issues involved. These positions are made public through press releases, white papers, and other statements produced by the group; and with the Internet, most groups maintain a presence on websites, blogs, and other social media platforms where such statements are posted. These statements may often include not only the position of the organization on the issue, but also what the organization hopes to achieve through the desired action (i.e., their objective). In other cases their objective has to be inferred from the position.

In addition to understanding a stakeholder's position (i.e., the policy action desired by the stakeholder) and objective (i.e., what the stakeholder hopes to achieve through the desired policy action), it is important to understand a stakeholder's interests and motivations. A position may be only one way of many different policy actions that would satisfy the real interests of the organization. In addition to the interests of the organization, the individual decision makers in the organization may have private motivations that transcend the interests of the organization. The head of an association or nongovernmental group, for example, may have a private interest in attracting new dues-paying members not only because it would expand the influence the group, but because it would enhance the leader's salary and social stature. Understanding interests and motivations is important because it offers many new avenues for attracting a stakeholder to join a coalition or for understanding why a stakeholder may decline offers that are in line with the organization's publicly stated positions.

One of the most important things to remember, therefore, is that a stakeholder group's trade objective may be completely tangential to their ultimate goal. Trade policy may simply be a vehicle for achieving ends that are totally unrelated to trade, economic policy, or general welfare. So, unlike the trade official who would usually be expected to keep his/her eyes firmly on the trade objective, other players may be pursuing a variety of goals totally unrelated to trade but using trade as a tool to advance their own domestic agenda. Nevertheless, they are on the field cannot be ignored as irrelevant to the process of winning the game.

How Does Each of the Various Stakeholder Groups Measure Success?

One of the critical things that a Commercial Diplomat must understand is that government officials measure their success very differently from corporate managers, and corporate managers measure their success differently from the managers of the business associations the corporations belong to. Similarly, journalists measure their success differently from politicians or academics.

Success in business is measured by how well the firm enhances revenues, profits, and market share. Success in the government is measured by the ability to obtain a decision on a desired policy measure, and that usually means getting a large number of individuals, or in some cases some very important individuals, to agree on the measure. Managers of business associations measure success by satisfying not only the needs of present members, but also prospective members. Their interests in the profits of the industry they represent are only derivative, insofar as the policy actions desired by their members is aimed at their collective profits. Politicians are primarily motivated by winning elections, and generally their advocacy of particular policies is explained by the views of their most influential constituencies. Journalists are of course interested in good reporting, but ultimately the test is whether the stories they write attract readers and subscribers. Academics are, of course, interested in their reputation and ultimately their ability to attract consulting contracts.

Table 6A below demonstrates the complexity of interests and motivations that one might expect to find in the context of a typical trade negotiation in the United States.

Table 6A

Interests and Motivations				
Individual Player	**Priority 1**	**Priority 2**	**Priority 3**	**Priority 4**
Trade official	Negotiate good agreement	Satisfy superiors	Satisfy legislators	Satisfy main pressure groups
Trade association representative	Get more members	Satisfy current members	Satisfy superiors	Get appropriate policies enacted
Journalist	Sell media	Build reputation	Get scoop	Get accurate information

National politician	Get votes	Get campaign donations	Get/retain support of major constituencies	Get defensible agreement
Regulator/ Bureaucrat	Protect turf and prerogatives	Promote own career/agenda	Satisfy superiors	Simplify/ ease workload
Corporate trade lobbyist	Establish/ promote own reputation	Promote corporation's interests	Promote industry interests	Promote broader coalition's interests
NGO activist	Promote NGO ideals	Attract new members/ donors	Promote visibility of NGO	Get "good" agreement
Union/Labor activist	Promote labor agenda	Attract new members/ Retain existing members	Get media visibility	Satisfy union bosses
State or municipal politician or official	Protect turf and parochial interests	Create alliances to increase leverage	Satisfy home constituencies	Build national reputation

Complex calculations of personal and organizational gain or loss are only one part of the psychological and political nexus in which the Commercial Diplomat must operate. Inter-agency rivalries, ideological differences between political parties, or competition for federal resources among states all add to the brew. Needless to say, a great deal of "horse trading" has always occurred in the political process surrounding the negotiation and approval of any trade agreement. What has recently changed is the diversity of tools and strategies available to the activist or official wishing to affect the outcome.

ANALYZING THE STRATEGIES AND TOOLS STAKEHOLDERS WILL USE TO EXERT INFLUENCE

In order to understand the politics surrounding a particular trade issue, a trade professional has to analyze not only the key stakeholders and their motivations and objectives, but also the strategies they are likely to pursue to advance their interests. An analysis of the strategies that such stakeholders are likely to pursue can provide insights into the political pressures that could be exerted by stakeholders on different sides of an issue and provide the basis for evaluating the influence that can be exerted on decision makers.

There are essentially two different styles of exerting influence on a foreign government's trade policy: formal and informal. What we want to address here are the more informal methods of exerting influence that are utilized not only by the trade professional, but also by the whole range of stakeholders at every level of government and society. It should be noted that these are used both in the foreign and domestic contexts.

There are also essentially two avenues for exerting informal political influence on governments: (1) directly targeting and influencing specific decision makers; and (2) indirectly applying pressure on the targeted decision maker by targeting and influencing legislators, other key stakeholders, or public opinion. These two methods are of differing utility depending on whether you are trying to influence a foreign government or your own. The trade professional needs to be aware of the trade-offs involved in utilizing these strategies, as illustrated in Table 6B.

Table 6B

Trade Diplomat Influence by Target Audience		
	Foreign	**Domestic**
Official/Legislator	Medium	High
Public/Voters	Low	Medium

Other stakeholders will have different trade-off relationships. For instance, as shown in Table 6C, a well-known international environmental NGO may have the following influence structure:

Table 6C

International NGO Influence by Target Audience		
	Foreign	**Domestic**
Official	Low	Medium
Public	High	High

Direct Methods for Influencing Governments

Speaking Directly to Individual Decision-making Officials

The most obvious way stakeholders can seek to influence a decision is to speak directly to decision makers or to a staff member. They may do this by visiting officials in their offices or by having side conversations during social events. The most effective trade diplomats or domestic trade policy advocates treat such efforts as a means of conveying information to the decision maker about some of the substantive issues raised by the decision, about the impact of the decision on the interests they represent, on the position and interests of other stakeholders who support their position, and why they believe a decision along the lines they favor is in the broader interest of the country or whatever geographic region covered by the government. Decision makers will also be interested in hearing from stakeholders on the type of political support they can provide in the legislature or in other forums where trade policy decisions might be challenged.

Domestic stakeholders will generally be more effective than foreign stakeholders in the political support they can provide. The value of their help will obviously also depend on their own ability to exercise political influence through relationships and influence with legislators and politicians, the press, voters, or other influential groups.

Influencing Legislators (Staff Members, Influential Supporters/Constituents)

Another approach stakeholders can take is to ask legislators to use their influence with the decision makers or to influence the outcome through legislative action. This strategy will obviously work better at home than abroad, although many companies, NGO's, or professional associations established abroad succeed in building a reputation and influence in the countries in which they are established or with which they do business. However, in some countries the decision makers will resent efforts by foreign stakeholders to mobilize legislators, and this strategy could backfire. In other countries it may be illegal for foreigners to lobby legislators.

Occasionally, legislators will want to support a particular trade initiative but lack the data or the rationale for doing so. By providing such data, stakeholders can boost their credibility with the legislator's staff and prepare the ground for more cooperation in the future. Any information provided to a legislator must be considered in the public domain and be readily quotable for it to be of any value to the legislator. Secret, confidential, proprietary, or sensitive information should almost never be distributed to legislative staff. An example of data that is usually difficult for a legislator to keep current is the number of jobs in the legislator's home district affected by the trade action, whether that involves jobs gained through expanded exports or jobs lost through increased imports.

Indirect Methods – Courting, Cultivating, and Shaping Public Opinion

In most countries, media plays a central role in shaping public opinion. Today, media takes many forms: print media (e.g., newspapers, books, magazines), television, radio, cinema, the Internet (e.g., websites, blogs, and social media), and wireless technologies such as mobile phones. The media is heavily influenced by "experts," "pundits," former and current officials, celebrities, and interest group policy statements, and the internet is making it easier and quicker to pass information across borders. Each form of media is given a different credibility value depending on the source or how biased that source is considered to be. A Nobel laureate trade economist will not necessarily attract much attention on the trade issue if he/she has taken a consistent stance for the last 20 years. However, if a well-known macroeconomist suddenly starts making pronouncements about trade, his opinion will get noticed and reported.

Using Experts and Studies

Hiring experts to prepare studies is another approach you can take. If the experts and the studies are sufficiently balanced, the media attention may be more or less what the sponsor had in mind. If not, the media can easily decide to totally destroy the credibility of the study, the experts, and the sponsoring organization.

A more subtle approach is to ally oneself with studies that have been carried out by others without receiving any direct financial support from the stakeholders with the most direct interests. This works particularly well if the study is by a high-profile university, think tank, or commission. It works less well if a consulting firm, even a highly respected one, carries it out.

The third approach is for the stakeholder to provide the study, along with full transparency on the study, the researchers, the sponsors, and the objectives. If the study is well done and presents convincing and solid data, it can be as successful as the other two methods, despite the obvious bias.

Op Eds, Columns, Stories, Letters to the Editor, Journal Articles, Think Tank Newsletters

Besides commissioning studies, there are a variety of other good ways stakeholders can get coverage for their issue in the print media, among them: opinion editorials (op-eds), guest columns, special interest stories, and letters to the editor. Op-eds are notoriously difficult to get published in some papers, particularly those with very high circulation numbers. However, smaller regional papers may be much readier to publish, particularly if the issue being discussed is directly related to local concerns.

The Internet, Email, Public Opinion Polls, and Direct Marketing

For many, the Internet has evolved into the primary source of information about everything. A Commercial Diplomat, or anyone hoping to influence public opinion on trade matters, cannot afford to overlook the pervasiveness of this media channel. However, because the Internet is a free and unregulated form of media, information may need to be verified for accuracy, including when the information was last updated and if the author of the information is credible. This is much different from traditional media channels.

Because the Internet audience is broken down into numerous sub-segments, such as demography, region, interests, ideology, occupation, etc., it is not necessarily a good "mass marketing" vehicle. However, it is very good as a mechanism for establishing support groups and connecting people with like interests. It can also be an excellent tool for mobilizing such groups once established. The Internet has been largely responsible for the success of grass-roots campaigns against the World Bank, the IMF, and globalization in general, which draw vast, amorphous, discontented populations into organized protest activity. More will be said later under the section on asymmetries as to why it is difficult to organize such campaigns in favor of something rather than in opposition to something.

Non-Internet based mass marketing is very expensive in most countries; therefore, social media is being utilized (i.e., Facebook and Twitter) to bring attention to policy issues to the general public. For instance, you can search for just about any policy matter on Facebook and you will find many interest groups expressing their views, direct links to websites that frame the issue (e.g., United States Trade Representative [USTR]), or even information on how to register to participate in webinars on policy debates relating to the issue.

Trade groups tend to form coalitions to undertake such campaigns. The objective of such campaigns is normally to influence the behavior of key governmental decision makers. These campaigns are usually most effective in countries where decision makers are actually responsive to public opinion.

Strategies for Reinforcing Political Influence

Coalition Building – the Role of Associations, Caucuses, and Alliances

Trade politics, like most politics, is a matter of coming up with a critical mass of supporters that is larger, more influential, or more powerful than the opponents' group(s). Coalitions are particularly important for carrying out informal trade diplomacy because of the complexity of the task and the diversity of people, agencies, and issues that need to be addressed. Coalitions provide the opportunity to divide up the labor while carrying a common message. Thus, USA*NAFTA, the coalition of trade associations in favor of the North American Free Trade Agreement, was able to divide up calls to members of Congress and organize funding for the grassroots campaign, speaking engagements, op ed drafting, and a variety of other tasks among 100 or so different groups with thousands of members.

Likewise, coalitions of countries can achieve a great deal more in official negotiations than any single country. Outside the official negotiations, these countries may also wish to continue to work together closely to manage the informal political process. Canadian, New Zealand, and Australian embassy officials in Washington, for instance, regularly communicate about their strategies and tactics for dealing with the United States.

The downside to coalitions is that they cannot always respond to new policy challenges as rapidly as one might hope due to policy differences and turf battles among the coalition members. Coalition management is time-consuming and exhausting work, which is rarely repaid with the affection and devotion of coalition members. Nevertheless, they are an indispensable and inevitable part of trade politics.

Individual trade associations may be able to wield more influence than one might expect when the issue at stake is precisely within their purview, particularly if the industry's largest players are members. The U.S. Coalition of Service Industries (CSI) is a good example of an industry association that wields enormous influence from time to time in the context of specific services negotiations. Likewise, U.S. Wheat Growers, Meat Producers, Dairy Producers, and Tomato Growers have all played critical roles at various stages of both bilateral and multilateral negotiations.

Establishment of Advisory Groups

What if trade associations and coalitions do not exist or are not strong enough to wield much influence on a specific topic or issue? One solution is for the government to create advisory groups that incorporate the key players and specifically solicit their input and advice. Even if the advice is contradictory (due to competitors arguing for different solutions, for instance), the government will have been able to gather important industry information and will be able to cobble together a policy more easily than if it was acting in a vacuum. More importantly, perhaps, is the notion that by inviting the main stakeholders to actively participate in the process, the government increases its credibility with those stakeholders and minimizes opposition to the negotiation and implementation of the agreement down the line.

ANALYZING PUBLIC OPINION AND THE MEDIA TREATMENT OF A TRADE ISSUE

Fortunately (or unfortunately), many decisions involving Commercial Diplomacy are of concern only to groups in society most directly involved in the issue. These decisions are often discussed behind the scenes without much public awareness and get little treatment in the popular press. At most, such issues may be discussed in periodicals that are focused on the particular industry or policy interest group that is most concerned about the issue. Other decisions, however, are of broad concern to the public and get discussed at length in newspapers, TV broadcasts, and radio shows. Public opinion, and by extension the media, can have a major impact on the policy outcome. In these cases, the Commercial Diplomat needs to understand the concerns that drive public opinion and must address these concerns by shaping both the proposed policy action and the advocacy message. The Commercial Diplomat must also analyze the views disseminated by the media either indirectly through the treatment of the issue in press reports and news broadcasts, or directly through editorials, in order to shape the further evolution of the story in the press through press releases, interviews, speeches, and other channels.

Media and Public Opinion Analysis: Questions to Ask

▶ Does public opinion play a role in the problem or any attempts to solve the problem?

▶ Has either the popular media or the specialized media covered the problem?

▶ Is the press likely to cover efforts to address the problem?

▶ What public information initiatives are available to shape public opinion?

Analyzing Public Opinion and Media Coverage

Elected officials are often motivated to support or oppose a policy based on what their constituents (i.e., the voters in their district) prefer. In contemporary society, the ready availability of public opinion polling and a variety of forms of direct communication between the general public and government officials means that individual citizens, when they act in large numbers, may influence the direction and outcome of public policy issues, including trade issues. The ever-present media – especially the immediacy of television – are constantly engaged in sending messages that shape the way the public views the issues of the day. With the growing number of global news networks, including CNN, international media coverage has expanded dramatically, and issues that once remained accessible or interesting only to a select few have now become subjects of widespread public debate.

International news coverage has exploded and sometimes trade-related concerns can quickly become politicized because of decisions made by broadcasters about what to cover in the news or other programming. Therefore, the next step is to assess what can be done to reduce the attention given to a particular issue so that negotiations can move out of the pressures of the limelight.

THE ASYMMETRIES OF TRADE POLITICS AND ITS IMPLICATIONS

Trade politics has a number of asymmetries that need to be understood by trade diplomats. These asymmetries makes it easier for stakeholders who want protection and to defend the status quo to mobilize political support and exert pressure on decision makers than for stakeholders who want to liberalize trade or to reform regulation to mobilize political support. Generally this means that private stakeholders need support from the government, which may want to pursue a policy of trade liberalization and regulatory reform for broader economic purposes.

Sources of Political Asymmetry Associated with Trade Liberalization

Differences in the Relative Distribution of Gains/Losses from Trade Liberalization

By now it is relatively widely known and discussed in popular literature that lowering tariffs and other trade barriers creates modest economic gains for the general population and for consumers overall, but may negatively impact smaller groups of firms and workers much more sharply. Consumer prices may drop 1%, but 200,000 people may lose their jobs. In a large or even medium-sized economy, the overall positive economic impact of the 1% decline in prices will completely overshadow the economic cost of 200,000 people temporarily being out of work. This means that the firms and workers that lose from liberalization or gain from protection are likely to have a much higher incentive to take action to influence decision makers than the consumers who stand to lose from protection or gain from liberalization.

Differences in the Identification of Winners/Losers from Trade Liberalization

As one can easily imagine, people who have lost their jobs are much more likely to identify themselves as losers from trade. Whereas, the much larger number of consumers who have enjoyed small gains in terms of cheaper prices or the much larger group of firms and workers who may gain from new opportunities are less likely to notice it, or attribute it to the absence of protection without having it brought to their attention. The much smaller group of people who are clearly conscious of the gains of protection or the loss from liberalization are, therefore, much more likely to seek to influence the trade decisions involved than the much larger group of consumers, firms, and workers who are less conscious of the impact of trade policy decisions on their economic interests.

Differences in the Time Horizon of Winners and Losers from Trade Liberalization (Short-term vs. Long-term Benefits and Losses)

New business opportunities that may emerge for firms in the export sector as a result of trade liberalization or in deregulated sectors as a result of regulatory reform are likely to take some time to emerge. This is partly because they are usually phased in, but more importantly because the new sales opportunities or jobs will emerge only after an entrepreneurial firm has recognized the new opportunity and has acted to take advantage of it. In contrast, the loss of sales and jobs from increased imports is usually far more immediate, as the firms involved seek to position themselves to meet the new competition. Similarly, the jobs preserved through new import protection when imports are surging is seen as much more immediate than the loss faced by consumers from increased prices or the loss of export sales and jobs in export industries that might result from future foreign retaliation. This greater sense of immediacy faced by those who could lose from liberalization or gain from new protection spurs them on to take action to influence decision makers, while those who would gain from liberalization or lose from protection see less incentive to act to obtain the future benefits of new business opportunities, jobs, and price reductions that will emerge in the long run. As Keynes observed, in the long run we are all dead. One is also reminded of the proverb that one bird in the hand is worth much more than two birds in the bush.

The Bias Inherent in the Mercantilist Calculus that Drives Trade Negotiations

Trade politics usually casts a mercantilist bias on trade negotiations (i.e., as a result of the dynamics generated by the politics of trade), which stresses that an increase in exports is considered to be a benefit for the country and an increase in imports is considered to be a loss for the country. An increase in exports is considered to be good because it increases jobs and foreign exchange earnings. An increase in imports is considered a loss because it is viewed as leading to a loss of jobs and an expenditure of foreign exchange earnings. This instinctive mercantilist view ignores the following from increased imports:

> ▶ The benefit of lower prices and improvements in quality that consumers can achieve from imports;

► The benefits derived from the acquisition of goods from imports that cannot be obtained domestically;

► The benefit of increased import competition generated by spurring domestic producers to increase their productivity; and

► The fact that the government has better ways of achieving full employment, as an economy cannot create more jobs than the number of available workers.

The mercantilist bias results in part because everyone has a tendency to apply their personal experience in managing a household to the management of the national economy, even though this is an inappropriate comparison in many ways. More importantly, the mercantilist bias flows from the asymmetrical politics of trade. To overcome this mercantilist bias in trade politics, a government has to undertake a focused campaign of making the public aware of the various benefits of imports discussed above.

The Political Bias Created By Bureaucratic, Nationalistic, or Other Interests

Those favoring protection often appeal to nationalistic sentiment to limit imports and foreign investment. After all, what can be more patriotic than preserving jobs for local citizens and preserving ownership of domestic assets for citizens? Keeping foreigners out has a certain nationalistic appeal to some elements of the population in every country. What is less obvious, however, is that protection may make a country weaker and less able to protect itself by making it poorer, less competitive, and less technologically advanced. Understanding these linkages takes a certain intellectual sophistication while populist slogans that seek to keep out foreigners communicate a message at a more emotional level.

Expanding trade increasingly means coordinating a wide range of policies with other countries, and this further increases the scope for nationalistic appeals in favor of protection and against liberalization of trade and investment. It also increases bureaucratic resistance by all the national regulators who now have to give up some power not only to foreign regulators, but also to trade officials.

Completely nontrade-related factors might also skew the political balance with respect to certain sectors or industries and thus trade outcomes. National security is frequently cited, for instance, to protect the U.S. shipping industry from foreign competition. Environmental and safety concerns have been used until very recently to block Mexican trucks from entering the United States as promised under the NAFTA. Federal broadcasting regulations, again sometimes justified on the basis of national security, have prevented the liberalization of the U.S. broadcasting market. In most countries, farmers have disproportionate political weight, not just because of the way the electoral system is set up, but also because of a national mythology surrounding the small family farm.

How These Asymmetries Lead to Imbalances in the Politics of Trade

In discussing the various asymmetries in trade politics we have noted how these asymmetries lead to differences in incentives by opponents and supporters to influence trade policy decisions and related decisions involving the reform of domestic regulations that limit competition. The asymmetries we discussed, however, result not only in differences in the motivation to act, but also to differences in the cost of organizing political action and differences in establishing legitimacy.

Motivation

Losers from trade liberalization will be much more highly motivated to prevent or redress such losses than winners will be to acquire or protect their gains. Proponents of protection will be more motivated to influence trade policy decisions through political action as a result of more concentrated gains from such action, the greater identification of the impact of trade policy decisions on their economic welfare, and the greater immediacy of the gains that can be obtained or the losses that can be avoided from political action.

Cost of Political Organization

Proponents of protectionist policies not only have a greater motivation to organize themselves politically to influence trade policy decisions, it also costs them less to organize such action. Because losses and gains are more concentrated among a smaller number of firms and unions, the cost of organizing political action is smaller than it is for the much more widely dispersed number of firms, workers, and consumers who would stand to gain from liberalization or lose from protection. It simply costs less to mobilize and organize a smaller number of stakeholders.

Stakeholders supporting protection will be ready to write letters, march, protest, sue, demand compensatory payments, etc. Stakeholders supporting liberalization will rarely do any of these things. Furthermore, they will often defend only the part of the agreement that directly benefits them, leading to fragmentation and lack of coherence in the pro-liberalization camp. Thus, it is much more expensive, time-consuming, and politically costly to organize a pro-liberalization campaign than an anti-liberalization effort.

Free Rider Problems

Free rider problems emerge when some stakeholders believe that they do not have to act to influence a trade decision because others with similar interests will act in any case. They, therefore, believe that they will benefit from actions taken by others without having to take any action of their own. Such free riding, however, is possible only when there are a large number of stakeholders who can potentially gain. Some stakeholders may decide to act in such situations on behalf of their interests even though a much larger group could potentially gain because they know that it would be difficult and costly to mobilize all stakeholders who might gain. The free rider problem is much less likely to occur when the number of stakeholders who might gain from joint action is small. This is because no one stakeholder may be willing or prepared to assume the cost of political action if other stakeholders who stand to gain from such action decide to be a free rider.

Since we saw that the gains and losses that come about from trade decisions that result in more protection or less liberalization are likely to be concentrated among a relatively small number of stakeholders, free riding is usually not an option. Given the wide dispersion of the gains that may result from the liberalization of trade or the avoidance of protectionist action, campaigns in support of trade liberalization or opposition to protection are usually characterized by a large number of free riders.

Appearance of Legitimacy

Increasingly trade policy has to focus on the use of domestic regulations as a cover for protection. The reform of such regulations is often desirable not only to liberalize trade and expand competition, but also to make such regulations more effective in achieving their objective. By raising questions about the protectionist aspects of such regulations, however, trade liberalizers open themselves up to the accusation that they are seeking to undermine the achievement of the various social objectives served by such regulations. Stakeholders who want to preserve the level of protection offered by such regulations, in contrast, can seek to portray themselves as merely trying to preserve the social objectives that led to the adoption of the regulations involved. They, therefore, can take on the mantle of social legitimacy, while their real objectives are to preserve their economic self-interests.

Summarizing the Asymmetries of Trade Politics

Table 6D

Schematic of Political Asymmetries of Trade Politics		
	Winners	**Losers**
Distribution of gains/losses	Wide distribution	Concentrated
Identification of gains/losses	Low	High
Time horizon of winners/losers	Long-term	Short-term
Motivation of winners/losers	Low	High
Cost of organizing winners/losers	High	Low
Risk of free riders among winners/losers	High	Low
Populist appeal	Low	High

Chapter 7

LEGAL ANALYSIS IN COMMERCIAL DIPLOMACY: ANALYZING DOMESTIC LAWS AND INTERNATIONAL AGREEMENTS

By: Laura Anderson, Jane Earley, Geza Feketekuty, and Irving Williamson[34]

I n all modern societies, a hierarchy of regulatory decisions, regulations, laws, judicial opinions, constitutional provisions, and international rules shape the actions governments take on trade and investment issues. There is, therefore, a close link between Commercial Diplomacy and legal analysis. Governments cannot discuss policy actions that affect trade and foreign investment without discussing the domestic laws and regulations, as well as the international rules that apply to such transactions.

The types of legal instruments that can affect international trade and investment decisions include domestic laws, regulations, directives, administrative decisions, and judicial opinions issued by governments at all levels – national, state/provincial, and local – and international trade rules adhered to by these governments. International trade rules are international legal instruments negotiated by Commercial Diplomats. International legal instruments include a wide range of treaties and other government-to-government agreements, in addition to decisions by international dispute settlement bodies such as the International Court of Justice or the Dispute Settlement Body (DSB) of the World Trade Organization.

In today's global environment, international trade rules increasingly shape and constrain domestic legal instruments and government actions. If trade policy profes-

34 The content of this chapter is substantially taken from the original training manual entitled *Legal Analysis in Commercial Diplomacy. Analyzing Applicable Domestic Laws and International Agreements* co-authored by Laura Anderson, Jane Earley, Geza Feketekuty, and Irving Williamson, which is available on the ITCD website, but has been further edited for the purposes of this textbook by Geza Feketekuty. The original manual can be found at www.commercialdiplomacy.org.

sionals are to be effective in resolving trade issues and negotiating international trade agreements, they have to be able to analyze laws related to trade, rule making, legal proceedings, and available dispute settlement mechanisms.

What Does the Trade Policy Professional Need to Know About Legal Analysis?

Every accomplished trade policy professional should be able to:

- ▶ Understand how a specific law or regulation affects the trade interests of a particular industry or constituency group;

- ▶ Understand the process of assessing the conformity of domestic laws and regulations with international trade rules;

- ▶ Identify the policy objectives served by particular laws and regulations;

- ▶ Understand when and how domestic regulatory objectives can be achieved in a less trade-restrictive manner;

- ▶ Work with Commercial Diplomats from other countries in crafting agreements governing trade and investment issues; and

- ▶ Understand the various venues and procedures available for resolving international trade and investment disputes.

What is the Purpose of this Chapter?

It is important for trade professionals to be familiar with the laws and legal procedures relevant to international trade because these provide the framework within which commerce is conducted and commercial disputes are settled. Basic legal knowledge can be critical to a Commercial Diplomat's ability to accurately assess the legal aspects of a dispute, as well as to find a satisfactory resolution. Of course, this chapter will not transform its readers into international trade lawyers or replace the need to include lawyers in commercial negotiations. Commercial Diplomats, even those who are trained lawyers, are well advised to consult lawyers with the appropriate expertise and to include them on their negotiating teams. They should, in particular, use such lawyers to obtain legal interpretations and opinions, to argue cases before dispute settlement panels or support governments where private entities are not allowed to appear before international tribunals, and to craft binding legal agreements. What this chapter will do is to help Commercial Diplomats work effectively with lawyers.

This chapter is also not intended to cover the legal analysis and the preparation of legal briefs leading to formal dispute settlement proceedings designed to assess the conformity of national laws, regulations, or policy actions with international trade agreements. These tasks are appropriately the work of trade layers with in-depth training in law, including international trade law. Much of the work of Commercial Diplomats involves identifying informal, non-litigious, negotiated solutions to trade problems. Upon closer investigation, some trade problems are found to be misunderstandings of facts by regulatory officials or misunderstandings of regulatory intent by business managers. In such cases, the role of the Commercial Diplomat is simply to clarify the facts or the regulations. In other cases, the problem can be solved through an accommodation, such as an adjustment in how a regulation is applied within the allowable discretion of regulatory officials. In still other cases, the officials involved may be willing to pursue a change in the applicable law or regulation based on the merits of the case. Indeed, the majority of issues that confront Commercial Diplomats are resolved well before they become candidates for formal international legal proceedings. Whatever the nature of the problem, however, the Commercial Diplomat needs to understand the laws and regulations that directly or indirectly impact on a trade issue being addressed.

Legal analysis and dispute settlement proceedings are an important component of Commercial Diplomacy and are closely linked to negotiations. The domestic legal provisions and international rules that apply to trade issues constitute an important element of the discussions carried out by negotiators charged with the resolution of trade disputes, whether or not such disputes arise from a violation of international trade agreements or international trade rules. Legal analysis can shed light on the relative merits of the respective positions advanced by the parties to a trade dispute and may also point to the options open to each side if a negotiated outcome is not achieved. If a dispute is referred to a WTO dispute settlement panel, and if such a dispute settlement panel determines that the measure in question is inconsistent with a country's WTO obligations, it will state in detail why the measure is inconsistent and recommend that the country bring its measure into compliance. Parties are generally expected to bring their measures into compliance within a reasonable period of time. There is some room for negotiations on what is a reasonable period of time and what must be done to comply. However, the Dispute Settlement Understanding (DSU) provides for arbitrators to determine the reasonable period of time if there is disagreement; it also provides procedures for determining whether any measures a country takes to bring it into compliance with its WTO obligations, in fact, meet the WTO requirements. Failure of a government to comply with a WTO panel decision can result in retaliatory trade action by the foreign government, not necessarily in the same sector as the complaint of conduct or in payment of "trade compensation" by the offending government to benefit the trade of the complaining WTO member.

This chapter will help trade policy professionals understand how laws are structured and interpreted, as well as how various domestic legal instruments (such as administrative decisions, directives, regulations, and laws) interact with and relate to international legal instruments (such as treaties and other government-to-government agreements).

Who Can Use this Chapter?

This chapter will be useful to any professional who is called on to work with trade-related policy issues. This includes professionals in government, especially those who are involved in negotiating trade agreements and in resolving disputes regarding policies or measures that affect international trade. Professionals in the private sector whose jobs or business relationships are affected by international trade agreements and disputes can also benefit from this chapter. This includes government relations experts, customs experts, and standards and certification professionals. Finally, this chapter will benefit other professionals in business and government who are not directly involved in trade policy-making but are nevertheless affected by trade policy decisions and negotiations. This can include supply management experts, human resources professionals, investment advisors, environmental and labor relations experts, and a whole range of business professionals who deal with international trade and business problems on a day-to-day basis.

NATIONAL LEGAL INSTRUMENTS THAT IMPACT ON TRADE

Why Governments Regulate Trade and the Role of Domestic Laws that May Impact on Trade

Governments use domestic legal instruments to regulate international trade and investment for essentially four reasons:

- ▶ To raise revenue (e.g., through tariffs on imports);

- ▶ To protect the national security (e.g., by prohibiting imports or exports that would aid hostile countries);

- ▶ To protect the health and safety of human, plant, or animal life (e.g., by subjecting imported products to food safety or quarantine requirements); and

- ▶ To promote economic growth and development (e.g., by subsidizing or protecting particular economic activities such as the creation of intellectual property).

Governments use a variety of domestic legal instruments to regulate international trade in pursuit of these objectives, including constitutional provisions, statutes, decrees, and regulations at the federal and sub-federal level as well as decisions of courts and administrative tribunals. The list of domestic legal instruments used to influence trade can also include quasi-legal standards and rules promulgated by industry associations. These legal instruments may apply to a country as a whole or to particular regions within the country, such as states, districts, provinces, and towns. The Technical Annex to this chapter contains a description of these domestic legal instruments.

Aside from the laws and regulations that are designed to regulate international trade, a wide range of domestic measures designed to achieve a wide range of domestic social objectives can impact on trade and can therefore become the subject of trade policy analysis and negotiation. Such domestic laws include laws designed to protect human health and safety, preserve social stability, stimulate economic growth, achieve higher levels of environmental quality, maintain ecological diversity, and preserve and support the infrastructure that supplies essential services such as finance, telecommunications, transport, energy, and so on.

The following are some broad categories of legal actions or non-actions that can impact on trade and therefore can lead to trade issues. In most cases the action involves a government measure that implements a law or regulation. Some of these measures are designed to regulate trade, while certain measures are designed to achieve other objectives but impact trade negatively for one reason or another. In a few cases a dispute arises because a government refuses to discipline discriminatory or illegal actions by its own citizens or companies.

Domestic Legal Instruments That Impact on Trade

Laws, Regulations, or Other Government Actions that are Designed to Protect Domestic Industries

The world of international commerce is intensely competitive, and governments everywhere at times adopt measures designed to protect their domestic industries or to give extra advantages to their exporters and investors. The WTO and other international trade agreements have attempted to curb such measures by negotiating limits on measures that restrict trade and by establishing rules that require governments to observe principles such as nondiscrimination and transparency in applying measures that affect trade. Large areas of policy action that potentially can affect trade are not covered by international trade agreements, and individual governments may interpret the agreements differently, or political pressures may lead them to skirt or ignore particular provisions from time to time.

Laws, Regulations, or Other Government Actions Relating to Noneconomic Objectives that Adversely Affect Trade

Governments often adopt measures to protect health, safety, social welfare, or the environment that may adversely affect the trade interests of another country. While governments have a right under WTO rules to pursue legitimate domestic social objectives, they are required to do so on a nondiscriminatory basis and to pursue the desired objective in a way that minimizes the impact on trade. In many countries, governments may require compliance with a standard set by private standards-setting bodies or industry associations. In such cases, the government is in effect delegating part of its regulatory functions and has become responsible for any actions by such groups that result in discriminatory treatment of foreign firms or adversely affects their commercial interests. Trade rules in such cases require the government to take action to ensure nondiscriminatory treatment of foreign firms, and failure to do so could lead to a trade dispute.

Government Failure to Take a Trade- or Investment-Related Action to Address Private Commercial Activity that is Adversely Affecting the Social or Other Objectives of Another Country

Commercial activities by a country's domestic firms may have impacts that another government views as inimical to its environmental, social, or other objectives. For example, developing country concerns that they were not capable of identifying and properly dealing with hazardous wastes exported by developed countries led to the negotiation of an agreement, referred to as the Basel Convention, which prohibits developed countries from exporting hazardous waste to developing countries.

INTERNATIONAL TRADE AGREEMENTS

International trade consists of many thousands of private commercial transactions between private actors – companies and individuals. Trade agreements among countries pursuing a market-oriented economic policy, and that includes most countries today, are not designed to establish negotiated levels of trade, but rather they enable commercial enterprises to take advantage of trade opportunities. Commercial enterprises that engage in trade naturally do so on the basis of private agreements. While the negotiation of such agreements entails many of the same diplomatic skills and acumen as the negotiation of the government-to-government agreements, this chapter primarily focuses on the government-to-government agreements.

This next section explores the scope, purpose, and content of international trade agreements and how they relate to the domestic legal instruments governments use to regulate international trade and investment.

The Rationale for International Trade Rules and Agreements

Governments negotiate trade agreements with each other in order to limit the use of domestic laws and regulations to restrict or distort trade. By doing so, governments limit their own ability to stimulate economic activity by discriminating against foreign goods, services, and firms and by favoring domestic ones. What they gain, however, is an increased ability to stimulate economic activity by creating an expanded opportunity for trade. Because promotion of trade is not the only objective of government policies, governments will provide in a trade agreement that they will not distort trade except when it is necessary to achieve vital social objectives such as the protection of health, the environment, national security, and in some cases workers' rights.

Governments may also enter into trade agreements with other governments because they find that such agreements enable them to accomplish certain objectives with respect to international trade that they cannot accomplish by national regulation alone. The international legal framework for regulating the actions of governments that affect the private conduct of trade consists of a network of bilateral, regional, and multilateral agreements among governments. Agreements such as the multilateral trade agreements administered by the WTO, and regional trade agreements such as

NAFTA, commit governments to avoid policy measures that limit international trade and to follow agreed principles and procedures when pursuing domestic policies that affect trade. Many regional agreements also limit government measures that restrict foreign investment. All of these agreements generally allow governments to impose measures that implement policies aimed at legitimate social objectives even if the measures otherwise violate the agreement and have an adverse impact on trade. However, the agreements commit governments not to pursue such measures for the purpose of protecting domestic industries from international competition.

Without such agreed "rules of the road" on when it is appropriate for governments to take actions that can restrict international trade, countries can be drawn into "beggar-thy-neighbor" trade policies, in which each country seeks to expand domestic production in an industry at the expense of its trading partners. They usually end up with fewer exports as well as imports as well as a sharp decline in national income as trade collapses. Governments learned this lesson the hard way during the 1930s when major trading countries including the United States, in the face of the Great Depression, instead of immediately taking action to increase trade and counter the global decrease in demand, raised tariffs to very high levels. The result of the decline in demand, compounded by the increase in tariffs, was a precipitous 66% drop in world trade between 1929 and 1934.

Second, governments may agree on a common approach to the regulation of certain activities in order to achieve mutually agreed objectives more effectively. Common areas in which such collaboration occurs include the preservation of the environment; the safeguarding of human, plant, and animal health and safety; and the protection of intellectual property rights. Governments have found that in order to achieve their objectives in such areas, international cooperation is vital. A lexicon of international agreements and a description of different kinds of international legal instruments is provided in the Technical Annex on Domestic and International Legal Instruments within this chapter.

Key Legal Principles Embedded in Most Trade Agreements

Two principles form the basis of most modern trade agreements between governments: the "Most-Favored Nation Treatment" principle and "National Treatment" principle. These principles were developed in a series of bilateral trade agreements negotiated by major trading countries in the half-century leading up to World War II. These same principles were adopted as the core of the GATT, which was subsequently negotiated at the end of World War II. The Most-Favored Nation Treatment principle is set forth in Article I of the GATT, and the National Treatment principle is set forth in Article III. Both of these principles seek to ensure that governments regulate trade in a nondiscriminatory manner and are described in greater detail below.

The GATT also contains some other key fundamental principles that are found in almost all modern trade agreements:

- ▶ A prohibition against quantitative restrictions (set forth in Article XI of the GATT),

- ▶ A requirement to observe specific commitments to assure predictability of expanded market access (set forth in Article II on tariff bindings), and

> ► A requirement to publish all laws and regulations that affect trade to promote transparency (found in Article X and in various other places in the agreement).

The WTO/GATT also contains a number of exceptions to allow government to take measures that serve legitimate social, political, health and safety, and national security concerns even thought they violate WTO/GATT rules. The GATT has sought to limit the use of exceptions by imposing requirements such as a need that they not be applied in an arbitrary or discriminatory manner or be a disguised barrier to trade. The principle that trade measures inconsistent with basic GATT principles "should be no more trade restrictive than necessary" can be found in jurisprudence derived from the GATT of 1947 as well as in a number of other WTO agreements. Most of the foregoing GATT principles are contained in the other WTO agreements as well as in most regional trade agreements, although not always in the same way. The complete text of the GATT of 1947 was incorporated into the WTO agreements.

Each principle is summarized below, although no effort is made here to capture the extensive body of panel decisions and scholarly literature interpreting these principles. The principles are discussed as they are found in the GATT and WTO since these are by far the most widely applicable trade agreements today.

Most-Favored Nation (MFN) Treatment: Under the GATT, and now the WTO, members must give to the products of every other member treatment no less favorable than they give to the products of any other country (with the exception of better treatment given as part of a customs union or free trade area). This obligation is comprehensive and covers both exports and imports. With respect to trade in goods, MFN applies to tariffs, fees, and nontariff measures such as licenses, customs formalities, etc. In other words, members must accord to the products of every member the lowest tariff rates and the least restrictive treatment for nontariff measures given to any other member.

National Treatment: Members must treat imported goods no less favorably than those produced domestically. This constitutes a broad prohibition against discrimination against like or similar imported products once they have crossed the border. The GATT applies National Treatment automatically to all trade in goods, while the General Agreement on Trade in Services (GATS) provides for the negotiation of commitments applying National Treatment to specific services.

Prohibition of Quantitative Restrictions: In general, members are not allowed to erect quantitative barriers to trade in goods, although there are a number of exceptions to this rule. For example, countries can use quantitative restrictions to limit imports under some circumstances when they face a balance-of-payments crisis or a serious threat to one of their industries. These extraordinary measures have become increasingly rare.

Predictability Through Binding Commitments: To give foreign companies the confidence to make investments in export-oriented production facilities, countries are prohibited from changing tariffs on which they have made commitments as a result of negotiations, with a few legitimized exceptions spelled out in various GATT articles.

Transparency: To give firms a clear idea of the rules they are likely to face and to encourage responsible government, members pledge to publish their laws and regulations that affect trade and to give notice of new laws and regulations, or changes in old laws and regulations. This is a core principle embedded in all WTO agreements.

Progressive Liberalization Through Negotiations: To encourage the future liberalization of trade, the GATT and WTO agreements contain provisions that encourage members to negotiate additional reductions in tariffs and other barriers to trade and to take on additional concessions.

Least Trade Restrictiveness: Members pledge that various regulations and measures enforcing mandatory product standards will not be more trade restrictive than necessary to fulfill a legitimate policy objective. This basic principle is embedded in a number of WTO agreements, although the extent of commitment and the degree of application of the principle to various domestic policy instruments varies considerably from agreement to agreement. This is a particularly difficult obligation to enforce given its subjective nature, although it provides a critical basis for the resolution of many bilateral trade disputes through bilateral consultations and negotiations.

There are also provisions for exceptions, most notably the general exception provided in Article XX of the GATT. This provision contains important conditions affecting the operation of the agreement. Article XX exempts from the operation of every part of the agreement several broad categories of measures as long as they are not "disguised restrictions" on trade and do not constitute "arbitrary or unjustifiable discrimination between countries where the same conditions prevail." Measures covered by Article XX include those necessary to protect human, animal, or plant life or health, and those "relating to the conservation of exhaustible natural resources." Also included are measures "necessary to protect public morals," and those "relating to the products of prison labor."

Not surprisingly, each of these principles is subject to a variety of qualifications and exceptions that are written into the text of the governing article of the GATT and the other agreements of the WTO. Moreover, while these basic principles are found throughout the WTO Agreements, they are often tailored to conditions applicable in that area of trade.

MAJOR TRADE AGREEMENTS, AND INTERNATIONAL ECONOMIC AGREEMENTS THAT COVER TRADE

The World Trade Organization (WTO)

The most important international legal instruments that Commercial Diplomats will encounter are the World Trade Organization (WTO) agreements. These agreements were signed in 1994 as the "Final Act of the Uruguay Round" and the "Marrakesh

Agreement Establishing the World Trade Organization." Today these agreements are the basic foundation of international trade law.

The WTO agreements were the result of numerous years of negotiations under the auspices of the GATT, which governed negotiations on trade in goods. After its founding in 1947, the GATT conducted successive "rounds" of multinational trade negotiations that brought about a progressive liberalization of tariff and nontariff barriers to trade in goods. The last round, the Uruguay Round, which lasted from 1986 to 1995, not only continued that pattern, but expanded the negotiations to trade in services and to trade-related issues in areas such as agricultural policy, intellectual property, and investment. The Uruguay Round also established WTO, an institution created to administer the agreements and to attempt to conduct negotiations on an ongoing basis.

In addition, the Uruguay Round produced the "Understanding on Rules and Procedures Governing the Settlement of Disputes (DSU)." The WTO agreement incorporated fundamental changes into the GATT's dispute settlement process, including the establishment of a Dispute Settlement Body (DSB) to administer dispute settlement proceedings, and an Appellate Body to hear appeals from the rulings of dispute settlement panels and to make panel decisions final and binding on parties to any dispute.

Over the past 16 years since the conclusion of the Uruguay Round, three fundamental properties of the WTO have become apparent:

- ► First, its scope is unprecedented, as its agreements touch on a wide range of its members' domestic laws and regulations;

- ► Second, the decisions produced by the Appellant Body and dispute settlement panels interpreting the WTO agreements have become a powerful and binding source of public international commercial law; and

- ► Third, its jurisprudence and scope will continue to expand in the future, as new agreements are concluded and the DSU process produces new decisions on the interpretation of the WTO agreements.

The WTO administers over 60 agreements, hosts ongoing trade negotiations and dispute settlement panels, reviews the trade policies of its members, and administers assistance and training programs. It does this through a small staff (in comparison with other international organizations) headquartered in Geneva, Switzerland. A Director-General heads the organization, which is administratively organized into Directorates, each of which serves the needs of one or more committees responsible for issues and agreements. Unlike many other international institutions, the WTO's professional staff largely provides a housekeeping and technical support function; WTO members acting collectively make all decisions.

Decisions in the WTO are made on the basis of consensus. Votes are theoretically possible but, in practice, very rarely used. In fact, Article IX of the agreement establishing the WTO provides that the WTO shall continue the GATT practice of decision making by consensus.

Ministerial-level government officials meet every two years at Ministerial Meetings to shape the work program of the WTO. Between these sessions, a General Council (essentially a super committee to which others report) oversees the overall performance of the WTO bodies, including its Dispute Settlement Body and the Trade Policy Review Mechanism, which conducts and publishes regular reviews of member countries' trade policies. The General Council has direct oversight of the Goods Council, the Services Council, and the Intellectual Property Council. Under these three Councils are a host of committees that service individual agreements; WTO decisions in individual areas are first discussed within these committees. Only member governments can be members of the various committees, but the WTO as an institution has established cooperative relationships with other multilateral institutions, several of which participate as observers in committee meetings and other WTO meetings. Countries in the process of acceding to the WTO can also participate as observers.

Regional Free Trade and Economic Integration Agreements

Governments enter into regional free trade agreements in order to promote trade among a select group of countries, which are generally – although not always – located in close proximity to one another. In their simplest form, free trade agreements facilitate trade by reducing or eliminating tariffs among their members. However, many such agreements go further, extending their scope to include preferences in such areas as standards, customs administration, and investment.

Many countries belong to one or more regional free trade agreements. The WTO estimates that over 193 regional trade agreements are currently in force. These agreements vary greatly in their scope of coverage as well as in the extent of the preferences that their members provide one another.   ·

Free trade agreements are intrinsically discriminatory and thus pose an inherent conflict with the WTO's principle of "most-favored nation treatment." Article XXIV of the GATT permits the negotiation of customs unions and free trade agreements in goods, but also sets out a set of specific conditions that such agreements must meet in order to qualify for the exception from "most favored nation treatment." The GATS has a similar provision.

Some of the more well-known agreements include the European Union (EU), the European Free Trade Association (EFTA), the North American Free Trade Agreement (NAFTA), the Association of Southeast Asian Nations (ASEAN), the Southern Common Market (MERCOSUR), and The Common Market of Eastern and South Africa (COMESA).

The European Union: The European Union (EU) is an economic and political confederation of 27 European nations. Its current members are Austria, Belgium, Bulgaria, Cyprus, the Czech Republic, Denmark, Estonia, Finland, France, Germany, Great Britain, Greece, Hungary, Ireland, Italy, Latvia, Lithuania, Malta, Luxembourg, the Netherlands, Poland, Portugal, Romania, Slovakia, Slovenia, Spain, and Sweden.

The EU was built through a series of treaties that consisted of binding commitments by its member states. The European Economic Community was designed to merge separate national markets into a single, common market that would allow the free movement of goods, services, people, and investment among its members. It was launched in 1958 by a treaty among Belgium, the Federal Republic of Germany, France, Italy, Luxembourg, and the Netherlands. The Treaty on European Union, which took effect in November 1993, provided the foundations for economic and monetary union and created a Common Foreign and Security Policy that expanded cooperation in judicial and police matters. More recently the countries of the EU have expanded the scope of the EU for all or some of its members to other areas.

Unlike most international organizations, the EU has the power to enact laws in certain areas that are binding on all citizens of its member nations. For certain policy areas (including trade), the EU member states have effectively relinquished part of their national sovereignty to the EU's institutions. In these areas, the member states work together through the EU institutions to administer their sovereign powers jointly. In other areas, the member states have agreed to cooperate, but they retain much more discretion and maintain the right to veto certain measures. In these areas, EU policies are administered largely by the member states themselves rather than through the EU institutions.

The EU is governed by five institutions: the European Parliament, the Council of the European Union, the European Commission, the European Court of Justice, and the European Court of Auditors. In addition, the EU heads of state and the Commission president meet at least twice a year in European Council Summits. Finally, the European Central Bank is responsible for monetary policy, including management of the euro.

The European Free Trade Association (EFTA): The EFTA was formed in 1960, largely in response to the development of the European Economic Community. Its founding members – Austria, Denmark, Great Britain, Norway, Portugal, Sweden and Switzerland – had two objectives: to eliminate tariffs within the association, and to promote trade with the EC. In subsequent years, several of its members left EFTA to join the EU. The current members of the EFTA are Iceland, Liechtenstein, Norway, and Switzerland.

The North American Free Trade Agreement (NAFTA): NAFTA, formed between the United States, Canada, and Mexico, took effect on January 1, 1994. A central element of the Agreement was the elimination of virtually all tariffs among its members by 2004. The NAFTA central oversight body is the NAFTA Free Trade Commission (FTC), which is chaired jointly by the trade ministers of the three parties. The FTC is responsible for overseeing the implementation of the NAFTA, as well as its dispute settlement provisions.

NAFTA incorporates several dispute settlement mechanisms. These mechanisms are administered by the NAFTA Secretariat, which maintains offices in each member country. The principle dispute settlement provisions available under the agreement concern investment disputes, reviews of anti-dumping and countervailing duty determinations, and matters regarding the interpretation or application of the Agreement.

NAFTA is supplemented by agreements on labor (the North American Agreement on Labor Cooperation) and the environment (the North American Agreement on Environmental Cooperation). Both agreements are supported by secretariats that oversee their operation.

The Association of Southeast Asian Nations (ASEAN): ASEAN was established in 1967 by Indonesia, Malaysia, the Philippines, Singapore, and Thailand. In later years, this group was joined by Brunei, Vietnam, Laos, Myanmar, and Cambodia. ASEAN is supported by a Secretariat, located in Jakarta. ASEAN's initial objectives were to promote regional economic development through cooperation in trade, banking, technology, agriculture, industry, and tourism. In 1992 its members agreed to create the ASEAN Free Trade Area. As a result, many tariffs among its members were phased out by 2000.

The Southern Common Market (MERCOSUR): MERCOSUR, the largest trade bloc in South America, was created in 1991 by the countries of Argentina, Brazil, Paraguay and Uruguay. In 2006 Venezuela was added as a full member. Associate members include Chile, Bolivia, Colombia, Ecuador, and Peru. In addition to promoting economic cooperation, MERCOSUR is gradually eliminating tariffs among its members.

The Common Market of Eastern and South Africa (COMESA): COMESA is Africa's largest trading bloc, promoting cultural and social affairs as well as increased cooperation and integration in all fields of development, especially trade, customs and monetary affairs, transport, communication and information technology, industry and energy, gender, agriculture, environment, and natural resources. COMESA came about after the signing of the Preferential Trade Area (PTA) in 1981. Because of the success of the PTA, the signatories established COMESA, which entered into force in December 1984. COMESA was considered as a step toward the African Economic Community. Current signatories include Burundi, Comoros, Democratic Republic of the Congo, Djibouti, Egypt, Eritrea, Ethiopia, Kenya, Libyan Arab Jamahiriya, Madagascar, Malawi, Mauritius, Rwanda, Seychelles, Sudan, Swaziland, Uganda, Zambia, and Zimbabwe. COMESA is now looking to expand its presence in the Middle East to enhance Arab-African trade relations.

The Asian Pacific Economic Cooperation (APEC): Established in 1989 by 12 economies, APEC now consists of 21 Pacific Rim countries. Members signing on to the agreement in 1989 include Australia, Brunei, Canada, Indonesia, Japan, Republic of Korea, Malaysia, New Zealand, Philippines, Singapore, Thailand, and the United States. Followed by Taiwan, Hong Kong, People's Republic of China (1991), Mexico, Papua New Guinea (1993), Chile (1994), Peru, Russia, and Vietnam (1998), APEC is now the premier economic organization in the Asia-Pacific region. APEC works closely with the private sector and other stakeholders to ensure that activities foster economic growth, raise the standard of living, and increase the quality of education for citizens. APEC member countries promote trade expansion through voluntary actions such as unilateral reductions in trade barriers as well as simplified customs procedures. At present, APEC accounts for 43% of world trade and 55% of global GDP.

Bilateral Free Trade Agreements: A large number of countries have negotiated so-called bilateral agreements. Most of these agreements, however, carve out significant areas of trade and provide for long implementation periods for the elimination of many of the trade barriers covered by such agreements, ostensibly leading to free trade between their countries.

THE ROLE OF LEGAL ANALYSIS IN NEGOTIATING INTERNATIONAL TRADE ISSUES

In addressing any trade policy problem, a Commercial Diplomat must follow certain steps. This section reviews these steps with a view to the role that legal analysis plays in each of them. A more detailed review of the steps involved is found in Chapter 14 on negotiations. The discussion here is designed only to identify the legal aspects of the issue being addressed.

- ► Verification of the facts.

- ► Analysis of the issue from the perspective of the host country's legal system.

- ► Review of relevant international obligations.

- ► Examination of the range of options for reducing or removing the impediment to trade.

- ► Consultations and negotiations with the foreign host government.

- ► Initiation of formal dispute settlement proceedings if warranted.

Verification of the Facts – Assessing the Legal Dimension of the Trade Issue

The first step is to identify the government policy measure that may be the source of the issue. In other chapters we have discussed the analysis required to determine the real reason why a country's exporters may not be able to enter or expand their share of a foreign market. For purposes of this chapter we will assume that the policy analyst has been able to determine that the impediment to trade is caused by a domestic legal measure or policy action in the host country, and the task at hand is to identify the legal provisions at the heart of the issue. This may require intensive factual research.

It is important to be able to describe the measure or activity in detail and to obtain copies of any official documents regarding the measure or activity. As part of this fact-finding stage, the Commercial Diplomat should consult with affected industry representatives, diplomatic officials, and other relevant experts to ascertain their perspectives on the measure or activity.

Analysis of the Issue from the Perspective of the Host Country's Legal System

The next step is to identify the governmental measures that are relevant to the problem. For instance, it is important to know whether the applicable laws or regulations are mandatory or discretionary (if the latter, the extent of administrative discretion allowed), and whether the governmental action in question is consistent with the country's own regulations and laws. To carry out this analysis, one must understand the legal system of the host country, including how its laws are made and how its constitution allocates authority. A note on legal systems is provided in the Technical Annex to this chapter.

Identifying the legal dimension of a trade problem is important because it will then allow us to organize our further analysis of the issue more efficiently and to concentrate on the most important legal issues. Stakeholders affected by the issue can waste a great deal of time and get distracted by ancillary issues and ineffective solutions when they do not take the time to clearly identify the issue at the root of a trade problem.

This analysis will set the parameters for the range of options that will be available in developing a strategy to address the problem. It will also provide guidance to the Commercial Diplomat on the agencies with whom consultations or negotiations must be conducted.

The first step in carrying out this legal analysis is to identify the various domestic regulations, laws, judicial rulings, and constitutional provisions in the host country that apply to the regulatory decision, policy, or action that creates the trade issue. The Commercial Diplomat also needs to determine how the decision or measure of concern relates to the policy objectives that underlie any applicable legal provisions. In order to accomplish these tasks, the Commercial Diplomat must understand how laws in other jurisdictions are made, interpreted, and enforced. This can mean knowing and understanding a country's political, administrative, and judicial system with some sophistication.

This domestic legal analysis of a trade issue will enable a Commercial Diplomat to answer a number of key questions.

- ▶ **First**, what is the legal nature of the problem?

- ▶ **Second**, what is the legal foundation of the problem? Is it the way a regulation is being implemented in a particular case, the language of the regulation, the underlying law, a judicial ruling, or a fundamental issue in the legal system arising from the language of the constitution?

- ▶ **Third,** are the policy objectives embodied in the regulation, law, regulatory decision, or measure "legitimate," and could the legitimate objective be achieved by other means?

- ▶ **Fourth**, is there a legal inconsistency between the measure and the domestic laws of the host country?

Answering these questions will enable us to identify the legal origin of the problem and to map out a possible solution to the issue we have identified.

Identifying the Nature of the Legal Dimension of the Trade Problem

Arbitrary Actions by Regulators: In many countries, regulatory officials have a certain amount of leeway in the manner in which they may implement a particular law or regulation. A trade problem may arise if, for instance, such officials act in a manner that disadvantages foreign companies or products. While such problems are theoretically the easiest to address as they do not require changes to laws or regulations, in practice it can be difficult to demonstrate that the actions at issue are arbitrary or discriminatory rather than reflective of a government policy encapsulated in a law or regulation.

Interpretation or Implementation of Domestic Law: A trade problem can result from the manner in which a particular law is being implemented through a regulation or directive, even in cases where the law is satisfactory. For instance, administering officials may adopt regulations that inadvertently or intentionally discriminate against foreign companies or products. Sometimes a regulation can be redrafted to reduce its adverse impact on trade while remaining faithful to the intent of the law. For example, when U.S. regulations require foreign refiners to follow more onerous procedures than domestic ones to meet a gasoline cleanliness standard, a WTO dispute settlement panel found them discriminatory and WTO-inconsistent. Subsequently, the United States modified the regulations to comply with the panel ruling without lowering the standards established in the law.

Domestic Laws that Impede Trade, Even if They do not Violate International Agreements: A trade problem can be caused by a substantive provision in a domestic law or even a provision in a country's constitution. Difficulties may arise based on the following:

► The particular provision represents a significant departure from the types of measures used by most countries that have similar policy concerns,

► The provision may represent a major departure from international norms with respect to the policy objectives it is designed to achieve, or

► The provision may simply represent an element of protection the country has not been prepared to relinquish.

Needless to say, when protecting domestic interests is the motivation for a measure, finding a solution is likely to prove far more difficult and time-consuming. Achieving changes in domestic legislation in most cases turns out to be a difficult process that may take many years to accomplish. Obtaining a change in the country's constitution is almost virtually impossible and can be achieved only in the context of broader constitutional reforms. To cite an extreme case, Mexico's constitution contains a provision that prohibits the Mexican government from subrogating its rights with respect to the treatment of foreign investors to any third party, including arbitration tribunals. This provision has been a major concern to U.S. investors and officials, and a great deal of time has been spent in finding a legal approach that would allow Mexico to accept some third-party process for resolving investment disputes.

Domestic Judicial Rulings: A judicial ruling can create a trade problem if it compels a government to take an action that would be inconsistent with its international commitments. This can occur when there is an inherent conflict between a domestic law and international agreements the country has negotiated.

Sub-national Laws: Most federal systems leave international relations to the federal authority and provide that federal regulations supersede nonfederal ones. However, many federal governments lack efficient institutional mechanisms or the political will to enforce compliance by sub-federal governments. As global commercial activity begins to affect more aspects of local and regional commercial life, pressures are increasing at the local and regional level to regulate international activity. These regulations can lead to international conflicts when a country's trading partners view the actions of sub-federal units as conflicting with the obligations of a national government under a treaty or multilateral agreement.

Failure to Implement Domestic Laws: Some trade issues can result from the absence of government action. For instance, a country's pharmaceutical or entertainment companies that rely on patent or copyright protection may suffer commercial harm in foreign markets where governments have not adopted adequate laws for the protection of intellectual property or where the laws exist but are not enforced.

Mapping Out the Hierarchy of Domestic Legal Provisions that Apply to the Policy Measure

Analysis of the legal provisions that have a bearing on a trade problem can identify the true legal source of the problem. It is not uncommon for a regulatory decision or policy measure that has been identified as the immediate trade problem to be the end result of a whole hierarchy of domestic legal provisions that have little to do with international trade. Thus, a decision on reimbursement rates for pharmaceuticals that discriminates against foreign producers may not be the result of a decision to protect the domestic industry. It may actually be the result of a law that requires government regulators to keep health costs to a minimum.

Solving a trade problem that results from the application of a regulation that is not spelled out in detail in the underlying law in most cases is likely to be less difficult than a trade problem that is caused by a measure embedded in the underlying law. This point can also be illustrated by an actual case. In the 1990s a regulation by the Japanese Ministry of Telecommunications decreed that international leased lines used to connect computers in different countries could only connect to a single computer in each country. This provision, which was designed to protect the Japanese telecommunications monopoly, made it difficult for database vendors to sell access to their U.S. databases because such databases were distributed among large numbers of computers in the United States. A fix to this problem could have taken a number of forms:

- ► A change in the application of the regulation to this case,

- ► A change in the wording of the regulation,

- ► A change in the law which sought to restrict the use of leased lines for intra-corporate networking, or

- ► A change in the underlying law and policy.

From the point of view of solving the problem with the least effort, it obviously makes sense to find a solution requiring the lowest level of legal change possible, although a decision to apply the regulation in a flexible manner with respect to any one situation may raise questions of fairness. While U.S. negotiators asked for a change in the regulation, the Japanese officials finally decided to solve the problem by making an exception for the specific circumstances that led to the dispute.

Where the decision or measure of concern is a local regulation of a municipality or province, the trade policy analyst may face another legal hierarchy. In unitary, nonfederal states such as France, where the central government controls governmental functions, it may be necessary to consider both the local ordinance and the national law that governs the ordinance. In federal states like the United States or Australia, national, state, or provincial governments may have parallel laws on the same subject, with a shifting line of demarcation between the two in some areas and overlapping jurisdiction in others. In large countries going through political transitions such as Russia and China, the demarcation of authority between national and provincial governments can be opaque.

While a trade problem can be caused by a law or measure adopted at any level of government, it is the central government as the signatory of the WTO Agreements that bears the ultimate responsibility for implementing the nation's obligations under the agreements. At the same time, direct legal action by the central government in many cases is not the most effective way of solving trade problems caused by sub-central level of government. The most effective course of action a central government can take in such cases is to point out the potential consequences for local commercial interests. To cite an example, when the Texas Legislature adopted a law that exempted local mini breweries from an alcohol tax, thus discriminating against beer brewed outside the state, U.S. trade officials persuaded the Governor and the Legislature to reverse their decision by pointing out that any retaliation by foreign countries injured by the measure would likely be focused on products produced in Texas.

Establishing the Relationship between the Trade-distorting Decision or Measure and the Objectives of the Underlying Legal Provisions

For purposes of Commercial Diplomacy, it is important to achieve a clear understanding of the relationship between the regulatory decision or policy measure and the objectives or purposes of the underlying domestic legal provisions. A review of the objectives of a law may reveal that the regulation or measure creating a trade problem is not the only way of accomplishing the requirements of the law, and that there are other ways of accomplishing the law's objectives and meeting its legal requirements. In such cases, the adoption of one of these alternative approaches to the implementation of the law can often eliminate or significantly reduce the trade problem. This is not to say that governments are always ready to embrace alternative solutions, but if they decide that they would like to accommodate trade concerns, the awareness of alternative approaches for implementing the intent of the law can help. Persuading another government to adopt a pragmatic solution could be strengthened even further if a Commercial Diplomat can show that a change in the way the regulation is drafted could enable the government to achieve its objectives more effectively from a purely domestic perspective.

There are several legal sources for establishing the underlying public policy objective of a law. These sources form what is called the legislative history of a law. Although the sources differ from country to country, and between common law and civil law systems, some sources are:

► The preamble to the legislation;

► Reports that accompanied the legislation, prepared by legislative committees that examine the legislation before it is submitted for formal adoption;

► Statements made during debate on the legislation by legislators supporting the legislation and reported in the legislative record;

► Articles in legal journals analyzing the issue at the time the legislation was being considered by the legislature;

► Statements made by regulatory officials responsible for administering the measure; and

► Interpretations made by judges, legal tribunals, and legal scholars or experts.

ANALYZING INTERNATIONAL AGREEMENTS: HOW DOES THE TRADE PROBLEM RELATE TO APPLICABLE PROVISIONS OF INTERNATIONAL AGREEMENTS?

The legal analysis of a trade issue requires a review of the relevant provisions of international agreements and treaties, in particular the rules of the WTO and any regional trade agreements that apply to the host country. We need to determine what international agreements the country has signed, and what commitments it has made under these agreements. The objective is to assess whether the targeted measure or the underlying laws and regulations constitute a violation of the rules and commitments established under such agreements. We also want to know whether any international agreement establishes norms or best practices that might provide a reference point for efforts to resolve the issue, or whether any of the provisions create an obligation by the host country to make best efforts to resolve the issue even if it is not strictly a violation of any of the agreements. A clear understanding of the international legal provisions that apply to the case will also allow us to evaluate our options more clearly.

The results of this analysis are likely to be critical to efforts by a Commercial Diplomat to deal with the issue for three reasons:

► A request for a change will appear much more legitimate if legal analysis can demonstrate that the targeted measure constitutes a violation of international commitments and rules, or that it represents a departure from international norms or best practices even if it does not violate an international agreement.

► Legal analysis can shed light on possible violations of international commitments and the availability of dispute settlement provisions such as the WTO dispute settlement system. Commercial Diplomats can use such information as negotiating leverage while pursuing a negotiated resolution of the issue. If the Commercial Diplomat can present a strong legal case, the chances for negotiating a favorable solution to the trade problem will be much greater than if the legal case is weak.

► Where international legal analysis establishes that the home country has a good chance of winning a dispute settlement case, the Commercial Diplomat can begin to assemble the facts and legal arguments for a case. Since dispute settlement procedures often establish tight deadlines, early preparation allows the legal team to be better prepared if a decision is made later to initiate a dispute settlement proceeding. Moreover, an early start will also facilitate the collection of relevant information during the bilateral consultations organized to resolve the issue on an amicable basis.

Where Can the Trade Policy Analyst Find Information Concerning the Provisions of International Agreements and Treaties?

Most of the key trade agreements and other important international agreements that have an impact on trade policy decisions contain provisions for the establishment of an organization to administer the agreement. These organizations have established websites that provide ready access to information about the agreement and the activities of the organization. The WTO, for example, at www.wto.org, provides, not only the text of all WTO agreements and rulings by dispute settlement panels and the Appellate Body, but also has an online Analytical Index. The WTO also makes available for sale through its website annotated documents on all rulings, thus providing an in-depth analysis of how panels have interpreted key provisions of the various WTO agreements. Leading legal scholars have also compiled annotated versions of each WTO agreement. The website www.worldtradelaw.net provides an extensive database of WTO provisions and summaries of all WTO dispute settlement and appellate body decisions. Subscribers to the site can enter any key word and obtain references and a commentary on all relevant provisions and dispute settlement decisions.

A list of Internet resources providing access to both trade-related and nontrade-related international agreements and treaties is provided at the end of this chapter.

What if More than One Provision of an International Agreement Applies or More than One Agreement has a Bearing on the Issue?

Trade issues are often very complex. Frequently, several provisions in one trade agreement or provisions in several different trade agreements may be relevant in determining whether a measure or practice is consistent with international trade rules. In such situations, the analyst needs to evaluate all relevant agreements and provisions.

If multiple international agreements are relevant, a complaining country will need to decide which one to use to pursue its complaint. Of course, the "offending" country also must be a party to the agreement for the relevant dispute settlement provisions to provide an option for resolving the dispute.

With respect to trade issues among countries that belong to the WTO, the WTO and its dispute settlement system is clearly the most important venue to resolve these issues. This is because members of the WTO have all agreed to "binding" dispute settlement. In essence, this means that they agree to carry out the decisions of panels convened pursuant to the WTO DSU whose reports have been adopted by the WTO membership. Therefore, in most cases, countries will use the WTO dispute settlement system, rather than dispute settlement proceedings available under other treaties and agreements, few of which have "binding" dispute settlement provisions. A description of other dispute settlement venues is provided in the Technical Appendix on Venues for Resolving Disputes within this chapter.

Countries that belong to regional free trade agreements modeled on the WTO dispute settlement system may also choose to pursue the complaint within the regional framework, either because they have a better case under the provisions of the regional agreement or because they want to keep the complaint "within the family." However, countries in most cases are not required to choose among alternative venues and may well decide to pursue the issue in parallel in more than one forum. In contrast, countries that belong to an economic union like the European Union are required to pursue any trade issue with another member country through the institutions of the economic union.

Investment issues are commonly addressed in Bilateral Investment Treaties (BIT) and Bilateral Treaties of Friendship, Commerce, and Navigation. On investment issues that involve the provision of a service, however, GATS provides a legal framework for commitments on the establishment of enterprises producing services and the treatment of such enterprises under domestic laws. The WTO has not yet agreed to tackle general foreign investment issues in areas other than services, although the WTO has adopted rules for trade-related performance measures that countries impose on foreign investors. These are addressed in the WTO Agreement on Trade-Related Investment Measures.

In addition to the BIT and WTO venues, NAFTA provides for settlement of investment disputes between investors and states. This novel form of dispute settlement is most useful when involving a federal government to pursue an investment dispute is preferable to using local courts.

On issues that concern product standards, a number of international agreements and standards organizations may be relevant. Examples include the WTO Technical Barriers to Trade (TBT) Agreement; The International Standards Organization (ISO) that promulgates commercial standards; various regional standards organizations; and sectoral organizations such as the International Telecommunications Union (ITU), the Codex Alimentarius (for food safety standards), the International Plant Protection

Convention (for plant pest risks), and the International Organization for Epizootics (for animal health).

Finally, The International Court of Justice is also a useful venue for some types of disputes. The International Court of Justice (ICJ) is the principal judicial organ of the United Nations. It was established in 1946 and is based in The Hague. The ICJ has two functions: (1) to settle legal disputes, which countries may submit to it in accordance with international law; and (2) to provide advisory opinions on legal questions, which may be referred to it by various international agencies. The ICJ has had very little involvement in trade issues, but its rulings could form a part of the body of international law that may be considered relevant in WTO dispute settlement cases in some situations. Because its proceedings are lengthy and because the Court may hear a dispute only if the countries involved have accepted its jurisdiction, it is rarely used.

What if International Agreements Appear to Conflict?

Different international agreements may at times appear to create conflicting obligations. In such cases, the Vienna Convention (described below) provides that countries should interpret treaties in ways that avoid conflict. When two agreements are between the same parties on the same subject matter, the most recently ratified agreement should take precedence.

Apparent conflicts have arisen in a number of areas between trade agreements and environmental agreements with trade provisions. In practice, while the WTO and the various environmental agreements operate independently, the WTO agreements have been interpreted to permit members to take measures to protect the environment even though the measures might otherwise violate the GATT.

Commercial Diplomats should be aware of other environmental agreements that incorporate trade provisions, including the following examples:

► 1973: Convention on International Trade in Endangered Species,

► 1982: UN Convention on the Law of the Sea,

► 1987: Montreal Protocol, the 1992 UN Framework Convention on Climate Change,

► 1989: Basel Convention on the Control of Trans-boundary Movements of Hazardous Wastes and their Disposal,

► 1994: International Tropical Timber Agreement, and

► 2001: Stockholm Convention on Persistent Organic Pollutants

A Final Word of Caution

Commercial Diplomats should have competent legal counsel examine any issues relating to the relationship between specific domestic legal instruments and international agreements for the following reasons:

► States implement treaties differently and accord them differing status nationally.

► Some jurisdictions give precedence to local laws over national ones in some situations (e.g., under the European principle of "subsidiarity").

► Some jurisdictions, such as aboriginal or native preserves, have virtually autonomous status within nations.

► Other legal systems may exist outside the national or sub-national ones that are parallel to, not subordinate to, national or local laws.

► There may not be any effective legal system in place.

INVOKING FORMAL INTERNATIONAL DISPUTE SETTLEMENT PROCEDURES IN THE WTO

A number of international trade agreements have formal dispute settlement procedures, including the WTO and many of the regional free trade agreements such as NAFTA. The dispute settlement system of the WTO is by far the most important of these systems.

The WTO's dispute settlement agreement is formally known as "the Understanding on Rules and Procedures Governing the Settlement of Disputes" (the DSU). The DSU lays out the procedures for settling trade-related conflicts in the WTO. It is overseen by the Dispute Settlement Body (the DSB), which is composed of representatives of each WTO member. The DSB establishes dispute settlement panels, monitors the implementation of the panels' rulings, and has the power to authorize trade retaliation when a country does not comply with a ruling.

Typically, a WTO dispute arises when either, (a) one country adopts a trade measure or takes an action that another country considers to be a violation of a WTO agreement; or (b) one country believes that, as a result of another country's action, it has been denied WTO benefits to which it is entitled.

A procedure for settling disputes existed under the GATT, which preceded the WTO, but it had no fixed timetables, rulings were easy to block, and many cases dragged on inconclusively for a long time. The DSU introduced a more structured process with more clearly defined procedural stages, subject to strict time limits. The agreement is premised on the notion that prompt settlement of disputes is essential to the effective functioning of the WTO. The DSU sets out in considerable detail the procedures and the timetable to be followed in resolving disputes. A case that runs its full course should normally require no more than about one year before the first panel ruling is issued, and 15 months if the case is appealed. If the case is considered urgent (e.g., if perishable goods are involved), then it is subject to shorter deadlines.

Under the DSU the country losing a case cannot unilaterally block the adoption of the panel's ruling. Under previous GATT procedures, rulings could only be adopted by consensus, meaning that a single objection (including one originating from the country that lost the case) could block the ruling. Under the DSU the situation is reversed; rulings are automatically adopted, unless there is a consensus to reject a ruling. Any country wishing to block a ruling must persuade all other WTO members to support its position (including its adversary in the case).

Although much of the WTO's dispute settlement procedure resembles a court proceeding, the preferred solution is for the countries involved to settle the dispute by themselves. Before a country can request the formation of a dispute settlement panel, it must consult with the offending party for a minimum period of 60 days. Even when a case has progressed to later stages, consultation, negotiation, and mediation remain options for resolving the dispute.

Initiating a WTO Case

Before invoking the formal dispute settlement procedures found in the DSU, WTO members are expected to make an effort to resolve the dispute through bilateral discussions in capitals. They often also resort to other dispute settlement mechanisms provided by the WTO agreements, since they are easier and quicker to use than the DSU process. These mechanisms include informal consultations, raising the matter in the meetings of the relevant WTO committee, and using some of the dispute settlement tools included in specific agreements, such as the Subsidies Agreement. Formal dispute proceedings in the WTO require careful preparation, including verification of facts and analysis of the validity of legal arguments. In order to avoid the unnecessary expenditure of legal resources, a party should ideally undertake much of the research and analysis that is required for preparing a panel brief before it gets to the point of making a final decision on whether to request a panel.

There is also a practical reason to begin the work of preparing a brief early in the process of resolving a dispute. Under the DSU the time frame permitted for the panel process is so tight that a party cannot normally do an adequate job of preparing an entire case in such a short period of time, especially given the limited resources available to most governments.

In deciding whether to request a panel, parties should also recognize that the panel process raises the profile of a dispute and normally generates increased media and public attention. Such developments may sometimes make it more difficult to settle the matter by negotiation. However, as more disputes are brought and as more developing countries, and small countries find that they can successfully bring a case, media attention may become a less important factor than the merits of the case in determining whether parties are prepared to settle.

The WTO negotiators were very cognizant of the fact that formal litigation is not always the best method of resolving trade disputes. They laid out a hierarchy of preferred outcomes in Article 7 of the DSU, which states that:

"Before bringing a case, a Member shall exercise its judgment as to whether action under these procedures would be fruitful. The aim of the dispute settlement mechanism is to secure a positive solution to a dispute. A solution mutually acceptable to the parties to a dispute and consistent with the covered agreements is clearly to be preferred. In the absence of a mutually agreed solution, the first objective of the dispute settlement mechanism is usually to secure the withdrawal of the measures concerned if these are found to be inconsistent with the provisions of any of the covered agreements. The provision of compensation should be resorted to only if the immediate withdrawal of the measure is impracticable and as a temporary measure pending the withdrawal of the measure which is inconsistent with a covered agreement. The last resort which this Understanding provides to the Member invoking the dispute settlement procedures is the possibility of suspending the application of concessions or other obligations under the covered agreements on a discriminatory basis vis-à-vis the other Member, subject to authorization by the DSB of such measures."

Consultations

Before taking any other action, the DSU requires the parties to a dispute to talk to each other to see whether they can settle their differences amicably. Consultations offer a country the opportunity to assess the merits of the other country's case and to clarify the facts of the situation. To facilitate this process, the complaining country may sometimes submit written questions to which it will seek a response from the defending country during the consultations. The parties may hold more than one round of consultations if they find the process informative, or if they think they may be able to reach a settlement. If consultations fail, a party can also ask the WTO Director-General to mediate or try to help in any other way.

Consultations are not always followed by a request for a panel. Sometimes the threat of action is more potent than the action itself, so that consultations may provide information and leverage for negotiations that lead to a successful resolution of the dispute. On occasion, a complaining party may learn from the consultation process about weaknesses in its arguments or damaging facts, which may lead it to decide not to press its case.

Panels

If consultations fail, the complaining country can ask that a panel be appointed. In order to facilitate the panel formation process, the DSU requires the WTO Secretariat to maintain an indicative list of individuals who are qualified to serve as panelists. All WTO parties are involved in the selection of a panel. The country against whom a case has been brought can block the creation of a panel once, but when the DSB meets for a second time, the appointment can no longer be blocked (unless there is a consensus against appointing the panel). Furthermore, DSU rules provide that, if there is no agreement on panelists within 20 days after the establishment of the panel, the Director-General of the WTO, at the request of either party, can determine the composition of a panel. This prevents a party from blocking a dispute settlement proceeding indefinitely by rejecting panelists.

Officially, panels assist the DSB in issuing rulings or recommendations. However, since panel reports can only be rejected by consensus in the DSB, their conclusions are difficult to overturn.

Steps in the Panel Process

A panel's final report is normally given to the parties to a dispute within six months of the panel's formation. In urgent cases, which include those involving perishable goods, the deadline is shortened to three months.

Following are the main stages in the panel process, as outlined under the DSU:

- ► **Before the first hearing:** Each side in the dispute presents its case in writing to the panel. These written submissions are essentially legal "briefs" in which the parties state the facts, the findings they want the panel to make, and the legal arguments supporting their position.

- ► **First hearing:** At the first substantive meeting of the panel, the complaining country, the responding country, and those that have announced they have an interest in the dispute, make their cases. The first hearing may run two to three days, with the panel meeting in several sessions.

- ► **Second hearing:** Following the first hearing, the parties will usually have two to three weeks to submit written rebuttals. One to two weeks later, the panel will hold a second meeting at which the parties present oral rebuttal arguments. During oral presentations, the panel may interrupt the presenter with questions. The panel may also at any time ask the parties to submit written responses to questions posed either during or outside of the hearing.

- ► **Experts:** If one side raises scientific or technical matters, the panel may either consult experts or appoint an expert review group to prepare an advisory report. Non-government experts are not otherwise allowed to participate in the proceedings.

- ► **First draft:** Within two to four weeks of the second hearing, the panel usually submits the descriptive sections of its report to the two sides, giving them two weeks to comment. This portion of the report does not include findings or conclusions.

- ► **Interim report:** The panel then submits an interim report to the two sides, including its findings and conclusions. The parties have one week to ask for a review.

- ► **Review:** The period of review may not exceed two weeks. During that time, the panel may hold additional meetings with the two sides. To ensure transparency, presentations to the panel are made only in the presence of both sides and all written submissions are provided to both sides.

▶ **Final report:** A final report is submitted to the two sides and, three weeks later, circulated to all WTO members. If the panel decides that the disputed trade measure is inconsistent with a WTO agreement or obligation, it will recommend that the measure be brought into conformity with WTO rules. However, panels do not tell parties to a dispute exactly how this should be accomplished. Instead, the manner of implementation of panel recommendations is left to the discretion of the country concerned, but, as is discussed below, a complaining party does have tools available if it not satisfied with a losing party's compliance. If the panel finds that the trade measure is consistent with the relevant WTO agreements, but that the measure has denied the complaining party WTO benefits, it may recommend a solution, but the defending country cannot be required to withdraw its measure.

▶ **The report becomes a ruling:** Once members have had 20 days to consider a panel report, the report can be considered for adoption by the DSB, unless it is appealed. The DSB must adopt the report within 60 days, unless there is a consensus to reject it. The adopted report, which may include a recommendation to bring a measure into conformity with the WTO, becomes a ruling of the DSB. A "reasonable" time is allowed to implement panel rulings.

▶ **Appealing a panel decision:** Either side can appeal a panel ruling. Sometimes both sides do so. Appeals must be based on points of law, such as legal interpretation. They cannot request reexamination of existing evidence or examination of new evidence. Appeals are heard by three members of a permanent seven-member Appellate Body set up by the DSB. Members of the Appellate Body have four-year terms. They must be individuals with recognized standing in the field of law and international trade, not affiliated with any government. The appeal can uphold, modify, or reverse any of the panel's legal findings and conclusions. Normally the appeals process should not last more than 60 days, and in no case may it last more than 90 days. Following a ruling of the Appellate Body, the DSB must adopt the panel report, as modified by the Appellate Body, within 30 days following circulation of the Appellate Body's report, unless there is a consensus to reject it.

Significance of Panel Decisions

Although much has been written about whether the GATT and the succeeding WTO Dispute Settlement Mechanism are based on a common law or a civil law model, it is probably fair to say that they operate as an amalgam of the two. Although each dispute settlement panel has reference to decisions of other panels in which similar arguments and facts have been presented, it is authorized to interpret the facts and arguments before it on its own authority as well as in light of prior or similar cases. This has given rise to a series of cases in which the broad principles set forth in the WTO agreements and the GATT of 1947 were generally agreed by specific panels to operate in specific ways, but panels are not formally bound by prior decisions or interpretations.

However, with the establishment of the Appellate Body, the process may be shifting closer to a common law model. The discretion of individual dispute settlement panels is constrained as rulings of the Appellate Body clearly carry more weight than prior panel rulings, and the Appellate Body frequently cites its prior rulings when addressing an issue.

Aftermath of a DSB Ruling

After DSB adoption of a report in which a country's trade measure has been found to violate its WTO obligations, the country is required to act on the recommendations in the report and bring the measure into compliance with its obligations. The DSU stresses that "prompt compliance with recommendations or rulings of the DSB…is essential in order to ensure effective resolution of disputes to the benefit of all members." The offending country must state its intention to comply at a DSB meeting held within 30 days of the report's adoption. If immediate compliance with the recommendation is impractical, the member will be given a "reasonable period of time" to do so. The DSU provides that the "reasonable period of time" can be: (a) the time proposed by the losing country, if the DSB approves; (b) a time period mutually agreed by the parties; or, (c) a time period determined through arbitration. The DSU also indicates that the period of time should not normally exceed 15 months. To date, in most WTO disputes the losing party has chosen to bring its measure into compliance.

If a losing party fails to act within a reasonable period of time, it is required to enter into negotiations with the complaining country in order to determine mutually acceptable compensation — for instance, tariff reductions in areas of particular interest to the complaining party. If after 20 days no satisfactory compensation is agreed, the complaining party may ask the DSB for permission to impose limited trade sanctions (i.e., suspend concessions or obligations) against the offending country. The DSB is required to grant this authorization within 30 days of the expiry of the "reasonable period of time," unless there is a consensus against the request. If the two sides cannot agree on what constitutes "a reasonable period of time" or the level of compensation, the complaining country may request an arbitrator to determine the "reasonable period of time" or the appropriate amount of compensation or trade retaliation to be authorized by the DSB. If a country has taken steps to comply with a panel's findings, but the complaining party does not feel that they are adequate, the complaining party can ask the original panel to review the measures adopted and rule on whether they are adequate to bring the losing country into compliance.

In principle, any sanctions should be imposed in the same sector as the dispute. If this is not practical, or if it would not be effective, sanctions can be imposed in a different sector of the same agreement or under another agreement. The DSU's basic objective is to minimize the chances of actions spilling over into unrelated sectors, while at the same time ensuring that sanctions are effective.

The DSB monitors how adopted rulings and recommendations are implemented. Any outstanding cases remain on its agenda until the issue is resolved.

TECHNICAL ANNEX ON DOMESTIC AND INTERNATIONAL LEGAL INSTRUMENTS

Domestic Legal Instruments

This section provides a description and examples of domestic legal instruments that have a bearing on trade. Governments at the national, sub-national, and local level can apply legal instruments that have an impact on trade. At the sub-national level there are a variety of legal instruments promulgated by sub-national entities, such as states, districts, provinces, or other units. The national legal system usually has means for determining when a national law or regulation supersedes a sub-national one, but in both national and sub-national systems the relationship between the various legal instruments is the same.

Constitutional Provisions

A constitutional provision is one set forth in the governing constitution, or other fundamental document(s) upon which a national legal system is built such as the U.S. Constitution or the Treaty of Rome. Constitutional provisions can be extremely detailed and can affect commercial relationships in many ways.

An example of a constitutional provision is set forth below. This example is from the Constitution of South Africa.

Conflicts that cannot be resolved.
148. If a dispute concerning a conflict cannot be resolved by a court, the national legislation prevails over the provincial legislation or provincial constitution.

Constitutional provisions and amendments for South Africa and over 100 countries can be found on http://right2info.org/laws.

With respect to international trade, constitutional provisions may assign responsibility for regulating trade to certain institutions in government or allocate responsibility between different branches of government. Constitutional provisions at the national level of government are also important for international trade because they may allocate authority over issues affecting international trade between the national government and sub-national levels of government.

Laws or Decrees (of National Scope and Application)

Laws are instruments that are generally the legal instrument of most importance to Commercial Diplomats since in most legal systems they are superior to all other domestic legal instruments except constitutional provisions. In modern legal systems, most laws are passed by legislative bodies and then approved by the head of government. Such laws are sometimes called statutes or codes.

There are also legal instruments that have the same effect as a law, but which are issued by the head government without the involvement of the legislature. These instruments are often called decrees and in the U.S. legal system, executive orders. They generally address matters where the authority lies inherently in the hands of the head of government or has been delegated to the position by the legislature.

Statutes, Codes, or Other Instruments Enacted by Parliamentary or Congressional Bodies

These are laws promulgated by parliamentary or legislative bodies. The following example is from an unofficial translation of Mongolia's Law on Unfair Competition.

> *Article 3. Dominance, Monopoly and Monopolistic Activities 1. Dominance exists when a single entity acting alone or a group of economic entities acting together account constantly for over 50% of supply to the market of a certain good or similar goods, products or carried out works and provided services.*

Another example from a sub-central level of government is provided by the following excerpt from the Corporate Tax Act of the Province of Alberta in Canada.

> *The Minister of Revenue may at any time make an assessment, reassessment or additional assessment of tax for a taxation year, interest or penalties, if any, payable under this Act by a corporation, notify in writing any corporation by whom a return of income for a taxation year has been filed that no tax is payable for the year, or determine the corporation's entitlement to and the amount, if any, of a refundable tax credit for a taxation year...*

Regulations, Rules, Licenses

Regulations, rules, licenses, or guidance are legal instruments issued by an administrative or regulatory body that has been given authority over a subject matter. The authority may come from a law or a constitutional provision or may have been delegated by a higher administrative body. Regulations are generally issued to provide specific procedures to implement a law or to provide details that are not addressed in a law. In many countries, there are laws governing the procedures to be followed in issuing a regulation and standards a regulation must meet. Courts may overturn a regulation when the procedures are not followed or the standards not met. Rules are generally more specific than regulations and often address how a regulation should be applied in a specific circumstance; sometimes rules are issued in response to requests from companies or other entities that must comply with a regulation. A license is a grant of authority to a specific entity to carry out an activity. For example, the customs authority in a country may grant a license to a company to import a fixed amount of a certain good. Licenses are usually issued pursuant to a regulation

The example below is a Canadian regulation pertaining to industrial design applications.

Industrial Design Regulations: P.C. 1999-2135 2 December, 1999...Her Excellency the Governor General in Council, on the recommendation of the Minister of Industry, pursuant to section 25a of the Industrial Design Act, hereby makes the annexed Industrial Design Regulations... 10 (1) An application must relate to one design applied to a single article or set, or to variants (2) If an application does not comply with subsection (1), the applicant or their agent must limit the application to one design applied to a single article or set, or to variants.

Many national regulations are available on a country's official website. For U.S. regulations, visit http://www.access.gpo.gov/nara/cfr/cfr-table-search.html.

Another example illustrates a state-level regulation from the United States – State of California, a very large sub-national (state) unit with a correspondingly large administrative sector:

Title 7. Harbors and Navigation....Division 2. State Board of Pilot Commissioners for the Bays of San Francisco, San Pablo and Suisun. (a) The Board shall meet on a regular basis at least once each month on the date and at a time and place specified by the President. (b) Notice of the date, time and place of a meeting of the Board shall be given at least ten days in advance of the meeting.

Court Decisions or Judgments

In most legal systems, courts can render decisions with effect on those government agencies, persons, corporations, or properties deemed to be within the jurisdiction of the court or tribunal. Court decisions are important legal instruments for Commercial Diplomats because in addressing any trade problem it is important to determine if the measure or action causing the problem can be successfully challenged in a court that has jurisdiction over the agency responsible for the measure or action.

The constitutional decision of the Estonian Supreme Court referenced below is an example of a court decision.

Petition of Tallinna Administrative Court to declare clause 4.6 of "Rules for trading in markets and streets" approved by resolution No 43 of Tallinna City Council of 10.12.1998, order No 386 of the Government of Centre district of Tallinn of 31.03.1995 and order No 123 of the elder of Centre district of Tallinna of 28.03.2000 invalid because of conflict thereof with Articles 3 (1), 31, 113 and 154 (1) of the Constitution.

Many national court decisions are available in whole or in part on a country's official website or websites that specifically addresses nations' court decisions.

Another example of a judicial decision is the following excerpt from a state level court in Australia, the Supreme Court of Tasmania.

West Coast Transport Pty Ltd & Anor v Adams Group Services Pty Ltd & Anor [2001] TASSC 94 (15 August 2001) 7 The considerations applicable to misleading and deceptive conduct under the Trade Practices Act (C'wealth) are similar to those under the Fair Trading Act. In James & Ors v Australia and New Zealand Banking Group Ltd & Ors (1986) 64 ALR 347 at 372, Toohey J said, in a series of propositions, that: "(2) The mere fact that representations as to future conduct or events do not come to pass does not make them misleading or deceptive: Bill Acceptance Corporation Ltd v GWA Ltd (1983) 50 ALR 242.

Quasi-governmental Regulations, Procedures, or Standards

These are regulations, procedures, or standards that in some countries are produced by governmental bodies, and in others by private sector bodies that have been given some authority by government. They most often concern product standards or very focused economic enterprise activity (export monopolies, for instance). The trends toward deregulated economies across much of the world may mean, however, that devolution of government functions to the private sector may become more pervasive. A special case is that of state-owned, state-invested, and state-supported enterprises. In dealings with these entities, the influence of government may be highly opaque, and there is difficulty in applying international legal norms.

Standards-setting Bodies

Voluntary and mandatory standards are set around the world by both government and nongovernment bodies. Information on standards-setting bodies can be found at http://www.nist.gov/index.html and http://www.iso.ch/iso/en/ISOOnline. openerpage.

An example of a private standard setting body in the United States is the National Fire Protection Association (NFPA), which describes itself at http://www.nfpa.org/ index.asp?cookie_test=1 as follows.

The mission of the international nonprofit NFPA, established in 1896, is to reduce the worldwide burden of fire and other hazards on the quality of life by providing and advocating consensus codes and standards, research, training, and education. The world's leading advocate of fire prevention and an authoritative source on public safety, NFPA develops, publishes, and disseminates more than 300 consensus codes and standards intended to minimize the possibility and effects of fire and other risks. NFPA membership totals more than 70,000 individuals around the world.

Industry association procedures/rules can serve the same functions as standards-setting bodies by promoting uniform procedures among their members. In some countries private associations are given authority to enforce adherence to the procedures by virtue of exclusive license coupled with membership. If a member does not comply, it can be expelled, and if it is no longer a member it cannot engage in business. In other cases, industry associations are given other authority. Below is an extract from a 1997 report by Philip Budwick, for the Economic Strategy Institute entitled "On the Waterfront: Japan's Restrictive Port Practices and Harbor Regulations." A copy of this report can be requested at http://www.econstrat.org/index.php?option=com_con tent&task=view&id=192&Itemid=47.

*Japan Harbor Transportation Association (JHTA). The JHTA exercises unilateral con-
trol over Japan's waterfront through its broad discretion to review and disapprove
virtually all aspects of a carrier's operations in Japanese ports. As the sole negotiating intermediary between carriers and the providers of port services, the JHTA also
controls the availability of maritime labor to serve ocean carriers, but cannot choose
port terminals that might be cheaper or more efficient for loading and unloading.
This system has made Japanese ports extremely expensive and inconvenient.*

*Restrictive Port Practices. In 1989, the JHTA levied a port tax on all cargoes using
Japanese ports and services in order to fund the Harbor Management Fund (HMF),
which had been created to subsidize waterfront labor and to help finance the
upgrading of port facilities to deal with rising imports. Carriers from around the
world complained that the new port tax was an unfair trading practice and that
the fee structure discriminated against foreign carriers. After formal complaints
from the United States and the European Union, the port tax was discontinued in
1992, and the remaining funds were pledged for labor purposes only. However, as
of 1994, only nominal amounts had been expended from the HMF, and the JHTA's
plans for disposition of the remaining funds still remains unclear.*

International Organization for Standardization (ISO)

The most important global standards-setting organization is the International Organization for Standardization (ISO), a nongovernmental organization that sets voluntary
standards, ISO has no legal authority to enforce the implementation of its standards.
ISO does not regulate or legislate. However, countries may decide to adopt ISO standards - mainly those concerned with health, safety, or the environment - as regulations
refer to them in legislation for which they provide the technical basis. In addition,
although ISO standards are voluntary, they may become a market requirement, as
has happened in the case of ISO 9001 quality management systems or of dimensions
of freight containers and bank cards.

   ISO only develops standards for which there is a market requirement. The work is
mainly carried out by experts from the industrial, technical, and business sectors that
have asked for the standards and that subsequently put them to use. ISO standards
are based on international consensus among the experts in the field. Consensus, like
technology, evolves, and ISO takes account both of evolving technology and of evolving interests by requiring a periodic review of its standards at least every five years
to decide whether they should be maintained, updated, or withdrawn. In this way,
ISO standards retain their position as the state of the art. ISO standards are technical
agreements that provide the framework for compatible technology worldwide. They
are designed to be globally relevant - useful everywhere in the world.

International Legal Instruments: Terminology

There are a very large number of treaties and other types of agreements governing
commercial relationships between states. New bilateral, regional, and multilateral

agreements are being negotiated all the time. Multiplied by the number of countries in the world, this creates a huge body of law.

There are many names for international legal instruments (e.g., treaty, convention, declaration, charter, agreement, protocol, memorandum of understanding). There is no agreed-upon nomenclature or set of official definitions for the various names given to international agreements, although certain names tend to be associated with certain types of agreements on the basis of state practice. There is also much more standardization of terms for agreements concluded under the auspices of particular organizations, such as the United Nations or the WTO, or regional organizations, such as the European Union. The UN Treaty Collection Office has developed a very useful "Treaty Reference Guide," which explains the various terms used to describe international agreements and how they are currently being used. Examples of points in the guide are summarized below:

> *The title assigned to ... international instruments ...normally [has] no overriding legal effects. The title may follow habitual uses or may relate to the particular character or importance... attributed to the instrument by its parties. The degree of formality chosen will depend upon the gravity of the problems dealt with and upon the political implications and intent of the parties.*

Fortunately, international legal instruments have common features and international law has applied basically the same rules to all of them. These rules have become part of international customary law and have been codified in the 1969 Vienna Convention on the Law of Treaties. Traditionally the term "treaty" has referred to the highest form of international agreement, but for the purposes of the Vienna Convention the term "treaty" is broadly defined to mean "an international agreement concluded between States in written form and governed by international law, whether embodied in a single instrument or in two or more." The key elements of an international agreement are: (1) it has to be a binding instrument (i.e., an instrument in which the contracting parties intended to create legal rights and duties); (2) it must be concluded by states or international organizations with treaty-making power; and (3) it has to be governed by international law; and (4) it has to be in writing.

As a practical matter, according to the Treaty Reference Guide:

> *Usually the term "treaty" is reserved for matters of some gravity that require more solemn agreements. Their signatures are usually sealed and they normally require ratification.*

> *"Agreements" are usually less formal and deal with a narrower range of subject-matter than "treaties." There is a general tendency to apply the term "agreement" to bilateral or restricted multilateral treaties. It is employed especially for instruments of a technical or administrative character, which are signed by the representatives of government departments, but are not subject to ratification.*

> *Agreements in regional integration schemes are based on general framework treaties with constitutional character. International instruments which amend*

this framework at a later stage (e.g., accessions, revisions) are also designated as "treaties." Instruments that are concluded within the framework of the constitutional treaty or by the organs of the regional organization are usually referred to as "agreements," in order to distinguish them from the constitutional treaty. For example, whereas the Treaty of Rome of 1957 serves as a quasi-constitution of the European Community, treaties concluded by the EC with other nations are usually designated as "agreements." Also, the Treaty of Montevideo of 1980 established the Latin American Integration Association (LAIA), but the subregional instruments entered into under its framework are called "agreements."

"Conventions" are [formal multilateral treaties with a broad number of parties] normally open for participation by the international community as a whole, or by a large number of states. Usually the instruments negotiated under the auspices of an international organization are entitled "conventions" (e.g., Convention on Biological Diversity of 1992, United Nations Convention on the Law of the Sea of 1982).

The term "charter" is used for particularly formal and solemn instruments, such as the constituent treaty of an international organization. The term itself has an emotive content that goes back to the Magna Carta of 1215. Well-known recent examples are the Charter of the United Nations of 1945 and the Charter of the Organization of American States of 1952.

The term "protocol" is used for agreements less formal than those entitled "treaty" or "convention". [Protocols may deal with a variety of ancillary or supplementary matters to a treaty such as additional rights and obligations, technical matters, and modifications.]

A "Proces-Verbal" is an instrument that contains a record of certain understandings arrived at by the contracting parties.

The term "declaration" is used for various international instruments. However, declarations are not always legally binding. The term is often deliberately chosen to indicate that the parties do not intend to create binding obligations but merely want to declare certain aspirations.

A "memorandum of understanding" is an international instrument of a less formal kind. It often sets out operational arrangements under a framework international agreement. It is also used for the regulation of technical or detailed matters. It is typically in the form of a single instrument and does not require ratification.

An "exchange of notes" is a record of a routine agreement that has many similarities with the private law contract. The agreement consists of the exchange of two documents, each of the parties being in the possession of the one signed

by the representative of the other. Under the usual procedure, the accepting
State repeats the text of the offering State to record its assent. The signatories
of the letters may be government Ministers, diplomats or departmental heads.
The technique of exchange of notes is frequently resorted to, either because of
its speedy procedure, or, sometimes, to avoid the process of legislative approval.

More complete information can be found on http://untreaty.un.org/French/guide.txt.

Types of Treaties

Treaties Governing the Operation of Treaties

The pre-eminent treaty that now governs the operation and interpretation of treaties is the United Nations Convention on the Law of Treaties. (Commonly referred to as the Vienna Convention because it was signed in Vienna on May 23, 1969. the Convention codifies the customary international law and the established practice that states had come to follow regarding the operation and interpretation of treaties.) Go to http://www.taiwandocuments.org/vienna01.htm for more information. A later convention, the 1986 Vienna Convention on the Law of Treaties between States and International Organizations or between International Organizations (1986 Vienna Convention), adds rules for treaties with international organizations as parties. In 2011 there are 41 parties to the Convention, but only 29 states, and it has still not entered into force. Information on this Convention can be found at http://www.taiwandocuments.org/vienna03.htm.

Treaties and Agreements (Multilateral, Regional, and Bilateral) Governing Commercial Relationships

There are a very large number of treaties and other types of agreements governing commercial relationships between states. There are over 295 commercial treaties and agreements to which the United States is a party. A list is provided on http://www.state.gov/documents/organization/143863.pdf. New agreements -- bilateral regional, and multilateral -- are being negotiated all the time. Multiplied by the number of countries in the world, this creates a huge body of international law. There is a large and specialized body of law pertaining to treaties and international agreements; it is accessible on the Internet from many sources; one of which is http://www.public-international-law.net/. A guide to treaty research can be found at http://library.law.columbia.edu/guides/Guide_to_Treaty_Research. The texts of treaties are also available on the Internet.

Treaties Governing Other Types of Relationships

Treaties that govern political, social, environmental, security, and other types of relationships between states sometimes have commercial implications that are often very important. Although most do not purport to alter or affect the obligations covered by the WTO Agreements, several have been the source of controversy and confusion because of their effect on commercial conduct. The WTO is at present examining the relationship between its requirements and those of several multilateral environmental agreements (MEAs) because of the potential implications of some of their trade provisions for conflict with WTO obligations. The relationship of other kinds of agreements to WTO obligations, such as those administered by the International Labour Organization (ILO), has also been discussed in several multilateral institutions, although a formal linkage to the WTO Agreements has not been established. Obviously, there is much room for overlap, as all international agreements can be considered to affect commercial relationships in some sense. This was recognized by the drafters of the GATT 1947 when they drafted GATT Article XX, which provides a general exception to GATT provisions for matters that fall within ten separate categories, "subject to the general requirement that such measures are not applied in a manner that would constitute a means of arbitrary or unjustifiable discrimination between countries where the same conditions prevail, or a disguised restriction on international trade." GATT Article XXI contains an exception for measures to protect national security. These exceptions, along with the rest of GATT 1947, are incorporated in the Marrakesh Agreements establishing the World Trade Organization.

The following is an illustrative list of the specialized sectors in which there exist international agreements whose legal implications may at some point touch on the types of commercial obligations embodied in the WTO Agreements.

- Investment
- Taxation
- Environmental cooperation
- Energy provision and use [SUCH AS?]
- Scientific and technical cooperation

- Fisheries
- Protection of endangered species
- Labor and social welfare
- Human rights
- Security arrangements

Decisions of Subsidiary Bodies within Treaties

When a treaty or agreement establishes a Secretariat and an organizational structure, it also sets in motion a process that will generate subsidiary bodies such as scientific, technical, or other operational entities within the administrative organization. The decisions of these bodies have force and effect derived from the terms of the treaty. Since it is generally these bodies that generate decisions at the level of detail that states can implement, their decisions are relatively important.

The example below is a press report of a decision established by the International Whaling Commission, shown on http://iwcoffice.org/conservation/catches.htm.

In 1982, the Commission took a decision, which came into force for the 1986 and 1985/86 seasons, that catch limits for all commercial whaling would be set to zero. That decision also stated that by 1990 at the latest, the Commission will undertake a comprehensive assessment of the effect of the decision on whale stocks and consider modification of the provision and establishment of other catch limits - See Schedule Para 10e.

Subsequently the Scientific Committee has developed and the Commission adopted the Revised Management Procedure (RMP) for commercial whaling. This has not been implemented, awaiting agreement from the Commission on the Revised Management Scheme (RMS) which includes additional nonscientific matters including inspection and observation.

At the 2003 meeting, as in previous years, the Commission did not adopt a proposal by Japan for an interim relief allocation of 50 minke whales to be taken by coastal community-based whaling.

As Norway has lodged objections to the relevant items in the Schedule, it has exercised its right to set national catch limits for its coastal whaling operations for minke whales. The Commission passed a Resolution calling on Norway to halt all whaling activities under its jurisdiction.

Decisions of International Tribunals

Decisions of international tribunals, such as the International Court of Justice, are binding on states that have agreed to their jurisdiction.

► International tribunals include the Law of the Sea Tribunal and the WTO DSB. An example of a decision by the International Court of Justice in a case brought by New Zealand against France in 1995 to compel France to end nuclear testing at Mururoa Atoll (provided by the New Zealand government) can be viewed at http://www.beehive.govt.nz/feature/summaryworld-court-new-zealand039s-bid-end-nuclear-testing-mururoa-atoll.

► An example of a mutual recognition agreement is the U.S.-EU Mutual Recognition Agreement on medical devices. This agreement is described in part on http://www.mac.doc.gov/mra/mra.htm.

Decisions Resulting from Investor-State Dispute Settlement

The World Bank International Convention on the Settlement of Investor Disputes (ICSID) and NAFTA provide for procedures for investors to address investment issues in an arbitral dispute settlement proceeding with the state that agrees to be party to such a procedure. Investor-state arbitration has become a rapidly developing area of international law. For example, Mexico has negotiated treaties with European States (such as the 1997 Mexico-Spain Agreement on the Protection and Promotion of Investment). States in Asia and Oceania have also agreed to investor-state arbitration of investment disputes. An agreement between the Republic of Singapore and Japan and one between Singapore and New Zealand both provide for investor-state arbitration.

Reports on NAFTA Arbitral Tribunals can be purchased on "The NAFTA Arbitration Reports," http://www.cmppublishing.com/Journals_NAFTA.html, ISSN: 1477-3422.

International Quai-governmental – International Standardization Agreements

As sources of law, international product standards can normally be assumed to be more advisory than binding on governments. However, previously governments were free to adopt whatever standards they wanted. The WTO Agreements on Sanitary and Phytosanitary Measures (SPS Agreement) and the Agreement on Technical Barriers to Trade (TBT Agreement) have, in order to facilitate trade, imposed obligations on WTO members based on international standards to the extent possible, particularly when failure to comply with a standard means the product cannot be exported or imported. Thus, under certain circumstances, international standards can be binding on a country. For example, one WTO Panel Report found the EU to be acting inconsistently with its obligations under the TBT Agreement because, without justification, it did not base a standard on an international standard. The Panel Report is available from the WTO website at www.wto.org, WT/DS231/R/, decided May 29, 2002.

The WTO SPS Agreement specifically recognizes certain international standardizing bodies as the source of international standards that members should look to. These include the Codex Alimentarius, the International Organization of Epizootics, and the International Plant Protection Convention. The International Organization for Standardization is referenced in the WTO TBT Agreement, but the agreement does not identify specific international standardizing bodies. Most international standardizing bodies are multilaterally organized and administered and have been credible sources of international standardizing processes for many years. Standards are also made by many other types of organizations; some international, some private, and some public. A list of such organizations in the United States would number in the hundreds; a list worldwide would be far larger. In most countries worldwide, the government has a role in making national and international standards. In the United States, this is mostly done by the private sector.

Following are links to some of the larger organizations, from which individual examples of standards can be drawn:

► The International Organization for Standardizaton (ISO), the source of ISO 9000 and more than 13,000 International Standards for business, government and society: http://www.iso.org/iso/home.htm

► American National Standards Institute (ANSI): http://www.ansi.org/

► National Institute of Standards and Technology (NIST): http://www.nist.gov/index/html

► European Committee for Standardisation (CEN): http://www.cen.eu/cen/pages/default.aspx

► Standards Council of Canada (SCC): http://www.scc.ca/

APPENDIX: INTERNET RESOURCES

Below are some useful links when researching legal aspects of Commercial Diplomacy.

Table 7A

Commercial Diplomacy Legal Research Internet Resources	
Trade-related Institutions and Agreements	
United States Trade Representative (USTR) descriptions and texts of many U.S. trade agreements to which the U.S. is a party	http://www.ustr.gov/trade-agree-ments
The World Trade Organization	http://www.wto.org/
North American Free Trade Agreement	http://www.nafta-sec-alena.org/
Organization for Economic Cooperation and Development (OECD)	http://www.oecd.org/
Asia Pacific Economic Cooperation (APEC)	http://www.apec.org/
Association of South East Asian Nations (ASEAN)	http://www.asean.org/
European Union	http://ec.europa.eu/atoz_en.htm
Mercosur	http://www.mercosurtc.com/
Trade agreements and information in the Western Hemisphere	http://www.sice.oas.org/
United Nations Conference on Trade and Development	http://www.unctad.org/
European Free Trade Association (EFTA)	http://www.efta.int/
Southern African Customs Union	http://www.sacu.int/
Arbitration and Mediation Resources	
United Nations Commission on International Trade Law	http://www.uncitral.org/
Hague Conference on Private International Law	http://www.hcch.net/index_en.php
International Centre for Settlement of Investment Disputes	http://icsid.worldbank.org/ICSID/Index.jsp
International Chamber of Commerce	http://www.iccwbo.org/

Other Resources	
Law and technology resources for legal professionals, posts legal news and resources	http://www.llrx.com/features/wto2.htm#I_C
Cornell Law School Legal Information Institute	http://topics.law.cornell.edu/wex/International_trade
Lex Marcatoria provides information on international commercial law	http://www.jus.uio.no/lm/
Juris International	http://www.jurisint.org/pub/
Index to Foreign Legal Periodicals	http://www.law.berkeley.edu/library/iflp/
American Society of International law	http://www.asil.org/
Austral-Asian Legal Information Institute	http://www.austlii.edu.au/
British and Irish Legal Information Institute	http://www.bailii.org/

Chapter 8

ORGANIZING YOUR RESEARCH

By: Leslie Eliason and Geza Feketekuty[35]

PLANNING YOUR RESEARCH

The multidisciplinary analysis that Commercial Diplomacy requires involves the collection of a great deal of information and the application of a variety of analytical tools. The Commercial Diplomat needs to have a command of the basic analytical tools in a variety of disciplines in order to grasp comprehensively the issues that need to be addressed in developing a successful strategy to obtain a desired outcome on a trade-related policy issue. Few Commercial Diplomats can develop a professional level of knowledge in all the required disciplines, and part of the analytical process is the identification of professional experts and professional studies that can fill in any gaps in professional skills and areas of knowledge.

The amount of information a trade policy analyst may need to collect to prepare a policy issue for decision by superiors can be quite large. In order to accomplish this task efficiently, the analyst will need to map out a well-organized research strategy. The first step is to list all the questions that need to be answered and the most likely sources of information from the Internet, libraries, professional or industry associations, think tanks, international organizations such as the IMF, OECD or the World Bank, NGOs, or individual experts. The analyst will also need to identify the analytical tools to assess the data and the extent to which the analyst's own professional skills and knowledge in individual disciplines and areas of knowledge will need to be augmented by professional colleagues with greater professional training in the area.

---

35 The content of this chapter is substantially taken from the original training manual entitled *Policy Analysis* co-authored by Leslie Eliason and Geza Feketekuty, which is available on the ITCD website, but has been further edited for the purposes of this textbook by Geza Feketekuty. The original manual can be found at www.commercialdiplomacy.org.

Your Research Agenda: Questions to Ask

▶ What information will I need to analyze all the issues I have mapped out both at home and abroad?

▶ What sources of information are available?

▶ What professional skills/expertise will I need to analyze all the issues?

▶ What professional experts can I consult to fill gaps in my own knowledge and skills?

The policy analyst needs to engage in a comprehensive and competent search of the available information. He/she then needs to apply creativity and imagination to generate new ways of thinking about the problem and innovative solutions that satisfy as many stakeholders and aspects of the policy dilemma as possible. Learning to deal with ambiguity in a responsible way is a critical aspect of the research process as well. As one well-respected policy analyst expressed:

Highlighting ambiguity should not be seen as an excuse for vague, wishy-washy, or unresearched analysis. Indeed, you will have to work harder to arrange the competing theories and facts intelligently. Additionally, highlighting ambiguity does not absolve you from drawing analytic conclusions.[36]

As an analyst you have a responsibility to find the appropriate balance between breadth and depth of analysis as well as between the details and the big picture. This is more of an art than a science. Knowing how to strike the proper balance for those you are advising is something gained through experience over time. You must be thorough and fair in your criticisms. You will learn to be equally skeptical of arguments and solutions you (or your boss) like as of those you (or your boss) dislike.

GETTING STARTED – LOCATING DATA AND INFORMATION

You will first want to familiarize yourself with the issue and how it arrived on your desk, including the background to the issue. You will also want to familiarize yourself with the current media coverage on the issue. A good place to start to reconstruct the broad outlines of the policy history is to use an Internet database such as LexisNexis (http://www.lexisnexis.com), which has global coverage of media, professional, legal, and other sources You might also want to consult the *Financial Times* website and archives (http://www.ft.com), which often offers more extensive background coverage on trade-related issues, commercial concerns, and economic developments, both national and international. *The Economist* also offers good background coverage on international trade issues as well as domestic economic and business news (http://

---

36 David L. Wiemer and Aidan R. Vining, *Policy Analysis: Concepts and Practice* (Englewood Cliffs, NJ: Prentice Hall, 1992), 2nd ed., p. 181.

www.economist.com). In some cases, there is a fee for access to the above-mentioned archives, but the cost is relatively low.

You will find many databases and information sources listed on the Institute for Trade and Commercial Diplomacy website (http://www.commercialdiplomacy.org), including a range of links to various sources by topic, region, and issue area. For additional lists, see the International Commercial Diplomacy website's at: http://www.commercialdiplomacy.org/links_external_topic_list.php.

Political, Institutional, and Policy-Related Data and Information

After having researched the background to a particular policy issue, it is time to start mapping the policy process, the institutional actors, and the political dimensions. Your search of the media outlets described above will help you begin to sort through what additional sources you will want to seek. In particular, you should identify the government agencies involved in/responsible for the policy and key private stakeholder groups that may have well-articulated policy statements. They may have websites and/or you may want to arrange to conduct informational interviews to learn more about the "insider's perspective."

Economic Data and Information

Specific trade and economic data can be found from a number of international organizations and agencies, including most UN agencies. Go to http://www.un.org for general access. The UN Conference on Trade and Development (http://www.unctad.org) maintains a wide range of data and information related to many trade-related issues. Of course, the World Trade Organization (http://www.wto.org) also provides direct access to much of the WTO's records and documentation.

For other economic and trade-related data, you may want to consult the International Monetary Fund's website (http://www.imf.org). For developing countries, there is a good deal of economic and trade-related information available from the World Bank (http://www.worldbank.org). The World Bank's statistics are available, often in downloadable form from their statistical databank (http://www.worldbank.org/data/). The World Bank's Research Unit also offers many comprehensive reports on trade, development, and economic trends on their website, including annual reports such as *Global Economic Prospects.*

The Organization for Economic Cooperation and Development (OECD) is another key international intergovernmental organization that compiles statistics and conducts country surveys in various sectors and policy fields (http://www.oas.org/en/default.asp). Depending on the issue, OECD can be an excellent source of data, information, and analysis.

Many regional intergovernmental organizations also may be important sources for your research, one of which is the Organization of American States (http://www.oas.org). The European Union maintains an official website with a sometimes overwhelming amount of information, data, and reports (http://europa.eu). APEC, the Asia-Pacific Economic Cooperation, maintains a tariff database covering its member states (http://egs.apec.org/resources/apec-tariff). APEC's website (http://www.apec.org) also provides information on current APEC issues and proposals.

Commercial Data and Information

Many governments maintain websites that provide information about commercial policies and practices in their country. You can also search for the websites of key actors (firms, sectoral organizations, and associations, etc.) that are involved in the commercial aspects of the policy under analysis. This may lead you to the names and even email addresses of officials or contact persons from whom you can solicit more detailed information through a direct inquiry. LexisNexis offers a database specifically tailored for company financial information that includes contact information and other details of both the United States and international corporations.

Many private companies and corporations maintain websites providing extensive information and documentation about their products and operations worldwide. Even where this information is not available electronically, most publicly traded companies are willing (sometimes required) to share information with interested parties as a way of attracting investors.

Industry association websites and documentation are another valuable source of information to the trade policy analyst. These associations can help the analyst capture a broader view of the activities and interests as well as patterns of companies operating in a particular segment of the international economy.

Legal Data and Information

There are many electronic databases specifically dedicated to legal data and information. Westlaw is perhaps the best known and most commonly used electronic database for searching U.S. law and precedents (http://westlaw.com). However, Westlaw also provides legal information for more than 60 countries (http://westlawinternational.com). LexisNexis also offers several legal databases that are searchable. For U.S. laws, regulations, and executive orders, etc., you may want to search the Government Printing Office's online database (http://www.access.gpo.gov/su_docs/), which also includes links to other official government sources including the Code of Federal Regulations, the Federal Register, the Congressional Record, the U.S. Code, Congressional Bills, the Catalog of U.S. Government Publications, and other databases. You can also find a pictorial directory of U.S. Congress members at this website.

When the legal aspects of a particular policy are a key aspect of the trade-related issue, the trade policy analyst should probably enlist the expertise of a legal advisor who is well versed in the particular aspects of law that are part of the dispute. The Commercial Diplomat may also want to engage a legal advisor who is knowledgeable about the domestic laws of any foreign countries who are parties to the dispute. An extensive list of international trade law sites that extends beyond the ones indicated in this textbook can be found on www.commercialdiplomacy.org.

Tracking Your Progress

As you begin your research, be sure to create a good system for keeping and recording not only the information you gather, but also the sources from which you gained the information or data. Not only will you want to cite your sources so that your client or principal can make his/her own independent assessment of the validity and reliability of the source, but also this information may be useful in crafting a strategy for achieving your desired policy objectives. It will also help to remind you of any potential biases that may come from the particular source. In other instances, it may be useful in negotiations to be able to point out to an opponent that the data you are citing came from his/her own domestic sources.

As a guide to some useful steps in the research process, consider the following sequence.[37]

> ► **Develop a working bibliography.** Collect your sources as you identify them and keep them in a common file (electronic if possible). These sources constitute your working bibliography.

> ► **Write for needed information.** You will probably identify a number of sources that you will want to track down. This may include contacting individuals or organizations with whom you will want to conduct interviews or from whom you will want to request further information.

> ► **Evaluate written sources.** Determine quickly the potential usefulness of a source. Some sources are more reliable than others. (See the section on assessing sources below.) Save important information in either hard or soft copy (photocopy, scanned, PDF files, etc.). Be sure to comply with copyright laws.

> ► **Determine whether interviews or surveys are needed.** Generally speaking, this will not be a major part of your research. However, you may want to conduct selected interviews with key stakeholders or individuals who are particularly knowledgeable about key aspects or stakeholders relevant to your analysis. They can help you pinpoint information that may be essential to a thorough analysis.

> ► **Draft each section of your analysis as you go along.** Breaking the project down into manageable parts will help you make progress on a large report. Get feedback early and as often as practical from your client or supervisor and from peers. Your presentation should pass what Eugene Bardach refers to as the "New York Cabbie" test. Can you explain your analysis and recommendations to a New York cab driver in the time it takes to go from downtown to uptown?[38] Also what may be obvious to you may not be obvious to your reader. Sharing your draft with other readers will help you identify where you need

37 Gregory M. Scott and Stephen M. Garrison, *The Political Science Student Writer's Manual* (Englewood Cliffs, NJ: Prentice-Hall, 2000), especially chapter 3.

38 Eugene Bardach, *A Practical Guide for Policy Analysis: The Eightfold Path to More Effective Problem Solving* (New York: Chatham House, 2000).

to be more explicit or develop greater clarity in your presentation. They may also help you identify holes in your argument or presentation.

▶ **Be sure to follow ethical standards regarding use of source material.** "You should directly quote from a source when the original language is distinctive enough to enhance your argument or when rewording the passage would lessen its impact. In the interest of fairness, you should also quote a passage to which you will take exception."[39] Acknowledge quotations carefully and quote accurately.

Assessing Sources

As you gather information and data, you want to assess critically whether the information is believable. Is it measured in a reliable and consistent fashion? Can you appropriately compare the data collected by different organizations or jurisdictions? Are the numbers you are using appropriate measures of the particular factor you want to assess? These are the typical questions that any researcher would ask of his/her sources.

The ready access and availability of information and data from Internet sources has dramatically improved our access to information from a much broader range of sources. However, this also brings with it the complication that not all information on the web is equally reliable or believable. Thus, the researcher must be vigilant in assessing and evaluating the information and data he/she gleans from a web search. How credible is the information?

To guide your assessment of sources, consider the following questions.[40]

Purpose of the Site

▶ Is the purpose of the site stated? What clues do you pick up on based on the tone and language used?

▶ Is the information designed to inform, persuade, anger, entertain, spark creative thinking, challenge conventional wisdom, or something else?

▶ Who is the target audience (e.g., age, education, income, nationality, etc.)?

Author or Creator of the Site

▶ Who is the author/creator? What makes them an authority?

▶ Is there an organization associated with the site? What is the relationship between the organization and the maintainer(s) of the site? What is the organization's reputation, political orientation, funding source, etc.?

---

39 Scott and Garrison, p. 83.

40 Adapted from Randall S. Clemons and Mark K. McBeth, *Public Policy Praxis--Theory and Pragmatism: A Case Approach* (Upper Saddle River, NJ : Prentice Hall, 2001), pp. 326-7.

- ▶ Does the site provide an email address, telephone number, or other contact information that would allow you to follow up on the data or information and its original source(s)?

- ▶ What is the domain name or URL extension (.gov, .org, .edu, .com)?

Documentation

- ▶ Does the site make clear the source of the information presented there?

- ▶ If there are statistics presented, are they presented fairly and clearly? Who gathered and analyzed them? Are the dates of the research, the number of people interviewed, the methods, etc., clearly stated, and are these methods professionally and appropriately applied?

- ▶ Are references provided?

- ▶ Does the site steer you to other quality sources that allow you to check its story?

- ▶ Does the information provided square with other sources you have found and with previous research and study?

- ▶ Has the information passed through any filters or checks such as peer review?

- ▶ Is the currency of the information adequate? Is it up-to-date? What is the date posted and the date revised?

- ▶ Is the general quality of the work impressive or are there many obvious errors, misspellings, etc.?

APPENDIX: INTERNET RESOURCES

Below are selected websites for trade-related policy analysis.

Table 8A

Trade-related Policy Analysis Internet Resources	
National Conference of State Legislatures provides information on current initiatives in the 50 U.S. states.	http://www.ncsl.org/
National Governor's Association provides information on initiatives and studies conducted by the governors of the 50 U.S. states.	http://www.nga.org/
Resources for the Future is an environmental and natural resource NGO that covers trade and environment issues.	http://www.rff.org/
Vote Smart is a bipartisan organization that provides information for political candidates in the U.S. regarding elections, campaign finance, voting records, etc. This can be a good place to find out about supporters and opponents in Congress.	http://www.votesmart.org/
The World Wildlife Foundation, another environmental NGO that tracks trade and environment issues, among other things.	http://www.wwf.org/
The Worldwatch Institute, another environmental NGO, is particularly engaged in sustainable development issues and publishes an annual "State of the World" report.	http://www.worldwatch.org/
Common Cause is a nonprofit, nonpartisan citizen's lobbying organization promoting open, honest, and accountable U.S. government.	http://www.commoncause.org/
National Public Radio	http://www.npr.org/
The CIA's World Fact Book provides geographical, political, and other information of all the countries of the world including excellent map access.	http://www.cia.gov/ or https://www.cia.gov/library/publications/the-world-fact-book/index.html
The U.S. Geological Survey provides the national mapping program that can be useful in assessing information on natural resources and economic development.	http://www.usgs.gov/

The U.S. Bureau of the Census	http://www.census.gov/
The Federal Register—the source for U.S. laws and regulations	http://www.gpoaccess.gov/fr/
U.S. Government Printing Office	http://www.gpo.gov/
U.S. House of Representatives	http://www.house.gov/
U.S. Senate website	http://www.senate.gov/
U.S. Department of Commerce	http://www.commerce.gov/
Registry to all state and local government websites in US.	http://www.statelocalgov.net/
The Financial Times	http://www.ft.com/
The Economist	http://www.economist.com/
The United Nations	http://www.un.org/
The World Trade Organization	http://www.wto.org/
The UN Conference on Trade and Development	http://www.unctad.org/
The UN Commission on International Trade Law	http://www.uncitral.org/
Pace Law School Institute of International Commercial Law provides the UN Convention on the International Sale of Goods (CISG) database and information on international commercial law and international arbitration.	http://www.cisg.law.pace.edu/
The Organization for Economic Cooperation and Development	http://www.oecd.org/
The International Monetary Fund	http://www.imf.org/
The World Bank	http://www.worldbank.org/
The European Union official website	http://europa.eu/
The Organization of American States	http://www.oas.org/
The Asia-Pacific Economic Cooperation	http://www.apec.org/
APEC Tariff Database	http://egs.apec.org/resources/apec-tariff
NAFTA Secretariat; trilingual site contains a complete text of the North American Free Trade Agreement including panel decisions, reports rendered, etc.	http://www.nafta-sec-alena.org/
The NAFTA Customs Website provides a broad array of NAFTA and customs related information	http://www.nafta-customs.org/

SECTION III

COMMUNICATING THE MESSAGE

Chapter 9

WRITING AS A PROFESSIONAL TOOL IN COMMERCIAL DIPLOMACY

By: Eve Connell, Geza Feketekuty, Sarah Givens, and Jill Stoffers[41]

C ommercial Diplomats – government officials and representatives of businesses, industry associations, and nongovernmental organizations – are routinely called on to inform and persuade decision makers or other stakeholders concerning highly complex issues. Good writing skills are essential for success in these endeavors. Whether exploring how to tackle a new trade issue or formally negotiating a consensus agreement, a Commercial Diplomat must clearly and persuasively articulate his/her country's and/or organization's positions. The difference between a well and poorly written issue paper determines whether a new approach to an issue receives fair consideration. Similarly, the difference between clear and muddled testimony can determine whether a proposed policy is supported or opposed, and the difference between a well and poorly crafted newspaper opinion article can determine whether the article will have an impact on public debate.

In short, a Commercial Diplomat's analyses and arguments are likely to be disregarded despite their merits if those analyses and arguments are not conveyed in an effective manner. For the Commercial Diplomat to succeed in obtaining governmental decisions favorable to the stakeholders he/she represents, he/she must be able to use effectively a wide variety of documents. Typically, these may include briefing memos, policy papers, white papers, advocacy letters, public testimony, speeches, press releases, and op-ed (opinion-editorial) articles.

---

41 The content of this chapter is substantially taken from the original training manual entitled *Writing Manual for Commercial Diplomats* co-authored by Eve Connell, Geza Feketekuty, Sarah Givens, and Jill Stoffers, which is available on the ITCD website, but has been further edited for the purposes of this textbook by Geza Feketekuty. The original manual can be found at www.commercialdiplomacy.org.

TARGET AUDIENCES AND WRITERS OF COMMERCIAL DIPLOMACY DOCUMENTS

The basic challenge for writers of Commercial Diplomacy documents is to convey complex issues in a concise, easy-to-digest manner and to convince the reader of the desirability of a proposed course of action. Writing on Commercial Diplomacy topics can be particularly demanding. Issues in trade negotiations run the gamut of critiques from social, economic, legal, and scientific experts. Moreover, the number of different stakeholder groups, each with its own particular interests in a trade negotiation, can be staggering. Accurately and effectively accounting for all of this information and opinion is a significant challenge.

The Target Audience

Like many other professionals, Commercial Diplomats have more documents flowing through their in-boxes than they can read. They must absorb a great deal of information in a limited amount of time, sometimes while traveling from one meeting to another, or even over the course of a meeting itself. Thus, documents need to be short, to-the-point, and effortless to read and understand.

As a general rule, documents are written in a way that allows the contents to be quickly determined. If a reader is conversant on a given topic, he/she appreciates a paper that can, at a glance, serve as a refresher on the most important points. On the other hand, he/she will only be irritated by having to wade through a difficult paper. A paper that is not presented effectively loses the attention of key decision makers. It also leaves the writer's boss unprepared, which can be an embarrassment or worse, and reflects poorly on the writer.

Not only do documents need to be highly focused, they also need to be carefully crafted and worded to convey the nuances of an organization's position. Such documents are read and re-read with painstaking care as readers attempt to extract every possible interpretation from them. When providing information about previously established or discussed policy positions, the use of wording contained in the original policy documents is essential. Repetition of phrases, statements of position, and rationales and explanations are part of the process of consolidating the policy positions within and among governments. Even in cases where policy decisions are not yet finalized, the repeated use of language borrowed from a well-written document contributes to the formation of a governmental consensus. Borrowed language becomes common language that is incorporated in final policy memoranda and formal, negotiated agreements. A Commercial Diplomat with great writing skills can thus exert influence over policy making that goes far beyond his/her authority.

The Writer

Writers of Commercial Diplomacy documents have the same time pressures that readers do. Commercial Diplomats often face a highly dynamic, constantly evolving commercial, political, and negotiating environment. This calls for rapid responses to unforeseen events, problems, and opportunities. The closer a staff person is to key decision makers, the higher the probability that he/she will be asked to write important operational documents under extremely tight deadlines. Likewise, the higher the rank of the decision maker, the higher the probability that he/she will not have much time to digest the content of a document. A Commercial Diplomat who wants to become influential must learn to write highly focused, tightly worded documents in a short period of time.

For a Commercial Diplomacy document to be persuasive, the writer must be careful to ground his/her own organization's position in a comprehensive and solid analysis that accounts for the interests of all substantive stakeholders. While some selectivity in the choice of facts and arguments is expected, omission of critical facts or arguments, or worse, willful distortion of facts and arguments, can quickly undermine the credibility of a document and even destroy the credibility of the writer and his/her organization.

Generally, documents in Commercial Diplomacy convey facts, provide an analysis of the facts, and put forth recommendations flowing from analysis, but they do not include personal opinions or judgments. Personal judgments are presented only when a writer is considered an eminent authority on a given issue.

OPERATIONAL DOCUMENTS USED IN COMMERCIAL DIPLOMACY

While there are only three basic functions of Commercial Diplomacy documents (to inform, to persuade or to instruct), there are a number of document types used to perform these functions. Commonly used documents include:

► Policy Papers	► Briefing Papers	► Op-eds
► Advocacy Letters	► Press Releases	► Cables
► Memoranda	► Emails	► Public testimonies

Each of these documents serves multiple purposes. For example, a memo can instruct a company's employees about a policy change or instruct government negotiators of the government's position on a particular issue. A briefing paper can keep a manager current on a particular issue, provide analysis and recommendations for a decision-maker, or simply help prepare a superior for a meeting. A cable can report the results of a meeting or instruct government officials to attend a public hearing and provide a summation. An advocacy letter, while ultimately meant to persuade, also serves to inform.

A skilled Commercial Diplomat will use all of these documents to achieve his/her objectives. Later sections in this chapter provide a detailed discussion of these operational tools explaining what they are, who writes them, when and how they are written, and why they are written.

COMMON ELEMENTS IN COMMERCIAL DIPLOMACY DOCUMENTS

Each operational document in Commercial Diplomacy takes its own form. Briefing papers, cables, and op-ed articles, for example, all follow different yet fairly standard formats, which are examined one-by-one later in this manual.

Whatever the nature of the document, it should be highly focused and well organized so that the reader can identify and extract essential information rapidly. Moreover, virtually all Commercial Diplomacy documents should contain the following elements:

- ► An introduction or "Issue" section that covers the most important facts, analytical conclusions, and recommendations.

- ► Carefully worded subheadings that point the reader to more detailed information.

- ► Bullet points that highlight quick overviews of essential information.

- ► Where a conclusion is appropriate, which is normally the case in all documents that are longer than a few pages, it should recap the key points and recommendations. A final conclusion section often enables the author of the paper to provide a more detailed explanation of recommendations than is possible in the introductory section.

The Introduction or "Issue" Section

Almost without exception, Commercial Diplomacy documents require an introduction that sets out the issue being addressed, the issue's importance at the present time, the most pertinent facts or analytical points the reader needs to know, and where appropriate, the key conclusions or recommendations of the document. The introduction, often titled simply "Issue," informs the reader what the document is about, why it should be read, and how its contents should be interpreted. While preferred styles vary, the introduction does not provide detailed descriptions of factual scenarios, detailed conclusions, and/or recommendations. Rather, it should provide a basic summary to help the reader identify the most salient messages, points, conclusions, or recommendations conveyed in the rest of the document.

This section is critical because it often determines whether a reader chooses to read the rest of the document. Moreover, the "Issue" section is often the only part of a paper read by someone without the time to review the entire document.

Generally, "Issue" sections are only one paragraph long and contain just a few sentences. Accordingly, writing a good "Issue" section requires a great deal of judgment about what facts, arguments, and conclusions/recommendations to include. All unnecessary words, such as modifiers, are to be avoided. The goal is to convey the material as concisely and clearly as possible. An introduction may have to be rewritten several times as the writer thinks through the issue or receives new information on the issue.

The Body

The organization of the body of a document depends on the nature of the document and, therefore, is addressed more fully in the discussion of individual body types. However, all well-written documents have some common characteristics:

- ► Sentences generally convey one major idea.

- ► Paragraphs are short and made up of closely related sentences.

- ► Changes in subject matter are noted by bridging language, either by new paragraphs or by subheadings.

- ► Subheadings provide a quick index to a document's contents.

- ► Bullet points provide a quick overview of essential information.

The organization of a well-written document leads the reader through an orderly progression of the most pertinent facts and analytical observations and to the conclusions and/or recommendations the writer seeks to convey.

The Conclusion

A conclusion section is necessary in some documents and not in others. Generally, a conclusion is necessary if a writer is making a recommendation to a superior or seeking guidance from a superior (e.g., in public testimony, advocacy letters, longer policy papers such as white papers or non-papers, and in policy memoranda). A conclusion is not appropriate in press releases. It may or may not be appropriate in briefing papers and instructional memoranda.

A conclusion summarizes the most important points covered. It provides a more complete summary of the key points and/or recommendations than is possible in the introduction; it also reinforces the most important message(s) of the document. However, because conclusions generally reiterate information or recommendations already provided, they are rarely necessary for relatively short, one- or two-page documents. A conclusion should not be used in lieu of a good "Issue" section. The most important points of a document need to be stated at the outset, even if they will be reiterated in greater detail in a conclusion.

Source Citations

Briefing memoranda, testimony, press releases, reporting cables, negotiating instructions, policy papers, white papers, and advocacy letters often incorporate material obtained from other documents without citation. Material from other sources is footnoted in such documents only if the writer wishes to appeal to the authority of the person cited. Incorporation of language from other sources is not considered unethical and is usually encouraged in policy documents because the repetition of language used to describe policy positions and their rationale is an intrinsic part of the consensus building process in policy formation and negotiations. Moreover, the repetition of language used by an organization to describe its position is often the most accurate way of describing that position. Of course, when the Commercial Diplomat turns to writing for either the popular press or scholarly journals, the conventional rules for the citation of published materials apply.

THE WRITING PROCESS – TIPS FOR WRITERS

Writing is a dynamic process that combines brainstorming, drafting, editing, revising, and formatting, among other elements. A writer should consider the following before drafting any kind of written communication:

What is the Purpose/Intent of the Document?

What should a reader do with the information provided? In order to maximize the efficiency of his writing, a writer must focus on the principal objective of the document. Focus enables a writer to 1) make decisions on which facts and arguments must be included (and which are less important and can be omitted), and to 2) organize content in a manner that will most effectively achieve the desired objective. The purpose of a document is usually to trigger a certain response from the target reader (e.g., getting the reader to approve a certain course of action, to make an informed decision on an issue, or to use a particular set of facts and arguments in presenting an issue to an interlocutor, etc.).

Who Will Be Reading the Document?

How much does the targeted reader know? What is the reader's position or role with respect to the issue? What is the expected attitude or point of view of the reader? Is the reader likely to agree or disagree with the view presented? A clear focus on the reader enables a writer to determine how much detail and background he/she needs to provide in order for the reader to understand the message conveyed. The writer must decide whether the use of professional jargon helps or hinders the reader's understanding of a document's message, and what tone a paper should take. An informal style is most appropriate for a close colleague, while a more formal style is appropriate for a document that will be widely read. A document addressed to a superior needs to show proper deference, while a paper addressed to more junior staff needs to convey a sense of authority.

What is the Writer's Role or Position?

What is the writer's position in relation to the reader (expert or preeminent authority, staffer, advocate)? An official document stating an organization's view on a subject is very different from a document designed to convey the views of an individual to a colleague. Official documents must reflect the view of the organization as a whole, while personal memos need reflect only the views of one person - the writer. Of course, a document prepared by an eminent authority on a subject will be given more weight than a document prepared by an unknown staffer - and outside of their own organization. Unknown staffers usually are not expected to express any personal views that contradict the position of the organization they represent. When they do express their own view – usually within the organization's own brainstorming and consensus building processes – they most likely will be expected to compile extensive supporting evidence for their positions. On the other hand, the views of eminent authorities and senior personnel need less supporting evidence to gain careful consideration.

In light of the above, what major questions, issues or arguments must be addressed in the document? What background information, reasons, supporting evidence, or examples does the reader need in order to take desired actions on the issue?

The Importance of Peer Review

Inviting a colleague or neutral person to review and offer feedback is a useful way to make sure that all necessary points are covered in any written communication. Peer review can help refine ideas, eliminate ambiguous or unclear language, and reveal stylistic, typing, and other errors. Peer review is particularly important when writing on issues that are politically sensitive. Getting feedback from an outside observer helps ensure that a document is clear, concise, focused, and appropriate to the situation. A cool-off period is also useful when writing about volatile topics; cooling off allows a writer to regain perspective before sending a communication.

Additional Guidelines

- ▶ Be prepared to revise documents several times before submitting them.

- ▶ Allocate time for peer review and feedback.

- ▶ Be aware of different formats and rules.

- ▶ Meet deadlines.

- ▶ Use acronyms and jargon appropriately, according to the audience and the type of writing.

- ▶ Consider how your phrasing affects tone and comprehensibility.

- ▶ Keep in mind that written correspondence frequently becomes part of a permanent record.

OPERATIONAL COMMERCIAL DIPLOMACY DOCUMENTS

Policy Papers

Policy papers officially state an organization's views on a public policy issue. Such papers are generally called "white papers" in the United States and "green papers" in Europe.

The terminology gets yet more confusing because Europeans use the term "white paper" for initial drafts of policy positions for public comment, while in the United States such a paper would be called a draft policy paper. In international parlance, draft policy papers submitted for discussion in international negotiations are often called "non-papers."

Regardless of the name affixed to them, policy papers all target groups of individuals with an interest or stake in an issue. They generally assume that readers have a basic familiarity with the topic in question, though not necessarily familiar with the specific details of the issue.

Initial drafts of policy papers are often distributed within an organization to generate agreement among relevant stakeholders. When presented as formal statements of policy, they inform individuals both within and outside an organization of that organization's formal position, as well as the rationale for that position. Governments often distribute such papers in multilateral meetings and negotiating groups to inform negotiating partners of the country's position and where possible to persuade them to adopt the positions advocated in the paper.

Policy papers are meant to:

► Serve as both a transparency and an advocacy function

► Alert readers to an important issue that has become a matter of public concern.

► Bring objective facts and analysis to the attention of the policy community.

► Instruct employees of the organization's position on an issue.

► Inform stakeholders outside an organization of the organization's views on an issue.

► Persuade all who have a potential interest in a policy (and/or the ability to influence that policy) that available factual and analytical information supports the organization's position on the issue.

► Establish the relative importance that the organization attaches to the issue.

Policy Paper Format

► **Introduction.** An introductory paragraph should describe the issue at hand, explain its importance, and summarize the intended policy action or proposed policy action that is the subject of the paper.

► **Body.** The body of a policy paper contains essential background information, the most pertinent facts concerning the issue, and a cogent analysis of the problem, challenge, or opportunity. The body also contains a section that provides the details of and rationale for an organization's policy position. In deciding what to include in the body, a writer must weigh carefully the information a target reader needs to know to accept the proposed policy action.

▶ **Conclusion.** A final summary paragraph is usually included in policy papers to emphasize the paper's conclusions, the most important aspects of the issue at hand, and/or the course of action advocated in the paper. However, depending on the length and purpose of a paper, this paragraph may be omitted. A brief two-page paper, for example, probably does not need a conclusion. A longer policy paper, on the other hand, usually includes a conclusion because it is important to leave a reader with a very precise and clear statement of what the writer wants the reader to do.

In any case, a conclusion should not be the place to introduce the most important messages of the document. This should be done in the introductory "Issue" section so that a reader who does not reach the end of a document does not miss the key point.

General Guidelines for Writing Policy Papers

▶ **Tone:** The tone of a policy paper is objective and should convey a sense of objectivity. A reader should come away with the clear impression that an organization's policy is the most reasonable course of action that flows from the facts and analysis presented in the paper. The writer naturally is expected to emphasize information that supports the organization's position, and every reader assumes that this has been done. However, the writer should avoid misstating facts or failing to address important information that does not support the organization's position. Glaring gaps and misstatements of fact risk destroying the credibility of a document. While such misstatements (or omissions due to oversimplification) may reinforce support among loyal believers, they ensure that a document will fail to convince others who need to be convinced. It is usually best for the writer to address arguments and information that contradict the document's conclusions, recommendations, or policy decisions, rather than leave it to the reader to draw his/her own conclusions, or worse have the reader conclude that omission of well-known facts and arguments is a tacit admission that contradict the paper's message.

▶ **Length:** The optimal length of a policy paper depends upon the purpose of the paper. Generally, it is best to keep papers within five single-spaced pages. Some topics, however, should be covered in just two pages, while a particularly complex or controversial issue may require more than five pages. If it is necessary to convey extensive background material it is preferable to attach separate appendices rather than to extend the length of the basic document. This way, readers pressed for time are not discouraged from reading the paper, and those who want to know more are able to satisfy their curiosity.

Advocacy Letters

The purpose of advocacy letters is to convince influential people or organizations to adopt a desired point of view or to support a desired course of action. In the context of Commercial Diplomacy, this means support for a particular policy that a government or multilateral institution might adopt or an action they might pursue. An addressee might be asked to endorse the proposed policy or course of action or to take some other kind of supportive action such as making a phone call to an influential person, writing a letter, or joining a coalition of interested stakeholders.

All advocacy documents need to be carefully targeted to the intended reader(s). Accordingly, the decision as to what to include in a letter should be guided by the interests, beliefs, and level of knowledge of the targeted individual(s) and/or organization(s). At the same time, it is best to assume that even if a letter is intended to be a private, confidential communication, it may be made available (intentionally or otherwise) to the public or individuals other than the addressee(s). It is prudent, therefore, to avoid comments or analysis that other potential supporters might find offensive or that might embarrass the writer or his/her organization.

Advocacy Letter Format

- ► **Opening Paragraph.** The first paragraph of an advocacy letter should lay out the issue, explain its importance, and provide a summary of what the addressee is being asked to do. In a few sentences the reader should understand the action that she/he is being asked to take and why she/he is being asked to take it.

- ► **Body.** The body of a letter expected to explain the issue and the requested action in greater depth. It should provide compelling arguments why the addressee should take a proposed action. The writer's own reasons for advocating a particular action are less important than the reasons the addressee would find it in her/his interest to adopt the desired course of action.

- ► **Final Paragraph.** The last paragraph is important in an advocacy letter. It provides an opportunity to reiterate briefly why it is important that the addressee act and, perhaps most importantly, to summarize with precise clarity the action that the writer is seeking from the addressee.

General Guidelines for Writing Advocacy Letters

Effective advocacy letters:

- ► Are short – preferably one page – and certainly no longer than two pages.

- ► Contain short and easy-to-read paragraphs.

- ► Use bullet points to highlight summaries of important information.

- ► Use attachments to convey complex background information.

Memorandums

Memorandums are a basic means for conveying information and for establishing a permanent, official record. Memorandums are the primary means of formal communication among members of an organization. They are used to remind readers of a deadline, event, or policy; to communicate information to many people simultaneously; to seek guidance; and to instruct, inform, and report results.

Memorandum writing combines elements of letter and report writing. The main difference between letter and memorandum writing is that the recipient of a memorandum usually works within the same organization as the writer, while the recipient of a letter usually works outside the organization.

Memorandums are used in a number of ways:

- ▶ A manager writes a memorandum to inform his/her staff of a proposed meeting.

- ▶ A senior government official writes a memorandum instructing a subordinate to follow a particular course of action in carrying out an assignment.

- ▶ A staff member writes a memorandum to make a recommendation to a superior or to seek guidance on handling a particular issue.

- ▶ A subordinate writes a memorandum to his/her superior to report on an event or to report the steps he/she has taken to carry out an assignment.

- ▶ A government analyst writes a memorandum for "the record" to document a particular organizational decision.

Memorandum Format

- ▶ **Header.** Memorandums are usually written on an organization's template or letterhead and begin with a to/from section as follows:

  TO: (addressee)
  FROM: (name of writer, usually followed by the signed initials of the writer)
  CC: (individuals other than the address who will be sent courtesy copies
  RE: (the subject of the memo). - A precise and focused one- or two-line description of what the memo covers. A reader should not have any question concerning the general content of a memo after reading this line.

- ▶ **Body.** Like other policy documents, memos begin with a paragraph providing a clear overview of what is contained in the document and why it is important. Similarly, the rest of the document is written so that information is easy to find and understand. A conclusion paragraph is only included if a writer deems it necessary (see discussion in the "Policy Papers" section of this manual).

General Guidelines for Writing Memorandums

- ▶ Memorandums generally cover only one issue or decision.

- ▶ The message of the memo is stated explicitly so that readers do not misinterpret the message and purpose of the communication.

- ▶ A memorandum needs to be sensitive to a reader's attitudes and positions on the subject.

Briefing Papers

Briefing papers and reports are concise summaries of issues and events. Briefing papers update readers on an issue's current status and get readers up to speed on the background of an issue. Briefing papers can take the form of an unsigned, unaddressed, self-standing report, or they can take the form of memorandums as covered in the previous section of this manual.

Briefing papers are targeted toward a specific audience and for a specific purpose. For example:

- ▶ In preparation for a meeting with a European Commission official concerning another country's agricultural trade barriers, a senior manager in a European agricultural industry association might ask a member of his/her staff to prepare a paper on current trade problems with that country.

- ▶ An Australian trade official might be assigned to write daily updates to his/her boss on trade disruptions resulting from regional political strife.

- ▶ The desk officer for Kenya in Uganda's Trade Ministry may be asked to prepare a memorandum for the Trade Minister on Kenyan-Ugandan trade issues in preparation for a meeting with the Romanian Trade Minister.

- ▶ A junior staffer might be asked to attend a series of meetings and provide a written summary.

Entry-level employees are frequently assigned to write factual briefing reports on what is said in a public hearing, updates on specific pieces of legislation, or background papers on a particular country's trade. More senior employees typically are asked to write briefing memoranda that include not only objective facts but also analytical conclusions that may require judgments based on experience. In any case, the information contained in briefing papers is frequently used in decision-making, for strategizing, and for making policy or action recommendations.

Briefing Paper Format

- ▶ **Issue Section.** The introductory paragraph, often titled "Issue," is by far the most important part of a briefing paper. After reading the very first sentence of a briefing paper, the reader should have a clear idea of the subject, and why it is important. A reader may not even finish reading the "Issue" section, let alone the rest of the paper, if the first sentence doesn't let her/him know why the information is important. Moreover, the reader must know whether any of the information contained in the memo is time sensitive. If so, the first sentence should state what is currently happening. The reader may postpone reading about an important issue if not informed that the issue demands immediate attention due to current events.

The "Issue" section should give the reader a good overall sense of the issue at hand, and present the most important message(s) of the briefing paper. If the reader doesn't have time to go through the whole document, the "Issue" section should provide enough information so the addressee, at a minimum, can go into a meeting knowing both the subject matter being discussed and the preferred outcome of the discussion. Although the content of an "Issue" section can vary based on the subject of a paper and the reader's relation to the issue, questions that could be addressed in such a section include:

- What happened most recently on the issue?
- Are negotiations moving along productively or they bogging down?
- Are there any events on the horizon that will force some action to be taken?
- What major players (trade ministers, members of congress or parliament, public interest groups, etc.) are involved in the issue?

▶ **Background Section.** The "Background" section follows the "Issue" section of a briefing paper. Here the writer can provide enough background for the reader to understand the most recent developments. If a reader has been following an issue for a long time, he may not need much detail, or perhaps only enough to provide a quick refresher on his organization's official position.

Though some readers may need a review of an issue's history, background sections should not be written as historical accounts. While a chronology of events may be important, the sequence of past events is often immaterial to understanding the substance of an issue. Accordingly, it is usually better to organize a paper around substance than chronology. A writer should decide what points to cement in the reader's mind and organize the paper around these points.

Background sections reiterate points made in an issue section only when a writer wants to elaborate further. If no elaboration is necessary, there is no need to re-state a point.

In describing the policy position of an organization to a superior, particularly the head of the organization, a staff person needs to use language that reflects the subordinated position of the writer in setting or articulating the policy of the organization. A staff person can remind a superior of the organization's or superior's past policy position on an issue, but should be circumspect in describing the current policy of the organization.

▶ **Outlook Section.** Many briefing papers include a third section titled "Outlook." This section is not a conclusion. Rather, it should contain information on relevant upcoming events and/or deadlines. It may also include analytical points on what is likely to affect an issue in the near future and on what a reader should be prepared to encounter.

General Guidelines for Writing Briefing Papers

The challenge in writing a briefing paper is to be thorough but also succinct. This requires a writer to judge what information to include and what to leave out. A writer must explain an issue in enough detail so that a reader gains a full understanding in a few pages (usually two to five pages).

Descriptive subheadings are useful for organizing a briefing paper because they force a writer to focus and they enable readers to extract information quickly. To be useful to a reader, however, subheadings must be immediately understandable and cannot leave a reader guessing as to their meaning.

Tone of Briefing Papers

Unlike op-eds or other journalistic pieces, a briefing paper need not entice the reader with juicy information, provocative statements, or descriptive language. Instead, briefing papers should simply lay out information and analyses in the clearest and most concise manner possible. Similarly, direct quotes from individuals are not used in a briefing paper unless the specific wording of the quote is important. Usually it is sufficient to state that X individual or organization "took the position that" the policy should or should not be supported.

Decision Memorandum

The Commercial Diplomat usually acts on behalf of an organization (i.e., a government department, ministry or regulatory agency, an industry association or enterprise, a nongovernmental organization). Therefore, before adopting a course of action on a particular policy issue, the Commercial Diplomat must seek the approval of superiors and other stakeholders with a role in the decision-making process. The approval process usually involves the submission of a decision memorandum to everyone who will be participating in the decision.

The senior manager empowered to make a decision for an organization is usually an extremely busy individual who does not have the time to read through a thick document and sort through voluminous data and information. A decision memorandum, therefore, has to be relatively short, to the point, and well organized. A somewhat longer paper may be attached to the decision memorandum to give the decision maker's staff additional details. The writer of a decision memorandum has to be highly selective in the choice of background information and analysis that is included in the memorandum. Such a memorandum should typically not exceed a few pages and may need to be as short as one page. While the attachment can be longer, it should include only information that is necessary for making a well-informed decision on the issue. The attachment itself should be in a format that makes it easy to read, with tables and back-up documents relegated to separate appendixes at the back of the paper. Typically, an analyst will collect several times as much data as should be included in the complete document, and the decision making memorandum itself should include only a small fraction of that data with only the most critical information.

Decision Memorandum Format

- ▶ **Introduction.** A good decision memorandum, above all, needs a concisely written introductory paragraph that describes the problem or opportunity from the point of view of the organization, why the issue is important to the organization, the key hurdles that need to be addressed in obtaining a desirable outcome, and the recommended course of action.

- ▶ **The Background Section.** The introductory issue section should be followed by a background section that provides the most relevant background information.

- ▶ **The Analytical Section.** This section provides the writer's own interpretation of the background data and analysis of the issues that is likely to have a significant bearing on the decision.

- ▶ **The Option and Recommendation Section.** Available options (if desired by the decision maker) and a recommended policy outcome, including the rationale for the recommended choice are outlined in this section.

- ▶ **The Strategy Section.** A recommended course of action for implementing the desired outcome is clearly stated in the strategy section.

Each of these sections should be subdivided into key topics with subheadings that provide an outline of the topics addressed. By doing so, the reader a provided with a quick overview of the main lines of the argument, allowing him/her to decide which paragraphs to read when time is limited.

Both the background section and the analytical section should cover the commercial and policy issues, the politics, the national economic effects, the relevant legal provisions, and the public relations aspects of the issue. All factual material, including numerical data, information about stakeholders and their interests and views, applicable laws and international rules, actions by policy makers, news articles, and opinion polls belong in this section. The analytical section should cover the writer's own interpretation and analysis of the data and information presented in the background section. Where we are dealing with a policy issue that involves a foreign government, the information and analysis presented in these sections will need to cover both the situation in the home country and abroad.

Each successive section of the decision memorandum should establish a solid foundation for the next section. Thus, the background section should provide all the information needed to support the analysis provided in the analytical section. The analytical section needs to provide support for the recommended policy outcome and every element of the proposed strategy for obtaining a favorable decision. Background information that does not support an element of the analysis presented in the analytical section can probably be left out of the memorandum without reducing its effectiveness. In fact, leaving unessential information out of the memorandum is likely to enhance its effectiveness. Similarly, analytical observations that do not directly relate to the policy options, the recommended policy outcome, or the recommended strategy should also be left out. On the other hand, elements of a recommendation unsupported by analysis, or analysis unsupported by key facts, may call for additions to the paper. Recommendations not backed by analysis are unlikely to impress decision makers unless you are the world's greatest authority on a subject.

Writing a Decision Memorandum: Questions to Ask

- ▶ What factual background does the decision maker need to make an informed decision?

- ▶ What analysis can I add to support the recommended course of action?

- ▶ What are the elements of my recommended course of action? How will that solve the trade problem and satisfy other policy requirements?

- ▶ What is my strategy for developing the necessary consensus among domestic and foreign stakeholders? For making the legal case? For managing institutional issues? For building broader public support?

Outline of a Decision Memorandum

- ▶ **Issue.** Describe the issue, with particular emphasis on the trade problem or opportunity and the key hurdle that needs to be addressed in obtaining a desirable outcome, and the recommended course of action. To the extent it is relevant, include brief description of the key policy issue, key aspects of politics at home and abroad, principal domestic and international legal considerations, and any other factors that have to be considered by a decision maker.

- ▶ **Background.** Summarize the key facts concerning the issue, including:
    - Nature of the policy measure at issue,
    - Amount of trade involved, applicable domestic laws and international rules,
    - Total output of the industry and the number of workers involved,
    - Known positions of various stakeholder groups at home and abroad, and
    - Position of the relevant foreign country government.

- ▶ **Analysis.** Provide your interpretation and analysis of the background data from the point of view of the interests of the organization you represent. For example, you would want to provide:

- An interpretation of the various laws and regulations as they apply to the case,
- An examination of the commercial interests of your organization and of other stakeholders,
- An assessment of the broad economic interests of the country,
- A critical evaluation of the measure at issue from the point of view of the social or other national objectives it is designed to achieve,
- An indication of alternative measures that may be available to pursue the legitimate policy objective,
- An analysis of the means of various stakeholders to exercise political influence, and their likely political influence,
- An identification of institutional obstacles in achieving a satisfactory outcome,
- A review of the current state of public opinion on the issue and the role of the media, and
- An evaluation of the most important obstacles to a satisfactory solution.

Not all of these factors will be relevant in every case. Your job as an analyst is to identify the ones that are most relevant for achieving a satisfactory outcome for your organization.

► **Recommendation and/or Options.** Provide an explanation and summary of the available options (if desired by your supervisors) and your recommendation for addressing the issue. You should include the steps required to implement the recommendation.

► **Strategy.** In some cases you may want to describe the strategy that your organization could follow to obtain the recommended outcome, including research, the establishment of political coalitions and other forms of political action, and media strategies.

Press Releases

Press releases are one- to two-page written announcements that resemble news articles and are sent to newspapers, wire services, television and radio stations, and other organizations that write or post news. Businesses, industry associations, non-governmental organizations, universities, government agencies, and others use press releases to make public announcements. The goal is to attract an editor's attention and generate a news story.

A good press release is easy for the press to use. It has a descriptive title and quickly answers the "Who, What, When, Where, Why, and How" of an event. Press releases, written like news stories in an "inverted pyramid" format, are most likely to be printed as submitted with little or no editing. Under the inverted pyramid, the most important information and quotations are placed at the beginning of the story, followed by less important details in descending order of importance. Well-crafted press releases ensure that corresponding news stories are accurate and take an angle that emphasizes precisely what it is the organization wants to publicize.

Press releases are commonly used to announce:

- A policy action,

- The release of a policy statement,

- An organization's position or official response to an event,

- An important meeting,

- A new piece of legislation,

- An organization or government's reaction to an action or policy statement by another organization or government,

- Breakthroughs or stalemates in negotiations,

- The appointment of a senior officer of the organization, or

- The findings of a new study or survey.

Press Release Format

- **Headline.** The headline should provide a descriptive title for the story that catches a reader's attention. It should be ten words or less and should both summarize the information contained in the release and make the reader want to know more.

- **Opening Paragraph, Abstract, or Lead.** A two-line opening paragraph, sometimes called an abstract or lead, must answer the "Who, What, When, Where and Why" of a press release. The body should provide the details.

- **Body.** The body of a press release is written in an "inverted pyramid" format. Editors typically cut stories from the end when they need to meet space constraints. By putting critical information at the beginning of a release, a writer ensures that this information makes it into the news article. A good press release includes at least one interesting, descriptive quotation from an expert or relevant public opinion leader.

Ideally, the body of a press release is structured in such a fashion that if a reporter were to terminate the story at the end of any paragraph, the story would still be meaningful. Unlike in other documents, paragraphs in a press release should not be constructed as sequential building blocks to an argument. A reporter is thus able to use excerpts from the original text regardless of whether the editor agrees to provide space for one paragraph, three paragraphs, or ten paragraphs.

► **Closing Paragraph.** The closing paragraph is the place to repeat an organization's contact information. Some organizations include a standard boilerplate paragraph at the bottom of each press release to provide basic information about the organization. For example, a cheese industry association includes the following information: "The American Cheese Manufacturer's Group (ACMG) is a private nonprofit organization that represents America's dairy farmers and cheese producers in 37 states."

► **Attachments.** Detailed background information or texts of lengthy legal and policy documents can be attached to the press release. The text of the press release should only include information you can expect a reporter to include in a news article. Information designed to educate the reporter belongs in the attachments.

General Guidelines for Writing a Press Release

► **Make it Newsworthy.** Press releases must be newsworthy and interesting in order to catch a busy editor's attention. Focus on what is newsworthy in the press release. Is the press release announcing something that is new? Is there a local angle to a national issue? Does the release announce something that will affect people's lives everywhere or just in a local area? Does the announcement have a bearing on a widely recognized and important event?

Press releases aimed at the popular press often bring out a human interest angle to help nonexperts understand the impact of an issue on average citizens. The use of catchy, "sound-bite" phrases to summarize complex issues in a few well-chosen words is particularly effective. When such phrases capture the public imagination, they are likely to be repeated over and over again with a powerful impact on public opinion.

► **Make it Usable by Journalists.** Write the news release in the style and format commonly used by journalists in your area. If the journalist has to rewrite your story, he may not convey the same nuances in the message, or he may misinterpret the issue altogether. In general, follow the journalistic convention of providing the "who, what, where, and why" of the story, and follow the pyramidal style of writing in which information is provided in decreasing order of importance.

► **Targeting.** Some news stories are of interest to the general public, while others are relevant only to targeted groups. Similarly, some stories are of national interest, while others are of interest only to certain regions or localities. An auto manufacturer's announcement of a recall due to faulty brakes, for example, is issued broadly to national wire services, major newspapers, and television and radio networks. The story is then further disseminated by regional and local news organizations. A press release announcing a ban of a pesticide, however, might only be released to news agencies that cover agricultural issues or to publications distributed in areas with a high concentration of farms. A release announcing the appointment of a new university president might only be sent to local and university newspapers.

In targeting stories to particular newspapers or other media, the organiza-tion releasing the story needs to ask itself not only who is most interested in the story, but also whom the organization seeks to inform or persuade. If the objective is to persuade a particular group of legislators, the press release should target newspapers read by both the legislators and their constituents.

Press Release Template

FOR IMMEDIATE RELEASE

CONTACT: Contact person
Company/organization (or department name if using letterhead
Area code and telephone number
Fax number
Email address and website address

HEADLINE: City, state, date, opening paragraph, the "Who, What, When, Where and Why" of the press release.

BODY: The body of the press release, including relevant information, what is new, unique, different, and detrimental about the item being announced. Use quotations from experts, staff, and customers. Each paragraph should be relatively self-contained, since a reporter may decide to use only some of the paragraphs. Sequence the paragraphs in the order of relative impor-tance, because you want the most meaningful material used if either the writer or the editor decides to cut your story to fit the space available.

If the release continues on to a second page:

► Restate contact information in paragraph form at the top of the second page.

► A boilerplate paragraph about the organization may be added.

Op-Eds

Op-eds are opinion pieces submitted to newspapers by private citizens, university professors, syndicated columnists, business leaders, politicians, community activists, etc. The views expressed in an op-ed article may or may not concur with the opinions of a newspaper's editors. Op-eds further public debate on an issue by giving writers with specialized experience or knowledge the opportunity to express their unique perspectives on an issue.

Short for "opposite the editorial page" op-eds are published on the page opposite the one that contains editorials written by newspaper staff. The term "op-ed" is also sometimes used to indicate the "opinion and editorial" section of a newspaper.

These opinion pieces are not to be confused with "letters to the editor," which are short, reader responses to issues a newspaper has (or has not) covered. Nor should op-eds be confused with "editorials," which are area newspapers' formal positions on topics and are written by newspaper staff.

The writing style of op-ed pieces is significantly different from that of briefing papers and policy papers. Op-ed pieces need to draw a reader in. One way to do so is to describe how an issue affects specific people. Drawing a vivid picture of a human impact pushes readers to consider an issue in a way that cold factual analysis cannot.

Op-Ed Format

► **Introduction.** An op-ed article needs to express the writer's opinion up-front. A reader should understand the writer's position after reading the introductory paragraph. While all op-ed pieces include a brief description of the writer (usually printed in italics at the end of the piece), the writer may want to re-emphasize near the beginning of the article his/her credibility or experience on the subject issue.

► **Body.** Like any writing piece, an op-ed is more persuasive if it offers multiple, descriptive examples to illustrate a point. It should also address why opposing viewpoints are wrong or misguided. The trick with an op-ed is accomplishing all this in a very limited space. Op-eds are generally no longer than 500 words – approximately one single-spaced typewritten page.

► **Conclusion.** An op-ed intended simply to influence opinion should end by reiterating or illustrating the writer's main point in a way that leaves a strong impression. If the goal of the piece is to mobilize people to action, readers should know precisely what the writer wants them to do. For example, readers can be asked to vote a particular way on an issue, to contact government officials, to write letters to a company, or to boycott a particular store or product.

General Guidelines for Writing Op-Eds

To get an op-ed published, first check the newspaper's website or contact the newspaper directly for particular requirements for submission. Such requirements might include length, deadlines, format, and the form in which an op-ed is sent (i.e., email, fax, first-class mail). You may also want to check on the ground rules that apply in the area or country where the newspaper is published.

It is prudent to read other op-eds in target newspapers before submitting an op-ed. This helps a writer determine the newspapers most likely to publish an op-ed on a particular topic and helps a writer craft his/her op-ed in a way that ensures it gets published.

Cables

Cables are official communications between governments and their representatives abroad. Historically, both business and government organizations have used cables to communicate between home and overseas offices. Though e-mail has mostly replaced cables, cables continue to be used to establish a formal record of instructions by a government to its representatives abroad and to transmit reports prepared by overseas representatives back to the home government. The following examples illustrate current uses of cables:

▶ The Japanese Embassy in Sydney sends a cable to the Japanese Ministry of Foreign Affairs to report the results of a meeting with Australian cattle exporters.

▶ United States Trade Representative (USTR) officials send a cable with negotiation instructions to members of the United States Permanent Mission to the World Trade Organization (WTO) in Geneva.

▶ The Ministry of Trade in Mexico cables official changes in trade policy to its commercial officers in embassies abroad.

While cables are normally addressed to specific officials, they are circulated widely within a government for information purposes. The distribution of cables is one of the hardest fought bureaucratic issues within a government.

Cable Format

▶ **Summary.** Cables begin with a summary paragraph that is labeled as such. This is a short recapitulation of the most salient information provided in the body of the cable. The "Summary" paragraph is similar to the "Issue" section used in briefing and policy papers, although it often is even shorter.

▶ **Body.** Cable writing does not offer the same formatting options as word processing. While subheadings can be used (and should be used when appropriate), they cannot be underlined or bolded. Similarly, the only way to make a bullet point is with a dash, and paragraphs cannot be indented. Since cables cannot be formatted, they must be tightly organized to ensure clarity.

Paragraphs in a cable are automatically numbered. Because cable text is usually printed in two columns per page using small type, long paragraphs are very difficult to read and should be avoided. Paragraphs can be one sentence in length or can be several sentences, but each numbered paragraph must contain only one idea. Historically cables have been extremely expensive to send, and because the number of words determined the cost, a short and almost cryptic style emerged as the standard. While cost is no longer an issue today, cables still should be as succinct as possible.

General Guidelines for Writing Cables

Cables are always sent under the cover of the principal person of the organization. For example, a cable from an embassy will always be "from" the ambassador, even though a lower ranking staffer most likely wrote it. A "drafted by" line identifies the name and title of the cable's author.

Emails

Virtually all documents covered in this chapter can be distributed by email. Electronic networks are the most efficient method of distributing documents to recipients today.

Emails take the place of both verbal and more formal written communication. They lend themselves to quick exchanges and generally are more informal and terse than written memorandums. However, emails incur the risk of miscommunication. Short, informal messages that lack the traditional courtesy of a letter may unintentionally offend a recipient. Even if the words in the email are similar to those in an informal verbal exchange, they lack the tone and facial expressions inherent to verbal communication. Without audio and visual clues, messages are easy to misread.

The writer of an email message needs to consider his/her relationship to the recipient(s). Colleagues with a strong working relationship are more casual with each other than those trying to build a new relationship. Likewise, cultural norms and organizational hierarchies need to be considered. A message sent between people at the same level can be much less formal than one sent from a junior staffer to a senior diplomatic official even if it conveys virtually the same information. Finally, because email is part of the written record, it is important to follow spelling and grammar rules.

In summary, email is a convenient tool for informal communication. To avoid misinterpretations, it is important for the writer of an email to be mindful of organizational hierarchies and clarity.

Public Testimony

Governments invite public testimony on issues to bring transparency and public participation into decision-making processes. Testimony is used to:

- ► Educate and influence legislators and the public,

- ► Inform and defend a position or person in an investigative hearing,

- ► Oppose, support, or offer compromise solutions for proposed legislation or regulations, and

- ► Attract public attention to an issue.

Typically, those who give testimony begin by making a prepared statement (which is usually made available in writing at the time of the testimony). Subsequently, officials presiding over the meeting are given an opportunity to ask questions and challenge the positions presented in the statement.

Often an invitation is required for testimony. One cannot arrive for a hearing or meeting uninvited and expect to testify. However, those wishing to testify can always contact a committee member's office.

Examples of Public Testimony

In response to allegations of corruption, the International Olympic Committee (IOC) heard public testimony. The testimony helped further the investigation and, importantly, introduced at least an appearance of transparency into the process. Regulatory bodies in the United Kingdom use testimony in determining gas taxes.

When preparing for bilateral or multilateral negotiations, the United States Trade Representative's (USTR) Office often holds public meetings and invites testimony from interested parties.

Oral vs. Written Testimony

Oral testimony given before a government body is different from written testimony submitted for the permanent record. Typically, oral testimony is a shorter, more focused version of written testimony. Obviously, both oral and written testimonies should convey the same message and present the perspective of the organization in a clear and easy-to-follow style. They should, however, be structured somewhat differently.

- ▶ **Effective oral testimony** is succinct and focused toward swaying individual officials and, to a lesser extent, media representatives. Oral testimony is prepared like a speech. In written form, five to six double-spaced pages is roughly enough material for a ten-minute oral presentation.

- ▶ **Effective written testimony** needs to be more detailed and include more examples than oral testimony. However, brevity is still a virtue. If a writer's message gets lost due to too many examples and arguments, the testimony does not serve its purpose. Appendices can be attached if it is truly necessary to provide further information or data.

In most cases, committee members expect to receive copies of both the shorter oral version presented during the hearing and the longer, more detailed written testimony submitted for the official record.

The Question and Answer Period

During the question and answer period, officials presiding over the hearing ask questions meant to challenge the positions of those testifying. Committee members agreeing with the position presented may ask easy questions or questions that allow the respondent to elaborate further on the benefits of his/her proposal. Conversely, committee members opposed to the views of the testifier ask tough questions meant to expose the weaknesses of a position. In cases where a committee member asks a question to which the testifier does not know the answer, it is best for the testifier to admit his/her ignorance and offer to provide an answer at a later time.

Written and Oral Testimony Format

- ▶ **Cover Page.** Because both written and oral testimony are distributed to relevant government officials, both versions should include a cover page that cites the name, title, and contact information of the testifier's organization.

A cover page should also include the date of the testimony, the name of the committee and its chair, and the title or number of the hearing or meeting.

► **Opening.** The opening of both written and oral testimony should include an acknowledgment of appreciation for the opportunity to testify. Next, the testifier usually introduces himself/herself, providing enough information about himself/herself and/or his/her organization to establish credibility on the subject of the testimony. Is the testifier a business, academic, or government expert? Is he/she testifying on behalf of an organization or an industry coalition, or on behalf of members? If so, how many and where are they? Are they voters in the committee members' districts?

► **Introduction.** The substance portion of testimony should begin with a clear statement of the testifier's (or his/her organization's) position on the issue at hand. Next, the testifier should summarize the points that he/she will make in the order he/she will make them. For example, a representative from a U.S. business or industry association testifying before Congress in favor of passage of Normal Trade Relations for China (NTR) might make the following points:

- Passing NTR for China will create 1.2 million new export jobs in the United States.
- Passing NTR for China will expand business opportunities for U.S. businesses.

► **Body.** The body of the testimony is ideally outlined in the introduction. A common technique is to restate each point, along with vivid examples to illustrate the point.

Continuing with the example used above, the businessperson testifying before Congress might restate the first point in the introduction in the following way:

- Passing NTR for China will create 1.2 million new export jobs in the United States. X and Y research firm estimates that granting NTR to China and opening its market to U.S. manufactured goods and services will create 1.2 million new high paid export jobs in the United States over the next two years, etc.

A common technique in the body of the testimony is to cite credible sources, such as experts or independent third-party studies, or to quote those who will be affected by the legislation or regulation in question. Testifiers frequently remind committee members how their constituents will be affected by a policy decision.

► **Conclusion.** The conclusion should tie together and summarize the main points of the testimony. It should clearly state the call to action: a yes or no vote, further investigation, immediate change in policy or procedure, more funding, etc. Committee members should have a clear idea of the basic message.

General Guidelines for Public Testimonies

When giving testimony, it is important to speak slowly and clearly and to stay within allotted time limits. It is a good idea to practice testimony several times to be confident in its delivery. Additionally, it is important to anticipate difficult questions and be prepared to answer them. Of course, it is also important to be sure that all studies, statistics, and reports are properly cited, particularly because they may be challenged during the question and answer period. Additionally, a testifier should be prepared to distribute several copies of his/her testimony at the hearing. The press and others in attendance frequently ask for copies.

Chapter 10

EFFECTIVE DATA PRESENTATION

By: Fernando De Paolis, Geza Feketekuty, Robert McCleery, and Moyara Ruehsen[42]

When asked for good examples of effective data presentation, a senior U.S. trade policy official replied, "Actually, some good examples can be drawn from the Ross Perot NAFTA 'informercials'. The effectiveness of his presentation made his points harder for us to refute, despite the lack of merit to most of his arguments." While the authors of this text by no means intend to teach readers how to mislead their audience, knowing how to present data and interpret graphs effectively are vital skills for policy analysts, legislators, and industry lobbyists. In this chapter we briefly describe some of the different types of graphs that policy makers can use to lend weight to a policy position. In the subsequent sections, the appropriate use of each type of graphical illustration will be explained, followed by a summary flow chart indicating what factors to consider before selecting a particular type of graph.

GUIDANCE ON EFFECTIVE PRESENTATIONS AND INTERPRETATION OF PRESENTED DATA

The Five-Second Rule

As readers, we have all experienced instances of ineffective data presentation, when we must stare at a diagram for an inordinate amount of time to decipher what the illustrator is trying to demonstrate. Sometimes the graph is drawn incorrectly. Other

---

42 The content of this chapter is substantially taken from the original training manual entitled *Working with Economic Data in Trade Policy Development, Advocacy, and Negotations* co-authored by Geza Feketekuty, Robert McCleery, Moyara Ruehsen, and Fernando DePaolis, which is available on the ITCD website, but has been further edited for the purposes of this textbook by Geza Feketekuty. The original manual can be found at www.commercialdiplomacy.org.

times too much information is squeezed into one diagram, or what looked clear in color is indecipherable in shades of gray. In general a good rule to follow is to design a graph that can be read easily within five seconds. If your audience cannot interpret what the diagram is trying to illustrate within five seconds or less, then the diagram is not effective. Occasionally there are times when a graph is more complex out of necessity. In these rare instances it is acceptable to violate the five-second rule provided that the accompanying explanatory text is completely clear. For public presentations, however, the five-second rule should be adhered to.

Working with Time Series Data

Time-series data is simply data measured over time; for example, the dollar-yen exchange rate over a ten-year period. This type of data is best depicted with a line graph, although there are exceptions that will be discussed later. Since a line graph is most appropriate in 90% of these cases, a simple rule-of-thumb is "With time, use a line."

Simple Line Graphs

All line graphs should read from left to right, with the oldest unit of time (earliest year, month, or week) at the far left of the diagram, and the most recent year to the far right. This is important to keep in mind when creating spreadsheets of data, which are used for creating graphs. It is typical (but by no means a rigid rule) to have the time variable in the first column and the variable being measured in the second column, with the earliest time period at the top of the spreadsheet and the most recent time period at the bottom of the spreadsheet.

Consider the example of Chinese exports to the United States over time. The two variables we are viewing are (1) China's exports to the United States, which may alternatively be measured as U.S. imports from China, and (2) time. The horizontal or X-axis is counting years, from a starting year to an ending year, as you move to the right. The vertical or Y-axis counts Chinese exports to the United States (in appropriate units, here in millions of dollars of value). Each point represents both a dollar amount and the year in which that trade occurred.

Figure 10.1
Line Graph: Total Exports from China

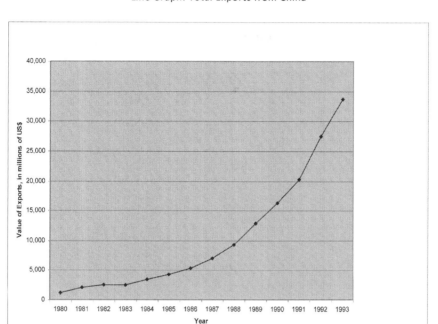

There are always tricks and traps to look out for when viewing graphs, particular time series graphs. For example, how did the illustrator choose the beginning and ending years in the series? For some series, it is possible to show either an upward or downward trend by a strategic choice of end points. For instance, consider the following series of U.S. inflation rates, as shown in the table below.

Table 10A

U.S. Inflation Rates

1982	'83	'84	'85	'86	'87	'88	'89	'90	'91	'92	'93	'94
6.7	3.2	4.3	3.6	1.9	3.6	4.1	4.8	5.4	4.2	3.0	3.0	2.9

Multiple Line Graphs

It is very easy, particularly with line graphs, to show a second, third, or even fourth variable in the same illustration, as long as the additional variables are measured in the same units (but even this limitation can be relaxed). Returning to our export diagram above, we could add Hong Kong's exports to the United States as a second line in our graph. The reason for doing so might be an assumption, based on other evidence, that a lot of Chinese products are shipped first to Hong Kong, then refined, packaged, or just transshipped and more effectively marketed to U.S. consumers. Generally, multiple line graphs should be limited to no more than four lines, even when the lines show up in different colors (as opposed to different shades of gray or different patterns of dashes, which are much more difficult to see). More than four lines is too much information, and the audience will not be able to appreciate the main point the presenter is trying to make.

Figure 10.2
Line Graph: Exports to the U.S. from China

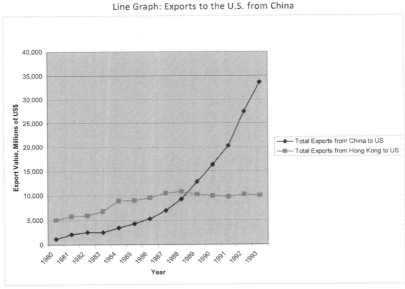

Manipulating Scales

Not all vertical or y-axis scales begin at zero, nor should they. Suppose we are interested in looking at changes over time in the Japanese yen/U.S. dollar exchange rate. Most foreign currency analysts (and trade policy analysts) are interested in depreciations and appreciations smaller than 5%. Yet such small changes would be difficult to observe if the vertical scale went from zero to 130. For the second half of the 1990s the line would almost look straight. So we must alter the range of the y-axis to "stretch" the graph and magnify movements in this exchange rate. We do this by choosing a y-axis range similar to the actual range of the data. If the exchange rate varied during the time in question from 105 yen to 125 yen/$, then an appropriate range for the y-axis scale would be 100 to 130 yen/$.

Another common and completely acceptable manipulation of y-axis scales is inversion. Inverting the vertical scale is extremely common with exchange rate diagrams. It is widely understood that an exchange rate diagram should illustrate appreciation of a currency with an upward sloping line and depreciation of a currency over time with a downward sloping line. However, if the Japanese yen is moving from 105 yen to 125 yen per U.S. dollar, then the yen is depreciating. Instead of inverting the exchange rate and having $/yen in place of yen/$ on the vertical axis (0.00813$/yen is less easily recognized than 123 yen/$) we should invert the y-axis scale, so the bottom of the vertical scale starts with 150Y/$, and the top of the scale ends with 80 yen/$. If we were trying to illustrate the movement of the U.S. dollar over time, then we would not need to invert the vertical scale.

Figure 10.3

Depreciating U.S. Dollar

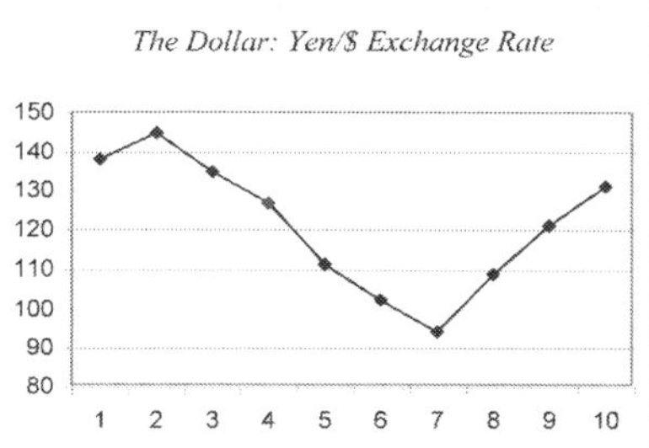

Figure 10.4

Appreciating Yen: Inverted Y Axis

Pie Charts

Line graphs are easy to interpret and can be extremely effective tools for illustration, but they are also limiting. The line graph of Chinese exports to the U.S. shown above does not tell us what kinds of products China is exporting to the U.S. Did the increase in export sales represent an increase in all of China's exports to the U.S., or was it largely an increase in one or two categories of exports such as textiles and toys?

Generally, the best tool for showing the relative size of the component parts of a total is the pie chart, but this can only be done with one variable. For instance, if we wish to see the composition of Chinese exports to the U.S., we can only graph exports for one year. We would use only one column of data: a variable called exports by category. If we wish to show how this composition has changed over time, we would need to create a pie chart for each year in the time series, or the first and last years. The downside is that each pie chart would likely be the same size. It is theoretically possible to make the pie charts successively larger as the total amount of exports increases, but this is generally not done. Absolute dollar amounts could be indicated on each slice, but an audience is unlikely to compare and contrast the dollar amounts among ten different pies. Therefore, pie charts are generally only good for graphing one variable and one point in time to illustrate the respective proportions of the component categories. These component categories should ideally not exceed seven or be less than three.

In the following examples, we have only five categories of traded goods. The shadings of each respective pie are sufficiently different from one another to be easily distinguished in a black and white publication. Note that both the absolute figures (in billions of dollars) and the percentages (in parentheses) appear next to each pie slice.

Figure 10.5
U.S. Merchandise Trade with the World by Product Sectors, 1998
Pie Chart: U.S. Exports (billion dollars)

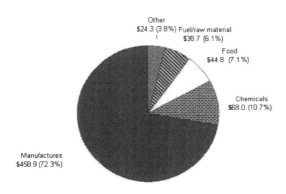

Figure 10.6
Pie Chart: U.S. Imports (billion dollars)

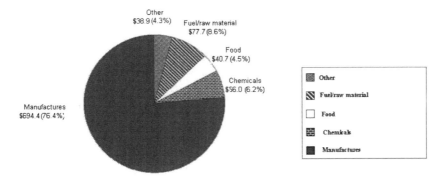

Note: Because of rounding, figures may not add up to the totals shown. Exports are domestic exports, f.a.s. Imports are not imports for consumption, customs value.

Source: Compiled from the official statistics of the U.S. Department of Commerce.

Vertical Bar Charts

As discussed earlier, there are exceptions to the rule of using line graphs for time series data. If the data is summary data, such as end-of-year trade balances, then a bar chart is perfectly appropriate and probably more effective. Whether one is looking at current account balances or merchandise trade balances or annual change in foreign reserves over time, the most appropriate illustration is a vertical bar chart, with years on the horizontal axis and the balance in financial terms on the y-axis.

Figure 10.7
Bar Chart: End of Year Trade Balances

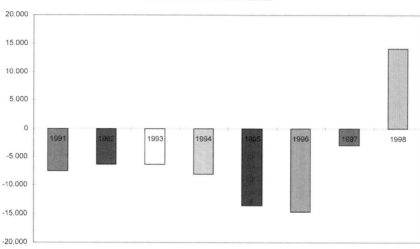

In general, bar charts are most commonly used when time is not one of the variables. Typically, there is one continuous variable (measured on the vertical axis), and one discrete variable (discrete categories such as countries, type of trade barrier, etc.) on the horizontal axis. For example, if we wanted to show which four countries filed the most complaints with the World Trade Organization in the past five years, we would illustrate this with four vertical bars, each bar representing one of the four countries. The height of each bar would indicate the number of cases filed during this five-year period.

There are several variations on vertical bar charts, such as clustered bar charts and stacked bar charts. These charts are used where there is one continuous variable and two discrete variables. In the example below of a clustered bar chart, the continuous variable is "percent of total," and the two discrete variables are "country" and "type of import."

This is a fairly clear diagram, but because of the amount of information in it, it probably would not pass the five-second test. At first glance, it would appear that Mexico accounts for a disproportionately large share of GSP (Generalized System of Preferences) imports to the United States, but upon closer inspection, the share of GSP imports is much smaller than Mexico's share of dutied imports into the United States.

Figure 10.8
Clustered Vertical Bar Chart: Share of GSP Imports for Top Shipping Countries

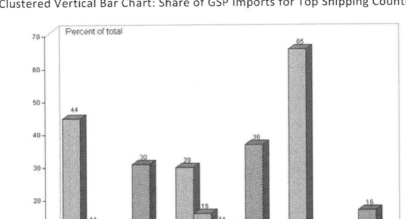

Source: U.S. Department of Commerce/Bureau of the Census

A stacked bar chart is also used when there is one continuous variable and two discrete variables. In the example below, the continuous variable is "U.S. dollar value of imports," and the two discrete variables are "type of agricultural product," and "year." Generally, when "year" is one of the two discrete variables, the bars represent the years and the stacks represent the other discrete variable. Another guideline is to limit the number of stacks. Two to four stacks is ideal. More than six stacks is often indecipherable.

Figure 10.9
Stacked Bar Chart: Chilean Agricultural Exports, 1989-1993

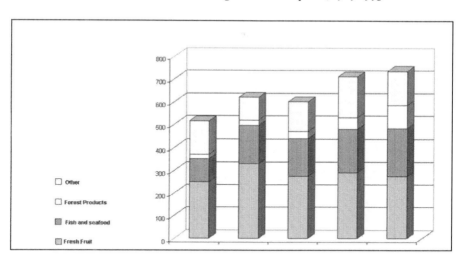

Note: Agriculture exports include agriculture, forestry, and fisheries products
Source: U.S. Department of Commerce

It is important to keep in mind when creating graphs that illustrations that look beautiful in full color on the computer screen may not look as wonderful when printed in black and white. There should be as much contrast as possible between the shadings of stacks and clustered bars to limit confusion and misinterpretation. Figure 10.10 below is an illustration of a stacked chart, where this rule was not followed. Upon close inspection it is easy to interpret, but this graph does not pass the five-second rule, and could be improved by either compressing the smaller categories into three categories (e.g., foreign investment earnings, services, and merchandise trade) or shading the stacks differently:

► as shown

► with clusters representing countries and bars representing type of import

► with five bars, each representing countries, and stacks in each bar representing type of import

► with three bars, each representing type of import, and stacks in each bar representing each country

Each of these different presentations puts a slightly different spin or emphasis on the diagram.

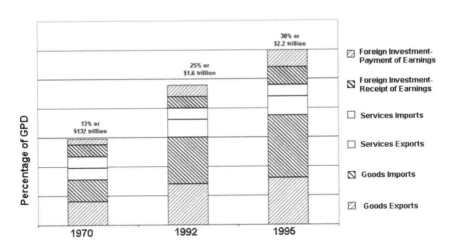

Figure 10.10
Stacked Chart: Trade as Percentage of Value of U.S. GDP

Horizontal Bar Graphs

There are times when vertical bars are inappropriate, such as when there are too many bars (when the discrete variable has more than six categories) to illustrate vertically. In this case a horizontal bar chart is more appropriate, but horizontal bar charts are not recommended if one of the variables is "time." It is counterintuitive for the audience to read consecutive time series data up and down rather than left to right.

Horizontal bar charts are also not recommended for clustered charts unless each cluster contains only two bars. In such a case, "time" is acceptable as a variable if one of the bars in the cluster is "year 1" and the other bar is "year 2." In this case, the clusters illustrate how each individual case has changed from "year 1" to "year 2."

Horizontal bar charts are useful for percentage changes over time, with negative changes illustrated by bars stretching to the left of the center line, and positive changes illustrated by bars stretching to the right of the center line.

Combining Lines and Bars

Combining both lines and bars can be very effective at times. In Figure 10.11 we see Mexico's account balance leading up to the 1994 Peso Crisis. In absolute terms, it was growing significantly over time, as evidenced by the hanging bars, but Mexico's economy was also growing during the same period. So, a more important question would be, how significant are these deficits measured as a proportion of Mexico's GDP? Both pieces of information are illustrated on the same diagram. By coincidence, the illustrator was able to use the same left-hand vertical scale to measure both $/billions and %/GDP. If the illustrator had wanted to use a separate scale for %/GDP, then this scale could be drawn on the far right side of the diagram.

Figure 10.11
Combined Line and Bar Chart / Mexico's Account Deficit 1988-94

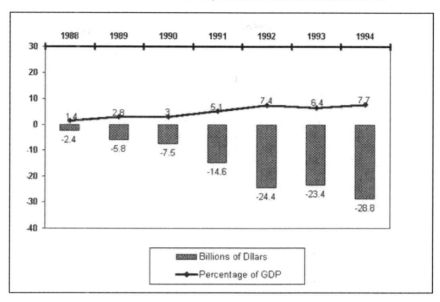

Source: Bank of Mexico

There are instances when superimposing a line and bar works well to illustrate causality. For example, what if we wanted to illustrate the impact of exchange rates on the trade balance? We could have bars illustrating the trade balance over time, and a line illustrating the country's trade-weighted exchange rate superimposed on top of the bars. The vertical scale (the exchange rate) in this instance should be adjusted for optimal visual correlation.

Area Diagrams

Area diagrams are seldom used because their utility is limited. There are instances, however, when they are visually effective. The most common use of area diagrams is with time series data divided into different component parts. In this instance, one of the variables would be a unit of "time," a second continuous variable would be measured on the vertical axis, and a third discrete variable would be represented by the different areas in the diagram. For example, let's say we wish to illustrate how the U.S. Commerce Department's budget has changed over time, both in magnitude and composition. The total dollar amount would be measured on the vertical axis (either in real or nominal terms), and each area would represent a discrete category of the budget. This is particularly effective if one wishes to illustrate how one budget category grows much faster than the others.

Scatter Diagrams

A scatter diagram is used when there are two continuous variables, neither of which is time, and one additional discrete variable. Three variables are the most that can be easily portrayed in a two-dimensional graph. If our discrete variable were "country" or "region," we could use a scatter diagram to show combinations of the other two variables for each country or region. For instance, suppose we want to show the relationship between trade barriers and economic growth for Southeast Asian countries. We could put a measure of protectionism like average tariff equivalent on the x-axis, growth rate or per capita growth rate of real output on the y-axis, and label each observed combination of tariff equivalent and growth rate with the name or a code for the corresponding country. Our scatter diagram would look like Figure 10–11.

Figure 10.11
Scatter Diagram: Protection and Growth, Southeast Asia

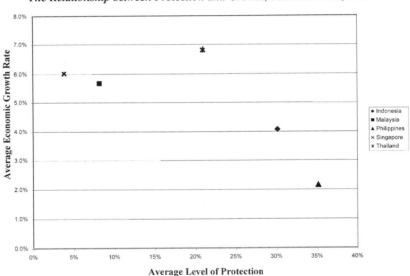

The Relationship between Protection and Growth, Southeast Asia, 1985-98

Using Objects

Most statistical software packages do not allow for fancy graphics, but other types of software can be used to create beautiful diagrams that illustrate a point more effectively. For example, in a cost-effectiveness study one could illustrate the cost of each option with stacked dollar bills. If the objective is to illustrate how a minor investment in Export-Import Bank loans yields a high rate of return, one could depict this with piles or bags of money.

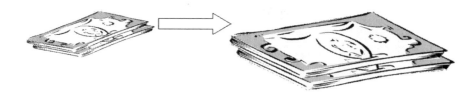

Figure 10.13
Example of Object Manipulation

Combining Text with Graphs

Another effective way to illustrate a point is with text highlighting key dates in a time-series line graph. For example, if we were looking at a trade-weighted exchange rate of the U.S. dollar over the past 20 years, we could insert dotted, vertical lines into the picture with accompanying text boxes indicating major currency interventions such as the Plaza Accord, the Louvre Accord, and the bilateral action of the United States Federal Reserve and the Bank of Japan in August 1995. Other crises such as the Mexican peso crisis are also worth noting, as this crisis and the subsequent bail-out loans were a principal element in the rapid depreciation of the dollar in early 1995.

Appropriate Use of 3-D

The use of 3-dimensional diagrams is becoming more frequent, largely because many illustrators and presenters think it makes their diagrams look more polished. Unfortunately, the addition of 3-D can distract the audience from the main points of the presentation. Also, 3-D can distort images. For instance, using 3-D with a pie chart can give the mistaken impression that the pie slices coming out of the page are larger than they really are. This is particularly true if there are many pie slices and the smaller slices are in the background. The only time 3-D is appropriate is when one wishes to graph three different variables with three different axes. For example, instead of a stacked bar chart, one might wish to show an index of protectionism for five different countries in four different time periods. A 3-D diagram would result in 20 different bars pointing out of the page, four rows with five country bars in each row. One caveat to creating such a diagram is that it sometimes requires ordering the dataset carefully so smaller bars are not obscured by much larger ones.

Summary

In summary, before deciding what kind of chart to use for the data at hand, clarify first how many variables there are. Are they continuous or discrete variables? Is a unit of "time" one of the variables? And what is the main objective of the diagram? These questions must be answered before the most effective type of chart can be selected. The following flow chart summarizes most of the choices discussed above.

Figure 10.14

Choosing the Appropriate Data Presentation

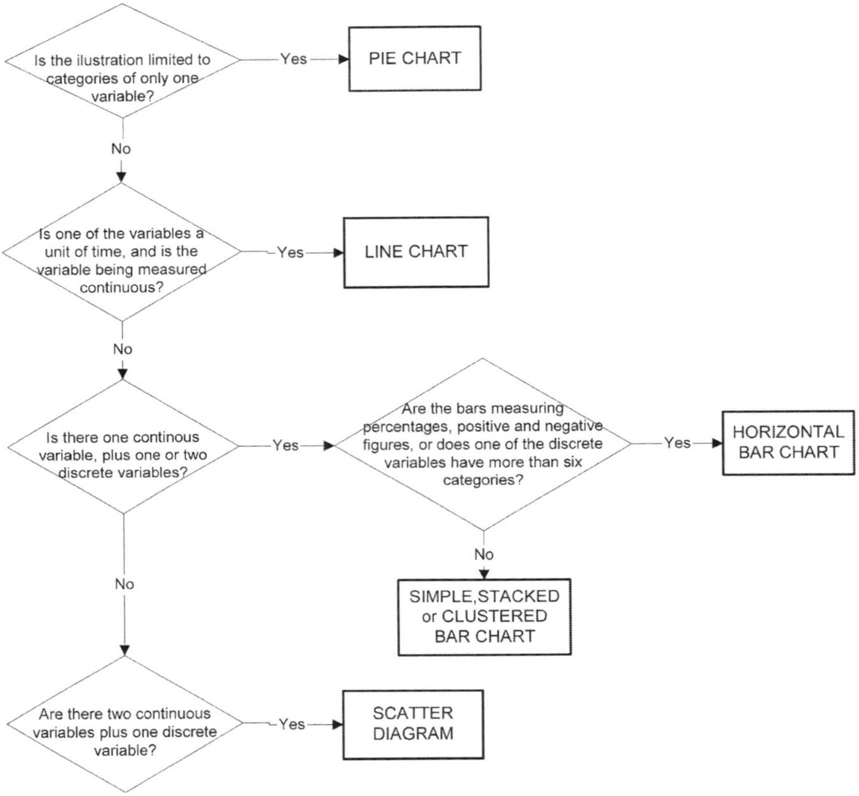

DATA SOURCES FOR TRADE POLICY ANALYSIS

Types of Data

The three types of data you will use most are:

► Trade policy data

► Macroeconomic data

► Microeconomic data

Key issues to consider in choosing data sources are consistency, level of aggregation, timeliness, reliability, and the screening or selection process for data in a source.

Trade Policy Data

Data on a country's trade barriers and policies can be extremely hard to find. The primary sources are GATT/WTO country studies

The advantages of these studies are their similar methodology across countries and the detail and extensive coverage. Disadvantages include their irregular publication (a country may be covered once every three to five years, thus the data you want may be four to six years old), their pro-trade and trade liberalization bias, and that they have been slow to include quantitative measures of the protectionist impact of nontariff barriers (NTBs), much less "domestic" laws and policies relating to government procurement, customs procedures, harmonization of standards, etc. The USTR publishes an annual trade review, covering trade barriers and "unfair" trading practices of key U.S. trading partners. They have been leaders in attempting to quantify the impact of NTBs, but the country coverage is limited. Most times the countries and products selected for attention reflect the specific U.S. commercial and political agenda of the time rather than a comprehensive list of a country's trade barriers. The text of published trade agreements, executive summaries, and new articles can be helpful, but be wary of generalizing from specifics or making specific claims based on generalizations. For instance, the initial ASEAN trade deal covered 40% of all "tariff lines" but barely 10% of regional trade, since most countries concentrated tariff cuts for partner countries on products not actually produced by their regional partners.

Macroeconomic Data

Macroeconomic data is usually easier to find, but still problematic. Definitions, methodologies, and oversight may be different in different countries. Exchange rate variations can make dollar-denominated data do odd things from year to year. Some data sources, such as the Penn World Tables, attempt to convert domestic currency figures to dollars at a hypothetical equilibrium exchange rate (usually based on purchasing power parity) rather than the current market exchange rate. International data sources such as the UN, IMF, WB, etc., have pros and cons. The main advantage is that data collection methods, sectoral definitions, etc., are presumably the same in all countries, with the international organization providing oversight and possibly technical assistance. The problems include the time lag before such data is published and the limited detail and fairly high degree of aggregation, making it less suitable for current policy debates. Examples include:

▶ UN yearbooks of national account statistics, industrial production, trade, etc.

▶ UN agencies such as ILO, FAO, etc., which follow international employment, agricultural production and trade, and other specialized issues.

▶ International Monetary Fund (IMF) data publications such as the International Financial Statistics Yearbook, Government Statistics Yearbook, Direction of Trade Statistics, etc.

National data in the home country language are an important source. The ability to read the language, particularly for laws and legal changes, is critical. The improved timeliness of national data should make it your primary source for bilateral as opposed to multilateral trade deals and disputes. You will need to investigate how the statistical services of the particular country are divided among government agencies; but ministries of trade, industry or commerce, finance, and census are good places to start. For the United States, the Bureau of Economic Analysis (under the U.S. Department of Commerce) is a good one-stop shopping place (for example, see the monthly Survey of Current Business and the annual National Income and Product Accounts). The Bureau of Labor Statistics Monthly Labor Review should be your primary source for national employment trends. Detailed surveys of manufacturing and service industries are published every three to four years. The Census Bureau also publishes data at the level of states, counties, and standard metropolitan statistical areas (SMSAs).

Academic studies can be great sources of data and analysis, but you must remember that the data has been collected, organized, and analyzed from a particular perspective to answer a specific question. If your perspective or purpose differs, the data and analysis may not be useful. Additionally, the process of searching can be tedious and time consuming. The title of a paper may or may not serve as a guide to the data it contains, or even reflect if data is used at all. Become familiar with the types of papers different journals publish, and do not bother with those that are purely theoretical.

As we all know, any Internet search today yields thousands of "hits." NGOs, think tanks, industry organizations, and private individuals place their ideas, numbers, and analysis in the public domain for you. When you use these sources you must try to judge their reliability and identify their "editorial bias." The Economic Policy Institute and the American Enterprise Institute will not agree on either the numbers or the implications of a trade policy initiative. Quoting such a source or using it without attribution will link you to that group in the eyes of the reader.

Final thought: Ask yourself what is the best available data. Ask yourself how much variation there is on a particular estimate. What do you think is the appropriate middle ground?

Microeconomic Data

Microeconomic data on specific industries can usually be found in statistics published by industry associations or industry studies prepared by academic or technical experts in universities, think tanks, and public research institutes such as the International Trade Commission in the United States.

Chapter 11

EFFECTIVE ORAL COMMUNICATIONS

By: Eve Connell, Geza Feketekuty, and Jill Stoffers[43]

C ommercial Diplomacy encompasses the entire analysis, advocacy, and negotiating chain leading to international agreements on trade-related issues. Commercial Diplomacy is all about persuasion, for which presentations play a vital role. The Commercial Diplomat must make effective use of such communicative advocacy tools such as public testimony, speeches, interviews, and debates. Learning to create and present public presentations effectively is critical to the Commercial Diplomat and his/her ability to negotiate effectively.

Public presentation skills are key to success in almost any profession, but particularly in Commercial Diplomacy. Effective communication with professionals in business, law, the media, academia, and politics is expected of the Commercial Diplomat. Public speaking skills are needed not only to make professional presentations at conferences and to the press, but also to build professional networks – another key to success in the business. In their work, Commercial Diplomats face a particular challenge. Much of their communication takes place with people from other cultures with different communication styles and native languages. This underscores the need to develop excellent public speaking skills.

Typical presentations by trade policy professionals require the audience to absorb a great deal of information in a short period of time. These presentations must clearly convey the essential information on complex issues. Working in a highly interdependent arena, Commercial Diplomats are required to clearly explain complicated issues such as:

---

43 The content of this chapter is substantially taken from the original training manual entitled *Public Speaking for the Commercial Diplomat* co-authored by Eve Connell, Jill Stoffers, and Geza Feketekuty, which is available on the ITCD website, but has been further edited for the purposes of this textbook by Geza Feketekuty. The original manual can be found at www.commercialdiplomacy.org.

► Commercial interests at stake,

► Domestic policy issues relevant to trade issues,

► Macro-economic impact of alternative policy options,

► Interests of stakeholders and their political influence,

► Applicable domestic and international legal provisions, and

► Impact of media coverage on public opinion.

The challenge is to convey the essence of the most important factors driving a case while convincing the audience of proposed courses of action. An accomplished professional in Commercial Diplomacy can often exert an influence far beyond his/her policy-making authority. This chapter provides the aspiring Commercial Diplomat with guidelines for making presentations in the field. Early sections cover distinguishing features of public speaking for Commercial Diplomacy and presentation basics. Later sections cover the particular characteristics of public speaking events, contexts, and concerns.

PRESENTATION SKILLS

To deliver a message effectively, the presenter must consider the following six factors, each of which we examine in detail:

► Audience and Context

► Content

► Language and Delivery

► Non-verbal Language

► Technology

Audience and Context

In developing a presentation, the speaker must first consider the audience. In addition to the age, gender, and ethnicity of the intended audience, the speaker should have a feel for its socio-economic and educational status; political party and/or religious affiliation; position on the presented topic; values and beliefs related to the presented subject matter; scope of knowledge; and expectation of the speaker, the topic, and the speaking event itself. An awareness of each of these "personal" factors will affect language, delivery, and content choices a speaker makes when designing a speech for public consumption. These are of particular importance to the Commercial Diplomat who speaks on sensitive topics that may also encompass cross-cultural issues.

The context of the event must be familiar to the speaker as well. Context includes the venue's physical space (e.g., auditorium lay-out, floor plan, podium), equipment usage (e.g., computer for PowerPoint slides, overhead projector, VCR/TV, microphone, lighting), speech format (e.g., individual speech, panel presentation, debate, media/interpreter presence), and timing considerations (e.g., progression of speakers, time limit of speech, time of day).

Whenever possible it is best for the speaker to practice in the event venue. Familiarity with one's surroundings, including equipment, lighting and audience proximity, can only help ease speaker apprehension. If it is not possible to practice in the actual event space, the speaker should simulate the environment as accurately as possible and practice delivering the presentation as he/she would to the audience. A dress rehearsal will enhance any speaker's final performance.

Content

Whether delivering an informal brief or formal, televised public hearing, the presenter typically is given a topic and parameters (theme, time limits, order of presentation, level of formality, etc.) to follow. In some cases the topic is thoroughly outlined. For example, a Commercial Diplomat may be asked to prepare a five-minute summation of committee hearings. Here the focus is narrow. The presentation should be short but hit all the main points of the issue. In another case he/she may be invited to speak to industry association stakeholders. This type of presentation allows the speaker to decide on the content, although there still are parameters of which to make note.

When developing content, carefully consider the following:

► **Who is the audience?** The content must be appropriate for the audience. Always keep in mind the audience's implied question, "What's in it for me?"

► **Discuss what you know.** You have been asked to present because of your expertise or knowledge.

► **Discuss what you find interesting.** The audience will immediately know if you are excited about the subject or not. Your enthusiasm (or lack thereof) will keep or lose the audience's attention.

► **Choose material that is new, noteworthy, or relevant.** This is especially important for "old news" subjects. Make the audience understand that this is not just the same old speech but that you have something new to offer – either in ideas, perspectives, facts, and analyses.

► **Take into account opposing viewpoints and address them in an appropriate way**: Compare and contrast, provide objective evidence to refute, and offer your supporting research or experience if facts are not available to support your views.

► **Refer back to the audience.** Remind them why they should be listening and what they should be taking away.

Opposing Viewpoints

Any prepared speaker will consider opposing viewpoints, especially when discussing sensitive and controversial issues. This consideration not only helps the speaker in the preparatory stages, but also aids a speaker in the question and answer period. Content should be chosen carefully to show that the speaker is an expert on the subject he/she is presenting. Take the following steps to prepare for opposing viewpoints:

► Brainstorm all possible arguments.

► Rank them in order of importance or magnitude.

► Address the major opposition in the body of the speech. Offer examples of why the view is inapplicable, unfounded, or misapplied.

There is usually at least one person who disagrees with all or part of your presentation. Remember to stay calm, present your information in a professional manner, and answer questions in a respectful, appropriate way. Practice answering tough, hard-hitting questions with rebuttals that illustrate your points.

Organization

At most engagements, the speaker is formally introduced. It is the speaker's responsibility to provide appropriate information to the conference organizers and media. A good introduction should include the basics: the speaker's name, title, position, authority on the subject, and the topic of the speech.

The key to a successful message is to organize content in a logical progression. Even the shortest "speech," such as a news brief or debate answer, should have an introductory statement, body, and a conclusion.

Introduction

The introductory section must include at least the following:

► **Grabber or hook.** The grabber or hook is the short opener that makes or breaks a speech. Grabbers can be questions, facts or statistics, a narrative, an introduction of a problem or a current issue. Speakers are encouraged to be creative but not to stray from the focus of the speech. The point is to draw audience members in and hold their attention throughout.

► **Purpose of speech.** The purpose statement comes soon after the grabber. The audience needs to know WHY the speaker is interested in the topic and WHY they should listen (audience members think, "what is in it for me?").

In the purpose statement you tell the audience what to get from the speech. Should they learn something? Should they agree with you at the conclusion? Should they take action?

▶ **Main idea or topic introduction.** The main idea or topic of a speech is WHAT the speaker will address.

▶ **Agenda for what is to come in the presentation.** The agenda is more specifically what will be covered and in what order (e.g. "my three main points today consist of..."). The agenda reveals HOW information will be organized and presented. A clear progression of numbered or lettered subjects and their divisions is very helpful. A solid agenda can smoothly lead both the speaker and audience into the main content section of the speech.

Body

The main content section must include, at a minimum, the following elements:

▶ Body "paragraphs,"

▶ Cohesive devices and transitional links, and

▶ Examples and details.

The body of any successful speech offers a clear progression of topics, with bold opening statements introducing each section. Limit yourself to four to seven main points. The audience will most likely remember only a few.

The points in the body of a speech need to follow the order of the agenda. Each section of the body should have a topic sentence that relates to the overall thesis. All facts, evidence, and details should carefully and clearly support the claims made in the speech. Links between sections must be clear and cohesive; remind the audience what it is you are talking about. For example, instead of saying "My next point is..." use a more content-embedded approach like "The second reason why it is imperative that China's human rights abuses are considered before allowing entry into the WTO is..." Remind the audience what you are discussing.

Conclusion

The concluding section must include, at a minimum, the following elements:

▶ Reiteration of main points and theme,

▶ Relation to current topics of discussion,

▶ Future implications, and

▶ Lead-in to the discussion or question and answer (Q&A) period.

As good speeches begin with an effective grabber or hook, they end by coming full circle. For instance, if you began with a question, quote, or narrative, reiterate its importance to your audience. It adds impact, reminds the audience of your main point, and ties together the entire presentation. Tie in the speech topic to current events, if relevant and appropriate. Give the audience something to "chew on." Most policy-oriented presentations end with recommendations and future projections. Remember to leave your audience with a message that offers lasting impact and naturally leads them into a discussion or question and answer period, if the event calls for such.

Question and Answer

Question and answer (Q&A) sessions can be grueling, entertaining, or both. Be calm, courteous, attentive, and focused on sending the correct information to the audience via this two-way communication process. After the last question and answer exchange, take additional time to sum up main points and ideas. This will ensure that the audience will leave the event with the speaker's words and ideas in mind, not the last question and answer that was discussed. For maximum impact and presence, repeat your theme, summarize the most important findings, and thank your audience for their time and participation.

Language and Delivery

Public speaking is personal. Even in official settings, a speaker's charisma, ethos, and character are revealed. Overall image and style, as much as content, construct a speech that carries weight and conveys professionalism.

A speaker's commitment and interest in a topic will shine through – or not – through language and delivery. Be clear on the kind of impression you hope to make, and try your best to convey this feeling with language, tone, and delivery. The language must be appropriate to the audience. Tone is also important. For example, the tone used when explaining a fait accompli is very different from the tone used when trying to persuade a group to change their opinion and take action. Likewise, the delivery of the presentation helps convey the message. There is a big difference between a conversational and an authoritative tone – the latter is more appropriate when discussing a controversial issue. Observe seasoned speakers to gain a sense of the impact of language, tone, and delivery; there may be some key elements you can make your own.

Language and Audience Attention

The language and delivery style of one's speech can make the difference between retaining and losing the audience's attention. One of the best ways to focus on language and delivery is to videotape speeches – your own and professional speakers – and review these two areas. Self-analysis is one of the most effective tools for marked improvements in presentation style.

Keep the audience engaged by using personal pronouns. Using "we" and "us" instead of "I" and "me" may keep the audience with you. Ask rhetorical or "active" questions. Use narrative to relate shared or familiar experiences. Likewise, carefully use jargon, colloquialisms, and other "non-standard" language. An audience that cannot understand or follow examples will not pay attention.

Thinking Out Loud

Spoken language is vastly different from written discourse. When preparing a presentation, think and speak rather than write speech notes. Jot notes in an outline format noting main points and underlining key words or phrases. If you must write down every word, make sure to practice enough in front of an audience (or into a tape recorder) so that it does not sound "canned." Try to imitate a conversation and get away from a stiff, stilted style. Even though speeches may be carefully planned, written, and read off of a teleprompter, the speaker should never sound like he/she is reading a script.

Vocabulary

Vocabulary choices need to be clear, concise, vivid, concrete and correct, especially in the world of international Commercial Diplomacy. Using correct language is vital to overall comprehension. This is especially true when working with speakers of other languages. A speaker must consider how to best promote imagery in the minds of her audience members - listeners need to see and feel the message. Check the meaning of all key words and be sure to clearly define and to not overuse acronyms and "industry specific" terminology and jargon, especially when working with the media and/or interpreters. It is vital to the integrity of the speech to speak clearly and concisely. Wordiness and convoluted sentences certainly confuse the audience and/or an interpreter. Such miscommunication leads to grave misunderstandings and potentially serious policy implications. Consider how lawyers speak at a deposition; they use strong and precise words, short, hard-hitting sentences and phrases, and vivid imagery. Make every effort to choose and use effective vocabulary.

Voice and Pronunciation: As for vocal quality and features, the professional speaker should be familiar with the following definitions:

- ▶ **Pitch:** vocal placement on a musical scale.

- ▶ **Volume:** voice's projection and loudness.

- ▶ **Rate:** speed of speech.

- ▶ **Vocal variety:** not monotone!

- ▶ **Articulation:** individual speech sounds.

- ▶ **Pronunciation:** saying words correctly.

- ▶ **Enunciation:** contextual articulation and pronunciation of words.

Non-verbal Language

Language choices aside, non-verbal cues add or detract from a presenter and his/her message. Body language, gestures, eye contact, posture, and poise communicate subtleties of a speaker's message. Consider examples of non-verbal behavior that aid in understanding:

- ► Direct eye contact with audience members conveys sincerity that words alone cannot.

- ► Moving out from behind the podium conveys honesty.

- ► Sitting comfortably conveys a sense of being at ease with the audience and the topic of discussion.

- ► Body language and other non-verbal cues add to the message being conveyed.

Unfortunately, these non-verbal components can detract as much as they add. Consider these examples:

- ► Jingling change in your pockets distracts the audience's attention from the message.

- ► Fidgeting conveys nervousness.

- ► Staring down at the podium conveys several messages: nervousness, dishonesty, and unpreparedness.

Paying close attention to these non-verbal cues when practicing a presentation will help you convey your intended message to the audience. Additionally, try to always offer natural facial expressions, gestures, body movements, and direct eye contact with audience members to make everyone feel comfortable. Pauses allow the speaker to collect his/her thoughts and the audience to absorb information. Professional attire should not be overlooked. Dress should never detract from the speaker or his/her message. Try not to completely subdue your personal style, but err on the conservative side by avoiding too much jewelry, loud colors and patterns, and inappropriate styles, especially when the speech is being televised.

There are also certain rules of etiquette in different regions. Eastern and western speakers have different styles. The onus rests on the professional to determine which style or mode of presenting works best for any given audience.

Technology

Professional presentations are enhanced with carefully used audiovisual (AV) equipment. However, simply preparing the content is not enough: Be familiar with all AV equipment before you attempt to use it in a professional, public forum, and always have a "Plan B" (e.g., handouts or backup for a PowerPoint presentation). If something can go wrong, it probably will. Remember that visual aids are effectively used to enhance the message, not to overtake the message; use them sparingly and effectively.

COMMON TYPES OF COMMERCIAL DIPLOMACY PRESENTATIONS

The most common types of speeches and presentations are meant to inform or to persuade – or both. These two main types of public speaking can be packaged differently, depending on the overall goals of the speaker. Negotiations, public hearings, and briefs certainly are more persuasive, while television interviews, panel presentations, and testimony may only serve to inform. Students and practitioners often have the opportunity to give basic informative and/or persuasive speeches; thus, a brief overview of each is covered.

Speeches to Inform

The goal of informative speaking is to impart knowledge. Consider informative speaking as a "teaching event." The audience is present to learn new and interesting information on important and relevant topics. Informative speeches include:

▶ Speeches of **demonstration**, which show an audience how to do something,

▶ Speeches of **description**, which tell an audience about the "physicality" of something, or

▶ Speeches of **explanation**, which introduce a new and often abstract concept.

Informative speeches can be effectively designed in six different ways:

▶ **Categorical** speeches are divided into segments or parts, such as the U.S. taxation system (federal, state, local).

▶ **Spatial** speeches represent topics as they occur in physical space (civic center floor plan).

▶ **Sequential** topics are introduced as a set of guidelines or a procedure to follow (decision-making guidelines within a governmental body).

▶ **Historical** topics are introduced from the earliest date to the most recent (events that led up to the creation of the WTO).

▶ **Comparison** speeches compare something old with something new (diesel fuel cars vs. electric cars).

▶ **Causation** speeches show how one condition generates or is generated by another (acid rain).

Speeches to Persuade

Persuasive speeches are the most lively and emotional speeches. Persuasive speeches are designed three ways:

- The **problem-solution** design is appropriate if an audience does not realize that a problem exists. The speaker introduces the problem and leads the audience to the solution.

- The **statement of reasons** design is best for audiences that agree on the topic and position but need more justification for adopting the intended solution. The speaker introduces the statement and then systematically provides supporting facts.

- The **comparative-advantages** design works best when an audience is unclear about which option to consider. The speaker compares and contrasts two possibilities to lead the audience to the best answer.

Audience considerations and attitude assessment are of utmost importance for the persuasive speech. Audiences may be neutral on the speech subject, opposed, hostile, apathetic, uninformed, informed, or ready to take action. The type of audience the speaker is facing – and the degree of controversy a speech topic may spark – will seriously affect a speaker's language choices, delivery style, and speech structure.

Public Hearings and Testimony

Governments invite public testimony to bring transparency and public participation into decision-making processes. Typically, those who give testimony begin by making a prepared statement (which is usually made available in writing). Subsequently, officials presiding over the meeting ask questions and challenge the positions presented in the statement. Examples of public testimony include:

- In response to allegations of corruption, the International Olympic Committee (IOC) heard public testimony. The testimony helped further the investigation and, importantly, introduced at least an appearance of transparency into the process.

- Regulatory bodies in the United Kingdom use testimony in determining gas taxes.

- When preparing for bilateral or multilateral negotiations, the United States Trade Representative's (USTR) Office invites testimony from interested parties.

Often an invitation is required for testimony; one may not arrive for a hearing or meeting uninvited and expect to testify. However, those wishing to testify may always contact a committee member's office.

Public hearings give committee members an opportunity to question those testifying. The questions are meant to probe and challenge and to draw out the positions of those testifying. In cases where a committee member agrees with the position presented, he/she may ask an "easy" question, or a question that allows the respondent to elaborate further on the benefits of his/her proposal. Conversely, a committee member opposed to a presented view is likely to ask challenging or complex questions that are meant to show weaknesses with the presented position. In cases where a committee member asks a question to which the respondent does not know the answer, it is best to admit it and offer to provide an answer at a later time.

Negotiations

People and agencies negotiate to achieve results they could not achieve on their own. Negotiations range from small, informal discussions to formal, orchestrated meetings, and include everything in between. We negotiate all the time, although we may not call it as such. A discussion among people from the same organization, such as a project team determining how to divide up work, is an example of a small, informal negotiation. A WTO meeting discussing trade and the environment is a large, formal negotiation. No matter what the size or scope, individuals can move toward successful resolution by using positive verbal and non-verbal language.

Approaching an issue from opposing viewpoints is implied at the outset of most negotiations. That said, verbal and non-verbal language assists in bringing parties closer together. Harmonizing verbal language includes:

- Using the term "partner" and "counterpart" instead of "opponent" or "adversary" when referring to negotiation counterparts.

- Asking open-ended questions to draw out the main points of your counterpart.

- Summarizing or restating the main points of agreement or disagreement, so that all parties are clear about what is being negotiated.

- Non-verbal language can also assist in bringing parties closer together: Consider sitting on the same side of the table as your counterparts rather than across from one another.

- Create a calm atmosphere: uncross arms, sit comfortably, and take deep breaths. This will calm you and add a calming presence.

- Show that you are listening: nod your head, make eye contact, take notes, and paraphrase.

The goal of the negotiation is to find a mutually agreeable solution. Verbal and non-verbal language can help set the right tone.

Briefs

Briefs are concise summaries used to inform others of issues or events. They can be used to update readers on current status or to provide background. They can be formal, such as a press secretary giving a brief to a press corps; or they can be informal, such as a junior staff member updating his/her boss on the content of a series of meetings. No matter the level of formality, a brief should include a short but strong introduction with a grabber, topic sentence, and agenda. Keep explanation of points clear and concise. Offer a conclusion with future projections and considerations of issue. Visit http://www.commercialdiplomacy.org/manuals/manual_writing.htm for information and tips for writing and submitting briefs.

COMMERCIAL DIPLOMACY-SPECIFIC ISSUES AND CONSIDERATIONS FOR PRESENTATIONS

Working with the Media

Working with the media can be a stressful experience, especially during times of crisis and when discussing sensitive topics. Some basic guidelines for speaking in front of the camera will aid the Commercial Diplomat during press conferences, interviews, and news briefs. It is important to remain calm (by breathing deeply, slowly, and consistently) and to stay on topic by focusing on the questions being asked. Remember to look directly into a camera and toward an "actual" audience.

Working with Interpreters

Working with interpreters takes some thought and planning.

- ► For information on working with interpreters: http://www.aiic.net/en/tips/conforg/10_golden_rules.htm.

- ► For additional information on conference interpreting guidelines: http://www.aiic.net

- ► For information on how to prepare documents for working with interpreters can be found at: http://www.commercialdiplomacy.org/manuals/manual_writing.htm.

PUBLIC SPEAKING SKILLS – TIPS AND GUIDELINES

Preparation Tips

- ► Conduct preliminary audience analysis.

- ► Investigate context of event.

- ▶ Consider expectations of speaker, event organizer, audience.

- ▶ Practice the presentation in the actual venue. If this is not possible, simulate and improvise!

Content Tips

- ▶ Choose content appropriate and relevant to the event, audience, theme (Why *this* topic for *this* group and event?).

- ▶ Establish professional credibility and authenticity early on in the speech (What is your expertise/authority on the topic?).

- ▶ Make sure main points and themes are limited for more impact and to avoid information overload.

- ▶ Be aware of the viewpoints of others. Address biases and prejudices, if appropriate.

- ▶ Acknowledge all sides of an issue, when appropriate.

Organizational Tips

- ▶ Organize content in a basic, easy to follow structure that includes a solid opening, body, and conclusion.

- ▶ Begin and end every speaking event with impact.

- ▶ Mention key points and main ideas to keep the speech theme consistent throughout the presentation.

- ▶ Use cohesive devices and transitions effectively within the body of a prepared speech. The audience will decide in the first few minutes of the presentation whether to listen to you or not. Catch their attention right away with an effective grabber or hook.

- ▶ Make sure main points are clearly stated at the beginning of the presentation in an agenda or preview.

- ▶ Use facts, figures, statistics and other sources to establish credibility but do not simply overwhelm the audience with a list of numbers. Communicate meaningful, useful, and relevant information.

- ▶ Maintain professionalism throughout the entire presentation. The audience makes judgments on you from the second you stand up until you take your seat after the question and answer period.

- ▶ The question and answer period should enhance the presented information. Announce at the onset that questions will be taken after the presentation.

► Restate questions into the microphone for the audience. Speak directly into the microphone when answering. If a particular question requires a lengthy response, be brief and concise and then offer to talk with that person after the presentation conclusion.

► Announce when the end of the question and answer period will be by stating "one final question."

Question and Answer Tips

► Mention at the start of the speech that the Q&A session will take place at the end of the presentation.

► Repeat the question back to the speaker to give time to consider the answer as well as to let all audience members hear.

► Keep answers clear and concise. Refer back to points made during the presentation.

► If you do not know the answer, try to redirect or redefine the question and discuss a related issue that you do know about. If this does not work, do not fake it. Say you do not know, offer to check into it, and follow up later with the questioner.

► Challenge assumptions made in question-formation.

► Take care with multifaceted questions. Be sure to answer all parts of the question(s).

► Focus on the main points of the presentation whenever possible.

Language and Delivery Tips

► Be clear, concise, and correct with all language usage.

► Consider non-verbal cues (eye contact, body language).

► Observe professional speakers in the field.

► Never read a speech - communicate directly to the audience. When reading, the voice is lost in the podium and eye contact is non-existent. Use notes in an outline form with key words and short phrases.

► Use a conversational quality to convey enthusiasm and spontaneity.

Use voice to underline and highlight main points. In practice, ask: "Is this the voice that I would like to listen to if I were in the audience?" If not, work on changing it through further practice and perhaps by audio taping yourself and playing it back for critique or by modeling your voice after admired speakers.

Technology Tips

► The use of audiovisual equipment is a necessary part of any good, professional presentation.

► Plan in advance (graphics, handouts, music) in order to become familiar with materials. Practice how to use them effectively and make changes if necessary; do not go overboard on graphics. The audiovisual aids are to enhance and support well-founded research.

► When using graphics, make sure that they are easy to read from all seats in the audience. It is best to use bullet points, short phrases, and key words only.

► Use a standard color scheme and format so each slide presented has the same "look." Too many colors, fonts, and images are distracting.

► Be prepared. Know how to use a microphone and the computers before the speech. As the speaker, do not turn and look at the screen. The audience does not wish to see the back of your head, and your voice will be lost behind you.

► Prepare Plan B - Power outages occur. Equipment explodes. Handouts get wet. Materials can be ruined. Always be ready with another way to deliver information effectively and professionally. And, if something does go wrong, remain professional. The audience assesses your credibility from the minute you enter the room until you leave, not solely when you are addressing them directly, from the podium.

Informative Speech Tips

► Be ready to impart knowledge and understanding to the audience.

► Choose an appropriate style and design to effectively organize and present.

► Use lists and numbers to explain factual information in a vivid and digestible manner.

► Offer new perspectives and insights for audience members to consider.

► Engage in lively question and answer or discussion periods.

Persuasive Speech Tips

► Communicate all information in a reliable and responsible manner.

► Establish credibility to speak on the subject early.

- ► Speak with charisma, enthusiasm, and above all conviction.

- ► Consider audience beliefs and values prior to speech construction.

- ► Be aware of audience bias and prejudice on current, controversial issues.

- ► Consider ethical consequences of decision-making.

- ► Choose speech designs appropriate for anticipated audience attitudes.

- ► Anticipate and prepare for opposition.

Working with the Media Tips

- ► Be clear on discussion topic ahead of time by contacting the television or radio station.

- ► Tell your story or somebody else will and not always correctly.

- ► Time is limited; be clear on key points that must be conveyed to the audience – both on and off camera.

- ► Use anecdotes and narrative to stimulate delivery.

- ► Be sure to look directly at the camera – and at the interviewer – for a natural gaze.

- ► Be conservative in dress and style – stick to solid colors. Wear contacts instead of glasses, if possible. If seated during a taped interview, do not cross legs. Sit on the front third of the chair to appear more alert and interested.

- ► Glance at note cards during breaks and commercials – never on camera.

- ► Practice answers to questions ahead of time. Anticipate the tricky questions and be ready with clear, concise, sharp responses (say it all in less than a minute!).

Working with Interpreters Tips

- ► Book interpreters/events in advance.

- ► Brief the interpreter in advance on the conference or event subject.

- ► Brief the interpreter in advance on specific technical terms, especially acronyms and abbreviations.

- ► Fully inform the interpreter in advance of expectations (from additional engagements to actual speech/presentation expectations).

- ► Offer briefings prior to the conference or event.

- ▶ Provide all resources, background information, and related topics.

- ▶ Get to know the interpreter – person, profession, voice, and language style.

- ▶ Keep a steady tempo, pauses and interruptions are uncomfortable.

- ▶ When working with a skilled interpreter, it is not necessary to stick to the manuscript.

- ▶ Do not use an interpreter if he/she is unclear or untrustworthy about confidential information.

- ▶ Employ the best professional as you would an accountant or legal advisor.

SECTION IV

STAKEHOLDERS AND THE TRADE POLICY DEVELOPMENT PROCESS

Chapter 12

UNDERSTANDING THE STAKEHOLDERS AND THEIR ROLE IN THE TRADE POLICY DEVELOPMENT PROCESS

By: Geza Feketekuty and Andrew Procassini[44]

C ommercial Diplomacy involves the application of advocacy tools to influence government policies that affect international commerce. Since government policy is the province of government officials and international commerce is the province of business managers, the dialogue between the two is at the heart of Commercial Diplomacy. Sound management of the relationship between government and business is crucial to good trade policy

In recent years there has been a growing awareness that trade decisions also affect broader interests of society in areas such as health, the environment, and labor standards. This non-economic dimension of trade policy has grown progressively as the trade agenda has expanded from barriers at the border such as tariffs and quotas to domestic regulatory measures such as environmental and health measures. These broader interests of society are often represented by public interest groups, who have increasingly demanded a role in the trade policy decision making process in their own countries, as well as globally. Beyond government and business, Commercial Diplo-

---

44 The content of this chapter is substantially taken from the original training manual entitled *Commercial Diplomacy, the Private Sector and the Public Policy Process – An Interactive Relationship* co-authored by Geza Feketekuty and Andrew Procassini, which is available on the ITCD website, but has been further edited for the purposes of this textbook by Geza Feketekuty. The original manual can be found at www.commercialdiplomacy.org.

macy therefore involves nongovernmental organizations that represent the interests of citizens as workers, as consumers, and as supporters of social objectives such as a clean environment and a safe community.

This chapter focuses on how these three groups in society can manage their relationships with each other as part of the trade policy decision-making process, and how Commercial Diplomats working for any government, business or public interest group can seek to influence the attitudes, objectives and actions of decision-makers in all three sectors, and thereby achieve desired policy outcomes. A key to effective management of the relationships involved is a basic understanding of the different roles, values, motivations, and objectives of actors in each of the three sectors. Effective advocacy has to be based on a sound understanding of potential partners or opponents. Achieving such an understanding is particularly challenging when it involves actors whose role and frame of reference is different than one's own.

There are considerable differences in how countries around the world organize their government, their economic enterprises, and civil society. These differences affect how much independence business and public interest groups have from the government, and conversely how much political influence either business or public interest groups can exert in trade policy decisions. Notwithstanding these differences, there are many similarities in the fundamental roles of business, government, and public interest groups in most countries, regardless of their economic and political organization. This similarity arises from the distinct roles played by each of these three sectors, which defines their basic objectives, motivations, and values.

This chapter is designed to help the aspiring Commercial Diplomat, as well as the practitioner, to understand the underlying relationship between government and business, and more broadly between government and civil society (i.e., all private organizations) in Commercial Diplomacy, and the tools by which these relationships can be managed. To the extent possible, the chapter identifies global best practices that hold true across a wide range of countries, and their distinct political and economic systems and cultures. The discussion of common elements and global best practices is supplemented by brief descriptions of institutional arrangements and practices in the United States, and to a more limited extent in other major countries. Finally, the chapter offers insights into the management of the government/private sector relationship at the global level.

The Role of Government, Business, and Interest Groups

The key to understanding the challenge in managing the relationship between government and business on one hand, and between government and public interest groups on the other hand is a profound appreciation of the differences in the respective roles, objectives, motivations, and values of actors in these three sectors. We will therefore focus initially on the unique mission of each, and how that affects their frame of reference.

Figure 12.1

Political Stakeholder Analysis

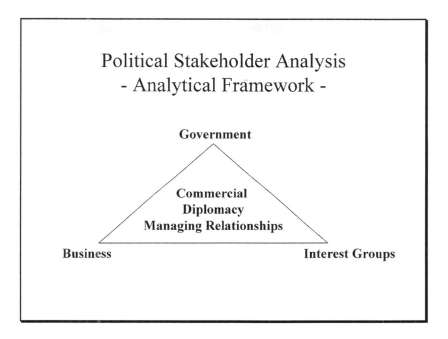

The role of business (i.e. the role of economic enterprises) is to efficiently organize production of goods and services. In free enterprise economies, which in different degrees now encompass most of the world, competition among competing producers is expected to result in the most efficient production of the goods and services consumers wish to purchase. Within this framework, business managers have the responsibility to make decisions on the allocation of scarce resources to the production of goods and services. Free market economies are based on the basic economic principle that competition among enterprises seeking to maximize their own profits will lead to the most economically efficient use of society's resources for producing the goods and services consumers wish to purchase.

In making production decisions, managers are required to obey the laws and regulations of the cities, counties, states, provinces, and countries in which they live. They may also choose to consider ethical aspects of their decisions, over and above the laws they are required to obey. They may do so for moral reasons, or because they believe that basic ethical values will shape the attitudes of employees, customers, the community and government towards the firm. For the same reason firms may choose to make financial contributions to charities or the arts in the communities in which they operate. Often firms are motivated as much as anything by the desire to create good will with the community; local, state, or provincial government; or national government (and in the case of the European Union, the EU Institution). This is considered an investment that can create tangible benefits.

If decisions made by business on economic grounds (i.e., if decisions based on the maximization of profit) result in socially undesirable consequences, it is the responsibility of government to establish laws and regulations that will encourage or mandate socially desirable actions and discourage or prohibit socially undesirable behavior by enterprises. It is thus the responsibility of government to identify public policy goals in areas such as the environment or human health which are impacted by decisions made by enterprises, and to pursue the achievement of such public policy goals through the promulgation and enforcement of appropriate laws and regulations. Similarly it is the responsibility of government to identify public goods such as education, police protection, defense, or medical care for the elderly that society does not wish to allocate on the basis of an ability to pay, and to provide for the production and distribution of these public goods.

Public interest groups help to crystallize public policy goals. They bring together private actors united by a common public policy goal. They give private actors the opportunity to exert a greater collective political influence on the public debate over a particular policy issue than they could achieve by acting individually. Public interest groups thus help to focus public policy issues for public debate and speak on behalf of members who share certain values or policy objectives.

Mission, Objectives, Motivations, and Values

An organization's mission will inevitably influence the objectives, motivations, and values of its staff and of its leaders.

In private market economies, the success of a business is measured in terms of its profits and/or its growth. It follows that the performance of individual business managers is measured in terms of their contribution to profits and/or growth. Business managers will therefore tend to support policies that advance their ability to generate higher profits or growth. It is also inevitable that in such an environment, where success is equated with economic performance, economic criteria will tend to feature prominently in the value system of business managers. (In state-run economies success is measured in terms of achievement of the production targets set by the state, and their managers will tend to support policies that will facilitate and enhance their ability to achieve these targets.)

In the government, success is measured in terms of the successful development, implementation, or enforcement of a government policy or program, all of which requires the consent and cooperation of a large number of officials, legislators, and ultimately voters. In other words, the performance of government leaders is most often measured in terms of success in building a political consensus in support of desirable policy goals. Government leaders will therefore tend to support policy actions that will help them to achieve this goal. It is inevitable that dedication to public policy goals and political skill will feature prominently in the value system of government leaders.

In public interest groups, success is measured in terms of success in focusing public attention on a public policy issue and/or success in achieving a political consensus in support of such a goal. An organization's ability to accomplish these goals is a function of the number of its supporters/members and/or the size of the financial contribution made by its supporters/ members. The performance of public interest advocates therefore is usually measured by the members and money they can attract, which in turn is a function of success in attracting attention to an issue or bringing about desired policy outcomes. Like government officials, public interest advocates live in an environment that values public policy and social goals, and these ideals are likely to feature prominently in their value systems.

Leaders in all institutional settings also have many things in common. They tend to value power, both as measured by the number of people or the amount of money under their stewardship and by the impact of their decisions on society. Bureaucratic turf is a fairly standard measure of status in organizations.

The implication of the link between organizational mission and private motivations and values is that successful advocacy in Commercial Diplomacy depends on a sound understanding of the different missions, objectives, motivations, and values of the different actors. In order to persuade a business leader on a course of action, one needs to emphasize how the desired action will enhance economic opportunities for the enterprise or industry (or minimize the economic losses that are likely to be incurred by the enterprise or industry.) In order to persuade a government leader on a course of action, one needs to emphasize how the desired action will strengthen political support for a policy outcome favored by the leader involved. In order to persuade a public interest advocate on a course of action, it is necessary to emphasize how the desired policy action will lead to increased public awareness and/or support for the desired cause.

The establishment of a good rapport between business and government requires a respect for the distinct roles and responsibilities of enterprise managers, government officials, and public interest advocates. Government officials should expect economic enterprises to make decisions on economic grounds, because only then will the most economically efficient producer prevail in the market place. If decisions based on economic criteria, within the existing legal framework, lead to socially undesirable outcomes, the fault is not with the manager of the enterprise but with the government for failing to develop the right legal framework. By the same token, business leaders should respect the role of government in pursuing social goals that have been delegated to the government. As individual citizens, business leaders have the right to advance their own social preferences, but once society has made a decision through the accepted political process, the principal concern should be the efficient and even-handed implementation of the policy.

There is sometimes a tendency among business professionals to view government officials as bungling bureaucrats and public interest groups as idealists, neither of whom understands hard economic reality. In return, there is a tendency among government officials and public interest advocates to view businessmen as morally deficient profit seekers. These negative stereotypes and attitudes get in the way of a sound understanding of the issues, and of a constructive engagement in the search of solutions that make sense from all three perspectives.

In summary, business, government, and interest groups are necessary for the smooth functioning of society. Both private and public goods and services are necessary for society to function and achieve the well being of its members. All three there-fore often play a role in the trade policy decision-making process, and Commercial Diplomats must be able to understand the contrasting missions, objectives, motiva-tions, and values of leaders in government, business, and interest groups.

The Political Marketplace

By its very nature, policy actions by governments are the result of a political process in which actors in all three spheres of society – business, government and public interest groups – seek to shape the outcome. There is no way other than politics by which the government can make decisions on policy goals and government programs. This is true regardless of the political philosophy and the political organization of a country. Even dictators need bureaucracies to administer the government, and all decisions within such bureaucracies involve politics.

In any political process, all actors impacted by a government decision will seek to influence the outcome through persuasion and the exercise of political influence. Some have likened the process to a political market place, within which advocates for alternative public policy goals and public goods compete for political support among the relevant decision makers. Everyone who wants to influence the outcome of a policy decision or the procurement of a public good has to allocate political capital to that objective, and the government adopts policy goals or public goods that receive the most political capital.

The advocacy tools used by Commercial Diplomats to advance a particular organization or country's interests can be seen as the means for participating in the political market place for policies and programs. This chapter shows how the effective management of the relationships among government, business, and public interest groups can contribute to success in the political market place for government policies and programs.

Commercial Diplomacy and Managing Relationships

Commercial Diplomacy involves the application of the tools of diplomacy to policy issues that affect international trade and investment, or to policy conflicts created by international trade and investment. The tools of Commercial Diplomacy include operational documents such as briefing memos, advocacy letters, policy white papers, press releases, and public testimony. It also includes consultations, negotiations, pub-lic speaking, and oral briefings. Commercial Diplomacy requires analytical skills in economics, politics, law, public policy, and public relations.

Commercial Diplomacy targets all policy measures that affect the flow of goods, services, information, people, and capital across national and regional borders. Policy measures addressed by Commercial Diplomacy include not only measures at the bor-der such as tariffs, quotas and visas, but also internal regulatory measures in policy areas such as labor standards, environmental issues, health and safety matters and competition policy. Today's international conflicts and issues are related to how differ-ent nations view each other's use of subsidies, industrial policies, industry standards, intellectual property practices and laws, and similar issues. These regulatory issues are often deeply embedded in a country's public policy goals in sectors such as telecommunications, transportation, pharmaceuticals, and medical equipment. The modern day treatment of trade policy thus goes far beyond the landing dock for imported goods and well into the heart of the institutional, regulatory machinery of nations.

In today's rapidly converging world economy, Commercial Diplomacy is an activity that is essential to the smooth functioning of economic activity and the resolution of policy conflicts among nations. International trade is well over 40% of the world's gross domestic product, and the sales of the foreign affiliates of corporations have exceeded that of world exports by 90%. In light of this high degree of economic interdependence, policy conflicts could prove highly disruptive. By the same token, achievement of desired public policy goals requires an increasing degree of cooperation on social issues such the environment and health.

Commercial Diplomacy makes an important contribution to continued improvements in international trade, foreign direct investment, and solutions to international non-market conflicts. These improvements are contributing to the achievement of world economic development.

Challenges in Commercial Diplomacy

The Commercial Diplomat must be able to achieve his or her objective, using acquired training and skills, by balancing the interests of all the major parties involved regardless of whether they represent government, business, or interest groups, at home or abroad. Without a balanced solution, no resolution of issues or conflicts can be expected to continue for very long. The primary challenge of the Commercial Diplomat is to succeed by obtaining long-term solutions to complex issues that require dedicated training and specialized skills.

It is clear from Table 12A below, that the knowledge and skills required to manage Commercial Diplomacy must include the economic, political, social, and international aspects of every issue. The Commercial Diplomat must also be able to balance home and host government, and business, and all aspects of related or private sector interest groups.

Summary Points for Commercial Diplomacy Professionals

► In order to manage the relationship between government and the private sector, including both business and public interest groups, Commercial Diplomats must develop a profound understanding of the differences in roles, and the resulting differences in objectives, motivations, and criteria for success.

► Differences in economic and political philosophy, and in the organization of government means that effective management of the relationships among business, government, and public interest groups requires a good understanding of each country's institutions and practices, even though the underlying relationships are fairly similar among countries.

► Effective management of relationships with the other key sectors in society, whether government business or public interest groups are critical to Commercial Diplomacy, which addresses policy decisions that affect international trade and investment. Managing these relationships is an important tool of Commercial Diplomacy.

► Effective management of relationships with the other key sectors in society, whether government business or public interest groups are critical to Commercial Diplomacy, which addresses policy decisions that affect international trade and investment. Managing these relationships is an important tool of Commercial Diplomacy.

UNDERSTANDING GOVERNMENT

Commercial Diplomacy is focused on governmental actions that affect international trade and investment, and it therefore involves governments. Understanding the functions and organization of government is therefore crucial to Commercial Diplomacy, and in particular, to the management of the relationship between government and business, and more broadly the private sector.

Government is responsible for carrying out whatever functions or tasks that society wishes to accomplish that cannot be left to the private market or to voluntary actions by the citizens of a country. Government is thus responsible for establishing the legal framework for economic activity, which defines the economic rights and obligations of businesses and consumers. Government is also responsible for regulating economic activity that potentially has an adverse social impact and for supporting the production of goods and services that create a social benefit beyond the market value (i.e., what individual consumers are willing and able to pay for). Government also serves as a producer of goods and services such as defense, policy protection, and public education, which are best provided by government for equity, efficiency, or social reasons. All of these functions of government potentially affect international trade and investment, and could become the subject of Commercial Diplomacy.

Organization of Government

Government is organized in a hierarchical fashion, with local governments at the bottom, national governments on top, and various intermediate levels of government in between. The allocation of responsibility among the various level of government, and their degree of independence from each other, varies from country to country. Most issues that are the subject of international negotiations on trade and investment are the responsibilities of national governments, and where that is not the case, the national government usually assumes the responsibility of negotiating with foreign governments. While this is usually the case, it is not always the case, and Commercial Diplomats need to identify those situations where that is not the case. Where lower governments have a great deal of independence from the national government, Commercial Diplomats may find it necessary to negotiate directly with officials below the national level.

Most governments are divided into three branches — an executive, a legislative, and a judicial branch. The executive is responsible for administering the government, managing programs, enforcing laws, and providing public goods and services. Managing trade policy is normally a responsibility of the executive branch of government at the national level. The other two branches of government are the legislative branch, which develops the laws, and the judicial branch, which interprets the laws and imposes penalties when laws are violated. In addition to the three branches of government, political parties play an important role in the formulation of laws by the legislature and key policy decisions by the executive branch. Members of political parties and legislatures also frequently use their political influence to intervene in specific decisions by the executive.

The relative weight and independence of the three branches of government and of the political parties varies from country to country, and these differences influence the way policies are developed and decisions are made in individual countries. Commercial Diplomats have the responsibility of familiarizing themselves with these differences.

The executive branch of government is usually divided into distinct departments, ministries, or agencies that have responsibility for different areas of policy concern – trade, finance, defense, foreign affairs, education, agriculture, commerce, etc. Most modern national governments are complex organizations. The development of policies and the administration of programs frequently require the involvement of a number of different departments that are impacted in one way or another by policy decisions. For example, an international trade dispute over sanitary standards in agriculture might involve trade, agriculture, foreign affairs, commerce, and health officials.

Sources of Political Authority

Political authority for governmental or legislative action in democratic societies is vested in the citizens of a jurisdiction, who elect legislators and in some countries, the President of the country. In parliamentary systems, the majority party or a coalition of parties that form a majority will elect a Prime Minister, who is then charged with managing the executive branch. In presidential systems like the United States, the voters elect a President, who is then charged with managing the executive branch. Political authority in non-democratic societies either flows from the leadership of a political party or from an individual with dictatorial powers. Where the authority is vested obviously makes a great deal of difference for Commercial Diplomacy. In order to influence policy decisions that affect trade or investment, the Commercial Diplomat will ultimately need to influence those with the power to determine the outcome.

Understanding Government and Government Officials

Commercial Diplomats who deal with either appointed or elected government officials need to understand the nature and objectives of government, the organizational objectives of the specific institutions these officials serve, and how the governmental role affects the personal goals, motivations, and values of the individuals involved.

The key to understanding government is to recognize that the role of government is to accomplish social objectives that cannot be achieved through economic activity in the market or voluntary actions by individual citizens or groups in civil society. Success in achieving these objectives requires the development of a consensus among a majority of individuals who can influence the adoption and implementation of laws, policies, or government programs. In other words, success in government is measured by success in the political market place. This is true regardless of the political organization of a country. The number of individuals in authoritarian governments is likely to be smaller than in democratic governments, but the principle is the same. Who those individuals are, of course, varies from country to country, and from issue to issue within each country.

The perspective of government officials is also influenced by whether they are elected or appointed, whether they are political appointees or civil servants, the branch of government they serve, and the area of government policy that falls within the organizational mandate of their department, ministry, agency, commission or committee. In the case of all elected officials, reelection to the post in which they serve is an overriding goal. Their actions are therefore heavily influenced by what they think they need to do to obtain the support of a majority of their constituents, and thus get reelected. Elected officials are also individual human beings who seek to obtain status and recognition through important achievements, and in the case of legislators that means being responsible for legislative action on significant laws or programs. Since success in accomplishing specific legislative tasks depends on winning support from fellow legislators, legislators are not only concerned about the views of their constituents, but also about the views of their fellow legislators. Individual legislators also have an interest in protecting the prerogatives of the legislature as an institution. Elected officials who are not legislators, such as governors, must also depend on others to make significant contributions within their area of responsibility, and they must, therefore, be concerned about their relationship with such individuals. This is, of course, why elected heads of government seek to appoint people they trust to key positions in their administration. All elected officials, as well as senior officials appointed to political positions in a government, tend to assign a high value to political skills and to political loyalty from associates and supporters. They spend a considerable effort building personal contacts and relationships, and they tend to view issues in political terms.

The executive branch of government is entrusted with the enforcement of laws, and the development and implementation of policy measures under those laws. The particular goals of the executive branch at any one point in time is set by the political leader in charge of the government, which could be a President, as in the United States, or the Prime Ministers, as is the case in all parliamentary democracies. The political program of the political party he/she represents, in turn, influences the leader's goals. These political programs are made up of a mix of policy objectives such as improved public health or improved access to foreign markets and actions such as the establishment of a public health program or the initiation of trade negotiations to achieve those respective objectives. Senior officials within the executive branch measure their success by their ability to obtain the support of everyone who can influence the development or implementation of policy actions such as the successful negotiation of a trade agreement. The bottom line for most government officials with decision-making powers is consensus in support of a particular policy measure or program. As individuals who dedicate their life to government, most officials, but particularly civil servants, tend to assign a high value to public service and to policy achievements. They tend to view the world from a policy perspective, and to respect public policy achievements.

The Link Between Organizational Responsibilities and Policy Perspectives

Officials from each government department or ministry are likely to approach policy decisions with a unique perspective determined by their role and responsibilities. Whatever differences may exist in political philosophy or organization among countries, officials with similar roles and functions are likely to approach issues from a similar perspective. This similarity in perspectives arises directly from their particular roles. Agriculture officials will be concerned about the impact on agriculture, trade officials about the impact on trade and on trade negotiations, foreign affairs officials about the impact on relationships with other countries, health officials about the impact on public health, and so on.

The Commercial Diplomat must be aware of conflicts within and between all government agencies and officials. If the Department or Ministry of Defense strongly supports a research and development tax credit for industry, the Department of the Treasury or Finance Ministry may oppose it because of an inability to raise a tax from a different source to offset the tax revenue shortfall. Trade officials may support an injunction against the importation of products that violate intellectual property rights, while the Commerce Department or Ministry of Industry will seek a result that still allows importation in order to complete an urgent program. Commercial Diplomats often have to play a facilitating role in resolving such conflicts among different government agencies.

Need to Understand Policy Rationales

Professionals in business organizations and public interest groups who are responsible for managing the relationship with the government need to fully understand the rationale for policy actions. A clear understanding of the rationale can help a Commercial Diplomat to enter into a dialogue with the officials responsible for policy measures that have an adverse impact on trade or investment, but are not explicitly aimed at restricting imports or foreign investments. Knowledge of the rationale enables the Commercial Diplomat to explore alternative ways of achieving the desired social objective.

Policy Instruments

Governments use a variety of policy instruments to accomplish their goals. These include laws, regulations, controls, taxes, tariffs, subsidies, grants, government procurement, and the provision of public goods and services. Each of these instruments can become the subject of Commercial Diplomacy.

Trade Policy

Trade policy is primarily the responsibility of officials within the executive branch of the national government responsible for administering the country's trade laws and negotiating trade agreements with other countries. Trade officials, however, do not have responsibility for all government policy actions that can affect trade. Policy actions by many different departments or ministries of the national government, by local or state/provincial governments can affect international trade and investment opportunities, and thereby become the focus of Commercial Diplomacy. In such cases, national trade officials frequently become intermediaries in the issue. At the same time the legislative branch can affect trade policy through legislation, hearings, and exerting pressure on officials.

Summary Points for Commercial Diplomacy Professionals

► The practice of Commercial Diplomacy requires an understanding of the structure and responsibilities of national government, its departments, and agencies.

► It is of the highest importance that the Commercial Diplomat understands the organizational goals of government departments, branches, and agencies, as well as the individual goals of elected and appointed officials involved in the issues to which he/she is professionally assigned.

► All organizations such as departments, agencies, as well as all officials, elected or appointed, and staff have conflicts. These must be determined and assessed by the Commercial Diplomat.

THE EXECUTIVE BRANCH AS A STAKEHOLDER IN TRADE POLICY

The Executive Branch and the Trade Minister

Here, the role of the executive branch as a stakeholder is examined with respect to the issue of trade and investment. The executive branch generally has a cabinet-level official or Minister responsible for trade. In the United States, the senior trade official is the United States Trade Representative (USTR), who has cabinet rank and who heads an office in the Executive Office of the President. In most countries the officials responsible for trade are located in a ministry with broader responsibilities (e.g., the Ministry of Industry, the Ministry of Foreign Affairs, the Ministry of Economy or the Ministry of Finance). In these countries the Minister for Trade also serves as Minister of Industry, Minister of Foreign Affairs, Minister of Economy, or Minister of Finance.

A junior minister or sub-cabinet official heads the trade office within these ministries. Only a few countries have a separate cabinet-level department of trade, headed by a trade minister, whose exclusive responsibility is trade.

The senior trade official (i.e., the senior most official exclusively responsible for trade matters) is generally responsible for setting and administering overall trade policy, and for representing his/her nation at the WTO, at the OECD when dealing with trade issues, and at all other bilateral and multicultural negotiations involving trade. The senior trade official may also hold positions on the boards of quasi-government organizations related to trade agreements and international financing. *The senior trade official is the prime manager of stakeholder interests with regard to issues involving international trade and investment, and serves as the principal focal point for efforts by other stakeholders to influence trade policy and negotiations.*

The list of stakeholders in the trade policy process can include the following:

► Other members of the executive branch, namely departments of commerce, state, treasury, defense, and others. These departments have interests but also have resources that can be applied to issues.

► Other branches of government including the legislature, the judiciary, sub-national governments, and their staff.

► Independent commissions and agencies such as the Internal Trade Commission, Export-Import Bank, the Overseas Private Investment Corporation, and the Trade and Development Agency in the United States.

► Business firm(s) or industry including all of its stakeholders, namely management, investors, employees, suppliers, and their foreign competitors.

► Nongovernmental organizations such as organizations representing labor, environmental, health, and other social interests.

► Foreign governments and their branches and agencies equivalent to those of the home ministries.

There are other stakeholders, but those named above should be considered the primary stakeholders. The role of the trade minister or senior trade official is to balance the interests of all the stakeholders over the issue life cycle.

Within the executive branch, trade officials are able to obtain a great amount of information related to the responsibilities of other departments and their views on trade issues. The trade policy staff is responsible for understanding the other branches of government and their position with regard to any specific trade issue. It is also the key organization in dealing with business and the issue.

Trade Officials and Business

Most trade issues can be related to a specific industry or business sector. Regardless of whether the domestic business is seeking to eliminate a foreign trade barrier to expand its exports to another market, is accused of dumping, or is seeking a defense against foreign competition, trade officials must understand the industry and its needs. The trade ministry will need the cooperation and collaboration of the industry with whom it is working. Without such an arrangement, the likelihood of winning on a trade issue is very small.

The trade ministry should strive to understand the following about the industry, to the extent feasible:

- ► State of the technology

- ► Product and process

- ► Sales by nation or by region

- ► Costs, fixed and variable

- ► Capital equipment costs

- ► Profits, to revenue and to investment

- ► Market share, totally and by region or country

- ► Pricing, nationally and globally

- ► Degree of local responsiveness

- ► Capacity utilization

- ► Many, many others

The above list is a very short one. Some sets of overall industry statistics provided by associations to their members may include up to 150 industry variables with as many as 50 or more available to the general public. The industry data, in fact, often reflects those items describing the business stakeholders such as number of employees, amount and type of supplies provided, investments made, competitors' ranking, including domestic and foreign, on a global basis.

The mass of information and its interpretation requires a close cooperative attitude between the trade ministry and the industry.

Trade Officials and Domestic Policy Interests

Most international trade and investment issues are inextricably intertwined with various domestic policy issues aimed at a variety of social issues such as health, safety, the environment, human rights, consumer protection, the operation of telecommunication and other networks, financial stability, support of farmers, food security, and so on. A government department or agency responsible for administering government laws and programs in that area represents each of these interests. Increasingly these policy interests are also represented by nongovernmental organizations that espouse the advancement of these goals in public policy. Support for the policy interests involved may also come from legislative committees with jurisdiction for these domestic policy programs, and individual legislators who have become champions of a particular social objective.

It is the responsibility of trade officials to take into account the needs of these policy interest groups at the same time as they are trying to satisfy the needs of the business interests involved. Trade officials must seek to balance the demands of the various groups in accordance with their degree of political influence and their ability to disrupt social consensus in support of a national position. The trade officials should also seek to understand their country's national interests and priorities that are important to the economy (or national security) of any industry. In countries that practice industrial policy, the trade official will often seek to relate trade policy objectives to a national plan.

The issues the trade official must address in this context are too varied to summarize here. In each case, the trade policy official must seek to identify

- ► The social objective at issue,

- ► The means by which the achievement of the social objective can be evaluated,

- ► The effectiveness of the regulation in question to achieve the desired objective, and

- ► Alternative means of accomplishing the same objective, should such alternative means better meet the needs of national trade policy objectives.

Trade Officials and the Issue Life Cycle

While trade officials are engaging the stakeholders, striving to understand their position and negative positions, they must also understand where an issue fits into the issue life cycle. At what stage is the issue? Which organizations are forming? Have customers or suppliers set up organizations and agendas to engage in the conflict?

Most issues go through a set of phases that have come to be called the issue life cycle. Understanding the pattern can substantially enhance the ability of an issue manager in Commercial Diplomacy to influence the evolution of issues that confront them. We will therefore begin by enumerating the stages in an issues life cycle, which are listed below.

Step one, sociopolitical change, is any trend, event, or controversy developing into the domain of public policy. This often originates in the social, political, regulatory, or judicial environments. It is a stage where the sensitivity of the observer to an emerging issue or trend is very important. For example, will the trend toward greater numbers of persons joining environmental groups mean the possibility of stronger environmental laws of enforcement? Should the persons involved begin to determine the size of the problem to arise? At this point, there needs only to be a sense that a new issue or trend is occurring.

At stage two, the observers, whether they be business or government or interest groups, attempt to research and define the problem. Are the members of environmentalist groups and their movements truly increasing? Is there a larger number of actions taking place? Can the problem be defined in terms of public policy? Are the environmental laws adequate? If not, why not? Are their supporters seeking objectives that are at odds with broader public policy concerns and need to be opposed? How should they be opposed? These are but a few of the questions to be answered on the way to stating the issue after defining the problem.

Table 12A

Stages of the Issue Lifecycle	
Stage Number	**Stage**
1	Sociopolitical change – a growing awareness of change.
2	Problem research/definition – the problem and issue become defined.
3	Organizations established – formation of opposing organizations around the issue.
4	Public agenda set – positions and opposition forces are set.
5	Public policy formalized – public policy debate and legislation or interest group actions.
6	Policy enforcement – agency enforcement and regulations or interest group negotiation and protests.
7	Policy challenges and in some instances, depending on a country's legal system and the issues involved, court cases to resolve conflicts.
8	Cycle renewal at end or any point in the cycle – the cycle reviews or can begin again at many points in the cycle.
9	Alternatively, the issue may be resolved, become irrelevant, or be judged unresolvable

Most important is the fact that an "issue" means a matter that is in dispute between two or more parties. This stage is reached when one party begins to assess an issue or trend and begins research to define the issue. *Each party will also begin to define the different parties that will be opposed to each other.*

As the actual and political parties in opposition are determined, their organizations can then be identified or established. Various private and public interest groups will take different sides of the dispute. Government branches and departments may also take positions, sometimes in opposition to each other. Eventually, the organizational lines of the dispute will be drawn and continue until the dispute is resolved.

At stage four, the policy agenda is set, that is, the list of public policies each group is hoping to have adopted. Which policies will each group oppose? What branches of government will be involved and what are their positions? Here in stage four, the policy agenda finally takes definite shape in terms of the lines of debate and who will be engaged in the debaters.

At stage five, the public policy is formalized into law or regulations. If the cycle does not achieve this point, it may die at stage four, or even an earlier stage. There is no assurance that the issues cycle will go completely through every stage.

The new law or regulation that was passed, or the new international trade agreement that was negotiated at stage five, is now enforced at stage six. The enforcement can either be acceptable to all sides or result in further dispute. At this point, appeals to the enforcement become stage seven, a policy challenge. The stage seven policy challenges can take place at the regulatory agency or in the appropriate court. If the new law or international rule is upheld, the cycle is over and another cycle on a different issue occupies the time and efforts of the individual parties. If the law, regulation, or international rule is found to be deficient in some way, the cycle will be renewed.

Knowledge of the issue cycle is important for Commercial Diplomats. It allows them to develop the strategy and tactics for pursuing their objectives effectively.

Trade Officials and Foreign Stakeholders

As government representatives, trade officials hold the unique position of being able to negotiate with a foreign government, which the business firm or industry cannot. These foreign governments constitute, in effect, another group of stakeholders that must be satisfied. Foreign government stakeholders, however, are merely representatives of a complex set of stakeholders in their own country, and in many cases the more effective approach is to reach through the veil of government negotiators and reach out to the key stakeholders in that country through direct contacts. By reaching out to the individual stakeholders in the other country, trade policy officials can expand the range of options for advancing the resolution of an issue subject to international negotiation. Such a strategy also opens up the possibility of direct contacts between other domestic stakeholders and their foreign counterparts as part of a process of developing a consensus in support of possible negotiated outcomes. (In addition, domestic stakeholders – whether firms, trade associations, or unions – are likely to have their own links across the border with their foreign counterparts. These linkages may be useful in increasing understanding and fostering resolution of issues being negotiated.)

Trade Officials and Domestic Stakeholders

While trade officials must seek to balance domestic and foreign stakeholder interests, they cannot lose sight of the fact that their principal responsibility is to represent the interests of domestic stakeholders, and that they cannot succeed ultimately if they cannot maintain the confidence of domestic stakeholders, including business, non-governmental organizations, legislators and other governmental entities. Maintaining close contacts with domestic stakeholders is crucial, and the private sector liaison function is therefore a critical one.

The Private Sector Liaison Functions

In the United States, a senior trade official is assigned the responsibility of maintaining contacts with the private sector and managing the consultation process with these groups. This is not an exclusive role, in as much each trade official responsible for a set of issues has the responsibility of identifying key stakeholders and communicating with these stakeholders. The head of the private sector liaison office, who is an Assistant United States Trade Representative, and the staff members in the private sector liaison office, have a broad responsibility for assuring that the private sector is adequately consulted and keeping track of their views on the principal issues facing U.S. trade policy makers.

Advice for Trade Policy Managers45

In closing, we want to focus on a few points of advice for trade policy managers on managing relationships with the private sector. The first point to remember is the importance of consulting key stakeholders. By consulting, you signal that you consider their views important and that any information they pass on to you at a minimum will be available to decision makers. In effect, by consulting the stakeholders, you make them part of the process.

The second point follows from the first. Convey to the stakeholders a real sense of participation. This can be achieved by (1) telling them that their interests and the information they have conveyed to you will be carefully considered in making any decisions, (2) by giving them information about the needs and views of other stakeholders that will have to be considered in making a final decision, and (3) by pointing out any national interest issues that may be at stake beyond the views of particular stakeholders.

Third, take advantage of opportunities where for exposing stakeholders directly to the views of other stakeholders, not only to corroborate your information about their views and needs, but also to expose them to the strength with which such views may be held and the emotional force behind them.

Fourth, arrange for studies, conferences, or hearings in which the objective facts related to the issue at hand are publicly aired and national interest issues are identified.

Fifth, maintain channels of communication as the issue moves through its various stages.

Sixth, you may want to communicate to stakeholders that their needs are more likely to be satisfied if they become constructive participants in the process than if they choose to oppose any effort to work out a viable solution to the issue.

---

45 NOTE: This description is derived from the situation prevailing in U.S. trade policy formulation, but will have many common elements with many if not most nation's trade policy formulation processes.

There are several reasons for following the practical steps outlined above. Stakeholders are much more likely to accept some kind of compromise if they are convinced that their problem, concern, or interest has been fully factored into a decision, rather than if they are left with the impression that they are not considered important enough to consult and that their problem, concern, or interest is not understood by the decision makers. Having been assured that their views are considered important and understood by decision makers, they are then more willing to accept that the interests and views of other stakeholders must be considered and that they may have to make some sacrifices in the national interest. This is not to say that all stakeholders are likely to be reasonable, but more often than not stakeholders participating in a process are likely to eventually accept an outcome that requires compromises, and perhaps even sacrifices on their part. Moreover, when confronted with the possibility that their interests may be ignored all together if they do not succeed in blocking a consensus may persuade many stakeholders not to take that gamble.

Summary Points for Commercial Diplomacy Professionals

► The focal organization of stakeholders in trade issues is the executive branch and the focal manager in these cases is the senior trade official.

► Trade officials must balance the interests of the executive branch department, other home government branches, the home business/industry, domestic policy interests, the foreign government, and the full range of stakeholders abroad.

► The most important tool of trade officials in seeking a balance of stakeholder interests is to establish a participatory process in which the tradeoffs among stakeholder interests and the national interest become fully transparent.

THE LEGISLATIVE BRANCH – A COMPLEX STAKEHOLDER

The legislative branch plays a key government role in trade and investment issues. The role of the legislature in the trade decision-making process is a subject for another manual. The discussion of the role of the legislature in this section is designed to describe the role of the legislature as an intermediary in the process whereby the government manages its relationship with the private sector and vice versa. (While the discussion in this section is informed by the organization of the government in the United States, many other governments have a strong, independent legislature. In countries where the legislature has far less power, the lessons of this section will be less applicable, although in those countries the ruling party secretariat may play a similar role.)

The key responsibilities of the legislature as they relate to the management of the relationship between government and the private sector are:

- ► Initiating, sponsoring, and passing trade and investment laws.

- ► Conducting hearings and obtaining findings regarding issues through the committee process.

- ► Influencing trade actions or negotiations by the executive branch through personal interventions by legislators.

Of these three functions, the most important with respect to the day- to-day manage-ment of the relationship between government and the private sector is the third, the direct intervention by legislators in issues being considered by trade officials on behalf of domestic business or policy interests. With respect to specific trade issues, indi-vidual members of the legislature, rather than the legislature as a whole, are usually the relevant actors. The members of the legislature may have *an individual interest, a party interest, a branch interest, and/or an electorate interest.* Their individual roles require as clear an understanding as that of the overall legislative body.

Politics and the Legislative Branch

As with the executive branch, the legislature and its members must understand the interests of other stakeholders, and of business and nongovernmental stakeholders particularly. The most important influence on a legislator's position is electoral poli-tics. In assessing an issue, the most important question a legislator may ask is "How will actions regarding the trade issue affect elections?" At the same time most legisla-tors believe they have a responsibility to act in accordance with the national interest and their own beliefs as well as the views of their electorate.

A second important influence can be the personal relationships between legisla-tors. In the past these were close. This is increasingly not the case in the United States and not usual in a parliamentary system.

A third influence is ideology. Many times, the party ideology is the reason for the legislator's position. Legislators frequently develop an ideological position in favor of free market policies that promote trade liberalization or fair trade policies that support greater government intervention.

A fourth influence is issue linkage. A legislator may well be inclined toward a pro-tectionist or free trade stance on a particular issue, but his/her vote may be swayed by advancing another cause of greater importance to the individual legislator, or may be swayed by an appeal from the President, Cabinet Officers, or a party leader.

Legislators and Actions by the Executive Branch

Legislators regularly seek to influence actions by the executive branch in the trade area. They do this individually or in groups that share certain interests. In the United States a group of legislators with a common policy interest may be frequently referred to as a caucus. Legislators seek to influence executive actions where it affects interests of constituents or where it touches on policy issues championed by the legislator. Legislators can exert considerable influence by virtue of their power to shape legislative provisions not only with respect to trade issues, but also with respect to a myriad other issues of interest to the executive branch, including the appropriation of funds for trade activities.[46] Whether the legislators establish an explicit link to such other actions or not, their potential ability to exert influence is often enough to elicit a positive consideration of favorable response to their intervention. Mobilizing legislators to intervene directly with the executive branch is one of the ways in which stakeholders in business or elsewhere can seek to influence actions by the executive branch.

Legislators and Making Laws

Trade issues that can only be resolved through the passage of laws ultimately will require action by the legislature as a body. The process whereby laws are passed is beyond the scope of this section, since the dynamics of the legislative process is a rich field by itself. It is worth noting, however, that one way that legislators can seek to influence executive actions is to propose the passage of a law that would require the executive to act along the lines being proposed by legislative proponents. A common tactic of private sector interests supporting a particular course of action by trade officials is to persuade a sympathetic member of the legislature to propose a law to that effect, and to obtain the support for such action by legislative allies. The credibility of this tactic hinges, of course, on the assessment by the executive branch of the likelihood that such legislation could actually be approved by the legislature as a whole.

Trade Staff

In carrying out both their political and legislative functions, legislators need information, and the most important source of such information is the legislative staff, whether they work for an individual legislator, for a legislative committee or the legislature as a whole. Some staff members are usually given the responsibility of collecting information for legislators on facts, analysis of issues, stakeholder interests and other matters. Staff also often serves as intermediaries with constituents and stakeholders. They are the objective tools that allow the legislators, the regulators, and the business and other interests to understand the issues most clearly. Their efforts are essential in establishing a firm objective foundation for legislative action. The staff of a legislator also plays another important role in helping constituents or stakeholders to understand the perspective the legislator brings to an issue.

Staff members, whether they work for individual legislators or legislative committees, play key roles in the resolution of trade and investment issues. Their role in sharing information on facts, positions, stakeholder interests, and other matters make them indispensable to the legislative process, and any stakeholder strategy needs to include them.

---

46 As relevant votes on trade issues in the United States have become less frequent, other forms of legislative leverage – the Senate's power to confirm Presidential appointments, the holding of public hearings, and occasionally passage of resolutions on particular issues – can be important means of influencing trade policy.

Summary Points for Commercial Diplomacy Professionals

► Legislators should be aware of the interests of stakeholders to the same degree as the executive branches of government, and maybe more so.

► The political influences on legislators must be understood and considered in addressing trade and investment issues under discussion between trade officials and private sector stakeholders.

► The views of legislators are influenced by the views of their constituents and their power in elections.

► The legislators' staff is indispensable to the successful insertion of legislators into the dialogue between the executive branch and the private sector on trade and investment issues.

BUSINESS

A Commercial Diplomat has to understand the role, organization, international strategies, and social function of business enterprises. Commercial Diplomats also need to understand how the economic philosophy of a country, the relevant laws and regulations, the ownership of the enterprise, and the structure of the industry affect the economic incentives of the enterprise and its managers. This chapter is devoted to exploring these issues with a broad brush.

The role of business enterprises is to organize production within the laws and regulations set by government. Regardless of the economic philosophy of a particular country, the production of goods and services is normally assigned to enterprises, which are expected to acquire the necessary inputs, organize production, and distribute the resulting goods and services to consumers, to other enterprises, and to government. Commercial Diplomats can expect the managers of these enterprises to advocate policies that facilitate their acquisition of inputs, their management of the production process, and their distribution of the output.

It is the responsibility of government to establish a legal framework for economic activity that will assure that decisions made by enterprises in their individual best interest are also in the best interest of society. The primary social responsibility of business therefore is to abide by the laws and regulations set by government and within that framework to make the most economically efficient decisions. An individual enterprise may also choose on a voluntary basis to establish higher social responsibilities for itself through codes of ethical conduct and philanthropic contributions to the communities in which it operates.

The country's economic laws, and regulations and the economic philosophy which underlies them, determine the choices available to managers in acquiring inputs, organizing production and distributing outputs, and the criteria by which their performance will be evaluated and rewarded. Thus, a country's laws can determine which outputs a firm may acquire and the prices it can pay for them, which production methods are considered suitable from a social point of view, and to whom and at what prices the goods or services produced by the enterprise can be sold.

The economic goals of an enterprise are determined in part by the ownership and corporate governance of the enterprise, and in part, by the structure of the industry. Enterprises owned by private shareholders are accountable to shareholders, whose objective normally is maximizing return on their investment. The economic objective of such enterprises is therefore primarily profit, or objectives linked to profits such as growth, share price, or market share. State-owned enterprises are accountable to the government in power, which may be interested in achieving a variety of social goals in addition to economic goals such as the production of desired goods and services with budgeted resources and the generation of income.

The remainder of this chapter will be devoted to an analysis of the different components of an enterprise, how the role of these subsidiary business units affects the interests and positions of their managers, and how the enterprise as a whole shapes its position on a particular regulatory issue or on a governmental policy decision that affects the international trade and investment interests of the firm. The chapter also examines the different strategies an enterprise might pursue in extending its operations to other countries, and how such strategies can affect the firm's management of its relationship with the home and foreign governments. Finally, we will explore the strategies a firm can follow to strengthen its support in the communities in which it operates.

Business Functions

In order to accomplish their economic responsibility, business firms perform a number of internal functions. The major functions of a hypothetical firm are production, engineering, marketing, sales, and distribution. Supporting or staff functions include legal, human resources, planning, communications, finance and accounting, government relations, and international operations. The managers of each of these functions within an enterprise have their distinct missions, concerns and criteria for success. A Commercial Diplomat must take account of these distinctions when dealing with the managers of these functions. A Commercial Diplomat also needs to know that every business function generally has a counterpart activity of government that is concerned with each function.

Government agencies and their regulations impact the business firm through their focus on the functions of the firm. For example, the tax authorities focus on the financial and accounting functions of the firm, while labor officials focus on the personnel function.

By understanding the organizational role and function of the managers impacted by policy decisions, the Commercial Diplomat is better able to relate to the business units involved.

Business and Industries

All enterprises are members of at least one industry, though some may span a whole range of industries. Membership in an industry is relevant for Commercial Diplomacy because some government regulations have an industry focus, while other more generic regulations place a heavier burden on some industries than others. Enterprises often form associations to deal with government as an industry. Industry associations are used by enterprises to pursue designated issues of common concern. Such associations, however, should never be seen as representing the full range of interests of the individual enterprises that make up their membership.

Examples of common industry-based regulations include transportation, telecommunications and broadcasting, energy, banking, insurance, medical, and legal services. Other regulations are applied across industries to serve broad social objectives such as public health, the environment, the safety of workers and consumers, the protection of consumer interests, and the functioning of networks. Economy-wide regulations become the focus of industry lobbying where they have a particular impact on a particular industry, as might be the case with respect to the impact of environmental regulations on the chemical industry or the semiconductor industry, the impact of electrical interference standards on the consumer electronics industry, or recycling regulations on the bottling industry. Industries will also lobby individually or with allied interests for tax provisions, health care programs, and other matters of broad application.

Organization of Business Along Geographic and Product Lines

The organization of business enterprises follows both geographic and product responsibilities. How these two forms of organization relate to each other differs from enterprise to enterprise. A Commercial Diplomat needs to be sensitive to the specific geographic or product responsibilities of an individual manager because managers can be expected to be knowledgeable and to speak authoritatively only with respect to regulatory issues that fall within their area of responsibility. Moreover, the interests of the different geographic or product units of an enterprise can vary significantly and can conflict. In the case of a complex enterprise the overall interest of the enterprise is frequently not clear.

In cases where the interests of the constituent units of an enterprise differ or conflict on a particular regulatory issue, general managers of the enterprise and government relations managers must determine how the firm should handle these differences. One strategy they can adopt is to allow the managers of the constituent business units to lobby the government in pursuit of their respective interests, while taking a neutral position at the overall enterprise level. An alternative strategy they can adopt is to establish and pursue an enterprise-wide position on such issues, by weighing the impact on the overall interest of the firm.

Firms with complex and contradictory interests on regulatory issues pose both difficulties and advantages for Commercial Diplomacy. Complex firms pose difficulties for Commercial Diplomacy, because it is difficult to establish the interests and motives of an enterprise with conflicting interests. They provide advantages for Commercial Diplomacy, because it expands the number of avenues for addressing the interests of the firm and persuading such a firm of the desirability of a particular course of action. A Commercial Diplomat who is seeking to convince the enterprise to change its opposition on any one issue, may be able to use the firm's interests in other areas to convince the firm that it is in its overall interest to change its position on the issue in question. Thus, a firm that is facing import competition in bicycles and is seeking to expand exports in motor cycles may find it in its interest to drop its opposition to an expansion of import quotas on bicycles if it will lead to expanded foreign market access for its motor cycles.

Business-government relations for enterprises with international operations are particularly complex because they need to respond to the regulatory requirements of the different governments that have jurisdiction in the countries where the enterprise is active.

International Dimensions of Business

The international dimensions of an enterprise are particularly important for the Commercial Diplomat. Enterprises that seek to acquire cheaper or higher quality inputs from other countries, or to sell the goods and services they produce in other countries, can pursue a number of different modes of entry. A description of each of the entry modes is given in Table 12B. Each mode of entry has its own advantages and disadvantages. It also has its own set of problems with regard to Commercial Diplomacy. Each one, for example, has a different level of market access and also a different level of investment and risk associated with it. The Commercial Diplomat is frequently involved with issues that develop because of the strategic choice made by a home business to pursue a host market by means of one or more of these modes.

Table 12B

Common Modes of Entry to Foreign Markets	
Mode of Entry	**Comments**
Export/Import	The business firm exports its products to agents in a foreign country for sale there. It may also import foreign products for sale at home.
Turnkey Projects	Some business firms specialize in the design, construction, and start-up of turnkey plants. This mode is frequently found in some industries.
Licensing Agreement	A licensing agreement is where the licensor grants the licensee the rights to intangible property for a specified period in return for a royalty. Occurs often in international markets.
Franchising	Franchising involves a long-term commitment involving intangible property and strict rules that the franchisee must agree to do business by.

Joint Ventures	A business firm that is jointly owned by two or more independent firms. A common mode of entering new foreign markets with at least one firm being foreign.
Wholly Owned Subsidiaries	The business firm owns 100% of the foreign subsidiary. It can set up a new operation or purchase an existing one.

The second area of note for the Commercial Diplomat is the *basic international business strategies* employed by businesses that decide to establish an international presence. There are four key strategies—global, international, multi-domestic, and transnational. Each of these strategies responds to different cost pressures and different pressures to respond to local requirements, whether they are private or regulatory. The importance of these strategies to the Commercial Diplomat is that trade and investment disputes are often created around these business strategies of an enterprise or industry.

In any world market where cost pressure on business is high and the local responsiveness is low, the firm would follow a *global* strategy. This is one where the firm may produce in a few countries to get economies of scale, while providing a standard product, with little local modification, to many world markets. If the cost pressures are low, and local responsiveness is also low, the firm follows an *international* strategy. This is one where the core competencies of the firm are transferred to countries where indigenous competitors lack these skills. Differentiated products developed at home are often offered in these markets. The third strategy is where cost pressures are low but the local responsiveness required is high. Here, a *multi-domestic* strategy is followed and the firm extensively customizes its product for each locale it markets in, although costs will vary and it often will have a high cost structure.

Finally, a strategy where both cost and local responsiveness pressures are high is called a *transnational* strategy. Here, the firm considers all world market conditions as so highly competitive that it must pursue rapid cost reductions, high local response, and transfer of core competencies, and therefore "do it all." This is the most difficult strategy, but the most probable in achieving global market success.

Closely related to *modes of entry* and *basic international business strategy* is the *nationality of the enterprise.* The Commercial Diplomat needs to take account of three perspectives with respect to the nationality of an enterprise. The first, is the perceived nationality of a firm from the perspective of the firm itself, the second is the perceived nationality of the firm from the perspective of the customers of the firm, and the third is from the perspective of the governments where the firm is active. Nationality with respect to the perspective of the firm is likely to be determined by the mode of entry and the international business strategy adopted by the firm. Thus, a firm that chooses an export/import strategy is likely to perceive itself, and is likely to be perceived by others, as having the nationality of the country in which its goods and services are produced. On the other hand a firm that chooses to organize its production on a global basis is likely to view itself as either having no nationality or having multiple nationalities by taking on the nationality of each country in which it operates.

A corporation is likely to view itself as having a particular nationality if its board of directors and top management, its strategic manufacturing and R&D organizations, and the largest number of sales and customers are located in the same country. In such cases the firm is also likely to view the same country as the nation of last resort in disputes. On the other hand, a firm that has customers, employees, investors, and subsidiaries in many different countries and has a multinational board of directors and top management team is likely to see itself as having no single nationality. Such a firm may also adopt a world language as its principal mode of internal communication, regardless of its historical roots. ABB, an international firm with Swedish, Swiss and German roots has thus adopted English as its working language, rather than Swedish or German. The Commercial Diplomat has no recourse but to consider in which mode the business firm believes itself to operate and if this is consistent over time regardless of issue.

Whatever the perceived nationality of the firm, governments have their own criteria for determining the nationality of an enterprise. The most common criteria used by governments historically were ownership and the nationality of the top management in the firm. The internationalization of stock ownership and a large rise in international mergers and acquisitions has confused the issue in more recent years. Many governments have therefore moved towards more multidimensional criteria for measuring nationality, such as the nationality of the local management, the number of local employees, and the presence of manufacturing and R&D facilities.

One concluding note is necessary here. The terms "global," "international," "multi-domestic," "multinational corporations," "multinational enterprises," and others are used so often and interchangeably that it is *absolutely essential* to understand the context within which any one of these terms are used. For example, a firm following a global strategy may consider itself as having a nationality, that is, it is a U.S. firm or a Japanese firm or any other. The Commercial Diplomat must understand his/her client and the government position with regard to nationality.

Corporate Governance

As the Constitution and subsequent laws provide the basis of government authority, so does corporate law and commercial practice govern the basis of a business's authority and governance.

One of the most important aspects of corporate law is the specification of corporate governance. A body authorized by law governs all corporations, which in most market economies is designated as the board of directors or the executive board. Every Commercial Diplomat should understand the different laws of governance in individual countries because they affect how an enterprise makes its key decisions.

The Role of Management

One of the most important functions of the board of directors is the selection of the highest level of management, generally the Chief Executive Officer (CEO), or if designated, the Managing Director (MD). Once the CEO has been selected, his/her fundamental responsibility is to establish corporate strategies and management strategies and their relationship to public issues. This is done at four levels—the enterprise level, the corporate level, the business level, and the functional level.

Objectives, Performance, and Rewards

Business is known for applying objectives and goals to its organizations, its management, and its employees. A well-known acronym among business firms is MBO, meaning "Management by Objectives." A business clearly has a more quantitative set of objectives than most other institutions, which are universally applicable to all businesses. These objectives follow the responsibilities of business on a one-to-one basis.

Table 12C

The Key Role of Management		
	Business/Policy Parameter	**Potential Public Policy Illustrative Concerns**
Enterprise Level	What is the role of the organization in society?	• Trade Policy • Environmental Policy
Corporate Level	What businesses are we in and should be in?	• Anti-Trust • Industry Regulatory Agencies
Business Level	How should we compete in a given business or industry?	• Federal Trade Commission • Federal Aviation Commission
Functional Level	Franchising involves a long-term commitment involving intangible property and strict rules that the franchisee must agree to do business by.	

The Responsibilities of Business

The responsibility of business is economic in nature. It is to be profitable in the production and distribution of private goods and services. Beyond this business has a responsibility to abide by the laws and regulations set by the government for economic activity. It is the responsibility of government to establish a legal framework for economic activity that will assure that decisions made by enterprises in their individual best interest are also in the best interest of society.

The primary social responsibility of business, therefore, is to abide by the laws and regulations set by government, and within that framework to make the most economically efficient decisions. Since the success of an enterprise depends on its reputation for good corporate citizenship, the successful enterprise also establishes norms of ethical behavior by its employees that go beyond the letter of the law and engages in philanthropic activities that advance the social interests of the communities in which it does business. Ethical considerations range from norms and morals to standards and expectations. Philanthropic activities strengthen a reputation for good corporate citizenship by contributing to the community and the quality of life. They are, in effect, those things that the public feels is "doing the right thing." It reflects a concern for customers, shareholders, suppliers, and all of the other stakeholders of the firm.

These four goals—make a profit, obey the laws, be ethical, and be a good corporate citizen—are the most that any corporate chief executive officer (CEO) can be expected to pursue. While some may believe that only the first two are responsibilities of enterprises, this section is based on the belief that all four are relevant in the practice of Commercial Diplomacy.

First, there are the *economic objectives* of the business firm. These are generally given as profits and other measures directly related to it. These objectives are: profits on sales, return on investment, market share, portfolio of products, rationalization of production, and market capitalization or share price. The total corporation or sub-units of the corporation may have quantitative objectives, whether domestic or foreign. The organization's objectives become the objectives of its management. Performance is relatively easy to measure over time, and the rewards are generally growth for the organization and the management is income, investment value, and market capitalization.

The corporation may also have a *legal objective,* that is, protection of its intellectual property, its defense in a consumer liability suit, or in an anti-dumping case. The *ethical objectives* relate to those that, although not required by law, are deemed important enough by management to be explicit. These may include, for example, installing the same plant safety features in its foreign plants as at home, although there is no legal requirement to do so abroad. The *philanthropic objectives* may include building community facilities in the foreign countries in which it operates, solely to become a good local citizen. A new public recreational facility for the community that is host to the factory may be such an objective.

In addition to organizational objectives, individuals in a business also have objectives. For example, functional managers may have objectives related to the their particular responsibilities and individual managers and employees within the firm may have personal objectives for achieving salary increases, bonuses, education, specialized training, community services, and many others. These individual objectives and their measure are as often qualitative as quantitative.

Summary Points for Commercial Diplomacy Professionals

▶ The responsibilities, functions, and objectives of business must be familiar to the Commercial Diplomacy professional, if he/she is to totally understand how the issues involved can affect the firm.

► The corresponding governmental activities; that is, agencies and regulators, should be known, and understood if the Commercial Diplomat is to understand their impact on the issue related to the firm.

► The Commercial Diplomacy professional must be aware of the international operations options and strategies of the business firm or industry. Since the international arena is the field of major interest to Commercial Diplomacy professional, it must be understood best of all areas of all corporate functions.

INTEREST GROUPS

Nature of Interest Groups

Interest groups are an essential part of the public policy process. They are organizations formed for the purpose of influencing government, business, and other sectors of civil society. An interest group provides individuals or a group with a means of articulating their interests and holding public officials, chief executive officers, and others accountable for their actions. It is also possible that if interest groups dominate a socio-political system, then public policy will be distorted in favor of the wealthiest, most well organized interest groups.

Interest groups may have economic, political, ideological, public affairs, religious, environmental, or any number of dedicated interests. Because of these varied interests, these groups are said to be the essential element in a pluralistic, democratic society. Furthermore, the place of interest groups in a pluralistic society differs from that in a corporatist society, even though one may believe that the same type of association or coalition exists in both types of society.

Business Interest Groups

Interest groups in the Commercial Diplomacy context are those that represent business's interests. It is important as a Commercial Diplomacy professional to clearly understand the organization of business interest organizations. Although business firms may belong to more than one association, this does not mean that all those to which they belong have the same political position. Multiple memberships in many organizations with different views on the same business issue are not uncommon in the United States. It is rare in countries with a corporatist foundation for their associations. The business interest groups can be divided into at least nine different categories worldwide. Examples of these different types of business interest groups are shown in Table 12D.

Table 12D

Business Interest Association by Type	
Association Type	**Example**
Broad Commercial	*Chamber of Commerce:* Voluntary membership, totally private, thousands of members but not all business. "Issue-by-issue" relationship with government.
Broad Industry	*Association of Manufacturers:* Typically represents large corporations and associations. Relates to government on an issue-by-issue basis.
Broad Industry-Specific	*Electronics Association:* Examples include the American Electronics Association, the Electronics Industry Association of the United States, the Electronics Industry Association of Japan (EIJA), or the ZVEI, the German electrical and electronics industry association. Many types of associations exist for other industries.
Segment-Specific Industry Associations	*Semiconductor Industry Association:* Segment-specific associations are independent of each other and do not have a hierarchical superior.
Research Associations	Research consortia.
Cartels	Cartels are explicitly illegal in the U.S. and their members many be punished by fine, imprisoned, or both. Cartels are legal in some countries.
Export Promotion Associations	Associations legislated to promote exports so as to not violate cartel laws.
Employers' Associations	The role of an employers association differs from country to country. In pluralist economic systems like the U.S. and UK, an employers association may act as an interest or advocacy group that can influence government policy through lobbying. In other countries (social economic systems like Sweden and the Netherlands), employers associations are part of an institutionalized system, whereby the association works together with government and trade unions.

In addition to company membership-type associations, there exist associations of business executives that comprise of CEOs, presidents, and vice presidents of functions. Professional societies of various types whose members often side with industry members are not part of a business interest group.

In general, associations made up of company members are the most active on political issues in a broad political setting, while professional societies are more active among the technical government agencies of the various cabinet departments or ministries.

Other Economic Interest Groups

Unions are the most typical interest group formed to advance the interests of workers in a particular industry or enterprise. Individual unions also frequently organize more all-encompassing labor organizations to represent the interests of their members vis-à-vis regional or national governments. A closely related type of economic organization is a professional association, representing the interests of particular professional practitioners such as doctors, lawyers, engineers, architects, pharmacists, scientists, or teachers. In many countries these professional associations have become quite powerful with respect to laws and regulations affecting their profession. Historically, guilds represented the interests of particular crafts. While some of these guilds survive, their power is much less than what it was in the past. A completely different type of economic association is represented by associations for pensioners or older citizens. As the average age has risen in developed societies, pensioners have increased their share of the voting age population, increasing their political power.

Social Interest Groups

The last few years have seen the rapid growth, in terms of both numbers and influence, of associations supporting a variety of social goals and causes. Such associations are typically made up of individual citizens who wish to advance a particular social goal. The causes supported by such groups include the achievement of better environmental conditions, improvements in public health and public education, consumer protection, nondiscriminatory treatment of minorities or women, developmental goals, right to privacy, transparency, worker rights, fair trade, and the achievement of ethical or religious goals. The creation of the Internet has given such social groups a powerful tool for reaching like-minded citizens over a wide geographic area, to influence voters and thus to impact policy

Social interest groups vary widely in their goals and tactics. While some social interest groups seek to persuade government in advancing their goals, other more radical groups are not willing to compromise and seek to radically restructure government or world organizations. A Commercial Diplomat who needs to address issues advanced by such nongovernmental organizations must determine what the underlying objectives of the organizations are in order to properly address their needs.

Structure of an Association

The typical structure usually includes the board of directors, and a paid executive director or president for administration. The typical functions include one for member recruitment, finance and accounting, communications, and member services such as insurance or retirement advice. A trade association would then have committees of members, with administrative support for areas of interest such as trade, technology, occupational safety and health, industry statistics, and others. Usually, the most important committee in Commercial Diplomacy is the government relations committee, which focuses on public policy and international trade and investment issues. Consequently, the structure is related to the traditional responsibilities and the government relations responsibilities of the specific association.

One example of the structure of a non-business association can be given by the Sierra Club, the oldest environmental interest group in the United States. This organization promotes pro-environmental policies in the public policy arena. By 1990, it had over one-half million members, and member recruitment is the responsibility of its headquarters group based in San Francisco, with a lobbying office in Washington, D.C. The Sierra Club has 15 regional field offices, 57 chapters which are basic member units, and 13 regional conservation committees. It uses a full range of political strategies to pursue its goals of preserving natural forests, national parks, and a broad set of environment issues. It is a politically powerful group.

Examples of key government-related activities of associations include the following:

(1) Performed by most associations:

- ► Inform members of legislative developments

- ► Help members express views to elected officials

- ► Inform members of government agency actions

- ► Testify before legislative committees

- ► Make recommendations on legislation

- ► Provide data to governments

- ► Analyze legislation at conventions

- ► Lobby and inform government of industry views

(2) Performed by some associations:

- ► Report court decisions

- ► Train members to become active in politics

- Collect and distribute funds to candidates

- Arrange plant tours for foreign visitors

- Sponsor courses on political participation

- Assist members with tariff and other trade issues

- Represent industry in tariff negotiations

- Assist government in foreign trade fair participation

Objectives, Performance, and Rewards

Interest group goals and objectives reflect the cause espoused by the group. A union is an association, which espouses employee goals; an environmental group espouses the goals of environmentalists. The objectives reflect the commitment of the group to political activity. Some may have narrowly focused goals, while others perceive themselves as major political participants with interests far beyond the group itself.

In terms of the business-type association, the single-issue coalition is the narrowest in terms of goals and political activity, while the broad commercial-type association such as a Chamber of Commerce has a wider range of goals and scope of political activity. Contrary to the casual assumption of many government officials, the primary purpose of a business association is not to expand the profits of its members; it is to advance the specific policy purpose that member companies have chosen to delegate to the association.

Association managers can increase their resources, and with it their power and salaries, by either expanding the number of members or by persuading existing members to increase their membership fees. The personal objective of association managers, therefore, is to pursue goals that will persuade more individuals or enterprises to join the association, or persuade existing members to increase their contributions. It is important, therefore, for Commercial Diplomats, to determine what strategy an association's current managers are pursuing, what goals underlie such strategies, and how members or potential members are likely to measure their achievement.

Interest Groups and the Management of International Economic Organizations

Increasingly organized interest groups, referred to as nongovernmental organizations (NGO's), have focused their attention on negotiations carried out by governments under the umbrella of international economic organizations such as the World Trade Organization and the World Bank, the administrative decisions made by such organizations, and the operation of panels charged with interpreting the agreements in specific cases. The notion has gained ground that NGO's represent civil society in international proceedings independently of national governments. It is argued that the participation of such groups helps close the democratic deficit inherent in decisions made by such organizations, in as much as such decisions are beyond the direct reach of domestic political activity, which is considered a core requirement of democratic governance.

Summary Points for Commercial Diplomacy Professionals

▶ Interest groups are socio-political entities that represent people with like views.

▶ There are many types of interest groups that could affect policy decisions on trade issues.

▶ There are several types of business groups and each is designed to advance a particular set of interests shared by the enterprises, mangers or business professionals that make up the group. No association represents the full range of interests of its individual members.

▶ Influencing government policy is the major focus of most interest groups, and therefore Commercial Diplomats must be alert to the social policy goals of association with a stake in a particular policy issue. In addition, a Commercial Diplomat must understand the strategies and interests of the managers of such organizations.

Chapter 13

A STAKEHOLDER'S GUIDE TO PROMOTING TRADE POLICY INTERESTS

By: Andrew Procassini and Geza Feketekuty[47]

BUILDING DOMESTIC CONSENSUS

In order to advance the commercial interests of the organizations they represent, Commercial Diplomats must frequently build consensus among diverse stakeholders on a desirable policy measure. Domestically, the challenge for the Commercial Diplomat is to build a consensus among private and government stakeholders who can influence the government's decision. Commercial Diplomats who wish to take the lead in developing the required domestic consensus on an issue can adopt a number of different strategies to pursue their goal. They are:

► Grassroots Campaigns

► Testimony

► Political Entrepreneurship

► Electoral Strategies

► Advisory Panels and Committees

---

47 The content of this chapter is substantially taken from the original training manuals entitled *Managing the Politics of Trade* authored by Geza Feketekuty and *Commercial Diplomacy, the Private Sector and the Public Policy Process – An Interactive Relationship* co-authored by Andrew Procassini and Geza Feketekuty, which are available on the ITCD website, but has been further edited for the purposes of this textbook by Geza Feketekuty. The original manuals can be found at www.commercialdiplomacy.org.

- ▶ Lobbying

- ▶ Coalition-Building and Collective Action

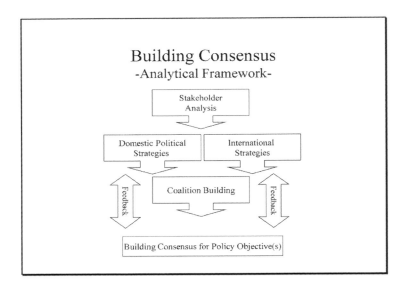

Figure 13.1

Building Consensus

Grassroots Campaigns

An important strategy is the use of a *grassroots campaign.* Grassroots campaigns are based on the connection between constituents and their elected representatives. Many interest groups engage in grassroots political activity in order to show the breadth and strength of their interests in the subject targeted. In recent years, the use of grassroots campaigns has increased enough to cause the number of political consultants who specialize in this approach to also increase. However, with their increased use, legislative leaders may have also become more astute in assessing the degree of impact of these campaigns.

In grassroots campaigns, there are a number of key elements necessary for their success. The first important element is that grassroots campaigns target *individuals.* They may be members of interest groups or other organizations; however, individuals are the objects of attention. The individuals are the *stakeholders* that have an interest in the issue and, therefore, have better knowledge of it than the public in general. Once the grassroots base of individuals is established, the program can then be put into motion.

The first step is planning and budgeting, and this is more important here than in most political approaches. The reason is that to reach thousands of people, the cost of staff, expenses, and communication (i.e., telephone, email, computers, training, conferences, as well as recognition programs and awards) all amount to extensive per-individual responding. The second step is the campaigner's ability for recruitment and motivation of volunteers for the campaign's network. Motivation is obviously tied to the individual's beliefs and his/her intensity. The identification of the individual in great detail, including personal identification, address, local political contacts and activity, legislative district, particular sensitivities to issues, and more, plays an important part in motivating the individual.

Following the planning and individual identification, the next step is to train and provide orientation for the individuals in the network. This step requires the generation of training materials on the issues, the campaign, how to participate, the goals to be attained, and more. Then, the materials are all communicated to the individuals with an appeal for action.

The appeal for action should be specific: who in government is to be contacted, how, where, when, and the position to be expressed. Talking points, various examples of letters, a call for personal experiences to be conveyed, are all part of the final action.

Finally, after the campaign is over, the individual participant must be thanked, informed as to the result, and appealed to for inclusion in the next campaign. The campaign manager must be prepared to maintain the individual as part of a pool of resources for future efforts. Eight essential principles for grassroots campaigns are listed below:

Essential Principles for Grassroots Campaigns[48]

1. Individuals must be motivated and recruited to participate.
2. They must be mobilized and trained in techniques of legislative communication.
3. Communication to participants should be frequent, factual, and objective.
4. Grassroots messages to legislators must reflect their understanding of the issues to be credible.
5. Appeal to action must be specific and clear as to issue messages, action needed, and action targets.
6. Grassroots, political action, and community relations programs should be closely coordinated.
7. Participants need frequent feedback to assure them of the value and effectiveness of their efforts.
8. Participants should be encouraged to provide their own feedback to program managers on responses from legislation.

Testimony

Executives often testify before legislative committees, regulatory agencies, administrative agencies, and courts. Testimony is important, not only because the information affects the decision, but also because it creates a record that serves several purposes. The testimony can provide new information to members of the legislature or other bodies who have not been lobbied, it can be the basis of a position statement to be

---

48 Charles Mack (1997), "Essential Principals," *Politics and the Practice of Government Relations.* Westport, CT: Acorn Books, p. 207. Permission requested.

built upon in future communications, it can be used to support the committee chair, or even be the news story for the morning TV news program. In fact, testimony can be part of a drama that has been totally orchestrated to effect support or opportunities for a specific issue.

Public testimony is an excellent tool for creating public awareness of an issue and getting an issue on the public agenda. Often the major obstacles to building a consensus on an issue are a lack of awareness of the importance of an issue or a lack of information about the costs of failing to adopt a particular policy measure, or the opportunities that might be generated through an international agreement. Public testimony helps to establish the importance of an issue and opens up a number of new channels for disseminating information about the issue. Aside from the public record of the hearing, which can be readily accessed by anyone interested in an issue, hearings are often covered by the newspaper and television. Initial coverage provided by journalists and television reporters present at the event can lead to wider secondary coverage by other journalists and television reporters. The wider the coverage, the more important the issue will appear to key actors in the public policy arena.

In addition to reporters, public hearings are usually also attended by junior staffers of trade associations, NGO's, corporations, and foreign embassies, whose job it is to monitor issues at hearings and to write regular reports to their head offices and memberships on issues that are on the public agenda. These reports in turn become key inputs into the briefing memoranda on current public policy issues prepared for top management and or reporting cables prepared by embassy staffs for their home governments. Anyone who wants to build a consensus for action on an issue, either domestically or internationally, has to pursue the best means of filling communication channels with information about the issue. Public testimony potentially is one of the best means for spreading the message.

Political Entrepreneurship

Political entrepreneurship is the active role by a high-profile individual who may be an organization's CEO or key executive in promoting a public policy issue through lobbying, media interviews, speeches, and participation in public advisory panels. The field of trade and investment has been ripe for political entrepreneurs. In semiconductors, the late Robert Noyce, co-inventor of the integrated circuit and a founder of Intel, became a political entrepreneur by spending virtually all of his time in the 1980s in Washington, primarily for the political solution to trade issues facing the semiconductor industry. The CEOs of MCI, Boeing Beach, American Express, and others during the late 1990s spent an enormous amount of time as political entrepreneurs in Washington pursuing their companies' cases. Increasingly, CEOs in other countries, from the European Community, Australia, Japan, and India, have been taking leadership positions on public policy issues, discussing the issues with key decision makers in their governments and participating in advisory groups. However, political entrepreneurs need not be businessmen. They can be any strong leader who makes the cause his/her own.

Political entrepreneurships can have wider costs and benefits for the CEO and the company. On one hand, political entrepreneurship can raise the stature of the CEO involved, and thus open new doors to business partnerships or favorable regulatory actions by government decision makers. On the other hand, extensive engagement in public policy issues can distract the CEO from the management of the firm or create the impression among shareholders or the Board of Directors that the CEO is not sufficiently focused on running the firm. This is a particular risk if the firm runs into problems or experiences a decline in profits or share price.

Electoral Strategies

Electoral strategies involve providing important electoral resources to candidates for office. Among these resources are endorsements, volunteer workers, and campaign contributions. There are a number of basic reasons for providing campaign contributions. These include an attempt to influence legislative voting, obtain access to officeholders – present or future, and finally to help a legislator with the right ideas to get elected. In many countries, however, it is a criminal offense to give a campaign contribution in return for a commitment by the legislator to vote in favor or against a legislative proposal. In most cases, what a contributor can expect is to obtain access to the legislator and an opportunity to make the case for a particular course of action. In some countries even this kind of lobbying is prohibited, although in most such cases legislators are nevertheless allowed to obtain information from knowledgeable individuals. In fact, even in countries such as the United States where lobbying is not prohibited, the best lobbyists treat their job as one of providing reliable information in a timely manner.

It is not necessarily important to be ideologically aligned with the legislator being financed. It is more important to understand how vital the legislator is to the issues that contributors want to influence and, therefore, to enhance the opportunity to obtain access at a crucial time. For example, the chair of a key committee, regardless of party, would be more likely to receive a contribution than a legislator who may be ideologically aligned but is not on a key committee and further has no interest in the contributor's issues.

The laws and practices related to campaign contributions vary significantly across countries and are one of the most debated aspects of any democracy. Political contributions are continuously under intense legislative debate, and the laws are continuously being modified.

Advisory Panels and Committees

Advisory panels and committees provide benefits to both the government side as well as the private side. For the business firm, participation on a panel provides information about possible decisions a government is about to make and, therefore, can also provide a way to put an issue on the agenda of the government if it is not there already. Furthermore, it raises the public awareness and reputation of the firms involved on the panel. From the standpoint of government agencies, the panel provides the government with expertise that can clarify the consequences of alternative proposal policies. From the government's viewpoint, it also provides a way of building support for its policy objectives. The advisory panel, if utilized properly by the Commercial Diplomat, can be a strong tool toward shaping the eventual legislative policy.

Lobbying

Lobbying is the personal provision of information to government officials including members of the legislature, commissions, staffs, and even the President or other head of government. Lobbying is the process of influencing public policy in much the same way as persuasion and requests or other forms of communication are intended to influence others for whatever reason. Lobbying takes place in all forms of organizations, although the term has primarily been used to describe the private sector's efforts to influence government. However, government agencies and bodies also lobby each other. For example, the executive branch of the government may lobby the legislature and vice versa, or one government agency may lobby another government department. Compared to other forms of influencing government -- such as testimony and advisory panels – lobbying is informal and behind the scenes.

Lobbying practices and laws governing lobbying vary widely among countries. Nevertheless, regardless of cultural, political, legal, and organizational differences among countries, every country has methods whereby stakeholders seek to influence government decision makers. This document is not designed to provide a comprehensive treatment of the specific approaches employed in different countries, but rather some general points that are likely to apply to any effort to influence government.

Reasons for Lobbying

There are many reasons for lobbying, but at the core is the attempt by individuals and organizations to obtain either benefits or relief from government. For instance, the private sector cannot by itself change trade policy. It must depend on government. Those organizations most desirous of change will lobby government for the changes they seek because they have no other recourse. Another reason is to gain an economic advantage or to nullify a sector opponent's gain. Unions will, therefore, lobby to place duties on imports in order to maintain jobs.

Another reason for lobbying is to single out a branch of government that will support a private sector goal that a different branch of government opposes. For example, an environmentalist interest group may seek national government control because local government control is inadequate. A different reason is to create new and different programs. All of these reasons and more can be attributed to the use of lobbying.

Applications

Lobbyists apply their efforts in a number of ways. Three specific applications would include the following. First, the lobbyist will attempt to influence specific legislation in his/her favor, whether it is to have it passed or failed. The lobbyist most often will attempt to modify legislation if a straightforward pass or fail action is not possible.

Another direction that lobbyists often pursue is to affect regulatory activity. The lobbyist may seek to strengthen or weaken a specific regulation or regulatory ruling that is pending. It may be virtually impossible to change a regulatory finding but it may be possible to modify its application to a particular case or set of circumstances.

Another target for lobbying activity is to shape executive branch policies, programs, and budgets. Finally, the lobbyist will also attempt to affect specific decisions regarding governmental appointments, contracts, grants, and other decisions that may have an effect but not as broad as the ones already mentioned. These then are the ways for the lobbyist to satisfy his/her needs to lobby: influencing and affecting legislation, regulation, policies, and personnel and fiscal decisions. In seeking to change a policy, a broad range of outcomes is available to the lobbyist and his/her clients.

Who Lobbies

Lobbying is done both by professionals who specialize in advancing the interests of their clients and by individuals and organizations that are affected by government decisions. The following list of lobbying scenarios provides an insight into the range of lobbyists and their activities.

- ► Legal counsel acting as lobbyists.

- ► Former government officials who have left office and now serve as lobbyists.

- ► Dedicated lobby firms and public affairs firms with lobbying skills.

- ► Government relations managers of organizations, such as business firms, and interest groups.

- ► Senior management of business firms and interest groups.

Personal Traits of Successful Lobbyists

As indicated earlier, lobbying is a face-to-face activity that involves personal persuasion. The personal traits and character of the lobbyist are, therefore, paramount in the qualities of a successful lobbyist. Among the many traits are personal integrity, strong communication and persuasive skills, and the ability to listen. They possess an intimate grasp of formal and informal procedures, political sophistication, intellectual capacity, and strategic skills. A second combination of abilities is as exhaustive, yet different. This list is shown below.

Abilities of a Successful Lobbyist49

- ► Defines the issues in any lobbying visit; determines at the outset what he/she wants.

---

49 Bruce C. Wolpe, Lobbying Congress and How the System Works, Congressional Quarterly. Washington, D.C., pp. 17-40.

- Knows the players.

- Knows the committees.

- Knows what the public rationale is on the issue.

- Prepares materials that are compelling.

- Anticipates the opposition.

- Is solicitous of political allies.

- Understands the process: the rules of procedure and the rules of compromise.

- Becomes cross-partisan eyes and ears.

- Observes the basic courtesies.

Lobbying Guidelines

The most skillful lobbyists and those with the best training do not commit the serious blunders of many neophytes and newcomers who attempt to lobby. A few admonitions are important here to keep in mind.

- **As a lobbyist for business interests, do not use "profits" as a motive for seeking help.** Profits are not easily understood and are among the least acceptable reasons for public policy change. Only a few industries have used profits as an element of argument and only because it was related to research and development expenditures. Pharmaceutical companies have used profits, and where it is possibly justified, the arguments have not always worked very successfully.

- **The lobbyist should always ask for what is desired at the end of a lobbying visit.** He/she never leaves the petitioned in doubt as to what is needed, and the lobbyists should, to the best of his/her ability, obtain a definite response as to whether the request will be granted.

- **Do not ignore precedence.** Precedence often controls process, so attempt to allude to precedence if it will assist the cause.

- **Never fail to tell the truth.** This is the basic criterion of integrity, and an untruth, once discovered, will affect all future statements and relationships.

- **Do not ignore staff.** Do the opposite. Spend as much time as necessary to prepare the staff of a committee or a legislator with the material required to obtain the desired results.

- **Do not spring surprises, especially when there is only one source and it cannot be supported.** Do not overextend the information in order to shock the party into action.

► **Do not discuss policy and political campaigns at the same meeting.** Lobbying for an expected outcome related to a policy affecting a client is not the time to discuss the congressman's reelection campaign, funding, or related subjects.

► **Do not ignore counterarguments to the case you want to make.** Indicate that there are contrary views and arguments and address them head on. Make it clear why you believe those counter arguments do not offset the reasons you have put forward for a particular course of action. Remember those opposed to your desired course of action, and if you do not prepare the person you are lobbying for those arguments, he/she may not know how to respond when those contrary views and arguments are put forward in debate.

Access and Timing

One of the most important advantages a successful lobbyist can have is access to the relevant officials. There are thousands of legislators, staffers, commissions, and others who can affect government policy. Knowing which ones are important for certain issues and, even more importantly, gaining access to them at critical times is highly valuable. At a minimum, the lobbyist must maintain access to a number of legislative committees, members who hold strategic positions such as committee or subcommittee chairs, and members who will work to solicit the support of others. In addition, key executive branch agencies are important. For trade issues, for example, trade officials should be targeted by former officials when access and timing are paramount.

Access should be synchronized to the stages of the legislative process. The timing of lobbying efforts should be in line with the process as it moves from committee staff to committee to floor. It should also be timed to affect those aspects that are still awaiting a decision; that is, on the fence, so to speak. It is here at opportune times that access is often gained by former politicians and government officials on fairly short notice. The access and timing aspects of lobbying are perhaps the most crucial and, therefore, among the greatest value of the best lobbyists.

Allies

One strategy that has great value is for lobbyists to enlist the support of not just a few isolated officials, but of an entire legislative group. The group then has the identity of a *Legislative Support Group* lending great weight to the lobbyist's cause. Support groups have been used widely in the United States on trade issues such as the semiconductor case when the Congressional Support Group for Semiconductors was formed. This group began with ten Senators and ten House members and proceeded to grow over the time the case was active. The use of an allied group of politicians and officials is a powerful representation of the support that an issue has gained.

Coalition Building and Collective Action

From the time a legislator, a government leader, or an interested organization intro-duces the draft of a new law to its final passage, a large number of alternative versions are likely to be considered. Those many alternatives are championed by as many minorities so that rarely is there a clear majority choice. The only means, therefore, by which a law can be passed by a majority is for a number of minorities to form a coalition and take collective action to support a single alternative. The same thing holds true for negotiations among government within international organizations.

At any given time, any number of coalitions may be active on a variety of issues. These coalitions are usually made up of interest groups representing industry asso-ciations, individual corporations, NGOs and other organizations. For example, unions and intellectual property rights groups may come together both separately and jointly in a coalition to have Outer Slobovia rejected for full membership in the World Trade Organization (WTO). Both unions and intellectual property rights groups condemn Outer Slobovia's policies. At the same time, business associations such as the peak association of the Chamber of Commerce and the National Manufacturers Association, each of them separately in favor of Outer Slobovia's acceptance, can also form a joint coalition that issues various public statements in support of Outer Slobovia's member-ship. The idea of coalitions is that they represent a joint point of view, although they may have a very different broad base of other interests. From minorities, a majority is built to support or oppose a policy being considered. The use of a single association as a coalition or a group of associations as an even broader coalition is a powerful political force when their resources and size and range of membership are considered. Although the range of differences within an association is such that not all members would support the same conditions for Outer Slobovia's entry into the WTO, the asso-ciation provides a means for building consensus on a set of conditions that can be used as a policy platform. Consequently, any political arguments are contained and only a unified position is shown.

"Ad Hoc" Coalitions

Hammering out a consensus among all members of an association is not the only means of solving an internal issue with an association. Oftentimes, with the approval of the association, an "ad hoc coalition" will be formed by some members to pursue a particu-lar issue as long as it remains within some pre-agreed guidelines. For example, assume that a group takes the position that intellectual property rights violations should be condemned, but that the condemnation should be mild and not impact entrance by Outer Slobovia into the WTO. This type of "ad hoc coalition" would cease to exist when the near-term decisions have been concluded.

The number of ad hoc coalitions at times increases at a rapid rate. Various groups make up ad hoc or "issue-specific" coalitions and these often break up after the issue is resolved. With the thousands of government relations offices in capitals and the wide range of communication channels available today via the Internet, ad hoc coali-tions can be formed by any type of group, can be effective quickly at low cost, and be terminated just as swiftly.

Coalitions are able to multiply their political forces in play by their combination of resources, but they may also be fragile if strong leadership differences begin to occur while the issues are in play. Organizations, however, that build strong coalitions, tend to be successful overall.

Communication tools that help coalitions maintain discipline and order in joint political operations are joint meetings, conferences, and exchanges of opinions. It also includes written forms of communication, such as white papers or other position papers and also on rare occasion an "amicus brief," where one group supports another to the extent of being a "friend" in court for another group.

Organizing and maintaining a coalition, especially of different interest groups, requires an intensive and focused short-term effort in order to obtain the desired results.

Coalitions: Summary

- ► Majorities are formed by combining minorities through the use of coalitions.

- ► "Ad hoc" or "single issue" coalitions are being more frequently employed today than ever before.

- ► Coalitions are powerful, but require good leadership and an extensive amount of disciplined effort of communication to keep the group together.

- ► Coalitions and collective action are essential for most successful public policy campaigns.

Policy Systems

Since the public policy process encompasses a highly diverse set of stakeholders, it is necessary to build consensus before a collective decision can be made regarding a specific policy or governmental action. This means involving committees or groups, both formally and informally, inside and outside of government. Furthermore, the number of persons that could theoretically be involved can reach well into the thousands. All of this appears to be a daunting set of conditions before collective decisions can be made. However, consensus and collective decisions in the public policy requires no more than 50 to 100 people, and sometimes less than a dozen well-placed people who are positioned to effect a successful outcome in a specific area of policy. *The persons, organizations, and procedures involved in building consensus in any given area of policy are called a policy system.*

There are probably 1000 *policy systems* that are active in the capital of a large country like the United States, although the related numbers of government, business, and interest group individuals could number in the tens of thousands. Also, although there are huge numbers of people affected by collective decisions, there are probably only 50 to 100 people in any of the 1,000 policy systems that will reach consensus and make the collection decision. As an example, in a trade area where expanded foreign market access is sought, the decisions on the U.S. side would involve no more than 100 people in a market access policy system. These 100 people would represent individuals from the USTR, Departments of Commerce and State, the appropriate committee of the House and the Senate, and affected business associations or firms. This relatively small grouping forms the policy system for reaching consensus on the issue. Two types of policy systems will be discussed here – iron triangles and policy networks.

Iron Triangles

When decision-making systems are strong and resistant to outside pressures, they are called iron triangles. An iron triangle can reach consensus and decisions quickly. It consists of a three-way alliance among a set of interest groups, a part of the executive branch, and a group of legislators and politicians. The three sides of the triangle reinforce each other with mutual influence. Iron triangles are common in many countries.

Policy Networks

A less formal policy system for reaching consensus quickly is a policy network. Rather than the triangle as described above, the policy network more closely resembles a net, which reaches out to important stakeholders, opinion leaders, and decision makers. When joined together, the policy network is able to achieve consensus quickly. A policy network generally includes a larger number of individuals with broader influence than the iron triangle. The policy network is less formal than the iron triangle, but both are informal mechanisms.

Leadership

Although iron triangles and policy networks provide a system of consensus, it is important to have a leader on the government side and one on the business community side as the system is operated. In the case of trade issues, a designated member of a trade ministry is usually in the best position to provide leadership for the government, while a designated member of the most affected business entity would be the leader on the business side. This arrangement works well in practice and is in line with either an iron triangle or a policy network system.

Policy Systems: Summary

- ► Policy systems are an essential means of building a strong consensus and reaching collective decisions
- ► Iron triangles and policy networks are the most-often-used systems.
- ► Agency and association leadership is necessary to manage and guide policy systems.

BUILDING INTERNATIONAL CONSENSUS FROM THE PERSPECTIVE OF THE PRIVATE SECTOR

In this section we explore managing the government-private sector interface at the global level, when nations work together in international organizations. Here governments lead the way since only they can represent a nation. No worldwide electronics manufacturing association or association of steel makers or even a true international labor union can represent/commit a nation in a formal agreement. Governments negotiate on behalf of all stakeholders and sectors, and governments alone can commit their countries in international trade and investment agreements. At the same time, building an international consensus among key private stakeholders can provide a powerful push to government negotiations, and private stakeholders who are successful in building global coalitions are often much more successful in achieving their goals than private stakeholders who leave it all to the government.

The work of the Commercial Diplomat in the international government relations role in a multinational or transnational corporation is the most complex and sophisticated one that can be experienced by the professional. One of the challenges faced by the manager of an international government relations group is the need to become acquainted with the stakeholders and their interests in countries around the world, the domestic decision-making process in these countries, and the practices and beliefs in these countries. The international government relations manager must learn to build coalitions with stakeholders abroad to influence their own governments.

At the international organization level, the international government relations managers must become acquainted with the secretariats of the various international organizations and the procedures of these organizations. Another challenge is the need to identify the key stakeholders around the world that are likely to be strategic in influencing the outcomes in multilateral negotiations and assessing their interests, concerns, and ultimately their degree of influence. The task of identifying stakeholders in other countries can be significantly facilitated if the enterprise has subsidiaries in the countries involved in the negotiation of an issue of interest to the corporation.

Major meetings of Ministers or other key negotiators are now frequently the occasion for extensive lobbying by major corporations, industry associations, and NGOs. While private sector representatives usually do not have direct access to the negotiations, they can meet with individual negotiators or groups of negotiators in informal settings and over lunches or dinners. The development of such international coalitions can be significantly enhanced if its members include corporations with a global reach.

Managing the Government Relations Activities of Foreign Subsidiaries

One of the issues an international government relation manager in a multinational corporation must confront is the degree of centralization the corporation should establish among its government relations offices around the world. Should the government relations department of each foreign subsidiary report principally to the head of the national subsidiary, or should such departments report and respond to the head of the government relations department of the parent corporation? To what extent should the firm pursue a coordinated strategy to particular trade and investment issues? The case for a coordinated approach is most persuasive with respect to global or regional negotiations that involve many member governments. A coordinated approach aimed simultaneously at all member governments participating in the negotiations is likely to be more successful than a decentralized approach under which each subsidiary pursues its own interests.

International Issue Coalitions and Associations

In order to influence global outcomes, an approach that can be adopted by the international government relation manager is to form global coalitions with stakeholders abroad with the objective of coordinated lobbying of member governments, their negotiators, and the secretariat staffs that support the negotiations. International issue coalitions can be very effective in achieving a desired outcome in international negotiations, as demonstrated by the intellectual property alliance during the Uruguay Round. The emergence of such global issue coalitions is a direct outgrowth of a growing tendency of corporations and NGOs to extend their lobbying activities beyond their own government to other governments participating in global and regional negotiations and the secretariats of organizations such as the WTO within which such negotiations take place.

The success of international issue coalitions has also lead to the emergence of international industry associations that seek to represent the interests of the industry in global negotiations. An example is the International Pharmaceutical Industry Association headquartered in Geneva, Switzerland, which is also the headquarters of the WTO. The same trend has lead to the emergence of global lobbying firms that devote themselves primarily to the representation of clients in global negotiations.

BUILDING INTERNATIONAL CONSENSUS FROM THE PERSPECTIVE OF THE GOVERNMENT

Coalition building is as central to successful negotiations at the intergovernmental level as it is to efforts by the private sector to build support for a particular policy or governmental action. The chapter on international trade negotiations will go into greater depth into the techniques for building coalitions in international trade negotiations at the government level.

It is worth noting in the context of this chapter that efforts by a government to build support among other governments for a new initiative increasingly has to reach out to private stakeholder groups as well as to the governments. As trade has become more and more important to domestic economic activity, and as trade agreements have increasingly affected domestic regulatory issues, private stakeholder groups have become more active in the trade policy decision-making processes of more and more countries. In other countries where private stakeholders have not become active players on a regular basis, they nevertheless constitute a potential source of influence if mobilized.

SECTION V

EFFECTIVE INTERNATIONAL NEGOTIATIONS

Chapter 14

EFFECTIVE INTERNATIONAL NEGOTIATIONS

By: Geza Feketekuty and William W. Monning[50]

N egotiations lie at the heart of international diplomacy. Parties (governments, businesses, and nongovernmental organizations [NGOs]) employ the art and science of negotiation to protect and advance their organizational and constituent interests. The skillful use of negotiation can advance a party's interests and help to avoid a less attractive alternative (e.g., trade wars, litigation, or protracted dispute settlement procedures under the WTO).

An effective negotiation process can lead to positive outcomes that can result in the promotion of important national objectives including economic development, new business opportunities, and environmental protection. Even for students and practitioners who may not aspire to the role of international trade negotiator, most professionals negotiate frequently in the performance of their jobs. Whether negotiating a raise, a vacation, or a promotion with a supervisor, or negotiating with peers and subordinates over work assignments, deadlines, or workplace conflicts, we negotiate all the time. No training manual can guarantee success in any particular negotiating setting, but everyone can improve their negotiating skills to increase the probability of successful outcomes.

International negotiations in the broad context of trade relations may include negotiations over prices, tariffs, and sales, or qualitative negotiations over broad principles related to the environmental, labor, health and safety, or other impacts of trade-related agreements.

The purpose of this chapter is to provide the reader and the practitioner with the following analytical and practical skills:

---

50 The content of this chapter is substantially taken from the original training manual entitled *International Trade Negotiations: Training Manual,* co-authored by William W. Monning and Geza Feketekuty, which is available on the ITCD website, but has been further edited for the purposes of this textbook by Geza Feketekuty. The original manual can be found at www.commercialdiplomacy.org.

- ▶ Problem identification and development of negotiation goals and strategies,

- ▶ Identification of parties (stakeholders) and their respective interests and priorities, and

- ▶ Development of multiple options (solutions) that will maximize the probability of positive outcomes for all parties to the process.

Development of specific skills in the following areas will also be addressed:

- ▶ Negotiation strategy,

- ▶ Pre-negotiation research and planning,

- ▶ Negotiation skills and techniques to be employed throughout the negotiation process, and

- ▶ Crafting and drafting durable agreements with an emphasis on successful implementation of the agreement.

THE ROLE AND DEVELOPMENT OF NEGOTIATIONS IN COMMERCIAL DIPLOMACY

This chapter addresses the negotiation of policy measures that affect international trade and investment. In the past trade negotiations focused primarily on tariffs, quotas, and other nontariff barriers at the border. In more recent years, negotiations have focused increasingly on domestic regulations in a wide range of policy areas that impact on trade. The reason for this shift is two-fold. First, many of the barriers at the border have been reduced or eliminated through trade negotiation carried out over the past few decades. Second, as a result of the increasing technological complexity of many goods, standards have become far more important. Third, the globalization of production networks and the process of deep integration have created a significant degree of dependence on foreign infrastructure and distribution networks.

The negotiation of trade-related domestic policy issues primarily centers on the reconciliation of trade-based economic objectives and broader public policy objectives such as health, safety, and the social welfare of disadvantaged groups in society. These different interests of society are reconciled through a complex negotiating process that takes place within and between domestic stakeholder groups such as businesses, unions, civic groups and government agencies, and ultimately between national governments. The special character of Commercial Diplomacy is that it encompasses both private stakeholders and governments, that it addresses both private commercial interests and public policy interests, and that the outcome is arbitrated through both economic markets and political markets. Negotiations in Commercial Diplomacy cover business issues, policy issues, broad economic and political issues, as well as legal issues.

Stakeholders in Negotiations

Negotiations in Commercial Diplomacy potentially involve a wide range of stakeholder. These include groups who represent the commercial, policy, political, economic, legal, and institutional/bureaucratic interests affected by trade and investment policy decisions. Each of these groups seeks to influence the policy outcome through negotiations. The most visible negotiations carried out in the trade policy arena are the negotiations between governments, either bilaterally or multilaterally. However, such government-to-government negotiations are preceded by intense negotiations within the individual countries on the country's negotiating position.

Negotiations often start within the individual firms, industry associations, government agencies, legislative committees, and nongovernmental organizations (NGOs) that have a stake, and they are followed by the negotiation and formation of policy-oriented coalitions among stakeholders for the purpose of influencing the policy outcome. The negotiations to form these coalitions can cross national borders and involve business leaders, academics, politicians, bureaucrats, and leaders of civil society from many different countries. Coalitions that cross national borders seek to influence the respective governments in parallel. Private stakeholders, whether acting on their own or as representatives of a coalition, negotiate with the various government agencies and politicians involved in the decision making process. Ultimately these government agencies and politicians negotiate with each other to arrive at a negotiating position for their country. Often these internal negotiations are much tougher and take a lot more time than the more visible government-to-government negotiations.

Each of the stakeholder groups involved in the trade policy advocacy, decision-making, and negotiating process brings their own motivations and interests to bear on the negotiations. As we shall explore more fully later, these interests and motivations are the key to a structured approach to negotiations that has the highest prospects for a satisfactory outcome. The interests and motivations that influence the positions of many stakeholders in the private sector are fairly straightforward and not too difficult to analyze. The interests and motivations of governments are often much more difficult to identify because governments represent all the various interests of society. Nevertheless, there is a great deal of consistency across governments with respect to the principal interests represented by government agencies and departments responsible for particular areas of government policy. The successful negotiator will prepare himself/herself by carefully analyzing the interests and political influence of each of the principal stakeholder groups.

How a Policy Issue Becomes Subject of Inter-governmental Negotiations

Most negotiations in Commercial Diplomacy are over the impact of specific policy measures on particular products or industries. The negotiation of such trade or investment-related policy issues typically starts as a negotiation between an affected enterprise or industry and the government responsible for the targeted policy measure. If the issue is not resolved at that level, the home government of the affected enterprise or industry may step into the dispute by initiating government-to-government negotiations. These types of negotiations usually go through a number of different phases that call for different negotiating attitudes and tactics.

Press reports often focus on high profile negotiations aimed at global or regional reductions in trade barriers or the resolution of highly charged trade disputes between governments. Most of the work of trade negotiators is focused on more mundane trade-related policy issues that concern particular firms or industries. A considerable amount of time of every trade official is taken up in addressing specific problems that arise from the application of domestic regulatory measures to internationally traded goods and services. Such problems can come to the attention of a trade negotiator as an affected entrepreneur raises the issue with the official responsible for a particular area of trade or trade with a particular country. Alternatively, the entrepreneur may first raise the issue with intermediaries such as legislators, party officials, or trade lawyers. If the trade negotiator is persuaded that the problem constitutes a legitimate trade issue, it may be added to the agenda of bilateral issues with the country concerned.

Initial consultations with officials of the other country may reveal that the problem is not really a problem. The perceived problem may be the result of poor communications between the foreign entrepreneur and domestic regulatory officials, or that the adverse trade impact is an unavoidable consequence of a legitimate regulatory action. Alternatively, initial consultations may reveal that the problem is a genuine trade barrier (i.e., that the measure was intended to restrain trade), or if the adverse trade effect was unintended, that the adverse trade effects could be reduced or eliminated through the adoption of alternative, less trade-distorting, policy tools.

The Negotiating Life Cycle of an Issue – How an Issue Evolves from Informal Consultations to Formal Global Negotiations

An enterprise that faces a particular regulatory barrier should ideally first seek to deal with the issue directly through consultations with the responsible officials in the host government. Such contacts will enable the enterprise managers and officials most directly involved in the issue to sort out how the existing regulations should apply to the specific facts in the case. It will also enable host country regulators to take into account any special factors that may need to be considered in the trade or investment proposal. In many cases the issue identified by an enterprise is created by a misunderstanding of the regulations by the exporter or investor or a misunderstanding of the specific facts related to the proposed export or investment. In other cases, the regulator may be able to make adjustments in how the regulation is applied to unique circumstances without sacrificing the regulatory objective.

A clear understanding of the regulatory issues will also better equip the prospective exporter or investor to communicate the nature of the issue clearly to the officials of the home government, if their intervention proves necessary. The willingness of an enterprise to expend the resources necessary to conduct such direct consultations is also usually a good test to the officials from whom they may seek help of how important the issue is to the enterprise. Small exporters, particularly small exporters in developing countries, may not have the resources to consult with the responsible officials in the importing country on a face-to-face basis. They could accomplish the same thing by contacting the officials involved through the mail or the Internet or by visiting the economic/commercial section of the nearest embassy or consulate of the host country.

The first contact is usually best approached as an informal information-gathering effort. After all, the enterprise managers may be ill-informed about the specific regulations or laws at issue or the administrative guidelines followed by the responsible officials. Conversely, the officials involved may lack adequate information about the production methods or business practices covered by the regulations.

The second step in the process, if direct consultations with the host government fail to resolve the issue, is to consult with the commercial/economic officers in the home country's embassy in the host country. The embassy may well be able to shed additional light on the issue or to intervene on behalf of the enterprise with host country officials. The embassy can also help alert officials in the home government with a potential stake in the issue through their regular reports to the home government. A wide range of officials in the home government eagerly read embassy reports on the problems faced by a country's exporters and investors in other countries. While embassy reporting cannot be a substitute for direct consultations with trade officials in the home country, it will facilitate the exporter or investor's task of briefing home government officials and of persuading to add the issue to their agenda.

At the third stage of the process the affected enterprise seeks to enlist officials in its home government in an advocacy effort. Trade and other officials at various levels of the hierarchy meet regularly with their counterpart(s) in other countries to discuss issues of common concern and mutual trade and investment problems. In this third phase of the process an issue can move step by step to more senior levels, starting with the desk officers responsible for trade and investment issues with a particular country and ending (for the most important issues) with the ministers or even heads of government. At some point during this process the nature of the discussions on the issue may move from an informal consultation process between specific officials to a formal country-to-country negotiating process. Efforts to resolve issues during this phase of bilateral consultations and negotiations is motivated by an implicit reciprocity – you help me solve one of my problems and I help you solve one of your problems.

Aside from the mutual back-scratching aspect of the bilateral consultation and negotiation process, the bilateral advocacy process enables officials from the two countries to weigh the trade effects of the measure, to explore the regulatory objectives served by the measure, and the potential for achieving the same regulatory objective through alternative, less trade-distorting measures. It also enables the two governments to test each other's perceptions regarding the applicability of various provisions and national commitments in international trade and investment agreements as well as the likelihood that one country or the other would lose a case submitted to dispute settlement. While even the best arguments put forward during such discussions may not be able to overcome strong political resistance, in a large number of cases these kinds of discussions do lead to mutually acceptable outcomes.

Problems that cannot be resolved through a mutual back-scratching process are then often incorporated in broader, formal negotiations such as multilateral trade negotiating rounds in the WTO or regional/bilateral free trade area negotiations. Such broader negotiating venues not only widen the potential for trade-offs among issues of interest to host countries, but it also makes it possible to negotiate rules for repetitive problems or to bring other countries into any effort to address the issue through a dispute settlement process.

An orderly sequential process for addressing specific trade issues, from direct contacts between the enterprises and the host government to bilateral negotiations and ultimately multilateral negotiations or dispute settlement, provides for the most efficient means for addressing trade-negotiating issues. The sequential process serves as a filtering device. Issues that are less difficult and less important are dealt with at a junior level of the government, while more senior officials or political leaders address the more intractable issues that raise difficult political or legal problems. Naturally, only the most important issues – those that are of major commercial or policy signifi-cance – make it to the higher levels of government.

One obvious point is worth making. Countries become engaged in negotiations on trade either because they would like to address a barrier to their exports of serv-ices in another country, or because another country seeks to engage the importing or host country in a negotiation over barriers to entry. As pointed out above, normally both countries engaged in a two-way trade relationship have trade or investment policy-related issues they would like to address with each other. Where that is not the case, and the issues being raised by the exporting country are not covered by commit-ments an importing country has made in a trade agreement, the importing country can simply refuse to negotiate. Current practice gives sovereign countries considerable leeway to agree or disagree on a trade matter on which it has not made a commitment. It is equally true that some importing countries in this kind of a situation may have nontrade reasons to engage in negotiations on trade issues raised by another country.

Problem-solving Phase of Bilateral Negotiations

Once the facts have been clarified, and a policy issue has been identified, the negotia-tion should move into a problem-solving phase.

A problem-solving approach, which suspends value judgments about who is right or wrong, encourages flexibility by the negotiating partners, maximizing the chances that an amicable resolution can be found that simultaneously preserves the policy objectives of the government and the commercial objectives of the enterprises involved in the negotiation. The best tactics to use in this type of a "win-win negotia-tion" will be explored later. Of course, some policy issues raised by exporters or inves-tors are without merit, while other policy actions taken by governments are not very defensible. In these situations, sometimes the best resolution is a graceful withdrawal before issues of face and prestige make such a withdrawal difficult.

If efforts to resolve the issue through a problem-solving approach fail, the nego-tiations may move into a third, more formal stage of negotiation during which the negotiators may increase the political and legal pressure on the other side. There is an increased risk at this stage that the negotiation may turn into a zero-sum game type of negotiation, in which one side or the other has to lose in order to secure a resolution of the issue. As we shall see later, zero-sum type negotiations are more difficult to conclude, and a successful negotiator will keep emphasizing the potential for a win-win outcome.

A negotiation that remains deadlocked may be referred to in a dispute settlement process. Many trade and investment agreements identify a process for settling disputes that cannot be resolved through negotiations. Some forms of dispute settlement, such as arbitration and mediation, are a structured and assisted form of negotiation.

Bilateral problem-solving negotiations go through several phases:

- ► In the first phase, the initial information-sharing stage, the parties seek to determine if there is a problem, where there is a genuine problem, the specific measure that is causing the problem, the policy objectives served by the measure, and the commercial problem created by the measure.

- ► In the second phase, the problem-solving stage, the negotiators seek to determine if there is a win-win solution that would reduce or eliminate the trade problem without compromising the policy objectives served by the measure. Ideally, less trade-distorting policy measures are available that can be substituted for the more trade-distorting measures, without compromising the desired policy outcome.

- ► In the third phase, the hard-nosed negotiating phase, the parties explore the positive outcomes that could be derived from solving the problem on one hand, and the negative consequences of not solving the problem. Positive outcomes could include an improved relationship between the two countries and the resolution of other issues where the importing country needs the help of trade officials in the exporting country (you help me and I help you). Negative outcomes could include a worsening of trade relationships, a negative impact on efforts to resolve other issues of particular interest to the importing country, and submission of the issue to a dispute settlement panel in the WTO if the complaining country believes it has a strong legal case under WTO rules.

- ► In the fourth phase, the dispute resolution phase, the parties submit their dispute to a dispute settlement process.

- ► In a fifth phase, the implementation phase, the parties may need to discuss the implementation of a solution or the fallout from a failure to solve the problem.

Many issues get resolved at the first stage, others at the second or third stage. Only a small percentage of cases go to actual dispute settlement, and only a fraction of those end up with some form of retaliation. The bulk of the issues are resolved because countries realize this is a two-way street, and in many cases both sides can gain – the exporting country with more exports, and the importing country with more imports of needed goods and services and better regulations.

The nature of the negotiating process and the negotiating tactics change as you move from the first to the last phase. At the beginning of the process, the emphasis is on win-win solutions. When you are seeking to obtain information from counterpart negotiators or to obtain their help in solving the problem, it would obviously be a mistake to approach them in a confrontational or hard-nosed way. As the negotiations move to hard bargaining and dispute settlement, the negotiations take on more of a zero-sum mentality. As we argue elsewhere, however, in most situations it pays to preserve a win-win mentality as long as possible, even as the negotiating process leads to hard-nosed bargaining and dispute settlement. After all, in many, if not in most cases, failure to resolve the issue is not the result of ill will by the trade officials on the other side, but rather the result of real difficulties in solving the many political, legal, policy, and public opinion issues that may stand in the way. By communicating to your counterpart negotiators that you understand their difficulties and that you and they face the same common challenge of finding a solution that meets the needs of both sides, you increase the chances that they will work with you rather than against you.

No matter how easy the solution to a problem appears, it is useful to remember that all *negotiated outcomes involve a cost.* Even if the solution is obvious and does not involve major difficulties to implement, the trade negotiator has to take the time to explain the problem to colleagues, superiors, regulatory officials responsible for administering the disputed regulation, and private stakeholders. Your counterpart(s) may have to ask for their support in solving the problem, thus incurring a reciprocal obligation to such stakeholders to help them solve one of their problems in the future. In other words, by proactively pushing for a solution, your counterpart(s) are likely to incur political costs. The more difficult the issue is to resolve, the higher the political costs incurred. As the political costs rise for the other side, so does the political cost for the complaining country.

One consequence of the escalation of political costs is that the issue is pushed to more senior officials in both governments, ultimately to cabinet ministers and heads of government. At each step of the way, the complaining country must consider whether the expected benefits from solving the issue warrant the increased human resource and political costs it will incur – costs in terms of the scarce time of the officials concerned, the expectation of reciprocal favors by the other government, or negative fallout for other issues being negotiated by the two governments. Obviously, only the most important issues survive this test.

Bilateral Negotiations Aimed at Mutual Reductions in Trade Barriers

In contrast to problem-solving negotiations, negotiations aimed at the mutual reduction of trade barriers between two countries usually cover a wide range of products and industries. Moreover, unlike the problem-solving negotiations that usually take place in response to a complaint brought by an enterprise seeking to export its goods or to invest abroad, negotiations between countries aimed at the mutual reduction of trade barriers are usually initiated by the governments involved. The two governments thus recognize from the outset their mutual interest in reciprocal reductions in trade barriers. One example is a bilateral free trade negotiation. Another example is a bilateral negotiation carried out between members of the WTO in the context of multilateral trade negotiations.

Bilateral negotiations aimed at the mutual reduction of trade barriers take place in an overall win-win framework, but they inevitably involve gains for some domestic stakeholders such as exporters or domestic consumers of imported products, and losses for other stakeholders such as domestic producers of competitive products in each country. Negotiators on both sides are expected to maximize the gains and to minimize the losses for their side. While economists would argue that both sides gain, whatever the impact on winners and losers in each country, the political economic reality is that losers are often in a position to block outcomes that do not take into account their interests. While winners can always trump losers where the potential gains are large enough, it is useful in a democratic society to persuade losers that the outcome is just. This usually means accommodating them in some way, while persuading them that a successful negotiating outcome is in the interests of the country as a whole. A good negotiator is able to gain their support through a combination of offers and threats – an offer to make less of a cut in the trade barrier than might be possible if they acquiesce and a threat to ignore their interests if they chose to oppose the agreement actively.

Negotiations over the mutual reduction of trade barriers thus always involve hard bargaining, *both at home and internationally.* In light of the stakes for winners and losers, they inevitably take on a zero-sum mentality. Negotiators in such situations must always remind themselves that the desired outcome is a win-win solution for the country as a whole, consistent with an acceptable distribution of gains and losses among stakeholders. The challenge of the negotiator is to achieve such an outcome for both sides, since both sides have to be satisfied with the outcome. The role of the negotiator is to let the other side know what is required to achieve a successful outcome, both in terms of the expected gains for exporters and what would constitute unacceptable losses for import competing industries. Equipped with information about each side's needs, the two negotiators then have the task of identifying an outcome that will maximize the potential increase in trade while meeting the domestic political requirements of each side.

The most important requirements for a successful outcome in such negotiations are a detailed analysis of the interests of stakeholders in both countries and comprehensive consultations with affected stakeholders on desired and achievable results. Good information about stakeholder interests in the other country will strengthen a negotiator's hand in negotiations with their counterpart(s) and provide the raw material for developing win-win solutions. Consultations with stakeholders will earn the negotiator the support of stakeholders when the negotiated agreement is tested politically at home.

Multilateral Negotiation of Trade Rules

Another typical negotiating format in trade is the multilateral negotiation of trade (or investment) rules. By multilateral we mean a number of countries meeting as a group to develop rules that will bind the participating countries. The rationale for such rules is that every member will be better off if all other members adhere to an agreed rule and avoid "beggar-thy-neighbor" policies that might benefit an individual country in the short run but would harm the country in the long run if other countries decide to pursue the same course. By its very nature, such a negotiation has to be approached as a win-win type of negotiation because in most such negotiations every country has to agree before the rule is adopted.

The various rounds of multilateral trade negotiations carried out under the auspices of the WTO are examples of such negotiations. Other examples are negotiations carried out by members of regional trade agreements such as NAFTA, the European Union, and Mercosur. Multilateral negotiations in other trade-oriented organizations such as APEC and the OECD follow similar patterns, although they typically result in voluntary best-effort commitments and "recommendations" rather than legally binding obligations of member governments.

Multilateral negotiations of rules usually go through several phases. In the first phase, the issue identification stage, one country typically identifies an issue or problem that it believes needs to be addressed through the formulation of a rule or some other form of common action. In order to persuade other governments to embark on an analysis of the issue that could lead to the negotiation of a rule, proponents have to demonstrate that

- ► The identified problem or issue is more than a one-time or rare event,

- ► It is potentially a problem for every (or most) countries,

- ► It is a more serious than a trivial problem for member countries,

- ► The nature of the problem and the potential remedy is fairly consistent over time and across countries, and

- ► The problem can be solved through a negotiated rule or agreement.

If the problem is rare, member countries will be reluctant to spend the time to analyze and negotiate the issue and to restrict their future freedom of action. If it is only a problem for one or some countries, but not for a majority of countries, it will be difficult to get an agreement to study the issue, much less to negotiate binding commitments. If the nature of the problem and the appropriate remedy changes from event to event, opponents will argue that while there may be a problem, rule making is not the answer.

In the second phase, the analysis phase, the negotiators analyze the nature of the problem and the potential remedies. This phase of the negotiation is designed to create a clear understanding of the problem and how it may be addressed. In the WTO an issue at this stage of the process will be entrusted to a study group. Members will study historical occurrences of the problem, identify patterns, examine analogies to similar problems that have been addressed through negotiated agreements, and evaluate principles that could serve as the basis for rule making. If member countries are persuaded by this work that the problem is serious, it is consistent over time, it is widespread among member countries, or it can be remedied through some form of agreement, then discussions will move toward the search for a negotiating framework to address the issue.

In the third phase, the pre-negotiation phase, member countries hammer out the terms and mandate for the negotiations. In the WTO the issue at this stage is often entrusted to a working group or a committee that has a formal standing within the organization. The work of the group is to define the problem to be addressed to identify the nature of the solution to be pursued through negotiations, the specific elements of the issue to be addressed, the components of a negotiated solution, and a timetable and venue for the negotiations.

In the fourth phase, the negotiating phase, member countries negotiate the actual provisions that will be added to the trade agreement. Such negotiations usually start with a consideration of negotiating proposals tabled by member countries. Where there are many such proposals, the Secretariat may be asked to compile the proposals into an integrated document and to provide members with an analysis of the various proposals. A discussion of these proposals can lead to a second tier of proposals that incorporate comments made by members during the review of the initial proposals or seek to bridge the gap between competing proposals.

Success in multilateral rule-making negotiations, like success in bilateral negotiations aimed at the mutual reduction of trade barriers, hinges on an in-depth analysis of stakeholder interests and comprehensive consultations with stakeholders. Success also requires proactive leadership in the negotiations in tabling analytical papers, policy white papers (which lay out the nature of the problem and proposed solutions), concept papers (which propose concepts and principles that can be used in framing rules or other negotiating solutions), negotiating proposals, and draft texts. A successful negotiator will also actively seek out multiple opportunities for informing the wide range of domestic and foreign stakeholders of the negotiating issues, the benefits to be derived from a positive negotiating outcome, the potential negotiating outcomes, and their rationale. The methods for communicating with stakeholders include use of websites, speeches, published articles, hearings, meetings with stakeholder groups, academic conferences, and intimate weekend seminars and roundtables with key stakeholders. One of the authors of this chapter used every one of these techniques in building a global consensus in support of negotiating the WTO agreement on services.

TYPES OF NEGOTIATIONS

While most day-to-day negotiations between governments on international commercial issues focus on commercial problems created by specific policy measures, the negotiations that get the most attention are comprehensive government-to-government negotiations that cover a wide range of products and policy issues. Examples are bilateral free trade negotiations aimed at removing most barriers to trade and investment between countries or the multilateral rounds of trade negotiations carried out under the auspices of the WTO negotiations. These negotiations typically address both the reduction and elimination of a wide range of trade barriers and the negotiation of trade rules. These negotiations by their very character have to be approached as win-win negotiations because no deal is possible without each party agreeing that the proposed agreement is in its interest. Rules-based negotiations, in particular, have to start from the identification of common interests that might be advanced through the adoption of the rule.

Another type of negotiation in Commercial Diplomacy is one in which one government seeks to eliminate, or at a minimum to moderate, a restrictive trade policy action by another government. On its face, this kind of negotiation is set up as a zero-sum game type of negotiation, and it takes extraordinary skill to convert it into a win-win negotiation. Assuming that the proposed measure has some degree of merit in light of the economic circumstances faced by the country involved, the trick is to show that negotiations can lead to a more balanced consideration of the interests of all parties involved.

Another type of negotiation might be one between a stakeholder left out of an agreement and the parties to a negotiated agreement. The aggrieved stakeholder could be a country adversely affected by a bilateral agreement between two other countries or a nongovernmental organization that believes its policy interests have not been adequately considered by the government and business representatives that worked out the deal. Commercial Diplomats representing parties not invited to the negotiating table need to consider what tactics might get them invited to the table. Ultimately, this means, that they need to consider how they might identify and mobilize potential allies with the necessary political influence.

Each of these various types of negotiations call for a different negotiating style and different negotiating skills:

> **Negotiations aimed at defining common interests.** This could involve the negotiation of a coalition, a common course of action, or common principles or rules. Each requires a soft sales approach that emphasizes common interests and engenders a great deal of mutual trust among negotiators on the genuine commitment of the negotiating partners to the advocated goals.

> **Negotiations over tariffs and quotas.** This type of negotiation may require a more hard-nosed approach that demonstrates to all stakeholders that the negotiated outcome was the best that could be achieved under the circumstances. Problem-solving negotiations fall somewhere in between. Each side to the negotiations must defend its interests but also has to be able to demonstrate that both sides can gain from both the policy and the commercial aspects of an agreement.

Understanding the nature of the parties and the subject matter of the negotiation is critical to the process of planning and preparation for a formal negotiation session.

Terminology

Terminology and descriptions of the various types of parties and form of negotiation follow:

> **Inter-governmental negotiations** – between governments – the government of Pakistan negotiates with the government of India.

- **Intra-governmental negotiations** – within and among one government – usually between government agencies, political parties, or with constituent groups.

- **Commercial negotiations** – between businesses, companies, corporations – this may include business negotiations related to contracts, sales agreements, investments, joint ventures, or may involve negotiations within a business or trade association.

- **Internal business negotiations** – within the business organization, company, or corporation – and include examples such as management, labor negotiations, human resources, inter-departmental, union negotiations, etc.

- **Nongovernmental Organizations (NGOs)** – business associations, trade associations, environmental, labor, human rights, development, etc., and may include inter-group (i.e., between and among other NGOs), NGO-business organization, NGO-governmental organization, or NGO-international government body (i.e., WTO, UN, WHO, ASEAN, etc.).

PREPARING FOR GOVERNMENT-TO-GOVERNMENT NEGOTIATIONS

The face-to-face negotiations are the culmination of a long and extended process of preparation. While many may think that the outcome of negotiations depends largely on the negotiating skills of individual negotiators at the bargaining table, good research and analysis and skillful shaping is often just as important, if not more important. A good negotiating outcome requires extensive analysis of the following:

- Commercial issues at stake for all sides,

- Economic impact on the respective countries,

- Trade-related domestic policy issues,

- Laws and international rules that apply, and

- Views and political influence of the stakeholders.

Identifying and Consulting Stakeholders

The first step in preparing for international negotiations is to identify the domestic stakeholders. Stakeholders are groups in society, both inside and outside the government, who will be affected by the negotiations and, therefore, have a stake in the negotiating outcome. A stakeholder will be impacted positively, negatively, or not at all, depending on how the issues discussed at the negotiating table relate to their interests.

By their very nature, international negotiations involve people who represent governments, businesses, NGOs, and other entities that have a stake or interest in the outcome of the negotiations. While the individual people involved in the negotiation process bring their own ambitions and self-interests to the table, their mission is to serve as representatives of their organizations, bureaucracies, or enterprises to whom they are accountable.

Involving domestic stakeholders in the preparation of negotiation is consistent with principles of good governance, since those most directly affected by the negotiations will have the best information on how various negotiating outcomes will affect trade and the achievement of regulatory objectives. Involving stakeholders is also required for practical political considerations. Those most affected by a governmental action will have a strong motivation to use the political process to ensure that the country's negotiating position reflects their interests.

Starting the preparation of negotiations with the identification and consultation of stakeholders also makes sense because stake holders are likely to be in a position to contribute and, in some cases, help collect basic information about the competitive strengths and weaknesses of national service industries, the problems exporters face in penetrating foreign markets, and the regulatory issues that are likely to arise in the course of the negotiations.

Asking domestic stakeholders to participate in the preparation of the negotiations also makes them feel like full participants in the process, making them loyal supporters of the negotiations as long as they can rationalize it as being consistent with their basic interests. At the very least, stakeholders included in the process will achieve a full understanding of the issues and the rationale for the negotiations, and they are likely to give the negotiators credit for including them in the process and for factoring their interests into the development of national positions, even if their interests are not fully satisfied. The final result is that they are much more likely to support the final agreement negotiated by the government if they are included than if they are not consulted.

During the Tokyo Round of Multilateral Trade Negotiations, the United States Trade Representative (USTR) developed an elaborate system of private sector advisory committees that were consulted before, during, and at the end of the negotiations. There were 45 committees, with a total membership of 600 private sector representatives. In addition to the formal consultations with these committees, Ambassador Robert Strauss consulted extensively with top business executives, labor leaders, members of Congress, and politicians. As a result of these efforts, he was able to obtain overwhelming approval of the Tokyo Round Agreements in the Congress. The Senate approved the Agreement by a vote of 96 to 3, and the House approved it with an equivalent majority. What was equally interesting is that the vast majority of advisors, including representatives of industries facing increased competition from imports as a result of the agreements, fervently spoke in favor of the Agreement at industry gatherings and public meetings.

Not every country has the resources to establish the same kind of elaborate system as the United States, but then, most smaller and less resource-rich countries do not have as many key stakeholder groups who are likely to have a substantive interest in negotiations. Every government has the ability to develop a consultative process appropriate to its economic and institutional circumstances.

We identified two categories of domestic stakeholders in the previous section – (1) the various government ministries and departments responsible for administering the regulations likely to be covered by the negotiations and (2) the enterprises producing the services likely to be covered by the prospective negotiations. The stakeholders in the government can include not only officials in the central government, but also officials at a sub-central level (e.g., states, provinces, etc.) where responsibility for the regulation of services is exercised at a sub-central level. Stakeholders from the services industries include both the various industry associations in services and the major enterprises producing services. Other stakeholders can include labor unions representing services workers, NGOs with a focus on services, and consumer groups.

Having identified the major stakeholder groups, the negotiator has to decide who should be consulted either individually or as a group, who should be invited to participate in meetings organized to discuss the negotiations, and who should be invited to join various consultative bodies established to support the negotiations. The consultation process should be built around three concentric circles.

The innermost circle should consist of the stakeholders within the central government (i.e., the key ministries and departments responsible for regulations covered by the negotiations). Each such ministry, department, or agency should be asked to designate an individual who will participate in an inter-ministerial or inter-agency group responsible for the negotiations. In many countries such a group is given decision-making power. In other countries the group can give formal advice to the trade negotiator but does not have the power to make decisions. Where sub-central governments have a key role in regulating services, the trade negotiators may also have to establish a separate forum for consulting officials from sub-central governments. However, such consultations will inevitably occur on a less frequent basis since the representatives involved may have to travel some distance to participate in meetings.

The second concentric circle is made up of representatives of key private stakeholder groups that are invited to participate in various advisory bodies. These advisory bodies can give negotiators direct feedback on proposed negotiating positions and serve as a vehicle for building consensus with the most influential private stakeholders. Such advisory bodies can also serve as sources of information on trade opportunities and problems, industry practices, and the most vexing barriers to an expansion of trade.

It is neither practical nor necessary to include representatives of every enterprise, industry association, union, NGO, or sub-central government in the consultation process. Optimally, negotiators should involve the most influential and interested individuals from these groups who will be respected by their peers by virtue of their reputation, who can influence the domestic political debate by virtue of their political clout, and who will spend the time to become informed by virtue of their interest in the negotiating outcome. Such individuals will often be found in the largest enterprises or most widely representative organizations, but not always. Since the objective of the negotiations is to expand trade, special care should be taken to include representatives of the most competitive industries that have a keen interest in expanding their exports. Ultimately, negotiators will have to count on their vocal support in building domestic political support in favor of the negotiations. It is also wise to include some vocal opponents to take some of the edge off their opposition.

The identification of the most relevant domestic stakeholder groups and of the most influential individuals in such groups is best accomplished by talking to academic and industry experts in the field and to journalists who cover services industries. By getting in touch with recommended individuals, trade officials can get a fair idea of the organization's potential interest and the contribution individuals at various levels in the organization could make to a consultative process. Ideally, an organization included in the consultative process would have interested individuals at both the top and middle levels of the organization as well as staff experts who can brief them and support their effective participation in meetings.

Consultations with key private sector stakeholders can take place either through private consultations with representatives of general business organizations such chambers of commerce, key industry associations such as the Banker's Association, key companies, labor unions and interested NGOs and companies. Most countries conduct such consultations to a lesser or greater extent. In addition to consultations with individual stakeholders, the government may choose to establish an advisory body or committee to provide organized advice to the government officials negotiating international trade agreements in services. Private advisory groups should be large enough to include representatives of the most important nongovernmental stakeholder groups. Such formal or informal advisory bodies can serve as a useful forum for building national consensus on the country's approach to the negotiations, for exchanging information on the progress of the negotiations, and for validating political support for any bargains struck during the negotiations. Such formal advisory groups have proven to be useful and practical in both very large developed countries and small developing countries such Sri Lanka, Kenya, and the islands in the Caribbean.

The third concentric tier is made up of all interested stakeholders, who may be invited to participate in briefings or conferences covering the negotiations. Individuals participating in such briefings and conferences will have an opportunity to become educated on the issues covered by the negotiations but will have only limited opportunity to provide direct in-depth feedback on negotiating positions. Public briefings by government negotiators can be held in hotels, chambers of commerce, or research institutes. The resource requirement for conducting such briefings is modest, particularly when the briefings are held in facilities that can be provided by a stakeholder.

Beyond these three concentric circles, negotiators will have to devise the means for informing the public at large on the evolution of negotiations. Since the press and the media have the widest reach, a core element of such a communication strategy is to brief the press on a regular basis through press releases, interviews, and press briefings. Negotiators can also publish reports or white papers on negotiating issues and establish a website with up-to-date information on the progress of the negotiations.

In practice, negotiators ideally would follow the sequence provided below, which includes steps in identifying and organizing stakeholders:

► Draft a letter from the Trade Minister or other senior trade official to other government departments, ministries, or agencies responsible for regulations that will be covered by the negotiations, asking them to appoint a senior official to an interagency committee that will review negotiating proposals. Organize an introductory meeting, in which members of the Committee are brought up to date on the schedule for the negotiations and the state of preparations for the negotiations.

► Identify appropriate sub-central officials and invite them to join an advisory committee of sub-central officials who will advise trade negotiators on regulatory issues within their jurisdiction. Invite them to an initial briefing on the negotiations.

► Identify private sector stakeholders, contact them through a phone call or personal visit, explain to them the nature of the upcoming negotiations, and invite their participation in a briefing session or conference on the negotiations. At that meeting, invite them to share their inputs into the negotiating process.

► Issue a press release on the briefing session or conference, and ask the press to publicize the conference indicating that any interested organizations are invited to send a representative.

► Based on initial contacts and consultations with relevant experts, identify prospective members of a private sector advisory body and send them invitations to become a member of the advisory body.

Assembling Information on National Interests and Issues

The next task of the negotiators is to assemble and compile background information on the country's exports and imports of services, competitive strengths and weaknesses of domestic services industries, foreign regulatory barriers that inhibit national exports of services to other markets, and regulatory issues that might arise in the context of negotiations. Crucial help in the collection of such information can come from the country's export industries, particularly the most successful exporting enterprises. Such companies are found even in the smallest developing countries.

Help in assembling this information can also come from a number of international institutions such as the International Trade Centre (ITC) in Geneva, multilateral development banks, and bilateral economic development assistance agencies such as the United States Agency for International Development (USAID) and the Canadian Economic Development Agency (CEDA).

Collecting detailed official statistics on trade in services is a challenge in every country because, unlike data on industrial trade, data on trade in services usually lacks sufficient detail to provide information on trade in specific services, much less a consistent time series. Available data are likely to be aggregated on a sectoral level (e.g., fee-based banking services, professional services, maritime transport services, etc.). Of course, the problem is even more difficult in small developing countries that lack the means for the organized collection of statistics on services.

To supplement the official statistics, negotiators should ask major exporters and industry associations in the individual services sectors to provide additional data that can provide insights at a product level. Asking stakeholders to supplement official data is particularly important for the newer information-based services and various professional services, which are often too new or too dispersed to be included in official statistics. This is particularly important because in most countries, both developed and developing, these services are often the ones that have the greatest potential for export growth if the right policies are pursued. In fact, the export potential in these services often hinges on domestic regulatory reforms in areas as such as telecommunications, air transportation, and financial services that might be included in a country's offer. Consulting businesses in these sectors are often a challenge in countries such as South Africa and India, where these industries are located in cities at a distance from the capital, but it is important that the effort be made.

Initial information on the country's competitive strengths and weaknesses is provided by the trade data. Sectors that export are likely to be relatively competitive, while sectors with large imports are likely to be competitively weak. Trade data, however, might not tell the full story. A sector in which a country has a potential competitive strength may not show many exports because foreign trade barriers or domestic regulatory constraints inhibit such trade, or simply because the industry has not explored export opportunities. Additional insights into competitive strengths can come from economic studies carried out by academic experts, assessments provided by industry experts, and a review of the export performance of other countries at a similar stage of economic development and economic circumstances. Such studies are often available from academic sources and from intergovernmental organizations such as the World Bank and the International Trade Centre.

Trade negotiators are unlikely to find the same kind of detailed quantitative data on trade, production, and prices of services that are available for goods. You cannot see a service crossing the border. Governments are, therefore, not able to measure the flow of services across the border in the same way that they can measure the flow of individual goods across the border. Instead, governments have to compile data on trade in services by periodically asking exporters and importers of services to fill out questionnaires. Since filling out the forms is relatively costly for market participants, only a limited number of exporters and importers are surveyed, and the published data are based on projections based on these sample surveys. Data on trade in services consequently lack the kind of accuracy and detail available for trade in goods. Data is generally available only for broad industry categories and for relatively long intervals. The shortcomings of the trade data is compounded by the difficulty of making a quantitative assessment of the degree of protection provided by regulatory measures. Negotiators in services thus lack the kind of detailed data that would enable them to estimate the impact of negotiated reductions in particular barriers on exports and imports of specific services. In order to make up for the lack of detailed official data, trade negotiators in services have to rely more heavily on information that can be provided by enterprises. Extensive consultations with industry are, therefore, particularly important in preparing for negotiations on trade in services.

In assessing the country's competitive strengths and weaknesses, a country must openly confront any competitive weaknesses that result from the country's own regulations. Onerous regulatory requirements may prevent the country's enterprises in a particular sector from increasing the economic efficiency of its operations or from introducing new and more competitive services and marketing techniques. In fact, most countries involved in negotiations in services found that domestic regulatory reforms were a prerequisite for the country's effective participation in the negotiations. In most cases, that entailed removing outdated regulations that made sense in the past in the context of different technologies and market structures but had outlived their usefulness. That also required the introduction of new regulations appropriate to a more market-oriented regulatory regime. In fact, as we have seen, many countries that liberalized capital controls and international financial transactions went through a subsequent financial crisis because they did not accompany liberalization with adequate fiduciary controls on financial transactions.

Information about foreign trade barriers is best provided by industry. The necessary canvassing of the industry can be done either by the trade negotiators themselves, by a consultant hired for the task, or by a general industry association. Insights into trade barriers can also be found in the surveys done by third countries, particularly third countries with large staffs. Fortunately, the results of many of these surveys and inventories of trade barriers in the principal countries are now often available through the Internet.

The greatest difficulty any country will face in collecting information about foreign barriers is to collect information about industries in which the country has no exports but potentially could export if foreign barriers are removed. How can we know whether the country's inability to export is due to foreign regulatory barriers or a lack of competitiveness of the country's enterprises in this sector? In such industries, private stakeholders are unlikely to be very reliable sources of information. What a small developing country in such a situation should do is to look for other developing countries at the same or slightly more advanced stage of economic development that might have developed successful exports in this sector. Officials and business managers in such countries may well be willing to share their information and insights and to serve as allies in the negotiating process.

The best sources of information about regulatory issues are as follows:

► Regulatory officials in the home government,

► Research institutes that specialize in regulatory issues,

► International professional bodies in areas such as architecture and accounting,

► International organizations such as the ITU (International Telecommunications Union) that are responsible for the development of technical regulations at a global level for individual industries, and

► International organizations with a wide economic mandate that regularly carry out regulatory studies for their members, including the WTO, UNCTAD, the World Bank, the OAS, and the OECD.

Assembling Information on Foreign Interests and Issues

Once we understand our own country's competitive strengths and weaknesses in services, our domestic stakeholders and their interests, and the foreign trade barriers that hamper our exports, we have to collect information about the countries with whom we will be negotiating. We need to understand the strengths and weaknesses of their services industries, their stakeholders and their interests, what difficulties the foreign government is likely to face in meeting our requests, and what they are likely to ask us to do. Information about what they may ask us to do, in turn, will enable us to identify the domestic regulatory issues we may have to face.

Understanding the foreign stakeholders and their interests is important because it will tell us something about the likely foreign reaction to our requests and the requests they are likely to make of us, even if we can gain no direct information on the thinking and evolving position of the foreign government. While it may not be possible to know precisely how the stakeholder interests will be reflected in the country's final negotiating position, it can give us some general ideas. Moreover, down the road, understanding the interests of the stakeholders who stand behind the government's position will enable us to enlist the support of the stakeholders with similar or converging interests, give us an idea where the other government can be pushed, and ultimately provide insights into possible win-win solutions to the negotiations.

In order to negotiate successfully, we also have to understand the interests and problems of those with whom we are negotiating as well as our own interests and problems. The reason for this is simply that a successful conclusion of a negotiation requires the consent of at least two parties, and that means that both sides to an agreement have to be satisfied that it meets their economic interests. Becoming familiar with the interests of our negotiating partners allows us to argue more effectively why our proposals will satisfy their economic interests. In many cases a government that has not taken the time to do a comprehensive analysis of its interests may not be even aware of how particular proposals could advance their interests. Ultimately, understanding the interests of our negotiating partners will help us to shape proposals that will meet their interests while also satisfying our own interest.

Collecting information about foreign stakeholders around the world sounds like a resource-intensive exercise that only large, rich countries could undertake, and it is certainly true that such countries can mobilize more resources to collect such information. However, most countries have commercial officers posted in embassies around the world who could collect this kind of information. The most successful exporting companies in the home country are another good source for this kind of information. Even most small developing countries have companies that have been successful in building markets overseas, and these companies are generally very knowledgeable about the views and interests of their counterpart(s) abroad.

Another key source of information accessible to anyone, even in developing countries, is the Internet. Most large countries, particularly democratic countries, have established a considerable degree of transparency with respect to the views and interests of their key stakeholders. They do this because it is an important tool for influencing the internal domestic debate on the issues. The United States, in particular, has a great deal of transparency as a result of its culture, legal environment, and a vigorous press. Most key industry associations, large corporations, unions, and NGOs in the United States maintain websites with information about the organization's activities and position on negotiating issues. Both companies and industry associations frequently prepare white papers to set out their views. The same is increasingly the case for principal stakeholder groups in other developed countries and the more advanced developing countries.

Analyzing the Data

In order to be useful, the information that is collected has to be organized in a coherent manner and analyzed. Collecting all the information needed to understand an issue can be time-consuming, but it is relatively easy compared to analyzing the data. New trade analysts often think that they have completed the work when they have compiled voluminous information. Developing an in-depth understanding of the relevance of the information for the issue at stake is far more challenging. Analysis consists of developing an understanding of how the information relates to the particulars of the issue at hand, how the information can be used to define the issue to maximize the chances for a successful negotiation, and ultimately how the information can be used to develop possible negotiating outcomes.

The following describes how information collected to prepare for negotiations on trade in services in the WTO can be used to prepare negotiating requests and offers.

- ► Information drawn from the export data, economic studies, industry surveys, and studies of other economies should lead to analytical conclusions regarding the services in which the country already has or could easily develop competitive exports.

- ► Information about foreign regulatory barriers and industry assessments of their relative importance, when combined with the analytical conclusions regarding potential export industries, can lead to conclusions regarding the foreign regulatory barriers that should be targeted in the requests submitted to other countries in the first stage of the negotiations.

- ► Import data, economic studies, industry surveys, studies of other economies, and inputs provided by domestic ministries or departments can lead to analytical conclusions regarding the services in which the country has weaknesses and in which liberalization commitments should only be made on the basis of long phase-in periods, or precluded altogether.

► Information on regulatory issues can lead to analytical conclusions on how requests and offers in particular sectors or with respect to particular horizontal measures should be framed.

► Information on the positions and interests[51] of both domestic and foreign stakeholders are crucial for the development of negotiating positions, the development of requests and offers, and the development of negotiating strategies and tactics.

Developing Domestic Consensus on Negotiating Objectives, Negotiating Strategy, and Negotiating Proposals

Analysis of the issues and of the stakeholders in a negotiation builds the foundation for the formulation of negotiating objectives, the development of a negotiating strategy, and the drafting of negotiating proposals. Negotiating objectives provide a sense of direction for the negotiations. A negotiating strategy provides a road map for getting to the desired negotiating goal. A negotiating proposal is designed as the first step in engaging others involved in the negotiation in a dialogue and for conveying one possible way of satisfying the negotiating objectives. The documents that set out a country's negotiating objectives, negotiating strategy and negotiating proposals provide a common frame of reference for the country's negotiating team and their stakeholders.

This section will examine in greater detail the purpose and content of documents that set out a country's negotiating objectives, negotiating strategy and negotiating proposals.

Establishing Negotiating Objectives

Once we have collected and analyzed the information described above, we are ready to develop a set of negotiating objectives. It is important to set out a clear set of negotiating objectives in order to provide a clear focus for both the preparatory work leading to a negotiation and to the management of the negotiation itself. The development of negotiating objectives is also the ideal way of building support by domestic stakeholders, particularly stakeholders who will have a crucial influence on the acceptance or rejection of the negotiating outcome by domestic decision makers and by officials who will have to implement the results. At the same time, the initial negotiating objectives may need to be adjusted or fine-tuned during the course of the negotiations as negotiators and their stakeholders learn more about the issues being negotiated and the constraints and interests of their negotiating partners.

---

51 *We will explore the implication of the differences between positions and interests later. Interests are the commercial interests, policy objectives, bureaucratic imperatives, or legal requirements that a negotiator must satisfy in a negotiation in order to obtain the approval of the home constituencies. Interests need to be distinguished from the negotiating position, which is what a negotiator is instructed to ask for at any particular phase of the negotiation. The negotiating position is dictated not only by the organization's interests, but also by the negotiating strategies and tactics of the parties.*

In order to develop our negotiating objectives we have to compile and analyze the information we have collected as discussed above, but we must also consult with our stakeholders. We have to go out and actively build consensus among the key domestic stakeholders who can influence a political decision on the issues covered by the negotiations. In effect, the negotiators have to build a coalition of domestic stakeholders who will support a political decision in support of a negotiating position. Coalition partners at home can include key officials from other government departments or agencies, key executives from corporations or trade associations, experts from academia or think tanks, and key legislators and their staffs.

The country's negotiating objectives should be set out in a statement that is approved by the political leadership. Who has to approve such a statement of negotiating objectives in the country varies according to the importance of the issues and the political structure of the country. Comprehensive multilateral negotiations in the WTO that may have far-reaching consequences for the country may require not only the approval of the country's trade minister, but also by the country's other top economic leadership and the head of government.

A statement of negotiating objectives need not cover technical details, but rather should set out some broad strategic objectives and a set of negotiating priorities. It may also set out an accompanying domestic policy agenda. As noted earlier, the ability of a country's enterprises to take advantage of the liberalization of trade barriers by other countries may well hinge on domestic regulatory reforms designed to remove unnecessary regulatory burdens, while assuring that regulations are in place to protect important social objectives such as the protection of consumers, the stability of the financial system, regulatory transparency, and so on. Moreover, the government may well find it desirable to ease the economic adjustment of import sensitive sectors and firms to increased competition from foreign firms. Such assistance could take the form of adjustment assistance programs designed to assist domestic firms in adopting more competitive technologies or business practices, or to assist workers in these industries to develop the skills needed in the export-oriented industries that are expected to benefit from trade liberalization.

Ideally, a country's negotiating objectives are formulated as part of a broader domestic economic development strategy. While most countries sooner or later need to face up to the connection between the domestic policy agenda and international trade negotiations, institutional issues often make it difficult to synchronize the domestic and trade policy-making processes in a seamless way. Linking negotiating objectives to broader domestic economic growth strategies is generally beyond the scope of responsibilities of trade officials and, therefore, requires leadership by the country's top political leaders.

Developing a Negotiating Strategy

In negotiations, like in war, good strategy is a critical factor in success, as has been demonstrated by numerous examples where the less powerful beat the more powerful through good strategy. Good strategy can also help the powerful to obtain their objectives without much conflict. The best generals are those who win a war with a minimum of bloodshed or even without fighting a battle at all.

Negotiations are a process rather than a discrete event that begins and ends with a formal negotiating session. The more successful a negotiator is in building support outside the negotiating room for the preferred negotiating outcome and in developing a broad international consensus on the basic legitimacy and fairness of the proposed outcome, the easier it will be for the negotiator to achieve the desired results at the negotiating table.

A negotiator's bargaining strength inside the negotiating room is determined as much by the number of stakeholders at home and abroad who support the negotiator's preferred negotiating outcome, and by the degree to which the wider stakeholder community considers the proposals to be legitimate and fair, as it is by the economic power of the country he/she represents in international negotiations or by the power of the organization he/she represents in negotiations at home. Support is built through the formation of coalitions of stakeholders dedicated to the achievement of particular negotiating outcomes. Legitimacy and fairness is built through wider public dialogue with policy experts, the press, and the public at large, provided, of course, that the proposal is not arbitrary and can be defended on the basis of widely held principles of what is fair and legitimate.

A negotiating strategy is a plan for building support for a desired negotiating outcome. It needs to identify the means for obtaining the support of potential allies and for minimizing and overcoming the opposition of potential opponents. Building support is a process of aligning interests, aligning negotiating proposals and arguments, and aligning supportive actions. A good strategy spells out in fairly specific terms how the desired negotiating outcome has to be adjusted to meet the interests of the targeted coalition of supporters. It needs to describe the arguments that should be made to potential supporters to win their support and the arguments that should be made to opponents to minimize their opposition or to win them over. It should lay out a menu of written and oral communications such as white papers, advocacy letters, testimony, press releases, speeches, conferences, and other communication tools that will be used to reach the targeted stakeholder communities. It should include steps that can be taken to establish and communicate the legitimacy and fairness of the proposed outcome. Finally, a strategy should set out the basis for a successful negotiating outcome by describing the possible elements of an outcome that could satisfy the interests of the parties to the negotiations.

A good strategy builds on the information that has been collected about the issues and the stakeholders in phase one of the preparations and the analysis of that information in phase two of the preparations. The better our information and the higher the quality of our analysis, the better we can make the negotiating strategy.

The development of a strategy for coalition building and legitimizing negotiating objectives is particularly important for smaller countries participating in international negotiations. To smaller companies or industries, it is important for seeking to influence governments at home or abroad on negotiating issues. Large and powerful countries can more easily afford to pay less attention to alliances and to considerations of legitimacy. As history has shown, however, even powerful countries or organizations are unlikely to remain successful if they do not seek the support of allies and fail to establish the legitimacy of their desired negotiating outcomes. Building consensus is a labor-intensive effort. Once it is built and the negotiated outcome is firmly rooted as the new paradigm, it is difficult to change. This is particularly true for negotiations on rules or negotiations that will create a new paradigm.

A good negotiating strategy that maps out the formation of coalitions and the establishment of the legitimacy of desired negotiating outcomes is also important for the negotiation of rules. After all, ultimately every country that will be bound by the rules will have to agree to them. This can only be achieved through a good strategy. Issue- and country-specific negotiations provide fewer opportunities for coalition building, and issues of legitimacy and fairness are often difficult to judge in such negotiations. However, the problems inherent in communicating the relevance of a complicated technical issue, or worse, a whole catalog of technical issues, can be overcome through the skillful packaging of the issues and the results. If the relevance of the issues involved and of possible negotiating outcomes is successfully communicated in ways that can be understood by the broader stakeholder communities, it is possible to bring to bear the benefits of good strategy, including the benefits of alliances and appeals to legitimacy to even the most technical and detailed negotiations.

Case Illustrating Use of Strategy in Negotiations[52]

A use of strategy in negotiations is provided by the one adopted by the U.S. negotiating team to use the OECD Study on Services as a stepping stone toward global consensus on the launching of negotiations on trade and services.

Specifically, the strategy consisted of the following:

▶ Using the study identifying real trade problems in services and to show that these trade problems were similar in kind to many barriers to trade in goods that had been successfully addressed in trade negotiations.

▶ Working with the private sector in the United States to identify services industries in key countries that had real interests in expanding trade opportunities abroad, and who could be persuaded to communicate those interests to their respective governments.

▶ Demonstrating the practicality of using traditional trade rules to address trade problems in services by (a) raising a number of regulatory barriers in bilateral trade consultations with individual countries and tying the resolution of these problems to other bilateral negotiations on traditional trade issues in goods, and (b) adding services to the agenda of bilateral free trade area negotiations with Canada and Israel.

▶ Establishing the legitimacy of negotiations on trade in services by (a) working with economists from a representative group of countries on the applicability to traditional trade theories to trade in services and the economic benefits

---

that could be derived, and (b) organizing weekend conferences of key opinion leaders from key countries to discuss the role of services in light of globalization and the new information technologies.

Building a global consensus on the launching of negotiation on trade in services was something beyond the normal challenge faced by trade negotiators, and it called for an extra level of effort. At the same time, the number of people directly involved and the resources that were used were quite modest. While this does not mean that any country could have accomplished the same thing, the techniques involved are generally applicable and can usefully be applied by any country, no matter how small.

For example, building global consensus in support of the negotiation of an agreement on trade in services was a multidimensional effort that required building support by a large number of stakeholder groups throughout the world and establishing the legitimacy of its objective, which was to reduce barriers and expand trade in services. While the United States led the early effort, changes in political leadership at the top resulted in a sharp decline of U.S. leadership during some years. During those periods, the momentum generated by the international consensus that had been built during the earlier years carried the effort forward on its own momentum and overrode new U.S. positions that might have reversed aspects of the consensus that had been built. International negotiations can be best visualized as an aircraft carrier; it takes a considerable amount of energy to get it moving, but once it is moving in a particular direction it is difficult to change its course.

Can any country develop the means for implementing a good strategy? Can a country with limited means mobilize enough resources to develop wide support outside the negotiating room for its desired negotiating outcome? Resources obviously do make a difference, and a small country could find it more difficult mobilizing consensus in support of a global undertaking, but not impossible. There are many examples where even one individual was able to move the world (e.g., Florence Nightingale and the formation of the Red Cross and Adam Powell and the Scouting Movement come to mind). A few talented individuals can devise and implement successful strategies if they have the requisite knowledge and skills. One can identify charismatic, knowledgeable, and energetic individuals in most countries, particularly in small countries, since individuals in small countries learn early on how to overcome the lack of power through the energetic application of knowledge and skill. Development of the right alliances can empower any country, as was demonstrated by the Cairns Group, which comprised both small and large countries that banded together during the Uruguay Round negotiations to achieve a breakthrough on agricultural trade reform.

Defensive Strategies

In the last section we looked at outward-looking negotiations aimed at solving a problem faced by exporters. In this section we will examine possible responses by an importing country to foreign requests for a change in its regulations. Our response to the foreign request will be influenced by the legitimacy of the request, the relative political and legal difficulty in responding to the request, and our relative bargaining power. The role of a negotiating strategy in this situation is to develop the means for increasing our relative bargaining power and the legitimacy of our position. In the final analysis, however, we need to consider that both sides have options, and we, therefore, have to consider the consequences of saying no. An important concept in evaluating such requests is the concept of BATNA, the Best Alternative to an Agreement.

The Power to Say No

Current ideas of national sovereignty give a country the right to say no to foreign requests, even when the foreign request is a request to honor commitments under trade rules. Saying no may have consequences, but as long as the country is prepared to live with those consequences it has the right to say no. There may be a number of reasons why we may want to say no. The request may involve an action that is inconsistent with our economic philosophy. Changing the targeted regulation may not be in our economic interest or it may be too difficult to change the regulation for political, legal, or even constitutional reasons. We may simply consider the request as not a legitimate request.

The power to say no is even stronger in multilateral trade negotiations in the WTO than in bilateral negotiations. Decisions in the WTO are made on the basis of consensus. In principle, consensus means that all countries that are members of the WTO have to agree. In practice, it probably means that the vast majority of countries and all important countries have to agree. This right to say no gives individual countries considerable leverage in multilateral negotiations carried out under the WTO umbrella. The same is true, of course, under regional and bilateral free trade agreements.

The question we want to address here is how we can minimize the consequences of saying no. The consequences of saying no will depend on the importance of the issue to the other country, the relative merits of their request and our decision to say no, and the relative bargaining power of the two sides (i.e., the relative strengths of the options available to the two sides involved in the negotiation). Just saying no is most likely to be a successful strategy when the issue is not particularly important to the other side, when we do not have important export interests in the other country, when the request of the other side is not backed by international trade rules, or it is not seen as legitimate by the world trading community.

Before exploring strategies we can adopt to strengthen our ability to say no while minimizing the consequences, it is useful to consider the issue of bargaining power. We are programmed to thinking that bargaining power is a function of the size of the country, but that is not necessarily true in the case of trade. What matters in trade negotiations is not the relative size of the countries but the relative size of their actual and potential trade. A large country may have little bargaining power if its imports are relatively small, while a small country may have a large amount of bargaining power if its imports are relatively large. Thus, India had limited bargaining power for many years, while smaller countries like the Netherlands, Chile, Switzerland, or Hong Kong had much more bargaining power than would have been suggested by their size. At the same time, a small country that has professionally well-trained negotiators who are successful in building the legitimacy of their case may have more bargaining power than a large country that lacks negotiators with those skills.

This brings us to strategy. How can we bolster our decision to say no? One obvious answer is to find allies, either in the other country, in third countries, or among opinion makers. Finding allies in a bilateral dispute is clearly more of a challenge than in multilateral negotiations, but it can be done. For example, if the other country feels it has a case under trade rules and initiates a dispute settlement proceeding, we can get other countries to submit a brief in support of our case. Other countries can also help strengthen the legitimacy of our case by speaking out in our behalf. In multilateral negotiations, building coalitions is the essence of the negotiating process just as it is in national legislatures. How do representatives from small and poor districts get a hearing in national legislatures?

The Consequences of Saying No – Moves and Countermoves

To better understand the consequences of saying no, we need to examine the options available to a country whose request we have refused. As we discussed in the first section, the essence of trade negotiations is the exchange of commitments that involve the mutual liberalization of barriers to trade. When we say no to a request from another country to help solve a problem faced by their exporters, they will be less inclined to help us solve a problem faced by our exporters. Two countries that trade actively with each other undoubtedly have a large number of mutual problems to address, and a country's willingness to help its trading partners is unlikely to depend on the resolution of a single issue. The net impact of saying no on any one issue, therefore, will depend on the relative importance of the issue and our response on all the other issues on the negotiating table. One way of minimizing the consequences of saying no on one issue is to be more helpful in solving another issue.

Another potential response of the country we have refused is to initiate dispute settlement proceedings if they believe that the measure at stake involves a violation of a commitment we have made in a trade agreement or a trade rule. We, therefore, need to consider the relative strength of both our legal position and theirs, as well as the consequences of losing the case. If we are confident that we can win the case, winning the case would bolster the legitimacy of our position and make it much more difficult for the other country to press their case or to take any action against us for refusing to address the issue. On the other hand, if we are likely to lose the case, are the problems associated with resolving the problem greater than the problems we may face if the other country is given the right to retaliate against us? Are we in a better position to address the issue domestically after we have lost the case than we are now?

On the other hand, the other country may decide not to wait for a dispute settlement ruling and take some form of retaliatory measure. There are a number of ways it may be able to do so legally under the trade rules by initiating an action sanctioned by the trade rules. For example, they could initiate a safeguard action on one of our export products that have been creating difficulty for their industry, or they may decide to initiate a stricter enforcement of a sanitary measure on one of our exported agricultural products. Beyond such actions within the rules, they could decide to take an illegal retaliatory measure that would put pressure on us while we initiate a dispute settlement proceeding against them.

We also need to consider responses by a country that is frustrated by our ability to block consensus in the WTO on adding a particular issue to the negotiating agenda or in concluding an agreement that has been under negotiation. One of those responses is to pursue the issues involved in other international negotiating venues in which we are excluded. While we may be able to avoid being bound by any such agreement, we may also lose our ability to influence the development of international norms on that issue.

Cooperative Defensive Strategies

The foreign request for a change in our regulations that affect their exports may well have economic merit, even from the point of view of the regulation of domestic enterprises. There may be a number of reasons why our country's regulatory agencies may have failed to reform regulations that may be outdated as a result of changes in technology, market structure, or system of governance. The reason may have been regulatory inertia, or political difficulties associated in overcoming the vested interests created under the existing regulatory structure. In such cases, the question we can ask is how we can use the external impetus to pursue regulatory reforms that are in our economic interest but difficult to implement. Many countries have developed the fine art of blaming foreigners for reforms that are desirable but politically difficult. It can be a useful tactic, but it is also a double-edged sword because ultimately the legitimacy of the reform depends on public belief that it is in the country's interest. China's use of the negotiations with WTO members on its readmission to the WTO, for example, was a classic case of a country making the most of negotiations with foreigners to advance a domestic regulatory and economic reform agenda.

In responding to a foreign request for a regulatory change, we should ideally first ask ourselves whether changes in the targeted regulations would ultimately be in our economic interest. Maybe the specific changes suggested by the other government would not be in our best economic interest, but an alternative set of changes that would address some of their concerns could be turned into a desirable reform. If the trade negotiators on the other side are doing their job well, they will present all the arguments why the desired change would not only remove a barrier to their exports but would also improve the performance of our economy or increase the competitiveness of our own industry.

PREPARING THE NEGOTIATIONS –BUILDING SUPPORT

The negotiating process begins with the first exploratory discussions of the issues with stakeholders at home and abroad. While these preliminary discussions are not what we normally consider as a negotiation, for all practical purposes they are a part and parcel of the negotiating process.

This section will examine the process for building supportive coalitions and for selling negotiating proposals to negotiating partners.

Building Supportive Coalitions

Trade negotiations are a process of progressively building consensus among an increasing number of stakeholder groups with diverse interests. Building coalitions among like-minded groups at home in support of particular negotiating proposals and agreements is a critical aspect of that process.

The negotiation of the services agreement in the WTO, for example, was advanced by a number of crosscutting international coalitions of stakeholders that supported the negotiation of a services agreement under the aegis of the global multilateral trading system. Business leaders, academics, and government officials from both developed and developing countries that favored an agreement met periodically to brainstorm the issues, to coordinate lobbying efforts, and to map out negotiating proposals and initiatives. It included stakeholders from such diverse countries as the United States, the European Community, UK, France, Sweden, Japan, Australia, New Zealand, Hong Kong, Singapore, Colombia, and Chile. Similarly, the working-level negotiators from many of these countries constituted an informal group called the friends of services, who regularly coordinated their interventions in the meetings of the negotiating group on services.

Once potential coalition partners have been identified, then it is important to reach out to them to discuss the pending negotiations and, where possible, to coordinate positions or even to draft joint negotiating proposals. A coalition partner may support efforts to prepare negotiations in some or all of the following ways:

► Help brainstorm possible solutions (options) to present in the negotiations;

► Reach out to their constituents (members) to involve them in collateral legislative, lobbying, media, or other supportive activities;

► Help to raise resources, including funds to advance various aspects of a concerted campaign that will support the negotiators; and

► Provide market, scientific, research, and other data in support of the negotiating objectives.

One of the most important skills a negotiator can have is the ability to build coalitions and alliances with other parties that have similar or at least compatible interests. This is particularly important for small developing countries with a limited amount of imports. In trade negotiations, the volume of current and potential imports gives a country negotiating power. In trade negotiations, buying power equates to negotiating power. Even large countries may have only a limited amount of negotiating power if the value of their imports is relatively small. On the other hand, even a small country can exert considerable negotiating power if it is a significant importing country. What a country cannot achieve on its own through a large volume of trade, however, it may be able to achieve as part of a coalition of countries that together can exert considerable negotiating clout.

Some countries limit their coalition-building efforts to regional neighbors. This can sometimes be a mistake because neighboring countries may not have the same economic interests on a particular issue, and the negotiation of a common position may, therefore, unnecessarily dilute the effectiveness of common negotiating proposals in advancing the country's economic interest. It may also be a mistake in spending too many resources in building coalitions with neighboring countries that lack much negotiating power. It would be much better in such situations to seek out influential countries in other parts of the world that have similar interests on a particular issue.

Coalition partners in broad stakeholder coalitions can include key officials from government departments or agencies, key executives from corporations or trade associations, experts from academia or think tanks, and key legislators and their staffs. International coalition partners can include officials from other governments, executives from foreign corporations and trade associations, and foreign academic experts.

The negotiation of the General Agreement for Trade in Services (GATS) was supported by a loose international coalition of officials, businessmen and academic experts who met periodically to map a joint strategy for advancing the negotiations, and who organized conferences and other events around the world to expand the consensus. This coalition was crucial in building up negotiating momentum and sustaining the negotiating process once the negotiations developed their own momentum. Negotiators should also identify members of the press who develop an interest in the negotiations and become educated on the issues and can be counted on to write informative, in-depth articles on the rationale for the negotiations.

Negotiators should ideally establish different coalitions for different purposes. Thus, a coalition within the government at home may be critical to the development of an interagency consensus, while a coalition of like-minded countries in the WTO may be equally critical to building support among WTO negotiators. International coalition building is particularly critical to smaller countries that can gain influence only through coalitions that include powerful countries. During the Uruguay Round, many smaller developing economies were able to exert considerable influence on the course of the agriculture negotiations through the Cairns Group of countries, named after the Australian city where they first met. The negotiation of the GATS during the Uruguay Round was significantly enhanced through the coordinated efforts of a group of small and big countries called the friends of services.

Equally important is contacting stakeholders with conflicting interests. Can they be approached and "neutralized"? Can you offer information, trade-offs, or other assurances that will minimize or eliminate their adverse influence on the negotiation process?

Negotiations need to be viewed as an interlocking chain of events that start with the formation of coalitions to explore negotiating ideas. The formation of supportive coalitions and the development of negotiating proposals should be treated as an interactive process. In order to succeed, a negotiating proposal has to receive the support of a coalition of stakeholders at home and a coalition of countries internationally that together is influential enough to prevail. Building a coalition and negotiating a common position among the members of the coalition is thus a steppingstone towards the negotiation of a successful outcome. Negotiating supportive coalitions at home is a key stepping stone toward the development of the country's initial negotiating position. Negotiating supportive coalitions abroad is a key stepping stone toward the negotiation of an international agreement.

Formally, the development of a negotiating position in the home country and the negotiation of an international agreement are two separate and sequential phases of the negotiation process. In reality, a successful outcome to negotiations is enhanced through international coalition building, while a national position is still being developed. Such an overlapping process allows negotiators to factor the interests of likely international coalition partners into the development of the country's initial negotiating position.

Developing Negotiating Proposals

The next step in the preparation of negotiations is the development of negotiating proposals. A negotiating proposal represents the opening position in a negotiation and should be designed to evoke responses from negotiating partners that will help frame the negotiations. In framing a negotiating proposal, a country (or stakeholder) needs to consider not only its negotiating objective, but also the views and interests of its negotiating partners. Like a game of chess, a negotiation is an interactive process of moves and countermoves, and the wise negotiator will think ahead to map out how the sequence of moves will eventually lead to the desired negotiating outcome. This is, of course, is the essence of a negotiating strategy.

How a proposal is structured depends on the nature of the negotiations. A negotiating proposal in a bilateral negotiation can take the form of a paper that describes desired changes in the regulation at issue.

Negotiating proposals can be submitted by individual countries or by a coalition of countries acting together. If the coalition is wide enough and representative of a cross-section of countries, it can have considerable influence on the negotiating process. On the other hand, strategically crafted proposals by individual countries could turn out to be just as influential. Countries that are proactive in submitting negotiating proposals and in crafting group proposals can achieve considerable influence in the negotiating process, even if they are relatively small countries. The key to exercising influence is to master the technical details of the issue, to develop an in-depth understanding of the needs and views of member countries, and to surface proposals that can serve as the basis for consensus.

A negotiating proposal should contain not only proposed language, but also the rationale underlying the proposal. The proposal should start out by placing it in the context of the negotiations. This should be followed by an analytical section that lays out the issues that need to be addressed, by a description of the proposed text, and a final section laying out the rationale and why the proposal is the right solution for the problems posed.

Selling the Negotiating Proposals

Once negotiators have developed a negotiating proposal, they must persuade stakeholders at home and abroad on the merits of the proposal. In part, this is done through meetings with stakeholders and conferences and, in part, in writing through the preparation of white papers, published statements, press releases, and websites. Such documents can be targeted at either the general public, the media, or through specialized publications serving particular services industries. Negotiators might also make public speeches to stakeholder groups, testify at legislative hearings, and post the white paper and other materials on the organization's website.

Internationally, bilateral consultations with foreign negotiators are the most common method of broadening support among negotiators. Negotiators also have the option of distributing the written text of oral interventions made at meetings of the negotiating group.

Each of the various types of written and oral methods of communication have their own requirements that determine structure and format.[53] A white paper, for example, should have a brief summary that briefly covers the what, where, when, and why; a background section that outlines the issues that give rise to the proposal; a full description of the proposal; and a section that describes what will be gained as a result of the proposal. This paper can serve as a handout at meetings with stakeholders and at conferences.

ELEMENTS OF INTEREST-BASED NEGOTIATIONS

What is interest-based negotiation? The theory and practice of interest-based negotiation is a relatively new addition to the academic literature related to international diplomacy. Many of the elements discussed in this chapter were developed and refined by the Harvard Negotiation Program and members of a growing consortium of academics and practitioners devoted to the development of negotiation as a science. We acknowledge those contributions as we seek to build upon them in their application to trade-related negotiations and conflict resolution in the international arena.

Interest-based negotiation is based upon a simple premise. No one wants to "lose" or sacrifice his/her interests in a negotiation process. In a "zero-sum" gain type of negotiation, one party succeeds at the expense of the other party, who makes all the concessions or compromises to the detriment of their interests.

By recognizing the fundamental human desire to be successful, the art and science of interest-based negotiations has evolved. By understanding the interests of all parties to a negotiation (often diverse interests), a negotiator can better formulate "positive-sum" approaches that allow all parties to advance and protect some, if not all, of their interests. Such "positive-sum gain" approaches to negotiations have been coined as "win-win" negotiations.

Traditional, competitive negotiations pit negotiators against each other as adversaries who seek to win concessions at the expense of their counterpart(s). Parties seek to discover the "bottom line" of their counterpart(s) in an attempt to extract the maximum concession possible. A party with "superior negotiating power" might be able to negotiate their counterpart(s) into submission, but such an approach often

---

53 For an extended description of the most effective structure and content of these various written documents and oral presentations, visit the website of the Institute for Trade and Commercial Diplomacy, www.commercialdiplomacy.org and look for the instructional modules on written and oral communications.

leads to *impasse* (the failure to reach an agreement) as parties become entrenched in intractable positions, or alternatively, the negotiation of an unequal agreement will leave a legacy of distrust and resentment.

Interest-based negotiation is rooted in the recognition that parties invariably have divergent as well as shared interests. By understanding the interests of all parties in a negotiation process, the skilled negotiator is often able to craft solutions (options) that will satisfy some if not all of a counterpart's interests, thus demonstrating the benefits of remaining engaged in the negotiation process. By working cooperatively in the quest for workable solutions, the skilled negotiator is able to articulate the interests and needs of not only his/her own party, but also of all other parties to the negotiation.

In the parlance of the authors of ***Getting to Yes, Negotiating Agreements Without Giving In***, the goal of interest-based negotiation is to move the parties away from judgmental, or predetermined positions, to a more pragmatic approach that recognizes that there are various ways of meeting the complex set of interests represented by both parties. Negotiators must develop the skill of evaluating the benefits of a negotiated agreement compared to the alternative conflict situations that are likely to emerge in the absence of negotiations.

In the development of an interest-based approach to the negotiation process, the negotiator who faces entrenched and positional negotiators can gain a negotiating advantage by employing an analytical and problem-solving approach. In fact, while the benefits of parties sharing an interest-based approach to negotiation become immediately apparent, it is the success of the technique with recalcitrant and positional parties that proves its ultimate efficacy.

In the following sections, the various elements of interest-based negotiation will be identified and discussed. Regardless of the nature of the negotiation, the setting, or the cultures involved, every negotiation will include the following elements:

- ► People (parties, stakeholders),

- ► Interests,

- ► Options or possible solutions to satisfy interests,

- ► A BATNA or best alternative(s) to a negotiated agreement, and

- ► Various objective criteria that may be employed to provide support for a proposal or to reduce the legitimacy or applicability of a proposal.

INTEREST IDENTIFICATION CHART

These elements are pulled together in the following Interest Identification Chart:

Table 14A

Interest Identification Chart				
People/ Stakeholders	**Interests**	**Options**	**Objective Criteria**	**BATNA**
For every party to a negotiation (in-cluding your own), you should know: (1) What govern-ment ministries or agencies are involved? (2) What non-government groups are involved? (3) What com-panies or industries are involved? (4) Who are the individuals involved? What special relationships or connec-tions might they have?	What are the interests of each of the parties to a trade problem? (1) What do they want and need to come out of a solution? (2) Who are they account-able to? What are the conse-quences of their action or inaction? Remember: Govern-ment ministries or agencies all have different interests to protect, as do indi-viduals.	What options are available to each of the negotiat-ing parties in trying to solve a specific trade problem? For example, (1) Should par-ties hold informal consulta-tions or call for a formal negotiation? (2) Should they refuse to negotiate until certain conditions are met? (3) Could one or more parties refuse to admit the need for negotiations?	Objective crite-ria are domes-tic, foreign and inter-national principles, rules and regula-tions that you would use to examine and solve a trade problem. Other examples of objective cri-teria include scientific studies, white papers, and/ or past trade problems that could be used as precedent cases. Remember: Different nego-tiating parties or groups may share the same objec-tive criteria, but they may interpret them differently.	A BATNA is a **B**est **A**lternative **t**o a **N**egotiated **A**greement. It is the option, strategy or plan that you and your negotiating team will use to solve a trade problem if negotiations fail and/or the par-ties are unable to reach a mutually beneficial agree-ment. A BATNA is **not** your preferred outcome. It is your final option. In many cases, all parties to a nego-tiation will keep their BATNAs a secret. By keep-ing your BATNA a secret, there is added pressure and incentive to reach an agree-ment.

Stakeholder Identification and Analysis (The People and Organizations)

Who are the Stakeholders?

The people and organizations involved in the negotiation process. A stakeholder can be defined as any person or entity that has a vested interest or investment in the outcome of the negotiations. A stakeholder will be impacted either positively, negatively, or not at all, depending on how the issues discussed at the negotiating table relate to their interests.

By their very nature, international negotiations involve people of different national, ethnic, racial, religious, and cultural backgrounds. These people, in turn, represent governments, businesses, NGOs, and other entities that have a stake or interest in the outcome of the negotiations. While the individual people involved in the negotiation process bring their own backgrounds, personalities, training, ambitions, and self-interests to the table, their mission is to serve as representatives of organizations, bureaucracies, or enterprises to whom they are accountable.

The parties most directly involved in international trade negotiations that cover trade-related policy issues are government representatives. Government representatives in formal international trade negotiations are usually from the ministries of foreign trade, economy, foreign affairs, or in the United States the Office of the United States Trade Representative (USTR), which is a cabinet level position within the executive branch of government. The USTR is appointed by the President of the United States and reports directly to the President.

Negotiations of trade agreements are often handled by government trade representatives. However, the broader process may include internal negotiations between different government agencies, political representatives, and nongovernmental interest groups. These interest groups include but are not limited to corporations or other enterprises, trade and business associations, labor unions, consumer groups, and nongovernmental organizations representing policy interests.

Negotiators engaged in formal inter-governmental negotiations are usually subject to the influence of multiple stakeholders. These stakeholders are not at the official negotiating table, but rather those who exercise their influence through official or informal contacts with negotiators, public testimony, speeches, press releases, lobbying, legislative initiatives, grass roots campaigns, or other political activity to ensure that their interests are protected.

Who are the Stakeholders and What is Their Influence on the Negotiation Process?

At the outset of developing a negotiation strategy, a good negotiator will identify all of the stakeholders and chart their interests, positions, and options. By understanding which parties (people and organizations) have an interest and potential influence on the negotiating process, a negotiator can generate a list of the interests that have to be accommodated in the course of either the internal or external negotiating process in order to achieve a successful outcome.

In international trade negotiations between governments, the stakeholder analysis needs to cover four sets of stakeholders:

- Private stakeholders in the home country,

- Government stakeholders in the home country,

- Private stakeholders in all foreign countries involved in the negotiations, and

- Government stakeholders in all foreign countries involved in the negotiations.

In some cases the secretariat of an international organization may become involved as a fifth set of stakeholders.

The Interest Identification Chart illustrates the universe of potential stakeholders in an international trade negotiation related to the removal of agricultural trade barriers between the United States and Europe. Referring to Table 14A above, examples of People/Stakeholders listed in column 1 are as follows:

U.S. Government Stakeholders

- U.S. Government Executive Branch

    o   U.S. Administration
    o   USTR
    o   U.S. Department of Agriculture
    o   U.S. Department of State
    o   U.S. Department of Commerce
- Other U.S. Government Stakeholders

    o   Members of U.S. Congress
    o   Members of U.S. Senate

European Union Governmental Stakeholders

- Executive Branch

    o   EU Commission
    o   DG for External Relations
- Other Governmental Stakeholders

    o   EU Parliament
    o   Council of Ministers
    o   Member States

Nongovernmental Stakeholders

- Growers of Export Crops

- Growers of Import Competing Crops

- Food Processors

- ► Manufacturers of Export Products

- ► NGO's supporting Family Farms

Other Stakeholders

- ► China

Identification of Potential Coalition Partners and Allies

An important aspect of the analysis of stakeholders is to identify those stakeholders who may serve as *coalition partners*. Coalition partners are those stakeholders with similar or shared interests whose participation in the process may add support and influence in the negotiation process. Similarly, it is important to identify potential coalition partners who may join with counterpart(s) in the negotiation process.

Once the potential coalition partners of all parties to the negotiation have been identified, then it is important to reach out to your allies and discuss the pending negotiations. A coalition partner may support your efforts in some or all of the following ways:

- ► Help brainstorm possible solutions (options) to present in the negotiations.

- ► Reach out to their constituents (members) to involve them in collateral legislative, lobbying, media, or other supportive activities.

- ► Help to raise resources including funds to advance various aspects of a concerted campaign which will support the negotiators.

- ► Provide market, scientific, research, and other data in support of the negotiating objectives.

- ► Equally important is the identification of stakeholders with conflicting interests. Can they be approached and "neutralized"? In other words, can you offer information, trade-offs, or other assurances that will minimize or eliminate their adverse influence on the negotiation process? Coalition partners or negotiating partners may include other governments, business organizations, associations, NGOs, elected officials, agency representatives, members of the media, or members of the academic or epistemic community.

Interest Identification of All Stakeholders

At the very heart of interest-based negotiations is the ability of negotiators to understand and discover the full range of their own interests and those of all counterparts and other stakeholders.

- ► *Interests* are at the very core of what drives parties in a negotiation. Interests underlie positions. Interests are the commercial interests, policy objectives, bureaucratic imperatives, or legal requirements that a negotiator must satisfy in a negotiation in order to obtain the approval of the home constituencies. Interests need to be distinguished from the negotiating position, which is what a negotiator is instructed to ask for at any particular phase of the negotiation. The negotiating position is dictated not only by the organization's interests, but by the negotiating strategies and tactics of the parties. The negotiating positions of the two parties define the parameters for the negotiations at any point in time. *In other words, the positions that parties take in negotiations are based on underlying interests.*

By better understanding your own party's interests as well as those of your counterpart(s), you will be better able to fashion proposals and agreements that can lead to a successful negotiation outcome. When parties adhere to a single solution as the only solution that will result in a successful negotiation, they invariably limit the broader range of possibilities that might also satisfy their core interests. Inexperienced negotiators talk about "finding common interests" to successfully solve a problem. While most negotiations are predicated on some recognition of broad shared interests (peace, trade relations, economic gain, etc.), many negotiations are successfully completed only when the negotiators' divergent or different interest(s) are identified. It is the ability to identify these divergent interests or varying priorities that can provide the basis for generating workable solutions between and among parties.

In the planning stages as well as at the negotiating table, the skilled negotiator will employ questions and active listening to learn what is really important to their counterpart(s): What are their real interests? By successfully identifying a party's key interests (multiple), more options can be generated that will satisfy some, if not all, of a counterpart's interests.

At the end of the day, all parties to a negotiation seek to satisfy their interests. If you can help a counterpart negotiator to satisfy some of the interests of the organization he/she represents while protecting and advancing your own interests, you maximize the probability of a positive negotiated outcome.

In international negotiations, interests may revolve around issues of:

▸ Economic interests,

▸ Domestic policy objectives such as environmental integrity and resource protection,

▸ National security,

▸ Domestic political considerations,

▸ Bureaucratic interests,

▸ National legal requirements, issues of legitimacy (recognition), or

▸ Moral or ethical standards

Examples: It is difficult to discuss interests in negotiations in the abstract. The following examples help to illustrate the identification of simple interests and trade-related interests.

1. A common example utilized to illustrate interests involves a fight between two children over a single orange. Both children want the orange. Neither child wants one half of the orange. There is no apparent solution to this *stalemate* (standoff or impasse). The solution is revealed when an adult determines the underlying interests of the two children. One child wants the orange to eat the sections while the other child wants the orange peels (skins) to squirt the residue into a candle flame. By identifying the children's *different interests* a solution is easily found: one child gets the orange peel, the other gets the inner sections.

2. In a trade dispute over tariffs on grape imports from country A to country B, the interests of the importing country may be to protect existing markets and manufacturers while the exporting country seeks to maximize sales and profits. Country B seeks to block grape imports and proposes to raise tariffs while Country A seeks to expand its grape exports and remove tariffs barriers. The parties take divergent and competing positions. By discovering that Country A has an interest in exporting grapes during nonharvest periods in Country B, while Country B is particularly worried about grape imports during the harvest season, then a negotiated agreement becomes possible.

How does a negotiator identify a party's interests? There are several tools that a negotiator can use in the planning process and at the negotiating table to determine a party's interests.

The use of the *'interest-identification chart,"* as illustrated above, is an indispensable tool for the development of effective negotiation strategies. A chart is created with vertical columns reflecting the following headings:

Table 14B

Interest Identification Chart Column Headings				
People/ Stake-holders	Interests	Options	Objective Criteria	BATNA

The columns are then filled-in with the names of the parties and interest groups who will be at the negotiating table or who may influence positions taken at the negotiating table. For each party listed on the chart, generate a preliminary list of the interests you consider to be compelling to each party. Be expansive in your charting, and list as many similar and different interests as you can think of for each party. *PUT YOURSELF IN THE SHOES OF YOUR COUNTERPART(S).* In other words, role-play within your team as part of the planning process. Designate some of your team members to role-play as if they represent your counterpart(s) in the upcoming negotiation.

► Ask your own team members/superiors to articulate what is most important to them in the upcoming negotiations. What do they seek to achieve and WHY?

► Ask your role-playing counterpart directly, "What are your interests? What do you care about most in these negotiations? What do you want to protect, advance, or gain from the process?"

► Fill-in the columns in the chart for each party, or constituent group by asking what are their key interests?

You will also use the actual negotiation process to learn from your counterpart(s) what their real interests are or how they prioritize their many interests. As your understanding of their interests expands in the course of the negotiations, you should continuously update the chart. What may be a number one interest to your team or group may be of secondary or minimal importance to your counterpart(s). By identifying the different weight or importance of various interests, the parties will be able to promote trade-offs or exchanges that will lead to their mutual satisfaction.

Practice Tip:

Another tool to help identify interests is to pose a series of questions on a piece of paper and then rate how a counterpart(s) might gain or lose based on his/her current perception of choices. Development of a *current perceived choices (CPC)* chart can be a powerful tool in understanding how various negotiation choices appear to a counterpart(s). Such a chart can help to uncover and identify the party's real interests. While the interest identification may sound elementary, party interests are often not revealed or obvious because of the power of articulated negotiating positions to obstruct or eclipse the parties from understanding and ranking core interests.

One of the most important skills to develop in the practice of international trade negotiations is the ability to learn from your counterpart(s) by listening, by asking focused questions, and learning to read "between the lines" (i.e., study the body language, emotion, and sense of importance or urgency that a party places on various negotiating issues or agenda items to discover underlying interests).

In trade negotiations, it can be safely assumed that all parties at the table seek to advance their economic interests, but there may be a multitude of other important interests that compel the parties to take the positions they do. Some of these interests in trade negotiations may include:

► Protection of sanitary and phytosanitary interests

► Protection of domestic standards

- Protection of the domestic labor force

- Protection of the environment

- Protection of political power and legitimacy of those engaged in the negotiations

- Protection of intellectual property rights or interests

- Protection of public health

- Compliance with international law or trade rules over a specified period of time

- Application of the same rules to other competitors

- Gaining positive media coverage or a public relations advantage

- Protection of political power

- Protecting national sovereignty

- Generating a perception of fairness, equal treatment, or shared burdens

This list is demonstrative and not exhaustive. It is intended to illustrate the multitude of interests that may influence the positions and attitudes of negotiators in a single trade negotiation. The ranking and prioritization of interests will differ between parties. It is in the recognition of these different priorities in the interest that the skilled negotiator can offer creative options (solutions) that maximize prospects for a negotiated agreement.

Framing the Issues

The interests of stakeholders is determined by the impact of the targeted policy measure on the commercial interests of competing enterprises and workers, the policy objectives served by the targeted policy measure, the broader economic impact of the measure, and institutional and bureaucratic interests. It is also shaped by the domestic and international legal provisions that apply to the measure.

A stakeholder's perceived interests may or may not coincide with that stakeholder's real interests, depending on the availability and accuracy of their information. A successful Commercial Diplomat therefore analyzes the issues not only to better understand the issues at stake, but also potentially to educate other stakeholders on their real interests where that reinforces the analyst's own objectives.

A complete understanding of the issues and of the perceived and real interests of stakeholders forms an essential basis for framing the issue for negotiation. In the course of preparing for negotiations, a Commercial Diplomat may find it necessary or desirable to redefine the negotiating issue periodically as more information sheds new light on the issue. For example, as you learn more about the policy issue underlying the targeted measure, you may find that your own understanding of the problem was faulty and that the more accurate information calls for a different approach to the problem. Or you may need to redefine the problem to reach out to potential coalition partners whose interests are similar but not exactly the same as yours. You may find that a better understanding leads you to recast the issue in terms that provide a closer legal fit.

Once you are comfortable that you have done all the necessary analytical work for framing the issue, you must build public support at home and abroad for the desired policy action. If you represent a private stakeholder group and your task is to align the position of your home government with your group's interests, you want to negotiate with the government with as much support from other stakeholder groups as possible. This may call not only for a coalition building strategy, but also for a public media strategy and a strategy for obtaining the support of knowledgeable and respected experts in the field. If you represent the government, you want to be sure you have strong public support at home for your negotiating position as well as active support from stakeholder groups in other countries that have the potential of swaying their own negotiators. This calls for an active strategy to reach out to stakeholders with similar interests in other countries and a foreign press strategy that will enable you to get your perspective accurately reflected in the foreign press.

What should be clear is that successful negotiations are preceded by a considerable amount of hard work to identify the issues and the interests of the key stakeholders, to develop and implement a strategy that will build broad public support at home and abroad, and to negotiate with domestic stakeholders in hammering out a negotiating position for the home government. Successful negotiations are like an iceberg. What you visibly see is only a fraction of what you do not see.

The international bargaining is not the end of the negotiating process either. Any negotiated agreement has to be sold to the home constituencies and implemented with their support. An agreement that is successfully negotiated at the bargaining table but ultimately fails to gain the support of the home government because it is opposed by key constituencies is a failed agreement. Similarly, an agreement that is successfully negotiated and approved by the home government is still a flawed agreement if the officials responsible for implementing the agreement fail to implement effectively, either because they do not have the capacity or because they lack commitment to the outcome.

Identification of Problems and Opportunities

What are the elements of the problem (dispute)? Negotiations take place when parties identify a problem or opportunity that they believe can be resolved or positively exploited through a negotiated agreement. As part of the planning in preparation for a formal negotiation session, it is crucial to identify the problem or opportunity presented and to thoroughly analyze and understand the history and nature of the problem. (Note: for purposes of this section, reference to a problem or conflict between parties will include opportunities as in business or commercial agreements.)

By understanding the nature of a problem or conflict, a negotiator is better able to anticipate the interests of a counterpart(s) and to advance proposals and options that may take into account the history of the problem between the parties.

► **History of the conflict.** What is the history of the conflict between or among parties? In a trade dispute, the history may include past practices, tariffs, quotas, dumping, or other trade-related practices that have defined a trading relationship. What has changed since the original conflict began? Have political parties or representation changed key players within administrations or effected businesses?

► **Identify multiple elements of the problem and break the problem down by breaking the problem into multiple parts.** Various solutions can be applied to different aspects of the problem. If part of the problem can be solved, this may build confidence among or between the parties to solve the outstanding issues.

► **Frame the key issues.** By breaking the problem down into its component parts, a negotiator can prioritize the most important issues and devote appropriate time and resources to solving those aspects of the problem that are essential to a solution.

Example: A dispute over the importation of genetically modified organisms (GMOs) from the United States to the EU may be easier to resolve if the larger problem is broken down into its component parts:

► Foods for human consumption or animal feed,

► Processed foods or fresh foods,

► More or less than 5% GMO content,

► Subject to labeling or not,

► Timetable for importation/implementation (30 days or three years?), or

► Products already tested by the Food and Drug Administration (FDA) in the United States or not?

Practice Tip:

Interview people familiar with the history of the conflict to learn the dynamics and particulars of the dispute.

What is the opportunity to be pursued through negotiations? As indicated above, many negotiations are prompted by parties seeking to resolve a conflict or seeking to avoid a conflict. The *opportunity* to be achieved in a negotiation is often more apparent in a commercial or business transaction where the parties seek to negotiate a mutually beneficial outcome.

In a trade dispute the parties must analyze the opportunity presented by a negotiation as compared to the alternative. The opportunity may be to avoid the consequences of a more protracted and costly dispute settlement process under WTO rules, or to avoid retaliation or penalties that may result from an adverse finding if your party is deemed to have violated established trade rules and requirements.

Other measurements of opportunity at the negotiation table may include:

► Preservation of the trading relationship,

► Nondisruption of other trade flows,

► Exploration of options that may be less costly than a full-blown dispute settlement procedure,

► An opportunity to learn of the other party or parties' explanation of conduct or position, or

► An opportunity to maintain status quo while exploring options at the negotiating table.

Why is a negotiated resolution preferable to other options? As will be discussed, *infra*, a crucial element of the negotiation planning process, is to determine the BATNA (Best Alternative to a Negotiated Agreement) of all parties. This process may be considered to be a "cost-benefit" analysis of negotiations. Some factors to consider in weighing the benefits and costs of negotiations are:

► How much time will be required to pursue a negotiation?

► Will there be travel required?

► What will be personnel costs in terms of research, planning, and preparation?

► Will a negotiation process be efficient in terms of time and cost as compared to a non-negotiating alternative?

Options and Possible Solutions:

Can You Identify Your Preferred Outcome?

Closely linked to your analysis of the problem and opportunities presented by a negotiation process is your ability to articulate your negotiating goals and objectives – or your preferred outcome. What is the ideal solution that would satisfy all of your interests? While it is unlikely that you will be able to attain all of your objectives in a negotiation, it is critical to be able to articulate with your team and allies exactly what solution, remedy, or objectives you are pursuing. If you do not have a vision of your preferred outcome, it will be virtually impossible to develop a comprehensive negotiating strategy; and just as you seek to break down the negotiating problem into multiple subsets, you will be far more effective at the negotiating table if you can break down your preferred outcome into multiple parts. Articulating different outcomes that would satisfy some or all of your interests will give you greater flexibility at the negotiating table.

Can You Really Describe What You Want?

Practice Tip:

Write what you want on paper. Spell out exactly the outcome that would be ideal, and do this for as many aspects of the problem that you can identify.

Does writing what you want on paper mean that you will share that with your counterpart(s)? Not necessarily, although in some situations that may prove advantageous. In the "dance" of high stakes negotiations, parties may prefer not to reveal what they consider to be their "bottom line" or the absolute last compromise that they would be willing to make.

Revealing your bottom line should not be confused with understanding what you are going to pursue in the negotiation. When asked what you want, you should be able to reply with an emphasis on key interests that you seek to satisfy as well as some options that will still leave you room to bargain or engage in the practice of trade-offs or mutual compromises.

Can You Describe Your Counterpart's Negotiating Objectives/Preferred Outcomes?

Just as it is important to be able to articulate and describe your broad negotiating objectives, it is important to be able to identify your counterpart's negotiating objectives. In a multilateral (multi-party) negotiation, the various parties may share some objectives while maintaining very divergent views or goals on various issues.

As part of the planning process, it is recommended to at least attempt to write down your counterpart's negotiating objectives. Put yourself in "their shoes." What does the problem look like to them? What do they want? By understanding what your counterpart(s) are seeking, you may be better equipped to fashion proposals that will empower them with their respective superiors and constituencies.

Even in high-stakes negotiations, parties will often arrive at the negotiating table without a clear vision of what they want. The ambiguity and lack of focus of a negotiating team can make the work that much harder for all parties. By asking questions of your counterpart(s), you can help to determine what their key interests and objectives may be.

By articulating what you consider to be your counterpart's key interests, you might explore, hypothetically, what you consider to be their key goals in the negotiation. Invite your counterpart(s) to correct your assumptions if you have made an incorrect assumption, and use this tactic as an opening to draw out your counterpart's negotiating objectives.

Remember, by learning from your counterpart(s) what their interests and negotiating objectives are, you are NOT making concessions or agreeing to accommodate.

You are simply expanding your understanding, conveying to your counterpart(s) that you respect the importance of the issue to him/her, and establishing an aptitude as a negotiator to collect valuable information and insight before fashioning proposals or modifying proposals that may already be on the table.

Practice Tip:

Never underestimate the importance of a particular issue or interest to your counterpart(s). What may not seem important to you may be very important to your counterpart(s). If you can incorporate language that addresses a key objective at little cost to yourself, then do it.

Example: In an air route and landing rights negotiations between the U.S. government and a Latin American country, the Latin American negotiators made it clear that they would need technical assistance to properly train their pilots and air traffic controllers. To the U.S. negotiators, this was of little consequence as the U.S. government was committed to providing the technical assistance. The U.S. negotiators were dismissive and sought to reassure the Latin American delegation that they had nothing to worry about and that there was no point in taking up time in the negotiations. As a consequence, the negotiations were bogged down by the harder issues of air routes, landing rights, etc., and a disgruntled Latin American delegation left the negotiations. Had the U.S. government team spent some time crafting language that affirmed its commitment to technical assistance, the Latin American team would have secured important text to take home and perhaps justify compromises made on other issues.

Authority of the Parties - Who are the Individuals at the Table and What is Their Authority?

What is your negotiating authority? A party's *authority* in the negotiation process indicates the authority to make a binding or enforceable commitment. *Limited authority* means that a party does not have the authority to fully commit their interest group to a binding decision.

It is essential to determine and clarify YOUR authority prior to entering a negotiation. Your authority is generally determined by your superior within a government bureaucracy, corporate organization, or NGO. You may be required to negotiate the terms of your negotiating authority within your organization, usually with a superior or with a committee of key stakeholders in your organization. It is not uncommon to represent your party with limited authority. Limited authority may require that any agreement be reviewed and approved by a superior or committee before you receive authorization to sign the agreement. A skilled negotiator will use his/her limited authority to explore all options for agreement but will remind your counterpart(s) that no final or binding commitments can be made until approval from a higher authority (not present at the negotiating table) has been obtained.

What is your counterpart's negotiating authority? And, while knowing the parameters of your negotiating authority is critical, determining the negotiating authority of your counterpart(s) is absolutely essential.

How do you discover the negotiating authority of your counterpart(s)? *You ask!* It is generally not in the interest of the counterpart(s) to mislead or deceive a negotiating partner regarding their authority. If their authority is limited, they will want to communicate that to protect their ability to test interim or provisional agreements without committing to conclude the agreement without approval from a higher authority.

Authority may also be deduced based on past practice, protocol, or prior agreement. It can never hurt, however, to clarify your counterpart's authority. The failure to determine your counterpart's authority, or yours, can lead to failure of the negotiations. A failed opportunity to conclude a negotiated agreement that represents the hard work of the parties is a wasted effort.

If you will be expected to gain approval of a higher authority before finalizing a negotiated agreement, you will need to agree to a time period during which you can seek approval or learn of concerns. It is also useful to ask your counterpart(s) to whom they will have to present the terms and conditions of an interim or final agreement. Is that person reachable? How long will they need to review a proposal or interim agreement? Can they be reached by phone, cable, fax, or email?

Practice Tip:

Keeping notes and copies of proposed agreements on a laptop computer will make it easier to forward text for review and approval during the negotiating process.

Use of Limited Authority Can be Used to Your Advantage

The use of *limited authority* may be used to your advantage. By making it clear that any final agreement or interim agreements must be reviewed by a person or a group that is not present at the table, you can use your limited authority to seek the input of superiors before agreeing to final language, text, or other commitments. Similarly, by knowing of your counterpart's limited authority, you can float "trial balloons" (exploratory proposals) that your counterpart(s) can be expected to convey to his/her superior. By obtaining feedback, questions, or other articulated concerns, amendments might be made during the course of the negotiation that may be missed under pressure to agree but which will enhance the quality of the agreement and its durability.

Negotiating Authority and the Importance of Speaking with "One Voice"

Closely related to a party's negotiating authority is the importance of a negotiating party speaking with one voice. A governmental delegation will most often be represented by a "head of delegation" who will also serve as the lead negotiator. It is of critical importance in negotiations for a team that may be composed of several members to communicate and reflect a unified position at all times. Nothing will undermine a negotiating team's credibility more than an aura of disunity, disagreement, or other forms of dissension. If disunity or disagreement is observed by a counterpart negotiator, that negotiator will move to exploit those differences or will simply be confused by the team's inability to present a unified and coherent proposal or response.

Practice Tip:

As part of your presentation and planning, be clear as to who will lead the delegation in the negotiations and who will speak on various agenda items. If there are questions during the process of an active negotiation, pass a note to the head of your delegation and suggest a break. Discuss differences, review proposals, and explore options within your team AWAY from the negotiating table.

OPENING, MANAGING, AND CONCLUDING NEGOTIATIONS54

This section explores the organization and choreography of opening, managing, and concluding a negotiation. A well-run negotiation follows a number of well established steps for choreographing the negotiating process. Some of the steps are designed to assure that the negotiating team is solidly grounded in terms of its relationship with the home constituencies. Other steps are designed to achieve an efficient organization of the negotiations and to create a positive feedback mechanism that will facilitate progress in the negotiations. Some of the steps in a well-choreographed negotiation can help minimize irritants that could distract and derail the negotiations and create a sequence of events that will allow negotiators to make progress on an incremental basis. The ultimate value of a well-choreographed negotiation is to create positive psychological and physical feedback mechanisms that will encourage participants in the negotiations to expand their horizon and to address the issues under discussion with a great deal of creativity.

Organizing the Negotiating Team

A governmental delegation most often consists of a "head of delegation," who serves as the lead negotiator, as well as experts on various issues and representatives of various departments and ministries. The head of delegation should organize the team well in advance of the start of negotiations, giving each team member a clear set of responsibilities. This will not only assure that every team member feels like a full participant who will take responsibility for the outcome, but it will also lighten

---

54 Much of the material in this and the next section is taken from a manual entitled *Negotiation in Commercial Diplomacy* coauthored by Bill Monning and Geza Feketekuty and available on www.commercialdiplomacy.org. The manual built on ideas developed by Roger Fisher of the Harvard Negotiating Project and disseminated through various books, including *Getting to Yes: Negotiating Agreement Without Giving In* by Roger Fisher and William Ury (New York: Penguin Books, 1991).

the load on the lead negotiator and assure better preparation of the negotiating issues.

It is of critical importance in negotiations for a team to reflect a unified position at all times. Nothing will undermine a negotiating team's credibility more than an aura of disunity, disagreement, or other forms of dissension. If disunity or disagreement is observed by a counterpart negotiator, that negotiator will move to exploit those differences or will simply be confused by the team's inability to present a unified and coherent proposal or response.

Drafting the Negotiating Instructions

In pursuing these discussions with domestic and foreign stakeholders, negotiators are usually acting under general guidance they have received from their superiors on the negotiating issues. Since no formal commitments are being made on behalf of the government involved during these discussions, they usually take place without formal negotiating instructions. Once the negotiations move from informal discussions to formal negotiations, however, negotiators become bound by negotiating instructions that receive all the necessary approvals from their home government. Most governments have a legally established procedure for approving such instructions that normally require not only the approval of superiors within the Trade Ministry (or Foreign Ministry) but also by other key departments and ministries within the government.

Negotiating instructions constitute the following:

▶ **A delegation of authority** by the political authorities of a government to its negotiators, giving them the authority to speak on behalf of the government, and

▶ **A script for the negotiations** that sets out the country's positions on the issues, the arguments negotiators should put forward in support of those positions, the information they should seek to obtain from negotiating partners, and what they may agree to during the negotiating sessions covered by the instructions.

The negotiating instructions should set out the country's opening position for the negotiations and spell out the flexibility that can be exercised by the negotiators. As a general rule, negotiators should be given some degree of flexibility in exploring possible negotiating outcomes but only a limited degree of flexibility to agree on an outcome that substantially differs from the negotiating position outlined in the instructions. After all, the instructions and the negotiating proposals on which they are based reflect carefully crafted compromises among stakeholder at home, inside and outside of the government, and these stakeholders should be given an opportunity to participate in the evolution of the country's negotiating position. Besides, it is normally advantageous to allow some time for reflection on new negotiating outcomes because it is usually difficult, if not impossible, to think through all the ramifications and implications of new compromise proposals. Of course, as the negotiations move to a final conclusion, the negotiators have to be given a well-defined range of outcomes that they are authorized to accept. Even then, it is common for negotiators to seek and obtain final instructions from their superiors before finally concluding an agreement.

Pre-negotiating the Negotiations

Every negotiation actually begins before the negotiators sit down at the negotiating table. Through phone calls, email messages, and other communications, the negotiating parties need to discuss and decide on the following:

► Meeting logistics (when, where, and who participates).

► Exchange of background information that can be reviewed before the negotiation session.

► The Agenda – a list of the topics to be covered in the negotiations and a sequence of topics and the amount of time that should be scheduled for each topic. A scheduling of different topics may allow the two parties to decide who should sit in during which portion of the negotiations.

► Rules of the negotiation.

► Confidentiality.

► Media contacts.

► Use of interpreters.

Negotiators can also use the pre-negotiation period to learn as much as possible about the expectations of their counterpart(s). By exchanging information about expectations, the participants can avoid being caught by surprise when the formal sessions are convened.

The Preliminary Steps of the Dance

Before launching into the negotiation proper – the substantive issues that have brought the parties to the table – the negotiators will want to go through a basic check list to insure a productive negotiating session.

► Introduction of team members. It is useful to build an early rapport with the negotiators on the other side even though there may be serious and contentious issues that divide the parties.

► Review of logistical arrangements, agreements on confidentiality/media issues, and the agenda.

► Review of mutual expectations regarding the objectives or desired results of the negotiating session – to exchange information, explore issues, identify possible solutions, and conclude a final agreement.

Opening Statements

An opening statement is an important "first intervention" in a formal negotiation, working group, or conference setting. The opening statement provides parties with an opportunity to identify key issues and interests as well as to articulate parameters for potential agreements. This is not a process where a party "reveals a bottom line", but rather an opportunity to stress the importance of the outcome to the interests of the party and to establish early in the proceeding exactly what the party making the opening statement has been directed to pursue by his/her nation or other organizational hierarchy.

After a few negotiating sessions, participants can grow weary of the repetitive enumeration of each side's views and positions on the issue. Nevertheless, a country's position, no matter how often it is repeated, remains one of the anchor points in a negotiation, and it is important to be clear about the starting point for each negotiating session. It is important for each negotiator to be able to report faithfully to his/her home government that the negotiating team clearly laid out the country's negotiating position in line with its negotiating instructions. This is an essential aspect of maintaining the confidence of the home government and of the nongovernmental stakeholders at home. No matter how confidential a negotiation is, information about the negotiations inevitably leaks out.

Repetition of the country's position also provides an opportunity to ask whether any aspect of the position has changed since the last session. Miscommunication and false assumptions can easily set a negotiation back, so it is always important to be very clear about the two positions that frame the negotiation. Patience is a key characteristic of a good negotiator, and a certain amount of repetition is the price you pay for being a negotiator.

Practice Tip:

Use your opening statement to clearly identify your key interests, to acknowledge your counterpart(s), and to employ some dramatic effect to underscore those key objectives that you may deem to be essential to your agreement. You put all parties on notice, you establish yourself as prepared and resolute, and you can also indicate areas where you think creative options or compromise might be appropriate.

Be attentive to your counterpart(s) as they make their opening statements. You convey respect without offering compromise, and you learn what is of utmost importance to them. There may be a use of terminology, phrasing, or nuance that you can incorporate in a proposal or later intervention that will resonate clearly with the other party.

Exploring the Positions and Interests of the Parties

The opening statements provide a platform for a subsequent exchange of clarifying questions on the respective positions and the underlying interests of the parties. A good way to start the process is for the head of each delegation to summarize the position of the other side and to seek confirmation that they understood the position of the other side correctly. This provides each side the opportunity to clarify and elaborate on their initial statement of the position and to ask clarifying questions of the other side.

As discussed earlier, negotiating positions need to be distinguished from interests. The negotiating position, which is what a negotiator is instructed to ask for at any particular phase of the negotiation, is dictated not only by the organization's interests, but by the negotiating strategies and tactics of the parties. Interests underlie positions. Interests are the commercial interests, policy objectives, bureaucratic imperatives, or legal requirements that a negotiator must satisfy in a negotiation in order to obtain the approval of the home constituencies. Interests are at the very core of what drives parties in a negotiation.

In trade negotiations, it can be safely assumed that all parties at the table seek to advance their economic interests, but there may be a multitude of other important interests that compel the parties to take the positions they do. The ranking and prioritization of interests will differ between parties. It is in the recognition of these different priorities in the interest that the skilled negotiator can offer creative options (solutions) that maximize prospects for a negotiated agreement.

The interests of stakeholders is determined by the impact of the targeted policy measure on the commercial interests of competing enterprises and workers, the policy objectives served by the targeted policy measure, the broader economic impact of the measure, and institutional and bureaucratic interests. It is also shaped by the domestic and international legal provisions that apply to the measure. A stakeholder's perceived interests may or may not coincide with that stakeholder's real interests, depending on the availability and accuracy of their information. A successful Commercial Diplomat, therefore, analyzes the issues not only to better understand the issues at stake, but also potentially to educate other stakeholders on their real interests where that reinforces the analyst's own objectives.

Active Listening

Active listening is one of the most important skills to be developed as a negotiator. It sounds like common sense, but many negotiators do not make good listeners. Negotiators often become so convinced of the wisdom of their own arguments, and become so intent on convincing others of their particular point of view, that they naturally tend to interpret what they hear through the prism of their own view of the issue and to think others agree with them when in reality they do not. A healthy degree of skepticism is, therefore, a healthy trait in a negotiator. When in doubt, ask to confirm what you thought you heard.

Another aspect of listening is to place information provided by other negotiators into the proper context. Is it information about the official position of the organization the negotiator represents or is it information about the underlying interests of the organization? Is it an argument why you or others should support the position the other negotiator is advocating? Is it a statement about the underlying beliefs of the organization your negotiating partner represents, or perhaps is it information about the personal views of the negotiator? It obviously makes a huge difference whether a statement provides information about the organization's position, belief, or interests, and whether it is an official view or a personal view.

Many years ago the American representative to the Development Committee of UNCTAD made the statement that the United States did not believe in special and differential treatment (S&D) as the right approach to economic development. Some delegates interpreted that statement as an indication that the United States would oppose S&D in the Doha Round, which was not what was said. The Ambassador did not say that it was the position of the United States to oppose the extension of S&D. A belief says something about a country's philosophical predisposition but not what it intends to do on an issue.

How can we tell what the negotiator meant? We have to listen for the introductory comment. Does the negotiator say, "It is my country's 'position'..." or does the negotiator say "It my country's 'belief'..."? Does the negotiator say that the country's objective is to expand opportunities for a particular group or avoid injury to another group, which are statements about "interests"? In private conversations the negotiator may be even more direct in describing the interests they are seeking to satisfy. Does the negotiator say that others should agree with a particular proposition "because" it would accomplish a variety of wonderful objectives? The word "because" is a tip-off that what follows is a recitation of reasons why other parties should agree to the proposition being advocated. Those reasons do not say anything about the country's own objectives or practices.

The most confident negotiators use the art of active listening to enhance their understanding of their counterpart's interests. Active listening is more than just listening. Active listening includes the act of communicating to a counterpart(s) that you have heard what they said. By communicating understanding, the negotiator is not accepting or acquiescing to a counterpart's proposal. By actively restating what the speaker has said, you communicate that you have indeed heard what was said.

Asking Questions – Information is the Basis for a Successful Negotiation

Combined with the skill of active listening is the skill of asking. This may sound like a basic tenet of negotiations at any level, but many inexperienced negotiators use every opportunity to advance their proposals, their options, and their ultimatums at the table. By failing to use the negotiation setting as an opportunity to learn, a negotiator will remain uneducated about his/her counterpart's interests.

Asking for information or clarification conveys interest and a willingness to understand the other party's interests.

- ▶ Questions can draw information from counterpart(s). Information that has not been offered or volunteered by a counterpart(s) in an opening or affirmative statement may be shared or revealed in response to a question.

- ▶ Questions and responses will contribute to *building the information base for the negotiations.* The broader and more complete the base of information, the better equipped a negotiator will be to fashion proposals, options, and solutions that can result in a successful outcome.

▶ Leading questions are those designed to get your counterpart(s) talking/sharing information. Examples of intentional "*leading questions* include:

  o "How did you arrive at that position?"
  o "What is your proposal based upon? If we understand the basis of the proposal, we will be better equipped to share it with our superiors, home office, etc."
  o "What information did you rely upon to reach that conclusion? Would you share a copy with us?"
  o "Please explain further..."
  o The use of the single word "*Why*" can be a trigger to uncover underlying party interests...

Patience in the negotiating process can give a negotiator the upper hand in terms of command of information, finding out what is really important to counterpart(s), and determining areas where trade-offs or compromise might be appropriate.

Sharing Information

In addition to asking good questions, the successful negotiator also is willing to share information with his/her counterpart(s). Negotiations are all about discovering mutual advantage, and a negotiator for the other side is only able to identify creative ways of meeting your interests or avoiding your more sensitive problem areas, particularly when the other side could meet your needs with little pain, if your counterpart(s) has a thorough understanding of your interests and problems. Withholding information goes against the grain because we are taught that information is power, and many negotiators, therefore, think that denying information to the other side will strengthen their negotiating position. The more likely outcome of withholding information about one's interests is a failed negotiation.

Identifying Your BATNA (Best Alternative to a Negotiated Agreement) and Your Counterpart's BATNA

As part of the negotiation planning and strategy development process, a party must compare the potential advantages of a negotiated solution to those alternatives available to the negotiator without negotiating.

Example: If an employee seeks to negotiate a raise with his/her boss, he/she can employ whatever arguments and reasoning he/she thinks should entitle him/her to the raise. The employer has the option to grant or deny the raise. The employee will have more leverage in the negotiation with his/her present boss if he/she introduces his/her BATNA – another job offer. This increases his/her negotiating leverage because if he/she does not get the raise he/she can pursue the other job. If the alternative job offer is good enough, he/she can forego the negotiation with his/her current boss all together and simply accept the new job offer.

As part of the planning process, identify what options are available to your team away from the table. The BATNA is NOT static. You can work to improve the strength of your BATNA by actively working to strengthen the availability and desirability of a walk-away alternative.

Similarly, it is essential to anticipate and chart the BATNAs that may be available to your counterpart(s). How can you keep them at the table if they have a strong BATNA? You can keep your counterpart(s) engaged in the negotiation process by introducing information (evidence or objective criteria) that will make their BATNA look less secure, uncertain, or less attractive than what might be negotiated at the table. The following provides some examples.

All of the suggested possible BATNAs include the option of the *status quo* or acceptance of the current situation. On balance, the exercise of this "walk-away" alternative would be the result of an analysis that the current situation is acceptable or preferable to the time, resources, and likelihood of securing a better outcome through negotiations.

Practice Tip:

Do not confuse a BATMA with an option that must be secured through the negotiation process. By definition, a BATNA is not an outcome that is achieved in the negotiation; it is an option that is pursued in lieu of negotiations or if negotiations fail to produce an outcome that is attractive as the BATNA.

Remember to chart as many BATNAs as you are able to generate for your party and for all other parties engaged in the negotiation process. Understanding your counterpart's BATNAs is of critical importance. Your job at the negotiating table is to display an understanding of the other parties' BATNAs and to show them why those BATNAs are NOT as attractive as they may present them to be. If you know your counterpart's BATNAs, you can introduce information (facts, evidence, or objective criteria) to undercut the attractiveness of their BATNAs. This serves to keep the counterpart(s) engaged at the negotiating table and gives you more leverage to pursue a negotiated outcome.

Use of Objective Criteria

The final element in the interest-based negotiation chart, is the category of *Objective Criteria.* Objective criteria represent a set of independent or external standards that are introduced to support the legitimacy or fairness of a party's proposed option or solution.

Objective criteria can be viewed as factual information drawn from any number of sources. The introduction of objective criteria at the negotiating table is a form of submitting evidence in support of your argument or proposal. The goal is to persuade the other parties that your proposal is reasonable and consistent with findings of independent, neutral experts.

For example, in a dispute over the value of manufactured steel that is the subject of an anti-dumping complaint, some of the objective criteria that would be essential to the prosecution and defense of the claim would be production cost, grade of steel, market value, and other costs. Some of this information will be within the province of the parties to the dispute while some of the information will be generated exclusively by scientists, academics, or other experts familiar with the industry and industry practices.

Objective criteria can also be understood as the introduction of *fair standards*. By relying on a non-party to the negotiations, who in the normal course of business produces scientific or market studies, the parties can agree on the standards or norms that will serve as guideposts in the negotiation process.

A party may be skeptical of your representation that a certain proposal is fair. If you can offer outside criteria in support of your proposal, it will convey legitimacy to persuade both your counterpart(s) and their constituency or superiors.

Some examples of sources for objective criteria include:

► Market values

► Prevailing wage rates

► Industry standards and practices

► Expert studies

► Academic research and reports

► Rules and regulations

► Precedent decisions (decisions made by legal or authoritative bodies on similar types of issues or cases

► WTO Dispute Settlement Body decisions: while not binding, may be instructive as to how the WTO DSB would decide a similar case

► Court decisions

► Arbitrator decisions and awards

These elements, present in every negotiation, represent the fundamental aspects to be considered in the development of the negotiation strategy and at the negotiating table. Use of the interest-based negotiation chart is an essential planning tool and road map that can be used throughout the negotiation process.

Review of Core Elements Present in the Negotiation Process

► People (Stakeholders)

► Interests

► Options (solutions)

► BATNA

► Objective Criteria

Listening to and Recording all Proposed Options

It is important to record all proposed options. The use of charts or posted paper is an effective means as it will preserve the proposal for ongoing review and comment and create a record of the session. Without agreeing or acquiescing to a proposed option that has been generated by your counterpart(s), you can gain valuable information and expose potential weaknesses by asking the contributor, "How did you arrive at that solution or proposal? What is it based upon? Is there a factual, scientific, or other objective basis for your proposed option?"

No matter how unacceptable or unattractive a proposal offered by the other side may be in its entirety or by itself, you might be able to come up with counterproposals that build on or combine various proposals they have offered. By studying all their proposals you may find a way of moving the negotiations forward by showing them that you are listening to their ideas and have found a way of building on them. You will be able to use this tactic only if you have been faithful in recording all their suggestions. Moreover, by studying the pattern of their proposals you may get some valuable insights into the direction of their thinking.

Finally, if the presenter can offer further evidence or criteria in support of their proposal (or if you can in response to a similar question), the information shared may be useful in winning support from constituents or superiors who may be skeptical. Further information or lack thereof can fortify or reduce the value of a proposed option.

Make Charts

The use of charts is time saving and will help you to organize your information, facts, and planning. Making the chart at the beginning of your research and planning process is essential. Assembly of a chart at the end of the process is of little utility.

Team-building and Brainstorming

Organize a *brainstorming session* where teammates all join in to generate options to satisfy all the parties' interests. Such a team-building exercise can help assure that all participants in the negotiation become fully engaged in searching out solutions. In this exercise, begin with work on your own interests and generate different options that will satisfy those identified interests.

Practice Tip:

An organized brainstorming session should include use of flip charts, white boards, or butcher paper (sheets of white poster paper). Designate one team member to act as scribe to list the options as they are suggested. Proposed options should NOT be judged or evaluated during the preliminary brainstorming session. Allow the ideas to flow freely. Create an atmosphere that welcomes any and all ideas no matter how extreme or unrealistic. During a second session, go through the list and invite constructive criticism and prioritize the best options by ranking them numerically.

Even an apparently wild or unorthodox proposal may trigger a more realistic modification that will have utility and may be applied in the formal negotiation session. By employing this tactic, a negotiator can engage team members constructively in the formulation of options for consideration, comment, acceptance, or refinement. A useful technique for eliciting a team mate's input is to ask, "What if we did x, or what if we agreed to do y?"

Practicing Role Reversal

Role reversal can be an invaluable tool in achieving a better understanding of the negotiations. Practice role reversal, and have members of your own team play the role of counterpart(s). Insist that they assume the role by speaking in the first person. Ask them directly what are their concerns, goals and objectives, or interests. What would work for them and why?

Creating Multiple Solutions to Satisfy Interests

One of the key elements to effective negotiations is the development of multiple options or solutions to satisfy party interests. The best negotiators distinguish themselves by their ability to create and generate multiple options in both the planning stage and at the negotiating table. This is the area of interest-based negotiation where a negotiator's creativity and capacity to think beyond a single solution is paramount. The shortcoming of many positional negotiators is that they become fixated on single solutions or positions that blind them to other possibilities. Such singular thinking can lead to stalemate and impasse in the negotiation process.

Take Breaks from the Negotiating Table – "Go to the Balcony"

Get AWAY from the table. This can be one of the most important and underutilized tools to increase your negotiating power. Negotiators, even when representing large organizations, often make commitments or concessions without discussing them fully with teammates or superiors. If you exceed your negotiating authority you can anger superiors, and depending on the severity of the breach of confidence and authority, you might even lose your job!

"Going to the balcony" is a term intended to mean the physical act of absenting yourself from a room by going out on the balcony, or going to a balcony where you might still observe the proceedings but from a more distant perspective. Taking a break allows parties to achieve a number of important negotiating objectives, including:

► **To review an oral or written proposal.** "You have obviously put a lot of time into developing this proposal, let us take a few minutes to review it..." Or, depending on the weight and volume of what has been introduced by your counterpart(s), you may need a week or a month recess for your economists, scientists, or other experts to review the proposal and the underlying data upon which it has been based.

- ► **To develop or formulate a response.** Thinking "on your feet" or in the heat of the moment may lead to unwise decisions and result in an incomplete formulation of a counterproposal or response. Take a break, leave the room, and work on the formulation of a response or counter-proposal that protects and advances your party's interests.

- ► **To regain your composure.** If you feel that a counterpart is moving too quickly, using intimidating tactics, or if you simply do not feel right about the pace of the negotiations, then it is your absolute right and prerogative to request a recess or short break. Use a break to regain your composure, talk with your teammates, and to evaluate what has transpired that made you feel uncomfortable or uneasy.

- ► **To allow for a counterpart to calm down or review a proposal you have made.** Yes, you can take a break to facilitate your counterpart's need to hear from his/her teammates, who might be supportive of a proposal you have made and will lend their voice to move a recalcitrant lead negotiator.

How do you get away from the table? You simply ask to take a break. For instance, say

- "We would like to take a short break to review your proposal…"
- "We would like to take a short recess…."
- "Perhaps it would be helpful if we take a break and allow all parties a chance to review and discuss the most recent proposal."

A mediator may ask that parties wait until someone has completed a presentation or answered a question on the floor before agreeing to a recess. You, too, might ask another party to postpone taking a break until you have completed a proposal or explanation.

Introducing a Written or Single Text Document

The "dance" of negotiation can involve protracted dialogue and discussion that may seem unproductive as parties restate positions and appear to offer nothing to advance the process. In most productive negotiation sessions, the parties will eventually reduce areas of agreement or consensus to writing. Once parties begin working on text there is often a qualitative change in the course of the negotiations. Parties begin working together to craft appropriate and acceptable text. To be effective, a written or single text proposal need not be long or address a long list of issues. It is useful to use text that has been agreed to as building blocks.

A negotiator can actually expedite this productive stage of negotiations by introducing a *written or single text* document. By offering text that describes a prior agreement or suggests a potential resolution, the parties will begin discussing terms in response to a written text. When a draft proposal or agreement is presented to a counterpart(s), it should be with the intent of *inviting their feedback*. There may be proposed changes that are minor and which make the document read better. These are obviously welcome changes and give your counterpart(s) a hand in the crafting of the document. They see *their* words in the document and are more likely to support and sign an agreement that has their input and "fingerprint." Some proposed changes might be fundamental and go to the very substance of the negotiations. Even if the proposed change is unacceptable, it can be used as a platform for exploring other variants and options that may satisfy all parties.

Examples of single text or written documents cover a wide range, including:

- ► Proposed agenda

- ► Proposed procedural rules related to confidentiality, security, timetable of negotiations, location, etc.

- ► Proposed substantive elements of an interim or final agreement

- ► Proposed text on consequences of a breach of an agreement

- ► Proposed text on alternative dispute resolution mechanisms

- ► Proposed text on implementation guidelines, deadlines, etc.

- ► Proposed text incorporated from other documents, prior agreements, applicable rules, guiding principles, etc.

To be effective, a written or single text proposal need not be long or address a long list of issues. Use text that has been agreed to as building blocks that can be linked to or constitute an interim or final agreement between or among parties. Obtain signatures or initials of the parties on individual text documents and proposals to indicate support. This can be done with the assurance that no final agreement will be signed if it is not acceptable to the party, but the act of signing or initialing the interim agreement or building blocks is to establish a "culture of agreement" and signing documents together.

Drafting Durable Agreements

The following outline provides the key elements that should be contained in an enforceable agreement.

- ► Title – include suggestion of achievement in title (e.g., "Trade Agreement Between Chile and Brazil"; "Agreement on Reconciliation of Multilateral Environmental Agreements [MEAs] and Trade Agreements Between the United States and the European Union").

- ► Preamble – one or several paragraphs.

- ► "Media statement" – describes the achievement in layman's terms and is designed to make it easy for media and the public to understand significance and key elements of agreement.

- ► Identification of parties.

- ► Numbered paragraphs dealing with procedural and substantive agreements.

- ► Implementation provisions.

- ► Penalty provisions.

- ► Conflict resolution provisions.

- ► Signatures of the principal negotiators along with date and location.

- ► Translator's declaration, if a certified professional translator translated the document.

SKILLS TO EMPLOY AT THE NEGOTIATING TABLE AND GOOD NEGOTIATING HABITS

This section addresses negotiating habits that help to facilitate good communications among the negotiators, create a positive atmosphere conducive to progress in the negotiations, and facilitate the identification of win/win solutions to the negotiations.

Use of Silence

One of the more powerful skills to be employed in the negotiation process is the tactical and timely use of *silence.* In many cultures, protracted silence creates a socially uncomfortable atmosphere. People will offer words and verbiage to fill the silence. Counterpart(s) may offer further information, concessions, or compromises simply to fill the vacuum.

Cross-cultural Dynamics, Gender, and Language as Variants Affecting the Negotiation Process

International negotiations necessarily involve cross-cultural interactions that may affect the flow of a negotiation and the understanding of various parties to process proposals and agreements. In the field of international trade law and practice, a *diplomatic culture* has developed that has served to minimize some of the barriers that cross-cultural dynamics may pose in business or other nongovernmental negotiations. Diplomatic culture can be described as the universal culture of professional diplomats who often speak in a common language (English, French, Spanish) even if that language is not the diplomat's native language. Diplomats often maintain common habits associated with international diplomacy including western dress, common educational backgrounds, and familiarity with procedures and protocols associated with international law or rule-making.

However, even those who present themselves as part of this diplomatic culture may maintain strong cultural identification and habits with their native culture. Culture is manifested in many ways including the orientation to time (monochronic vs. polychronic); the decision-making process; the formality of the negotiation process; the formality of decisions (oral agreement vs. written contract.); the importance of age, language, and preferences; and attitudes toward food, music, sports, body language, etc.

Combined with cross-cultural issues that may affect the negotiation process is the difference in the role of men and women in various cultures. Gender dynamics may be of little importance or of profound significance depending upon the culture.

Language and the choice of language used in international negotiations is also an important variant in the potential success or failure of a negotiation process. Today, the diplomatic culture increasingly relies on English as the common language for inter-governmental negotiations. This may, of course, vary if all participants are South European, Latin American, or from a Francophone country or the former Soviet Union. The important lesson to be learned with respect to language as a variant in international negotiations is that people possess varying degrees of fluency.

Negotiators often are confused or misunderstand the intent of a counterpart negotiator even when negotiating in a shared common language. When negotiating with parties who do not share a common language, the potential for misunderstanding increases. Even with skilled, professional interpreters, a literally accurate interpretation may not convey the meaning or nuance intended by the speaker.

How can a negotiator be sure that his/her words are being understood as they are intended? Speaking slowly, rephrasing what the counterpart negotiator has said in the negotiator's own words, reviewing written text, and the use of interpreters (oral) and translators (written) represent nonexclusive options to minimize error or misunderstanding.

Practice Tip:

Never assume that a counterpart(s) has understood a proposal as intended, especially when using interpreters. Repeat, review, and invite your counterpart(s) to articulate their understanding of your offer, proposal, etc.

You can prepare to negotiate with a foreign counterpart by reading about the culture. This preparation is important and should be considered to be part of the planning and preparation stage of the negotiation process. A negotiator, however, must be cautious not to become too confident about his/her knowledge of a counterpart's culture. Businesses often employ an agent who is indigenous to the culture with whom negotiations are being conducted. The agent is someone who speaks the native language of the counterpart(s) and is familiar with the customs, culture, politics, economics, current events, and social practices of the culture. Such an agent is indeed someone who is a native of the country and the culture with whom the business is negotiating. Government negotiators usually rely on the services of their embassy or consular personnel who are based in the foreign country where negotiations are to be held.

Dealing with Dirty Tricks and Ultimatums

Most serious negotiators bring a level of sophistication and professionalism to the negotiating table, but there are always circumstances where a desperate or aggressive negotiator will employ dirty tricks, ultimatums, or intimidation. The key to dealing with unprincipled negotiators is to *recognize and identify* the tactics being used. By being mindful of the types of tactics that are sometimes used, you can evaluate the impact that such tactics are having on the negotiation process and utilize one of the following techniques:

- ► **Identify and focus on the tactic.** Explain to your counterpart(s) that you do not appreciate intimidation, abusive language, or ultimatums. You can also convey that you remain fully prepared to continue in a good faith negotiation but will not accept conduct that is disrespectful or designed to intimidate. In many instances, identification of the perceived tactic will result in a denial by a counterpart(s), but often you will realize a change in behavior as well. By clearly articulating what you perceive to be unacceptable behavior changes the atmosphere of the negotiation and registers that you will not succumb to such tactics.

- ► **Utilize counter-tactics to counteract the behavior.** In the face of an ultimatum (a "take-it-or-leave-it" offer), you can request a break to review the offer. Return to the table to draw the party back into the negotiation by asking them how they arrived at that final offer. Use questions to draw a counterpart(s) back into the game of a give-and-take negotiation.

- ► **Make contact with the counterpart's superior.** In the most egregious case of disrespectful, demeaning, or insulting attacks by a counterpart, indicate that you will not participate in a negotiation where such behavior is manifest. A party can refuse to continue in a negotiation where such tactics are employed and contact the offending official's superiors to request that the offending personality be replaced at the negotiating table before the process continues.

- ► **Demand respect for your team.** By treating counterpart(s) with a modicum of respect, you can appropriately demand that respect be reciprocated.

Often, the tactics described above reflect the conduct of a highly emotional, defensive, and inexperienced negotiator. While such tactics may have worked in some instances, you need to make it clear that such conduct is unacceptable in the present negotiation.

Building a Reputation

At the end of the day, a negotiator will be evaluated as fair or untrustworthy. If you gain a reputation as being unfair or unprincipled, this reputation will follow you and will be difficult to overcome. There is a difference between appearing tough but principled and being unscrupulous and unprincipled. You build your reputation as a negotiator in large measure by your ability to follow through and implement commitments made during negotiations.

As discussed earlier, building rapport and a good working relationship with your counterpart(s) will generate long-term benefits. Remember that you are dealing with people who have their own professional aspirations, honor, and pride. Often, the key ingredient in building a strong working relationship is to build a friendship away from the negotiating table. Sharing meals, gifts, and providing hospitality to negotiating partners who have journeyed to your city will translate into more productive work at the negotiating table. Your ability to reach out to the people at the table, regardless of the severity of conflict between principals, demonstrates a maturity and confidence that will win respect and help the parties to navigate the difficult terrain of the negotiation.

Creating a Win-Win Mentality

Bilateral negotiations aimed at the mutual reduction of trade barriers take place in an overall win-win framework, but they inevitably involve gains for some domestic stakeholders such as exporters or domestic consumers of imported products, and losses for other stakeholders such as domestic producers of competitive products in each country. Negotiators on both sides are expected to maximize the gains and to minimize the losses for their side. While economists would argue that both sides gain, whatever the impact on winners and losers in each country, the political economic reality is that losers are often in a position to block outcomes that do not take into account their interests. While winners can always trump losers where the potential gains are large enough, it is useful in a democratic society to persuade losers that the outcome is just. This usually means accommodating them in some way while persuading them that a successful negotiating outcome is in the interests of the country as a whole. A good negotiator is able to gain their support through a combination of offers and threats – an offer to make less of a cut in the trade barrier than might be possible if they acquiesce and a threat to ignore their interests if they chose to oppose the agreement actively.

Negotiations over the mutual reduction of trade barriers thus always involve hard bargaining, both at home and internationally. In light of the stakes for winners and losers, they inevitable take on a zero-sum mentality. Negotiators in such situations must always remind themselves that the desired outcome is a win-win solution for the country as a whole, consistent with an acceptable distribution of gains and losses among stakeholders. The challenge of the negotiator is to achieve such an outcome for both sides since both sides have to be satisfied with the outcome. The role of the negotiator is to let the other side know what is required to achieve a successful outcome, both in terms of the expected gains for exporters and what would constitute unacceptable losses for import competing industries. Equipped with information about each side's needs, the two negotiators then have the task of identifying an outcome that will maximize the potential increase in trade while meeting the domestic political requirements of each side.

The most important requirements for a successful outcome in such negotiations are a detailed analysis of the interests of stakeholders in both countries and comprehensive consultations with affected stakeholders on desired and achievable results. Good information about stakeholder interests in the other country will strengthen a negotiator's hand in negotiations with his/her counterpart(s) and provide the raw material for developing win-win solutions. Consultations with stakeholders will earn the negotiator the support of stakeholders when the negotiated agreement is tested politically at home.

CONCLUSION

Success in negotiations depends not only on innate bargaining skills and on the power of the countries involved, but also on a detailed and comprehensive analysis of the issues, persuasive oral and written communication skills, and the ability to build alliances. These are skills that can be learned and mastered by any competent professional in the field. Even when a relatively small country has provided the necessary training for its trade negotiators, they are able to have considerable influence on any negotiating outcome.

Successful negotiations follow certain guidelines that create an atmosphere of trust conducive to a search for win-win solutions and an orderly sequence for addressing the full range of outstanding issues in a negotiation. When these guidelines are followed by the participants in a negotiation, they create a positive feedback loop that adds a dynamic momentum to the negotiating process.

GLOSSARY OF TERMINOLOGY USED IN NEGOTIATION, MEDIATION, AND ARBITRATION

Agreement. A coming together of minds; a coming together of opinion or determination; the coming together in accord of two minds on a given proposition; in law, a concord of understanding and intention between two or more parties with respect to their relative rights and obligations or duties. The parties may confirm an agreement in the form of a written contract. An agreement may be verbal in nature.

Alternative Dispute Resolution (ADR). A method of resolving disputes that does not involve using the official (governmental) court system. ADR can be understood to include negotiations, mediation, or arbitration. Parties to a formal legal proceeding may agree to ADR (mediation or arbitration) during the course of litigation of a claim or dispute.

Amendment. An addition, deletion, or change in a document. Making an amendment may include proposing new or different language in the proposed terms of a contractual agreement prior to reaching a final agreement.

Arbitration. The submission for determination of a disputed matter to private persons selected in a manner provided by law or by prior agreement (contractual-arbitration clause, arbitration provision). The *arbitrator* is the person who arbitrates the dispute. An arbitrator acts as a private judge and is often selected by the parties to a dispute based on the arbitrator's subject matter expertise (construction, trade, employment). Arbitration is more formal than mediation. The arbitrator usually has *decision-making authority.*

- **Binding arbitration.** The parties to an agreement agree to be legally bound (committed) to the ruling of the arbitrator. The arbitrator renders a decision in the case and the parties must abide by that decision. There is no legal appeal or recourse following a binding arbitration decision unless there is evidence of fraud, conflict of interest, or some other recognized conduct that would invalidate the arbitration. The arbitrator provides a decision that may include a formal "finding of fact," application of legal precedent, assessment of witness credibility, and award or other relief.

- **Nonbinding arbitration.** The parties agree in advance to submit their dispute to a nonbinding arbitration. The arbitrator's decision will not result in the losing party having to commit to any remedy. The purpose of a nonbinding arbitration is for parties to obtain a "preliminary view" of how the case might be handled by a court (judge) or a formal arbitration. A nonbinding arbitration can be useful to educate the parties as to the relative value of a case for settlement purposes.

Authority

- **General.** That which authorizes the agent to do everything connected with a particular business. Authority is the "power to make a decision" or "to make a binding commitment."

- **Limited.** Limited authority means that the agent or representative of a government or business entity has precise instructions regarding commitment that can be made to reach an agreement. Government representatives must often clear the terms of an agreement with a higher authority. In the United States, a treaty agreement must be ratified (approved) by two thirds of the members of the U.S. Senate.

BATNA - (Best Alternative to a Negotiated Agreement). The "walk away" alternative to a negotiated agreement – the status quo or other options that can satisfy a party's interest without negotiating with a counterpart(s). A strong BATNA gives a party more negotiating power at the negotiating table. One measures the strength of a proposed option or solution against the attractiveness of the BATNA. A party anticipates the counterpart's BATNA and introduces objective criteria (facts) to make the counterpart's BATNA look weak.

Bilateral Negotiation/Agreement. Between two people or parties (government, businesses, NGOs). A multilateral agreement is among three or more people or parties.

Caucus.

- **Noun.** A meeting with one's own team members or associates or with a mediator or a representative of another party in a confidential setting – a meeting held away from the negotiating table.

► **Verb.** To caucus—the act of caucusing, of meeting privately with one's own teammates or associates.

Civil Law. A system of law based on codes and statutes developed by a legislative, parliamentary body.

Client. The person or party upon whose behalf or in whose benefit one negotiates. A lawyer represents a client. An agent may represent a business or government client.

Common Law. The system of law based on usages, customs, and judicial decisions (precedent legal decisions) as distinguished from civil law.

Compradore. An intermediary, agent, or advisor in a foreign country employed by a domestic individual or company to facilitate transactions with local individuals or businesses in the foreign country.

Conditional Agreement. An obligation that only comes into effect if a certain condition is met. A party's obligation to perform a certain task or commitment may be dependent on the counterpart's performance of a certain task or obligation first. A seller's obligation to deliver goods or services to a buyer may be conditioned on the buyer's delivery or presentation of a down payment, letter of credit, or some other means of payment.

Consideration. The inducement to enter into a contractual agreement. The cause, motive, price, or impelling influence that induces a contracting party to enter into a contract. Some right, interest, gain, advantage, benefit, or profit to one party, usually the promisor, or some forbearance, detriment, prejudice, inconvenience, disadvantage, loss or responsibility, act or service given, suffered or undertaken, by the promissee. In a contract for goods or services, the seller offers his/her goods for money paid by the buyer. The goods provided by the seller represent consideration. The money paid by the buyer represents consideration.

Contract. A promissory agreement between two or more persons (parties) that creates, modifies, or destroys a legal relation. An agreement, based upon sufficient consideration, to do or not to do a particular thing. A contract must be signed by the parties to the agreement.

Counterpart. An opponent or adversary in a negotiation. The other party or parties with whom one is negotiating. A seller's counterpart will be the buyer. The counterpart is not necessarily adversarial in outlook.

Escape Clause. A provision in a bilateral or multilateral commercial agreement permitting a signatory nation to suspend tariff or other concessions (temporarily violate their obligations) when imports threaten serious harm to the producers of competitive domestic goods (see General Agreement on Tariffs and Trade – GATT Agreement, Article XIX, and U.S. Section 201 of the Trade Act of 1974).

In an employment contract or other personal service contract, an escape clause may be included to relieve one or both parties of their commitments (obligations) after some prior notification (usually written) or upon the occurrence of some event or circumstance.

Fraud. An intentional deception or representation known not to be true. To falsely represent facts knowing them to be wrong for the purpose of gaining an advantage or other result. The use of an intentional misrepresentation to induce another person to act in reliance on that false information to his/her financial or other detriment. Proof of fraud in a commercial agreement may relieve the party who has been defrauded from obligations under the agreement. Proof of fraud may subject the party who has perpetrated the fraud to fines, penalties, or criminal prosecution.

Impasse. A stalemate in negotiations. The parties are unable to move forward. The parties to a negotiation refuse to make concessions or explore options that could lead to an agreement. An impasse in negotiations may be broken by mutual agreement, by bringing a mediator into the negotiation, or by suspending negotiations for a period of time while the parties explore or review their positions within their own organizations, governments, or corporations.

Interests. Interests are what compel people to negotiate. Interests lie behind positions. Interests may include a party's desire for economic security, military security, political recognition/legitimacy, sovereignty, political autonomy or representation, sustenance, or specific underlying goals that motivate the person or party to seek concessions or acceptable solutions to a dispute, problem, or business opportunity.

Interim Agreement. A partial agreement pending a final agreement. An interim agreement may be a partial agreement related to certain aspects of a complex negotiation. An interim agreement may bind the parties to certain conduct pending the outcome of an ongoing negotiation or dispute settlement proceeding.

Mediation. Involves the participation or inclusion of a "third party" neutral to help the parties to a conflict negotiate an agreement. The process of mediation is usually voluntary. The mediator has no decision-making authority. A mediation is less formal than an arbitration. A successful mediation results in the parties reaching an agreement, usually made enforceable by a written agreement (contractual). The mediator may meet privately with individual parties in caucus meetings (caucuses). The mediator helps the parties to negotiate an agreement, but because of the voluntary nature of the process, a party may leave the mediation and pursue other remedies or recourse if desired. A means of "alternative dispute resolution."

Non-negotiable Demands. Offers or proposed solutions for which the party making the offer will accept no other solution. Non-negotiable demands are intended to give the counterpart no negotiating power. A "take-it-or-leave it" offer may appear to be a non-negotiable demand. Non-negotiable demands may lead to *impasse*, or blocked negotiations where no agreement can be reached.

Objective Criteria. A set of fair standards. Facts, scientific evidence, precedent legal decisions, expert opinion or testimony, or other information that may be introduced to support a party's proposed offers, proposals, or solutions. Objective criteria can also be introduced to demonstrate that a counterpart's position, proposal, or offer is unreasonable by comparison to established values, holdings, market rates, or other criteria.

Offer

- ▶ **Noun.** A proposal or presentation of an option or solution for settlement of a negotiation or a component of a negotiation.

- ▶ **Verb.** The act of presenting a proposal for consideration by one's counterpart.

  - o **Acceptance.** The act of agreeing to an offer; to accept or agree to the terms that have been offered. To create a valid and enforceable contractual agreement there must be proof of an offer and an acceptance with some form of valuable consideration exchanged between the contracting parties.

Opening Statement. A preliminary statement or introduction of a party's interests in a negotiation, mediation, arbitration, or court proceeding. An opening statement may include matters of protocol including introduction of team members, greetings to counterparts, and an articulation of the broad aspirations/goals of the party. In contrast, closing statements involve a summation of facts, conclusions, achievements, or positions taken – a re-articulation of a party's interests.

Options. Possible solutions in a negotiation. By generating or creating multiple options (solutions) the negotiators (parties) may create more opportunities for settling the dispute or solving the problem. A good negotiator will create or generate multiple options as part of the preparation and planning process. These options can then be presented for consideration at the negotiating table where one's counterparts can also be invited to generate multiple options or solutions to the problem that is the subject of the negotiation.

Party/Parties. The person or organization that participates in a negotiation or signs a contractual obligation. The parties to a contract or a negotiation are the people or representatives of organizations, corporations, or governments whose interests are being discussed, negotiated, or effected.

Positions. Parties present positions in negotiations that may set forth a desired outcome, solution, or quantitative proposals. A party to a negotiation may become fixated on one position while refusing to look or consider other options or solutions. A party may present "an opening position" with the intent of amending or changing that position in exchange for a specific concession or offer from the other party.

Proposal(s). An offer made in the negotiation process. A suggested solution or element of an agreement. A proposal is generally presented by one party to another for consideration or response. A proposal may be presented verbally or in writing. A proposal may be presented at the negotiating table or may be communicated to another party in writing via various communication mechanisms (telefax, email, mail, etc.).

Counterproposal. A party's response or reply to another party's proposal. The counterproposal may modify or amend the text or content of the original proposal. A counterproposal may add conditions or elements for consideration of the original proposing party.

Reciprocity. Equally binding obligations. If one party makes a concession on tariffs or terms of trade, the trading partner(s) is expected to make an equivalent concession or adjustment. The terms and conditions of a negotiated contract usually set forth reciprocal obligations, responsibilities, or duties. A *quid pro quo* is an exchange of items, services, conduct, or actions designed to compensate one's counterpart for his/her actions, payments, contributions, etc.

Settlement. The negotiated resolution of a dispute. An agreement reached between or among parties to a dispute that may include future obligations or commitments. A settlement agreement may be enforceable in a court or before another tribunal.

Stalemate. See *impasse.* A moment in the process of negotiations when the parties can make no further progress.

Tribunal. A formal hearing or forum for the investigation or resolution of a dispute or conflict. A tribunal may be established on behalf of a national entity or an international body or commission.

(See also *The Dictionary of International Trade*, Edward G. Hinkelman, 9th Edition, World Trade Press, Novato, California, 2010, which can be purchased online at online e-stores or directly from http://www.worldtradepress.com/Dictionary_of_International_Trade.php.)

Acronyms

APEC	Asia-Pacific Economic Cooperation
BATNA	Best Alternative To a Negotiated Agreement
CD	Commercial Diplomacy
CPIL	Code of Public International Law
DC	Developing Country
DSB	Dispute Settlement Body
DSM	Dispute Settlement Mechanism
FTA	Free Trade Area
GATS	General Agreement on Trade in Services
GATT	General Agreement on Tariffs and Trade
GMO	Genetically Modified Organism
ICDP	International Commercial Diplomacy Project
ILO	International Labour Organisation
IMF	International Monetary Fund
LDC	Least-Developed Country
MEA	Multilateral Environmental Agreement
MFN	Most Favored Nation
NAFTA	North American Free Trade Agreement
NGO	Non Government Organization
NTB	Non Tariff Barrier
NTR	Normal Trade Relations
OECD	Organization for Economic Cooperation and Development
RTA	Regional Trade Agreement
SPS	Sanitary and Phytosanitary
TRIPS	Trade-Related aspects of Intellectual Property Rights
UNCTAD	United Nations Conference on Trade and Development
WIPO	World Intellectual Property Organization
WTO	World Trade Organization

GLOSSARY

SECTION 1

TERMS RELATED TO TRADE POLICY AND NEGOTITIONS

Accession. The process by which countries join the World Trade Organization (WTO) (1995) and, previously, under the *General Agreement on Tariffs and Trade (GATT)* (1947) (See Sec. II). The length of the accession process varies, depending on the conformity of the applicant country's trade practices with WTO norms. Details on WTO accession can be found at http://www.wto.org/english/thewto_e/acc_e/acc_e.htm. Individual WTO members and the applicant country also usually negotiate a "price of admission" – tariff concessions or other obligations including the reduction of quotas and other trade-distorting policies – to compensate for benefits that have accrued over the years through multilateral WTO negotiations in which the applicant country did not participate. The basic requirement for accession is that the applicant country's trade policies must provide nondiscriminatory and predictable treatment for all other WTO members; in return, the country becomes part of the organization that makes world trade rules, and also enjoys by right of international obligation the benefits of these rules for its exports.

ACP Countries (African, Caribbean, and Pacific). Refers to 79 countries (as of July 2011); most of them former colonies of member states of the *European Community* (Sec. II) – receiving preferential tariff treatment as well as EC financial and technical assistance under the *Lome Convention.*

Administrative Review. In *unfair trade* cases, a mechanism for parties to a case to appeal a ruling on subsidization, dumping, or injury to an administrative authority in the importing country.

Ad Referendum. Refers to delegations' acceptance of the outcome of a negotiation on a provisional basis, pending final approval by governmental authorities.
Ad Valorem Duty. See *duty.*

Ad Valorem Equivalent (AVE). A specific duty expressed in terms of a percentage of the value of the product in question. For example, a duty of $5 per ton on a product valued at $50 per ton has an AVE of 10%. When tariff negotiations are conducted on a percentage-reduction basis, AVEs must be calculated in order to permit proportional cuts in specific duties.

Agreement on Implementation of Article VI of the GATT. See *Anti-dumping Code.*

Agreement on Implementation of Article VII of the GATT. See *Customs Valuation Code.*

Agreement on Interpretation and Application of Articles VI, XVI, and XXIII. See *Subsidies Code.*

Agreement on Trade-Related Aspects of Intellectual Property Rights (TRIPs). Annex 1C of the Marrakesh Agreement establishing the WTO, signed in Marrakesh, Morocco, on April 15, 1994 covering all aspects of *intellectual property rights* protection. See *Trade-Related Aspects of Intellectual Property* Rights and *intellectual property rights.*
Agreement on Technical Barriers to Trade. See *Standards Code.*

Aide Memoire. In diplomatic parlance, refers to a written outline or summary of the main points of a proposed agreement.

Andean Trade Preferences Arrangement (ATPA). A nonreciprocal *preferential arrangement* established by the Andean Trade Preference Act of 1991, under which the United States grants duty-free treatment for a ten-year period to certain imports from Bolivia, Colombia, Ecuador, and Peru. The ATPA is intended to expand economic alternatives available to Andean countries that are engaged in combating drug production and trafficking. Eligible articles are the same as those under the *Caribbean Basin Initiative,* except rum.

Annecy Round. The second *GATT Round* of multilateral trade negotiations, held in Annecy, France, from April through October, 1949. The Round dealt with institutional matters and the accession of new members, but did not make significant progress in reducing trade barriers.

Anti-circumvention Duty. A term used by the European Union for penalty charges imposed on the output of Japanese screwdriver assemblies in Europe; subsequently found in violation of GATT rules by a *dispute settlement* panel. See *circumvention.*

Anti-dumping Code. Formally known as the Agreement on Anti-Dumping Practices. A code negotiated under the auspices of the GATT during the *Kennedy Round* (1963-67) and subsequently renegotiated in the *Tokyo Round* (1973-79). The code interprets the provisions of GATT Article VI, specifying the procedures signatory countries must follow to verify *dumping* allegations and providing the basis for the imposition, collection, and duration of anti-dumping duties. For an updated list of the parties to this Code, visit www.wto.org.

Anti-dumping Duty. A penalty charge on imports to protect domestic industry against disruptive pricing practices by foreign firms (see *dumping*). An anti-dumping duty is supposed to be set equal to the margin of dumping, defined as the difference between *fair value* and the actual sales price. GATT Article VI permits members to levy anti-dumping duties, while the GATT *Anti-dumping Code* attempts to standardize and discipline importing governments' activities in this area. See also *circumvention* and *injury test*.

Appellations of Origin. (Also referred to as "geographic indications of origin.") The name of a country, region, or locality designating a product's origin – such as Champagne or Camembert – and having the same function as a trademark or brand name. International negotiations on protection of *intellectual property rights* seek to resolve differences among countries' eligibility requirements (or lack thereof) for use of appellations or origin.

Applied Tariff Rate. The tariff rate actually used to determine the amount of duty owed on a particular import transaction. Applied rates may differ from *bound rates*. Arrangement on Guidelines for Officially Supported Export Credits. See *Export Credits Arrangement*.

Assimilation. A term referring to *national treatment* in the protection of *industrial property*. See *Paris Convention*.

Assists. Inputs to production – including blueprints, designs, tools and dies, and development engineering – provided by an importer to a foreign manufacturer for use in producing merchandise for purchase by the importer. The value of assists may be subject to import duties on grounds that they would have been reflected in the sale price if they had been obtained commercially by the foreign manufacturer.

Authors' Rights. A term used primarily in Latin American countries to refer to copyrights.

Auto Pact. (Formally known as the Automotive Products Trade Agreement.) A bilateral agreement signed in 1965 between the United States and Canada, providing duty-free treatment of most automotive products. The Auto Pact was augmented in 1988 by the Canada – United States Free Trade Agreement, which required phasing out remaining auto duties by 1998.

Balance of Concessions. An agreement in which one country reduces tariffs on its imports from another country in exchange for an equivalent or similar reduction from the second country. See also *reciprocity.*

Balance of Payments Consultations. The WTO permits countries to levy quantitative restrictions in times of acute deficits in their balance of payments. Countries invoking this provision take part in balance-of-payments consultations with other WTO members to justify the restrictions and specify plans to improve the payments deficit (see *Committee on Balance of Payments Restrictions,* Sec. II*).* GATT Articles XII and XVIII require such restrictions to be temporary, but often they remain in place for years. (Article XVIII, which provides more flexible and lenient conditions, may only be invoked by LDC members). The 1979 GATT Framework Agreement legitimized use of non-quantitative restrictions for balance-of-payments purposes (see *import surcharge).*

Base Price or Basic Price. See *Common Agricultural Policy.*

Basic Instruments and Selected Documents (BISD). An official compilation of documents in hardcopy, updated at irregular intervals in supplemental volumes, containing decisions, waivers, and reports adopted by the GATT Contracting Parties and subsidiary bodies. The BISD comprises the body of GATT "case law" from 1947-1995.

Berne Convention. Formally known as the Berne Convention for the International Protection of Copyrights. Signed in 1886 and revised in 1971, the Convention requires *national treatment* in the protection of *intellectual property rights* by signatory countries. The Berne Convention specifies rights of authors in more detail than the *Universal Copyright Convention (UCC)*, and its minimum term of protection is longer than under the UCC. See also *Paris Convention.* Not to be confused with the *Berne Union* (Sec. II).

Bilateral Investment Treaty (BIT). An agreement between two countries providing for nondiscriminatory treatment of direct investments. A BIT usually contains provisions for prompt and adequate compensation in the event of expropriation, guarantees on free transfers of investment earnings, freedom from *performance requirements,* and mechanisms for resolving disputes such as third-party arbitration. As of 2009, the United States had 40 BITs entered into force and seven not yet ratified. Countries that do not have BITs with the United States may instead be covered under free trade agreements.

Bilateral Restraint Agreement. See *export restraints.*

Binding. A formal commitment specifying maximum levels at which a WTO member's tariffs on a given product will be set. Tariff bindings provide a major element of stability to international trade by limiting large, unpredictable changes in tariff levels since other WTO members may be entitled to *compensation* if a country raises a tariff above the *bound rate*. Many LDC members of WTO have bound few of their tariffs, however, and others – applying "ceiling bindings" at rates much higher than prevailing tariff levels – retain considerable leeway to change tariffs at will.

Blair House Accord. A bilateral agreement between the United States and the European Community, concluded in November 1992 at the Blair House in Washington in an effort to resolve longstanding U.S.-EC differences on agricultural trade issues that had been blocking conclusion of a comprehensive agreement in the GATT *Uruguay Round.* Through the accord, an incipient *trade war* over oil seeds was averted when Brussels effectively froze subsidized soybean production at current levels, while Washington withdrew a threat to impose 200% tariffs on European wines. In addition, the accord stipulated that the final Uruguay Round text should require countries to reduce their tonnage of subsidized grain exports by 21% over six years.

Blockade. An interdiction of international shipments to or from a particular port or country by the military forces of another country. Any nation seeking to impose a blockade must proclaim its intention to do so in order for the action to be valid under international law. Moreover, the 1856 Declaration of Paris requires that a blockade must be effective and maintained by sufficient force in order to be internationally recognized. See also *embargo.*

Blocked Exchange. A restriction forbidding the unlicensed purchase of bills of exchange, currency, or negotiable instruments denominated in a foreign currency in order to prevent depletion of foreign currency reserves. See *exchange controls.*

Border Tax Adjustments. The remission of taxes on exported goods, including sales taxes and value added taxes, in order to ensure that national tax systems do not impede exports. The WTO permits such adjustments for indirect taxes --based on the economic assumption that such taxes are largely passed on to consumers – but not for direct taxes (e.g., income taxes assessed on producing firms). The United States makes little use of border tax adjustments since the federal government relies more heavily on income (or direct) taxes than do most other countries.

Bound Rates. *Most-favored-nation* tariff rates resulting from GATT negotiations and thereafter incorporated as integral provisions of a country's *tariff schedule.* The bound rate may represent either a tariff reduction or a commitment not to raise an existing tariff rate (see *binding*).

Bounty or Grant. A form of *subsidy.* As used in U.S. trade legislation, the term refers to an economic inducement by a foreign government to a manufacturer within its territory to encourage exports. Such inducements may include operating subsidies or forgiveness of debt; loans and loan guarantees at below-market rates; provision of goods, services, raw materials, or capital at below-market prices; or absorption of production or distribution costs.

Bovine Meat Arrangement. Formally known as the Arrangement Regarding Bovine Meat. An agreement negotiated in the *Tokyo Round* to promote expansion, liberalization, and stabilization of international trade in beef, veal, and live cattle, as well as to improve international cooperation regarding such trade. The arrangement is supervised by the *International Meat Council* (Sec. II). Signatories included Argentina, Australia, Austria, Brazil, Bulgaria, Canada, Colombia, Egypt, the European Community, Finland, Guatemala, Hungary, Japan, New Zealand, Nigeria, Norway, Poland, Romania, South Africa, Sweden, Switzerland, Tunisia, the United States, and Uruguay. This agreement was terminated in end-1997.

Boycott. A refusal to deal commercially or otherwise with a country, firm, or individual. A party to a "primary boycott" is one that refrains from trading with the targeted country. A "secondary boycott" is one in which parties to a boycott attempt to induce other countries to adhere to the boycott, often as a condition of continued trade relations with them. See also *embargo* and *sanctions.*

Bretton Woods System. The general term for the international monetary and financial system established after World War II to foster full employment and price stability while allowing individual countries to attain external balance without having to resort to trade restrictions. It takes its name from the July 1944 conference of 44 countries meeting in Bretton Woods, New Hampshire, to plan for postwar reconstruction and economic stability. The Conference laid the foundation for the *International Monetary Fund* and *World Bank* (Sec. II). A third specialized agency envisaged at Bretton Woods --the *International Trade Organization* (Sec. II) did not materialize, and the less powerful GATT took its place. See also *World Economic Conference of* 1927 and 1933.

Brussels Tariff Nomenclature (BTN). See *Harmonized System.*

Buyback Arrangements. See *Countertrade.*

Buyer Credits. See *Export Credits.*

Call. A request by an importing country for consultations with an exporting country concerning products whose shipments during a specified period are at or near a limit specified in a textile agreement. See *Multifiber arrangement (MFA).*

Caribbean Basin Initiative (CBI). A nonreciprocal *preferential arrangement* established by the United States in 1984 to promote economic development in Caribbean countries; it was made a permanent program in 1990 under the Caribbean Basin Economic Recovery Act. Trade programs under CBI remain vital elements in U.S. economic relations with Central American and Caribbean countries. Under CBI, U.S. duties are eliminated on all imports from beneficiary countries except textile and apparel products, canned tuna, footwear, certain leather goods, and certain watches and watch parts. As of 2011, current beneficiary countries include Antigua and Barbuda, Aruba, the Bahamas, Barbados, Belize, British Virgin Islands, Costa Rica, Dominica, El

Salvador, Grenada, Guatamala, Guyana, Haiti, Honduras, Jamaica, Montserrat, Netherlands Antilles, Nicaragua, Panama, St. Kitts and Nevis, St. Lucia, St. Vincent and the Grenadines, and Trinidad and Tobago.

Caribbean-Canadian Common Market (CARIBCAN). A nonreciprocal *preferential arrangement* established by Canada in 1986 to extend tariff preferences to Commonwealth countries in the Caribbean region. Beneficiary countries are Antigua and Barbuda, Bahamas, Barbados, Belize, Dominica, Grenada, Guyana, Haiti, Jamaica, St. Kitts and Nevis, St. Lucia, St. Vincent and the Grenadines, Suriname, and Trinidad and Tobago. Under CARIBCAN, Canadian duties are eliminated on all products imported from beneficiary countries except textiles, clothing, footwear, luggage and handbags, leather garments, lubricating oils, methanol and alcohol, and tobacco products. Product eligibility requires 60% local content. More information on CARIBCAN can be found at the Caribbean Trade Reference Center, http://ctrc.sice.oas.org/Trade/caribcan/Caribcan_e.asp.

Cartel. A group of producers (or producing countries) entering into a collusive arrangement to regulate pricing, production, or marketing of goods by members. The aim of a cartel is to restrict output in order to raise prices; cartel members thereby gain the profit advantages of a single monopoly, but since they continue to function as separate entities, without the offsetting efficiency gains, a monopoly may achieve through economies of large-scale production. Cartels are illegal in the United States but are more common in other countries. The *Organization of Petroleum Exporting Countries,* or *OPEC* (Sec. II), is a prominent example of an international producer cartel.

Central and East European Countries (CEECs). CEECs include all Eastern Bloc countries west of the post-World War II border with the Soviet Union, the Independent states in former Yugoslavia, and three Baltic states: Albania, Bosnia-Herzegovina, Bulgaria, Croatia, the Czech Republic, Estonia, Germany, Hungary, Kosovo, Latvia, Lithuania, Macedonia, Montenegro, Poland, Romania, Serbia, Slovakia, and Slovenia. Belarus, Ukraine, Moldova, and Russia are members of CIS and not included in the CEECs. Ceiling Binding. See *binding.*

Centre William Rappard. Built in 1923 for the International Labour Organization (ILO), in 1977 it became the secretariat for the General Agreement on Tariffs and Trade (GATT) and is now the headquarters of the WTO in Geneva.

Check Price System. A device used by a government agency to avoid charges of *dumping* in foreign markets by establishing floor prices for exporting firms.

Chicken War. A *trade war* that occurred in 1962-63 between the United States and the European Community. Prior to 1962, U.S. chicken exports had entered many European countries at a bound tariff rate. Adoption of the *Common Agricultural Policy* imposed minimum import prices on all imported chicken, nullifying prior tariff concessions and causing an estimated $26 million in losses to U.S. poultry farmers. When attempts to achieve a negotiated resolution failed, the United States imposed retaliatory duties on European trucks, brandy, and other products.

Circumvention. Measures taken by exporting companies to forestall or evade the payment of penalty charges in an importing country such as *countervailing* or *anti-dumping duty.* Examples include false labeling, *transshipment,* and screwdriver assembly. See also *diversionary dumping* and *downstream dumping.*

Civil Aircraft Agreement. Formally known as the Agreement on Trade in Civil Aircraft. The only sectoral agreement covering manufactures to result from the *Tokyo Round* negotiations. Under the agreement, signatory countries eliminated tariffs on civil (i.e., nonmilitary) aircraft, engines, and components; established rules covering governments' involvement in civil aircraft purchases; and applied the GATT *Standards Code* and *Subsidies Code* to the aircraft sector. Code signatories are proscribed from pressuring airlines to buy from particular suppliers and may not grant or deny landing rights in attempts to influence aircraft purchases. There are currently 31 signatories to this agreement. For a full list of signatories, visit www.wto.org.

Clearing Agreements. See *Countertrade.*

COCOM List. A list compiled by the *Coordinating Committee for Multilateral Export Controls* or *COCOM* (Sec. II), designating strategic or sensitive products to be denied exportation to potentially hostile countries. The COCOM List encompassed the International Atomic Energy List; the International Munitions List; and the International List, which includes both military items and *dual-use goods.* A uniform control procedure, known as the International Import Certificate-Delivery Verification System was established by *COCOM* (see Sec. II) member countries to prevent diversion of restricted products.

Code of Conduct. An international agreement establishing standards of behavior by countries, corporations, or individuals deemed desirable by the international community. Such codes are essentially normative statements of principle and, unlike treaties or commercial agreements, have no binding force. Not to be confused with *GATT Codes.*

Codex Alimentarius. See *Codex Alimentarius Commission* (Sec. II). The compilation of minimum grades and standards for raw and processed food products published by the Commission is known as the Codex Alimentarius. Upon adherence by a government, all "codex standards" become minimum standards by that country. See *sanitary and phytosanitary measures.*

Column 1 Rates. U.S. tariff rates that have been established through international negotiation and approved by Congress. Column I rates are applied on a *most-favored-nation* basis and are usually subject to *binding* in GATT.

Column 2 Rates. U.S. tariff rates assessed on imports from countries not receiving *most-favored-nation* treatment. Most Column 2 rates date from the Smoot-Hawley Act of 1930 and are substantially higher than Column 1 rates.

Commercial Counterfeiting. A deceptive trade practice involving trademark piracy, false labeling, or other fraudulent means of claiming manufacture by a reputable producer. See *Counterfeit Code.*

Commodity Agreement. A formal international arrangement among exporters and importers of a commodity. Such agreements have often been advocated by commodity exporting countries for the purpose of stabilizing price fluctuations, but few arrangements have been successful in doing so. The United States currently participates in commodity agreements covering coffee, wheat, jute, rubber, lead and zinc, tropical timber, copper, and cotton. Of those, only the International Natural Rubber Agreement currently contains economic stabilization measures. See *international commodity organization, buffer stocks,* and *export quota agreement.*

Commodity Control List. A listing of products subject to *export controls* administered by the U.S. Department of Commerce. The list includes items on the multilateral *COCOM List* as well as those subject to unilateral U.S. restrictions.

Common Agricultural Policy (CAP). The system of production targets and marketing mechanisms maintained by the European Union to manage farm trade within the EU and with the rest of the world. Article 39 of the *Treaty of Rome* established the CAP in 1961 for the European Community as a mechanism merging the individual member states' agricultural policies into a unified program to promote regional agricultural development, fair and rising standards of living for the farm population, stable agricultural markets, increased agricultural productivity, and methods of dealing with security of food supply. The main categories of CAP market management and support mechanisms are:

- ▶ **Support Prices** covering most grains, sugar, milk, beef, veal, pork, certain fruits and vegetables, table wine, and fishery products.

- ▶ **External Protection** without price supports, applying to eggs, poultry, certain fruits and vegetables, flowers, and wine other than table wine.

- ▶ **Deficiency Payments** or supplementary product aid to producers, covering olive oil, some oilseeds, tobacco, sheep meat, tomatoes, and raisins.

- ▶ **Flat-Rate Aid** based on acreage or output, covering durum wheat, cottonseed, flax seed, hempseed, hops, and dehydrated fodder.

- ▶ The CAP was designed as a policy that relied extensively on trade measures to maintain and stabilize internal prices. Thus, two of the most prominent features of the CAP in terms of its effects on international trade are the *variable levy,* and *export subsidies* to promote exports of farm products that cannot be sold within the EU at target prices. The CAP mechanisms for managing the domestic market and regulating imports are based on a variety of price concepts, the main types of which are:

► **Target Price.** An optimum wholesale price established with reference to the income requirements of EC farmers and consumer interests as well as to world market prices. The products concerned are grain, sugar, milk, olive oil, rapeseed, and sunflower seed. When the commodity price falls below the target price, the EC intervenes to purchase supplies and raise prices. To encourage distribution, the target price for a commodity in an area experiencing shortages may be reduced by the cost of transport from areas within the EC where excess supplies exist.

► **Guide Price.** Corresponds to the target price, but applies to beef, veal, and wine.

► **Base Price or Basic Price.** Corresponds to the target price but applies to pork.

► **Norm Price.** Corresponds to the target price, but applies to tobacco.

► **Threshold Price.** A minimum import price for grain, sugar, milk products, and olive oil, calculated so that the imported product (after payment of transport costs) cannot be sold at less than the target price. The difference between the world price and the threshold price is covered by a *variable levy.* The threshold price for grain is computed by subtracting from the target price the costs of inland transportation from the nearest ocean port to the EC market center showing the greatest shortage of the commodity.

► **Gate Price (also known as a "Sluice-Gate Price" or "Lock-Gate Price").** A minimum import price established for pork, poultry, and eggs. The gate price is derived by computing the cost of feed adjusted quarterly in relation to world market prices and other factors constructed to represent producer costs in the non-EC country with the highest technical efficiency. When the price of an imported product falls below the gate price, a *supplementary levy* is imposed to neutralize the presumed price advantage of the foreign producer.

► **Reference Price.** A minimum import price established for fruit and vegetables, wine, and certain fishery products. The reference price is established in relation to EC producer prices in a way similar to the gate price but modified to reflect the special characteristics of the relevant commodity markets. A *countervailing charge* (not to be confused with a *countervailing duty*), may be levied in addition to the normal customs duty to cover the difference between the entry price of an imported product and the reference price.

► **Intervention Price.** The price at which EC intervention agencies are obliged to purchase commodities offered on the market. The products concerned are grain, sugar, butter, powdered milk, certain cheeses, olive oil, rapeseed, beef, veal, pork, and tobacco.

EC member states were large net importers of most agricultural products. While variable levies under the CAP isolated EC producers and consumers from world market forces, it was not seriously disruptive to world trade for products in which the EC was a net importer. Since the 1970s, however, a combination of CAP price incentives and technological advances led to increased agricultural investment and domestic production increases at a time when European demand for farm products was stagnant or falling. The EC consequently went from a net importer to a major net exporter of grains, sugar, meat, and poultry, leading to escalating trade frictions with other countries. At the same time, the CAP was beset with problems arising from monetary fluctuations, costly subsidies, overproduction, and high price support levels.

Still currently in force under the European Union, CAP's agricultural subsidies have represented up to 48% of the EU's budget. At present, CAP has been substantially reformed, and it is anticipated to decrease significantly after 2013.

Common External Tariff. A uniform tariff schedule applied by members of a *customs union* or *common market* to imports from nonmember countries.

Common Market. A group of countries formally committed to the unrestricted movement of goods, services, and factors of production traded among themselves. Features of a common market include elimination of tariffs and other barriers to internal trade, including harmonization of national standards that regulate the sale and distribution of goods; establishment of a *common external tariff*; and abolition of capital controls and restrictions on labor mobility among members. A common market may seek to harmonize macroeconomic policies or promote political unification, but this is not a necessary feature. See also *customs union* and *economic union.*

Comparative Advantage. Relative efficiency in production of one particular product or class of goods over another class of goods. Differences in comparative advantage among countries are the basis for mutually beneficial specialization. In principle, an international trading system organized around the concept of comparative advantage should increase worldwide efficiency and standards of living. In this sense, it is the basis for viewing international trade as a "win-win proposition" rather than the "winners and losers" model assumed by *mercantilism.*

Compensation. Trade concessions granted by a WTO member to offset the disadvantage caused to other members whose exports are affected by its withdrawal or suspension of previously agreed trade concessions or *bindings.* Compensation usually takes the form of reductions of tariffs on other products of commercial interest to the countries being compensated. See also *consultations* and *dispute settlement.*

Compensatory Tax. An import levy applied by the European Union to certain agricultural products when the import price is below a reference (or minimum target) price and reflects an export subsidy. Not the same as a *variable levy.*

Competitiveness. The ability of a nation or firm to sell competitive goods or services in international trade. Several aspects of competitiveness are involved in shaping international trade patterns, and can be categorized as:

> ▶ **Price Competitiveness.** Determined by the interaction of four factors leading to competitive prices on world markets: real input costs (material prices, wage rates, and the cost of capital); productivity; profit margins; and the exchange rate. Most firms have some control over the first three factors but have no control over the exchange rate. Government monetary and fiscal policies may directly or indirectly affect the first and fourth factors, while industrial targeting seeks to influence the second and third. Changes in competitive factors do not always occur in unison; shifts in one of the factors can be offset by movements in the opposite direction by another factor.

> ▶ **Technological Competitiveness.** Representing the ability to provide leading-edge technical capabilities, superior performance characteristics, fuel economy, or reliability. Technological competitiveness can sometimes be more important than price competitiveness in international trade, particularly in advanced-technology industries such as telecommunications equipment and aerospace.

> ▶ **Commercial Competitiveness.** Reflecting the vigor, creativity, and effectiveness of firms' entrepreneurial activities, including marketing and distribution and the provision of associated services that increase buyer value.

Apart from such fundamental aspects of competitiveness, firms and governments sometimes try to manipulate competitive outcomes by engaging in *competitive policies and practices,* or in *unfair trade practices.*

Competitive Policies and Practices. Actions by governments or firms to affect their competitive performance in international markets. Such actions can be legal (e.g., government-to-government lobbying or export promotion) or illicit (e.g., bribery or deceptive trade practices), and some are subject to multilateral agreements (e.g. tied to aid or concessional trade finance). Such practices may be undertaken by nations or firms to compensate for or bolster their underlying *competitiveness.* Illicit practices on the part of individual firms are usually termed "unfair business practices," as distinguished from *unfair trade practices,* which are actionable under multilateral trade rules.

Complementation Agreement. An agreement between a manufacturing firm and two or more governments to reduce or eliminate duties on specified items produced by the firm in one of the signatory countries. Complementation agreements are usually granted to induce a firm to establish manufacturing facilities in one of the signatory countries by ensuring access to all of the signatories' markets for its output.

Compulsory Licensing. A term used in the context of *intellectual property rights,* primarily with regard to licensing of pharmaceutical patents. It refers to the legal authority to compel a holder of a patent to license production to a local firm as a condition of patent protection and sale in that country. Compulsory licenses may be granted by a government allowing local parties to use a patent, copyright, or trademark with or without the owner's consent, and are usually granted on grounds of national security or overriding national interests or of nonworking by the original owner. Proponents argue that compulsory licensing can lead to increased competition and reduced prices by encouraging production among a larger number of producers. Critics argue that such measures have the same trade-distorting effect as a *local content requirement* or *performance requirement.*

Compound Tariff. A combination of a specific *duty* and an *ad valorem* tariff on the same imported item (e.g., $100 per unit plus 5% of the assessed value). Sometimes called a "mixed tariff."

Computed Value. (Not to be confused with *constructed value.)* An alternative method permitted by the *Customs Valuation Code* for establishing the value of imported merchandise for customs purposes when neither the *transaction value* nor the *deductive value* can be determined. The computed value is the sum of various production costs and charges associated with preparing goods for export, together with imputed profit and overhead.

Concession. An agreement to reduce import restrictions, such as through a tariff reduction or *binding,* granted in negotiations in return for equivalent concessions by trading partners. See *reciprocity.*

Conditional MFN. The granting of *most-favored-nation* treatment subject to the recipient country's compliance with specific terms or conditions. Because all members of the WTO are expected to accord unconditional MFN treatment to other members, conditional MFN is normally applied only to countries that do not belong to the WTO.

Confrontation and Justification. In negotiating parlance, refers to the process of defining country positions through multilateral cross-examination. Following confrontation, or questioning of a country's policy position or negotiating offers by other countries, the country being confronted is expected to respond with justification of its stand on the points raised.

Consensus. In WTO parlance, the outcome of a negotiated decision among contracting parties in which sufficiently generalized support for a position is achieved to permit action. A decision in the WTO is made by consensus if no party formally objects to the decision and is almost always achieved by avoiding rather than utilizing voting. Because membership in the WTO is a contractual arrangement, members cannot normally be bound through voting procedures in "majority rule" fashion. As a result, virtually all WTO decisions are made by consensus except decisions on amendments, waivers, and accessions. In any given case, a dissatisfied WTO member must decide whether the issue warrants expending negotiating capital in blocking a consensus. Consensus decisions in the WTO are not necessarily optimal; one former negotiator referred to the WTO consensus process as a "balance of dissatisfaction." See also *reverse consensus.*

Constructed Value. *See fair value;* not to be confused with *computed value.*

Consular Fees and Formalities. Special charges and procedures, such as documents that must be approved by a designated official, required by importing countries as a prerequisite for permission to import merchandise. Cumbersome consular formalities are especially widespread among developing countries, and because substantial fees are often charged for required authorizations, they can function as a significant *nontariff barrier* to trade. See also *customs and administrative entry procedures.*

Consultations. Any WTO member that believes its trade interests have been adversely affected by changes in the trade policy of another member, or by failure of another member to live up to its obligations, may request consultations with the offending country:

> ► **Article XXII** of the GATT stipulates that contracting parties must be receptive to requests for consultation "on any matter affecting the operation of the Agreement" (i.e., even if no violation of GATT rules or commitments are at issue). Article XXII consultations are important because they give members an opportunity to negotiate solutions to trade problems on a bilateral basis within the framework of the GATT. Should bilateral consultations under Article XXII fail to resolve a dispute, one or both of the parties may "raise the ante" by invoking Article XXIII.

> ► **Article XXIII** of the GATT also provides for bilateral consultations as a prerequisite for invoking the multilateral *dispute settlement* process if a WTO member believes that the actions or inaction of another member have caused *nullification or impairment* of benefits expected under GATT. As such, Article XXIII consultations represent a higher threshold of "seriousness" since they can culminate in multilateral review and recommendations from the *GATT Council* on how to resolve a dispute.

Similar provisions are contained in other agreements of the WTO, such as the GATS.

Consumer Subsidy Equivalent (CSE). The percentage by which consumer prices on an item are affected by direct or indirect government supports to producers.

Contingent Reciprocity. See *selective reciprocity.*

Contracting Party (CP). Formal term designating a signatory to the GATT (the term "member" of the GATT was often used informally). As signatories, contracting parties accepted specific *obligations* and benefits of the General Agreement and agreed to follow GATT rules in conducting their trade policy. Because of the *most-favored-nation* principle, all CPs received the benefit of lower tariffs and trade barriers that have been negotiated in GATT as well as recourse to GATT procedures for settling disputes with other members. CPs need not be independent, sovereign countries – Hong Kong and Macau are GATT members, for example – but must be autonomous in setting their trade policies. When written in capital letters, "CONTRACTING PARTIES" in GATT documents referred to the collective membership of the GATT, acting jointly rather than in their individual capacities. This entity was the only legally recognized body in the old (pre-WTO) GATT, as the Agreement itself makes no provision for a secretariat or for any subsidiary organs. The WTO, in contrast, is a legally recognized entity with a formally established institutional structure through which its members make decisions and carry out the other activities of the organization. As in the old GATT, GATT members can include sovereign countries as well as customs territories or groupings of sovereign nations such as the EU that have undertaken WTO obligations jointly.

Conventional Duty. A tariff or customs duty arising out of an international agreement, as contrasted with an "autonomous duty" unilaterally levied by a government.

Convention on International Trade in Endangered Species of Flora and Fauna (CUES). A multilateral agreement signed in 1973 to suppress international trade in endangered species of wildlife and plants. Signatories committed themselves to interdict exports or imports of species listed in the agreement, with limited exceptions.

Convention on Settlement of Investment Disputes Between States and Nationals of Other States. A multilateral agreement signed among World Bank member states in 1965 that established the *International Center for Settlement of Investment Disputes* (Sec. II). Signatories committed themselves to recognize decisions and arbitral awards in investment disputes and referred to the Center as binding.

Copyright. The exclusive right of authors, composers, playwrights, artists, publishers, or distributors to publish and dispose of their work for a specified time. Copyright protection varies from country to country , and its enforcement is a major issue in international negotiations concerning *intellectual property rights (IPR)*.

Counterfeit Code. A draft agreement initiated in the closing stages of the *Tokyo Round* but never concluded that would have addressed *commercial counterfeiting* problems in international trade. The initiative set the stage for subsequent work in the *Uruguay Round* on protecting *intellectual property rights (IPR)*.

Counterpurchase Contracts. See *Countertrade.*

Countertrade. An international commercial agreement in which a buyer pays for purchases wholly or partly with something other than money. Countertrade transactions can take various forms:

Counterpurchase contracts obligate the foreign seller to purchase from the buyer goods and services unrelated to the goods and services sold.

► **Reverse countertrade contracts** require the importer to export goods equivalent in value to a specified percentage of the value of the imported goods.

▶ **Buyback arrangements** obligate the foreign seller of a plant, machinery, or technology to buy from the purchaser a portion of the subsequent production during a specified time period.

▶ **Clearing agreements** between two countries stipulate that each signatory is required to purchase certain amounts of each other's products over a specified period using a designated "clearing currency."

▶ **Switch trading** involves a purchaser in one country assigning to a seller in another country an obligation due from a third party as compensation for goods purchased.

▶ **Swap schemes** involve parties exchanging equivalent goods at different locations to minimize transportation costs.

Countervailing Charge. A charge in addition to normal import duties that may be imposed under the European Union's *Common Agricultural Policy* on imports of certain fishery products, fruits and vegetables, and wine, to match the difference between the reference price and the entry price (for fishery products and fruits and vegetables) or the free-at-frontier price plus customs duty (for wine).

Countervailing Duty (CVD). A special duty levied on imports to enable domestic producers to compete on an equal footing with subsidized foreign producers. CVDs are levied in addition to normal tariffs in an amount necessary to offset government subsidies in the exporting country. U.S. trade law empowers the President to levy CVDs equal in amounts to any "bounties or grants" extended by other governments to exporters, although the law does not specify what kinds of government practices should be considered actionable; see *export subsidy*. GATT Article VI permits and regulates the use of CVDs; additionally, signatories to the GATT *Subsidies Code* are required to meet an *injury test* before levying CVDs on imports from another signatory nation. Because foreign subsidies usually reflect broader government policies and programs, countervailing duties are frequently the object of intense and sometimes acrimonious bilateral diplomacy. CVDs are not used as a remedy to *dumping,* which refers to pricing practices by foreign firms.

Countries in Transition (CITs). In 2000, the IMF listed the following countries as transition economies: Albania, Armenia, Azerbaijan, Belarus, Bulgaria, Cambodia, China, Croatia, Czech Republic, Estonia, Georgia, Hungary, Latvia, Lithuania, Kazakhstan, Kyrgyz Republic, Laos, Macedonia, Moldova, Poland, Romania, Russia, Slovak Republic, Slovenia, Tajikistan, Turkmenistan, Ukraine, Uzbekistan, and Vietnam. In 2002, the World Bank defined Bosnia and Herzegovina and Yugoslavia as transition economies, and in 2009 added Kosovo, and Mongolia. Also, according to the IMF, Iran is demonstrating early stages of a transition economy.

Country of Origin. For purposes of customs administration, the country in which an imported product was manufactured, produced, or grown. When goods pass through more than one country in the manufacturing process, the country of origin does not change unless the product has been substantially transformed. In general, a product is considered to have originated in the country in which at least 50% of its final value was derived, although higher percentage thresholds are sometimes used. In the case of goods entering the United States under the *Caribbean Basin Initiative* or the *Generalized System of Preferences,* lower levels of local value-added may be allowed in establishing eligibility. See *rules of origin.*

Coverage. The extent of applicability of a trade action, agreement, or policy.

Cross-licensing. An arrangement in which a firm grants a license to another firm to exploit proprietary rights in its *patents, trademarks,* or *trade secrets,* in exchange for similar licensure to use intellectual property rights of the recipient firm.

Cross-Retaliation. *Retaliation* in one sector of trade, such as agriculture, to counter unfair actions or violations of agreements affecting trade in another sector, such as services.

Currency Controls. See *exchange controls.*

Customs and Administrative Entry Procedures. Formalities applying to customs clearance of imported goods at national ports of entry, including health and sanitary certificates, certificates of origin disclosing the name and location of the manufacturer, and consular invoices. Such procedures can result in increased import costs that inhibit trade even when not intended to do so. See also *Kyoto Convention.*

Customs Classification. The determination of the appropriate category in which a traded product is classified for tariff purposes. Also refers to the coding system or "nomenclature" used by customs officials as a guide in determining which tariff rate applies to a particular item. See *dutiable status.*

Customs Harmonization. International efforts to increase the uniformity of customs procedures, such as valuation, nomenclature, and enforcement by participating countries. See *Harmonized System.*

Customs Territory. The geographical area within which a country's customs authority is empowered to impose duties and controls upon foreign merchandise entering the territory .The customs territory does not necessarily encompass all the territory over which the nation asserts sovereignty. The customs territory of the United States, for example, does not include the Virgin Islands, American Samoa, or various foreign trade zones established within the United States. On the other hand, a country's customs territory may extend to other sovereign states. Monaco, for example, is part of the customs territory of France.

Customs Union. A group of countries that have agreed to eliminate barriers to trade among themselves while harmonizing their tariffs on imports from nonmember countries into a *common external tariff.* A customs union represents a level of economic cooperation intermediate between *a free trade area* and a more closely integrated *common market.* Unlike a common market, it does not provide for free movement of capital and labor among members.

Customs Valuation. The process of appraising the value of imported goods on which duties are to be assessed according to the *tariff schedule* of the importing country.

Customs Valuation Code. Formally known as the *Agreement on Implementation of Article VII of the GATT.* A *GATT Code* establishing rules for the determination of value for customs purposes, designed to provide a fair, uniform, and neutral system of valuation, and to preclude use of arbitrary or fictitious values as a disguised form of protectionism. The cornerstone of the Code is the presumption that the actual sale price – or *transaction value* – will be used whenever possible for valuation purposes; the *deductive value* or the *computed value* methods may be used in cases where the *transaction value* cannot be determined. The code was originally signed by 40 contracting parties. For more information on the Customs Valuation Code, visit www.wto.org.

Customs Value. A method of valuing imported goods that excludes shipping costs from the final price.

Decoupling. A concept aimed at making government agricultural programs trade-neutral by breaking the link between assistance to farmers and farmers' decisions to produce and sell agricultural products. Direct income supports are a form of decoupled assistance.

Deductive Value. An alternative method of valuing imported merchandise for customs purposes, permitted under the *Customs Valuation Code* if none of the methods for establishing *transaction value* is appropriate. Under the deductive value method, the customs value is determined by using the first sale price of the goods in the importing country and deducting certain costs incurred after importation. It is not normally used on goods destined for further processing or manufacturing within the importing country (see *super deductive).* An alternative to the deductive value method is *computed value.*

De Facto Member of GATT. Prior to the creation of the WTO in 1995, this was a term for countries that had a former dependency of a GATT member that since attaining independence had applied the GATT on a de facto basis, pending final determination of its commercial policy. Based on its previous association with the GATT as a colony or protectorate of another member, a de facto member could become a full Contracting Party without engaging in lengthy *accession* negotiations --simply by notifying the Director-General of its intention to accede.

Deficiency Payments. Government payments to compensate producers – usually farmers – for all or part of the difference between domestic market price levels for a commodity and a higher, governmentally guaranteed price. See *variable levy.*

Degressivity. The characteristic of a trade restriction that diminishes in severity over time. A degressive measure could take the form of an import quota with a "growth provision" to enlarge progressively the amount permitted to be imported, or a tariff the rate of which automatically declines according to a specified timetable.

Demarche. A formal diplomatic communication of a country's position on an issue, presented to an official representative of another country.

Derogation. In negotiating parlance, an exemption from part of an agreement demanded by a country as a condition for its acceptance of the remaining obligations or commitments.

Developed Countries. See *industrial countries.*

Developing Countries or Less-Developed Countries (LDCs). Within the GATT articles, numerous references are made to "developed contracting parties" and "less-developed contracting parties," but few criteria are given for establishing which category a particular country belongs to. As in most GATT decisions, such a determination is achieved by consensus. For all practical purposes, countries designate themselves as developing countries claiming thereby that they should be given special and differential (i.e., more favorable) treatment in trade negotiations. However, individual developed countries may or may not accept the self-designated status of a particular country as being a developing country. See also *industrial countries, newly industrialized economies (NIEs),* and *least developed countries (LLDCs),* as well as *graduation.*

Within GATT articles, numerous references are made to "developed contracting parties" and to "less-developed contracting parties," but few criteria are given for establishing which category a particular country belongs to; as in most GATT decisions, such a determination is achieved by consensus. See also *industrial countries, newly industrialized economies (NIEs),* and *least developed countries (LLDCs),* as well as *graduation.*

Differential Exchange Rates. See *multiple exchange rates.*

Dillon Round. The fifth *GATT Round* of multilateral trade negotiations, held in Geneva

from May 1959-July 1962. The Round focused on revision of the GATT agreements and the addition of new countries. Tariff reductions, which were based on *item-by-item negotiations,* averaged roughly 10% on $4.9 billion of trade among the 45 participating countries. The Round was named for C. Douglas Dillon, then U.S. Under Secretary of State, who led moves to launch the Round.

Direct Tax. A tax charged on all forms of income including wages, profits, interest, rents, and royalties, or on the ownership of real property. Under GATT Article VI and the *Subsidies Code,* the rebate of direct taxes on exported products – but not of *indirect taxes* – can be considered an *export subsidy* and penalized by a *countervailing duty.* The direct tax/*indirect tax* distinction in GATT creates a disadvantage for U.S. firms, since other countries tend to rely on indirect taxes while the United States relies more on direct taxes for revenue purposes.

Disciplines. In GATT/WTO parlance, refers to members' substantive obligations undertaken by members to refrain from discriminatory trade practices. Generally refers to the key principles upon which GATT rules are based, notably *nondiscrimination, national treatment,* and *transparency.*

Discrimination. Inequality in trade treatment accorded by an importing country to one or more exporting countries. Some forms of discrimination may be sanctioned by GATT, such as preferential tariff rates for imports from LDCs or from partners in *a free trade area.* Discrimination may also involve trade restrictions that apply to the exports of certain countries but not to similar goods from other countries (see *selectivity* and *grey area measures).* The opposite of discrimination is *most-favored-nation (MFN)* treatment.

Dispute Panel. See *panel of experts.*

Dispute Settlement. The process of negotiation, consultation, conciliation or mediation, and resolution of trade policy conflicts between GATT Contracting Parties usually through a negotiated compromise between opposing claims. GATT Articles XXII and XXIII establish the basis for procedures a Contracting Party may follow --sometimes including referral to an impartial *panel of experts* or *working party* of countries not involved in the dispute --to obtain redress if it believes its benefits under GATT have been impaired. See *consultations.*

Diversionary Dumping. Sales by a firm at *less than fair value* in a foreign country where the product is further processed and exported to a third country. See also *downstream dumping.*

Domestic Content Requirement. A requirement that foreign firms selling a particular product must use goods produced within the importing country as a specified minimum percentage of their inputs. Similar measures relating to inward direct investments are referred to as *local content requirements.*

Domestic Subsidy. Government aid to a domestic manufacturer, grower, or producer to maintain or increase production. Common incentives include direct payments, tax relief, and low-interest loans. As distinguished from an *export subsidy,* a domestic subsidy is not explicitly or solely directed at exports, although it may nonetheless have a significant trade impact. GATT Article XVI establishes substantive obligations or disciplines only regarding the use of export subsidies, not domestic subsidies. The GATT *Subsidies Code* recognized that domestic subsidies are widely used for the promotion of social and economic policy objectives, but requires signatories applying them to "seek to avoid" creating adverse affects on the trade interests of other signatories.

Double-Column Tariff. A *tariff schedule* listing two duty rates for some or all commodities. In any given case, the applicable rate depends on the exporting country's trade relationship with the importing country.

Downstream Dumping. Sales at below cost in a firm's home country to a downstream producer that further processes the product and exports it. Similar transactions involving a downstream producer located in another country are referred to as *diversionary dumping.*

Draft Final Act (DFA). See *Dunkel Draft.*

Drawback. Also known as duty drawback. The partial or total reimbursement of import duties by a government when the imported goods are re-exported or used in the manufacture of exported goods. Drawback can also refer to the refund of a domestic tax upon exportation of an article that has been subjected to it. Drawbacks may be considered *export subsidies.* See also *duty remission.*

Dual Pricing. The selling of identical products in different countries for different prices. When not based on factors such as differences in shipping costs or exchange rates, dual pricing is often presumed to reflect *export subsidies* or *dumping* practices. See also *price discrimination.*

Dumping. The sale of a product in a foreign market at *less than fair value,* presumably in order to capture or hold market share, or for other economic motives (see *price discrimination, predation,* and *shakeout).* Different forms of dumping can be categorized as:

▸ **Sporadic or distress dumping**. The disposal abroad of unanticipated inventory accumulations of a given product. Such dumping follows no fixed pattern, although it can be expected to be prevalent in the early stages of an economic downturn or business-cycle contraction.

▸ **Persistent dumping.** An ongoing dumping effort over an extended time period, usually reflecting a desire to compete in a foreign market that is more price elastic than the exporter's home market.

▸ **Predatory dumping**. A willful effort to undersell foreign producers in their home market, for the purpose of eliminating rivals and establishing *market power.*

▸ Dumping is widely considered to be an *unfair trade practice* because it can disrupt markets and injure producers of competitive products in the importing country. When dumping occurs, adversely affected firms in the importing country may seek redress through imposition of an *anti-dumping duty.* See also *diversionary dumping* and *downstream dumping.*

Dumping Margin. In a *dumping* investigation, the percentage by which the price charged in the importing country's market falls below a product's *fair value.*

Dunkel Draft or Dunkel Text. Efforts to conclude the *Uruguay Round* in 1991 culminated in December of that year with the tabling of a "Draft Final Act" (DFA) by GATT Director-General Arthur Dunkel, embodying all of the rule-making agreements under negotiation in the Round. In some portions of the DFA – commonly referred to as the Dunkel Draft or Dunkel Text – the texts had been fully negotiated among participating countries; in others where this was not possible, Dunkel put forward his own proposed solutions after extensive consultations with delegations.

Dutiable Status. A determination made by an importing country's customs authorities whether a particular article is subject to duty and, if so, at what rate. The dutiable status is determined by "classifying" the merchandise (i.e., determining into which category of the tariff schedules the product falls). See *customs classification.*

Duties Collected. A criterion for evaluating the comparability or *reciprocity* of concessions in a tariff negotiation. Refers to the amount of duties collected for a particular product at a specified duty rate over a given time period.

Duty. A tax imposed on imports or exports. Duties can be "ad valorem" (applied as a percentage of value), "specific" (applied on a quantitative basis, such as dollars per ton), or "compound" (a combination of both). See also *tariff.*

Duty Drawback. See *drawback.*

Duty Remission. A system allowing a firm to import goods into a country for processing and, when exported to a third country, to receive a repayment of duties paid at the time of the original importation. Unlike *drawbacks* , duty remissions do not require that the exported products contain elements of the imported product. Duty remissions may be considered *export subsidies.*

Duty Suspension. A temporary , unilateral reduction in tariffs. Duties are sometimes suspended to ease shortages of needed imports or "to lower the cost of products not available domestically."

Dynamic Asian Economies (DAEs). In OECD discussions and publications, this term has been used to refer to Hong Kong, South Korea, Malaysia, Singapore, Taiwan, and Thailand. As such, the term is broader than and may eventually supersede *NIEs.*

East-West Trade. In the parlance of the 1970s and 1980s, trade between the *former East Bloc countries* (the East) and industrial and developing countries outside the East Bloc (the West).

Eco-labeling. Government or privately sponsored labels or markings (also known as eco-seals or green seals) signifying that products or packaging are "environment-friendly," allowing consumers to discriminate among products in terms of their environmental impact. Labels signifying "dolphin safe" tuna are an example. See also *eco-packaging.*

Eco-packaging. Refers to national regulations and programs to encourage recycling or reuse of product packaging and containers together with associated labeling designed to promote use of "environment-friendly" packaging. Discussions in the GA TT *Group on Environmental Measures and International Trade* have addressed application of eco-packaging and labeling requirements in ways that do not discriminate against foreign products.

Economic Union. The highest level of economic integration between sovereign countries in which members proceed beyond the requirements of a *common market* to unify their fiscal, monetary, and socio-economic policies. Belgium and Luxembourg, for example, have been joined in an economic union since 1921.

Embargo. A prohibition upon exports or imports, either with respect to specific products or to specific countries. An embargo is usually applied for political reasons, although it may also be intended for economic or regulatory (e.g., environmental or sanitary) purposes. The term also applies to an official edict prohibiting entry or departure from the nation's ports of vessels flying the flag of a particular country. In cases where ports are closed only to commercial vessels of the targeted nation, a "civil embargo" exists. When ports are closed to military or public vessels as well, the condition is a "hostile embargo." Both an embargo and a *blockade* are particular forms of a broader category of economic countermeasures known as *sanctions.*

Enabling Clause. Part of the 1979 *Framework Agreement* providing a legal basis in GATT for *industrial countries* to grant tariff preferences to LDCs. The enabling clause amounted to a permanent waiver of the GA TT *most-favored-nation* provision for the *Generalized System of Preferences (GSP).* LDCs sought agreement on the enabling clause as a key objective in the *Tokyo Round* but were obliged to accept inclusion of language in the agreement that also recognized the *graduation* principle.

Enterprise for the Americas Initiative (EAI). A program launched in 1990 as a vehicle for defining a new U.S. economic relationship with Latin America, including eventual free trade within the Western Hemisphere. The three pillars of the EAI are trade, debt, and investment. See *Framework Agreement (2).*

Enterprise Zones. See export processing zone.

Entities. In the context of the GATT *Government Procurement Code,* refers to government departments or ministries and their subsidiary agencies as well as state-owned monopolies or other *state trading enterprises.*

Environmental Dumping. Refers to an unfair trade practice whereby an exporter achieves a cost advantage over its rivals in foreign markets through inadequate environmental protection in its home country. A similar concept, referring to inadequate labor regulations, is referred to as *social dumping.*

Environmental Trade Measures. Trade measures applied by importing or exporting countries in conjunction with environmental policies. In 1987 parties to the *Montreal Protocol* enacted a series of restrictions to curtail trade in products employing ozone-damaging chemicals. Within GATT, international discussions on such measures are conducted in the *Group on Environmental Measures and International Trade* (Sec II). See also *Green Round.*

Escape Clause. A provision in a bilateral or multilateral commercial agreement permitting a signatory temporarily to suspend concessions it has granted when imports threaten harm to its domestic workers or firms producing competing goods or services. Also used in reference to procedures in the United States for applying for *import relief.*

Exceptions. Products specifically exempted from an international agreement to liberalize trade through multi-product duty reductions or other commitments. Exceptions are usually made by importing countries to protect workers and firms engaged in production of *sensitive products.*

Exchange Controls. The rationing of foreign currencies and other instruments for settling international financial obligations by a country facing balance-of-payments difficulties. Exchange controls require importers to apply for prior government authorization to obtain the foreign currency needed to bring in designated amounts and types of goods. Since such measures can easily be manipulated by governments to restrict imports, they are often viewed as *nontariff barriers* to trade.

Exhaustion. Refers to the doctrine that protection of *intellectual property rights (IPR)* is "exhausted" or confined to the country in which protection is granted. The exhaustion principle specifically implies that IPR holders may not seek to curb *parallel imports* from other countries. In the *Uruguay Round* IPR negotiations, some LDCs demanded international extension of the exhaustion principle in order to ensure access to industrial country markets for goods they produced under license.

Exonerated Cargo. Otherwise dutiable merchandise permitted duty-free entry into certain countries in furtherance of a particular government policy. The exonerations are in effect licenses to import specified quantities of the desired articles – usually raw materials or unfurnished goods not available locally but deemed essential to local industry. Imports in excess of the quantities authorized in the exoneration may be prohibited or may be permitted only at high rates of duty.

Export Controls. Regulations or restrictions applied to exports by the government of the exporting country to limit foreign access to sensitive technologies, or to protect domestic producers and consumers from temporary shortages of certain materials. See: *COCOM List* and *export restrictions.*

Export Credits. Deferred payment arrangements provided by exporters for goods or services sold internationally. Official export credits are deferred payment arrangements financed or underwritten by an exporter's government and can have the same effect as an outright export subsidy. Export credits are generally divided into short term (less than two years), medium term (two to five years), and long-term (over five years) credits. They may take the form of "supplier credits" extended by the exporter or "buyer credits," in which the exporter's bank or other financial institution lends to the buyer. Export credit agencies may give official support to both supplier and buyer credits. Such support may be limited to "pure cover" – insurance or guarantees given to exporters or lending institutions – or it may take the form of "financing support," including direct credits, refinancing, and interest subsidies. All major industrialized countries are signatories to the OECD *Export Credit Arrangement.* See *Group on Export Credits and Credit Guarantees* (Sec.II).

Export Credit Arrangement. Formal title is the Arrangement on Guidelines for Officially Supported Export Credits. An international understanding negotiated under the auspices of the OECD providing the institutional framework for an orderly *export credit* market. Its purpose is to prevent an "export credit race" in which exporting countries compete for sales to third-country markets on the basis of their financing terms rather than on the basis of providing competitively priced goods. The Arrangement deals with actions and policies of official export credit and insurance agencies and covers only the conditions or terms of insurance or guarantees. It limits trade finance subsidies, setting standards for minimum interest rates, maximum repayment periods, and down payments. The Arrangement took effect in April 1978 and included all OECD member countries except Turkey. It replaced a less elaborate understanding that had been in effect among a more limited number of countries since 1976. See also *Berne Union* (Sec. II).

Export Duty. A tax imposed on exports. Although export duties are sometimes a convenient source of revenue, in some circumstances they can discourage exports and place producers at a competitive disadvantage in world markets. The United States is constitutionally proscribed from imposing export duties; resource-exporting countries such as Canada, Australia, and many LDCs tend to favor them. See also *export restrictions.*

Export Enhancement Program (EEP). A system of agricultural *export subsidies* maintained by the United States. The EEP, which is linked to stock disposal policies, is partial and discretionary in nature. Payments are not automatically accorded to all exports of a given commodity or to all commodities, and payment rates may vary widely from sale to sale. Congress restored $1 billion in EEP export subsidies in mid-1992 as a result of failure to conclude a *Uruguay Round* agreement covering foreign agricultural trade practices.

Export Guarantees. Assurances by an exporter's government that financing provided by a private lender will be repaid with official funds if a buyer defaults.

Export Performance Requirements. See *performance requirements*.

Export Processing Zone. A special form of *free trade zone* in which certain exemptions from duties and regulations are granted as an inducement to export-oriented manufacturing. Usually a manufacturer within the zone may import equipment and raw materials free of duty for goods that are ultimately exported as finished products. Other inducements may include abatement of taxes on profits derived from export sales or relaxation of minimum wage regulations. Also known as "special economic zones," "enterprise zones," and "industrial free zones."

Export Quota. A specific restriction or ceiling imposed by an exporting country on the value or volume of certain exports. Some international *commodity agreements* explicitly indicate when producers should apply such restrictions. Export quotas are also often applied in *orderly marketing agreements* and *voluntary restraint agreements.*

Export Quota Agreement. An arrangement arising under an international *commodity agreement* whereby each participating exporting country is allocated a portion of the global market for the commodity. The purpose of the arrangement is to maintain price stability and ensure producer incomes.

Export Restitution. Certain payments made under the European Union's *Common Agricultural Policy (CAP)* to exporters of processed agricultural products made from raw materials for which the processor paid higher than world prices. In principle, restitution payments are not supposed to subsidize exports, but only to lower their selling prices to the levels that would have prevailed in the absence of CAP price distortions.

Export Restraints. Also referred to as bilateral restraint agreements. Quantitative restrictions applied by exporting countries to curtail shipments of *sensitive products* to a specified foreign market for a fixed time period, usually pursuant to a formal or informal agreement with the importing country (see *voluntary restraint agreement* and *orderly marketing agreements.)* Their economic effects – unlike those of "traditional" trade restrictions such as tariffs or import quotas – include significant benefits to established foreign producers. VRAs and OMAs have no explicit sanction under GATT (see *grey area measures).*

Export Restrictions. While usage varies, this term is often used to denote quantitative limits or charges on exports purely for domestic purposes, such as protecting producers and consumers from temporary shortages of certain materials, promoting processing of raw materials within the producing country, or bolstering export prices by limiting supplies in world markets. They are thus distinguished from *export restraints,* which are designed primarily to forestall frictions with the exporting country's major trading partners. U.S. efforts in the *Tokyo Round* to have GATT rules and disciplines extended to export restrictions were largely unsuccessful. See also *export controls* and *supply access.*

Export Subsidy. Any form of government payment or other benefit provided to domestic producers of goods destined for sale in foreign markets. Examples include preferential government financing, income tax holidays, and rebates of *direct taxes* on exported products. Reflecting the belief among the founders of GATT that export subsidies can distort normal trading patterns, GATT Article XVI proscribes export subsidies on non-primary products that result in lower prices in foreign markets than prices charged for the "like product" in the domestic market. The *Tokyo Round* yielded an agreement that extended Article XVI by banning all export subsidies by *industrial countries* on manufactured and semi-manufactured goods (see *Subsidies Code).* See also *domestic subsidy* and *countervailing duty.*

Fair Trade. International trade involving shipments that do not benefit from government assistance. Fair trade and the related concept of *unfair trade practices* are almost always used in the context of policies or practices affecting exports, while *free trade* usually refers to the absence of barriers to imports (see also *free trade).*

Fair Value. The benchmark against which selling prices of imported merchandise are compared in a *dumping* investigation. In U.S. practice, fair value is generally expressed as the weighted average of the exporter's home market prices or prices to third countries during the period of investigation. In some cases it is the "constructed value" – a derived figure used if there are few home-market or third-country sales of the product in question, or if the number of such sales made at prices above the cost of production is so few that they provide an inadequate basis for comparison. See also *dumping margin.*

Financing Support. See *export credits.*

Floor prices. See *buffer stocks.*

FOGS. See Functioning of the GATT System.

Former Centrally Planned Economies. See *countries in transition.*

Former East Bloc Countries. Countries that comprised the now-defunct East Bloc (i.e., those "dominated by international communism" in the language of the U.S. Trade Act of 1974), many but not all of which have now abandoned central planning and moved to establish market economies. Includes the East European countries *(CEECs),* the former Soviet republics *(NIS),* China, Mongolia, North Korea, Vietnam, Laos, Cambodia, and Cuba. In the parlance of the 1960s, these countries comprised the "Second World," between the industrialized "First World" countries and the underdeveloped "Third World." See *countries in transition.*

Formula Approach. A tariff negotiating procedure in which a general formula for calculating tariff reductions on all products is agreed by the participants, with limited exceptions allowed for sensitive items. The most straightforward formula approach is a *linear reduction,* although more complicated formulas have been used. Negotiations based on a formula approach tend to achieve tariff cuts across a broader range of products than *item-by-item negotiations*, but are vulnerable to becoming bogged down by demands for exceptions. See also *harmonization.*

Forum Shopping. Refers to the ability of countries to take advantage of differing procedures for *dispute settlement* under GATT and various *GATT Codes* by pursuing a trade complaint in a venue in which it believes it can exploit procedural or tactical advantages.

Four Dragons or Four Tigers. See newly industrializing economies (NIEs).

Framework Agreement (I). A package of agreements negotiated during the *Tokyo Round* dealing with (a) differential and more favorable treatment for LDCs; (b) trade restrictions applied for balance-of-payments purposes; (c) safeguard actions for "infant industry" development purposes; and (d) the process of *dispute settlement* in GATT. The agreement took its name from the paragraph in the *Tokyo Declaration* calling for "improvements in the international framework for the conduct of world trade." The GATT Contracting Parties adopted the four texts making up the Framework Agreement in November 1979. See also *enabling clause* and *graduation.*

Framework Agreement (2). Also known as a Trade and Investment Framework Agreement, or TIFA, a bilateral agreement establishing a mechanism for consultations on trade and investment policy in conjunction with the *Enterprise for the Americas Initiative (EAI).* The EAI framework agreements set up intergovernmental councils to discuss and negotiate the removal of trade and investment barriers. The councils also serve to prepare for subsequent stages of trade liberalization, including the possible negotiation *of free trade agreements (FTAs).* Since the EAI was launched, the United States has concluded TIFAs with the following countries:

► **Africa.** Angola, Common Market for Eastern and Southern Africa (COMESA), East African Community (Kenya, Uganda, Tanzania, Rwanda, Burundi), Ghana, Liberia, Mauritius, Mozambique, Nigeria, South Africa, West African Economic and Monetary Union (Benin, Burkina Faso, Guinea-Bissau, Mali, Niger, Senegal, Togo)

► **Americas.** Caricom (see Caribbean Community and Common Market), Uruguay

► **Europe and Middle East.** Algeria, Bahrain, Egypt, Georgia, Iceland, Iraq, Kuwait, Lebanon, Libya, Oman, Qatar, Saudi Arabia, Switzerland, Tunisia, Turkey, Ukraine, United Arab Emerites (UAE), Yemen

- **South and Central Asia.** Afghanistan, Central Asia (Kazakhstan, Kyrgyzstan, Tajikistan, Turkmenistan, and Uzbekistan), Nepal, Pakistan, Sri Lanka

- **Southeast Asia and the Pacific.** ASEAN (see *Association of South East Asian Nations*), Brunei, Cambodia, Indonesia, Malaysia, New Zealand, Philippines, Thailand, Vietnam

Framework Initiative. Also known as the New Economic Partnership. An initiative launched by the United States in May 1993 to address bilateral trade problems with Japan.

Free List. A list of goods that have been designated as free from tariffs or licensing requirements by an importing country.

Free Riders. In the context of the *Uruguay Round* discussions of a proposed *Multilateral Trade Organization,* refers to provisions to ensure that participating countries would not have the option of "free riding" – signing only some of the Uruguay Round agreements while avoiding the obligations of others – but instead would require countries to accept or reject the results of the Round as a "single undertaking." See *non-application.*

Free Trade. International trade that is unhampered by restrictive measures such as tariffs or nontariff barriers. An ideal concept that plays a role in economic theory similar to that of the "perfect vacuum" in physics, since, except within economic unions, virtually no international trade is genuinely free of governmental interference. In practical terms, trade policy deliberations in all countries do not normally concern questions of whether free trade should be pursued, but rather of how much and what kind of government intervention is needed to serve the national interest. See also *fair trade.*

Free Trade Agreement. An agreement between two or more countries establishing a *free trade area (FTA).*

Free Trade Area (FTA). A group of two or more countries that agree to remove barriers affecting substantially all trade with each other, while each maintains its own schedule of tariffs and other regulations on imports from nonmember countries. Because some goods such as farm products may not be traded in significant quantities between partners in an FTA, coverage of "substantially all " of their trade does not necessarily mean trade barriers are eliminated in all sectors. Indeed, agriculture is exempted from coverage in many FTAs.

Free Trade Zone. (Not to be confused with *a free trade area* or *free trade agreement.)* A designated area within a country in which goods can be imported, stored, or processed without being subject to customs duties and taxes. Also known as a "foreign trade zone," a "free port," or a "bonded warehouse." See also *transit zone* and *export processing zone."*

Functioning of the GATT System (FOGS). Designation for a negotiating group in the *Uruguay Round* that dealt with measures to strengthen the GATT process, particularly by improving surveillance of members' trade policies, encouraging greater involvement of trade ministers in the GATT, and strengthening GATT's relationship with other international organizations such as the IMF. See *Trade Policy Review Mechanism.*

Further Processing Method. See *super deductive.*

Gate Price. See Common Agricultural Policy.

GATT Codes. Agreements negotiated under GATT auspices to remove or lessen the trade-distorting effects of *nontariff measures* by prescribing signatories' rights and obligations concerning use of such measures as well as countermeasures that may be applied in response. Only the signatories of a GATT Code are bound by its terms. During the *Tokyo Round,* codes were negotiated governing subsidies and countervailing duties, standards and technical barriers to trade, import licensing procedures, customs valuation, and government purchasing policies. In addition, the existing GA TT anti-dumping code was revised.

GATT Panel. See Panel of Experts.

GATT Round. A cycle of multilateral trade negotiations conducted under the auspices of the GATT. Each Round has constituted a series of interrelated bargaining sessions among the participating countries to achieve mutually beneficial agreements reducing tariffs and other trade barriers. The agreements reached at the conclusion of each Round become new GATT commitments and thus amount to an important step in the progressive liberalization of the world trading system. Eight Rounds have been initiated under *GATT* auspices since 1947:

- ► *Geneva Round* (1) 1947 (First Round)
- ► *Annecy Round* 1949 (Second Round)
- ► *Torquay Round* 1950-51 (Third Round)
- ► *Geneva Round* (2) 1956 (Fourth Round)
- ► *Dillon Round* 1959-62 (Fifth Round)
- ► *Kennedy Round* 1963-67 (Sixth Round)
- ► *Tokyo Round* 1973-79 (Seventh Round)
- ► *Uruguay Round* 1986-94 (Eighth Round)

From 1956 to 1962, all GATT Rounds took place at GATT headquarters in Geneva, until the Tokyo Round. Subsequent rounds were named after the city or country in which the ministerial declaration launching the negotiations was signed. The efforts resulting from the Uruguay Round led to the creation of the WTO.

GATT Standing Committee. A permanent body of GATT members that dealt with a specific area of trade policy, including the Committee on Trade in Industrial Products and the Agriculture Committee (both were subsumed by the *Uruguay Round* negotiations under *Track* 1); the *Committee on Tariff Concessions;* the *Committee on Balance of Payments Restrictions;* the *Committee on Trade and Development;* the *Textile Surveillance Board;* and various *GATT Code* Committees.

General Tariff. A tariff that applies to countries that do not enjoy either preferential or *most-favored-nation* tariff treatment. Where the general tariff rate differs from MFN rate, the general tariff is usually the higher rate. See *Column 1 rates* and *Column 2 rates.*

Generalized System of Preferences (GSP). A system of tariff preferences applied by *industrial countries* to selected manufactured and semi-manufactured goods from developing countries in order to facilitate LDC exports and economic development. GSP was originally propounded by *UNCTAD* (see Sec. II), and was sanctioned by GATT in 1971 despite contravening the *most-favored-nation* principle of equal treatment for all GATT members. The United States began according *GSP* treatment to most LDCs in 1976, the last of the major *industrial countries* to do so. *GSP* was given permanent standing in GATT by the 1979 *Framework Agreement. GSP* tariff treatment is not subject to either *binding* or *reciprocity* and thus represents an autonomous, unilateral grant by the preference-giving country. In accordance with the *graduation* principle, *GSP* treatment is also intended to be temporary, with individual LDCs expected to relinquish benefits as they develop.

Geneva Rounds. The first and fourth *GATT Round* of multilateral trade negotiations held in Geneva, Switzerland. The "First Round" involved the actual drafting of the GATT itself as well as tariff negotiations among the original contracting parties. The Preparatory Committee met in October and November of 1946, and drafting of the General Agreement took place between January 20-February 28, 1947. Tariff negotiations lasted from April-October, 1947. The "Fourth Round" took place from January-May 1956.

Geographic Indications. See *appellations of origin.*

Global Quotas. Explicit limits set by a country on the overall value or quantity of goods that may be imported from or exported to all countries during a given period.

Government Procurement. Government policies and procedures for purchasing goods and services. Procurement policies can be construed as *nontariff barriers* if they discriminate in favor of domestic suppliers when imported goods are price-competitive and are of comparable quality.

Government Procurement Code. A *GATT Code* negotiated during the *Tokyo Round,* prohibiting signatories from discriminating against or among the products of other signatories in certain types of government procurement covered by the Code (i.e., purchases valued at more than $150,000 special drawing rights [SDRs] by specified government *entities* listed in the Agreement. Exceptions include contracts for most services, construction, procurement related to national security, and purchases by political subdivisions. The Code seeks to increase *transparency* in signatories' regulations and practices regarding government procurement and to ensure that they do not discriminate against foreign suppliers or products. It contains detailed rules on the way in which tenders should be invited and awarded. Signatories include Canada; the European Union (Austria, Belgium, Bulgaria, Cyprus, Czech Republic, Denmark, Estonia, Finland, France, Germany, Greece, Hungary, Ireland, Italy, Latvia, Lithuania, Luxembourg, Malta, The Netherlands, Poland, Portugal, Romania, Slovak Republic of Slovenia, Spain, Sweden, and the United Kingdom); Hong Kong, China; Iceland; Israel; The Netherlands (with respect to Aruba); Japan; Norway; South Korea; Liechtenstein; Singapore; Switzerland; Chinese Taipei; and the United States. There are also 23 observer governments to this Agreement, including Albania, Argentina, Armenia, Australia, Bahrain, Cameroon, Chile, China, Colombia, Croatia, Georgia, India, Jordan, Kyrgyz Republic, Moldova, Mongolia, New Zealand, Oman, Panama, Saudi Arabia, Sri Lanka, Turkey, and Ukraine.

Graduation. The principle that *developing countries*, as they advance economically and become more developed (i.e., through industrialization, increased production and export earnings, or rising living standards), should assume greater responsibilities and obligations within GATT. As enunciated by the GATT *enabling clause,* graduation specifically implies that donor countries will remove or "graduate" the more advanced developing countries from eligibility for preferential treatment under the *Generalized System of Preferences (GSP).* The United States has graduated from the U.S. GSP program, the following countries: Croatia and Equatorial Guinea (2011); Trinidad and Tobago (2010); Malaysia (1998); and Hong Kong, Korea, Singapore, and Taiwan (1989).

Grandfather Clause. A provision in the GATT and other trade agreements permitting signatories to retain domestic legislation that was in effect before the agreement was signed, even though it may be inconsistent with certain provisions of the agreement. Only charter members of GATT may take advantage of its grandfather clause; they are, however, expected to bring their legislation into conformity with GATT provisions as soon as possible.

Green Room Consultations. Informal meetings at the WTO Headquarters of countries that are viewed as playing a key role on a particular issue. Such meetings take their name from a conference room adjacent to the Director-General's office that used to have green wallpaper.

Green Round. A term referring to a proposed *GATT Round* of multilateral negotiations meant to address *environmental trade measures.* This Round never materialized as such, but the Doha Round of trade negotiations was the first-ever round of negotiations to include an "environmental or green chapter." This was also the first-ever round of negotiations to encourage members to conduct environmental reviews at the national level.

Grey Area Measures. *Import relief* measures taken outside the scope of GATT rules by countries seeking to protect domestic industries from injury arising from factors other than foreign *unfair trade practices.* The main forms are *voluntary restraint agreements (VRAs)* and *orderly marketing arrangements (OMAs).* Negotiations on *safeguards* in the *Uruguay Round* aimed at bringing grey area measures within the scope of GATT rules and disciplines.

Group on Negotiations of Goods (GNG) and Group on Negotiations of Services (GNS). See *negotiating group.* The establishment of separate GNG and GNS groups was agreed at the outset of the *Uruguay Round* to maintain the formal appearance, insisted upon by developing countries, that negotiations in the areas of goods and services were not linked.

Guide Price. See Common Agricultural Policy.

Harmonization. Cutting tariffs in a way that results in greater uniformity in rates applied to most items within each country's tariff schedule. Most harmonization negotiations have employed a *formula approach* for achieving relatively large cuts in high "tariff peaks" and smaller cuts in lower tariffs. This approach contrasts with *linear reduction* formulas, which call for equal percentage cuts in all tariffs.

Harmonized System (HS). A system of tariff nomenclature for *customs classification* negotiated within the *Customs Cooperation Council* (Sec. II). Participating countries classify goods for customs purposes on the HS basis up to a level of product specificity denoted by six-digit codes. Countries are free to introduce national distinctions – for tariff or statistical purposes – for more detailed product breakdowns beyond the six-digit level. The United States adopted the Harmonized System in the Trade Act of 1988. The Harmonized System superseded the Brussels Tariff Nomenclature (BTN) classification system.

Havana Charter. A multinational agreement concluded at Havana in 1948 that called for establishment of an *International Trade Organization (ITO)* (Sec. II) to govern world trade. The ITO never came into force, primarily because of opposition in the U.S. Congress, leaving the "provisional" GATT as the sole institution providing a foundation for the multilateral trading system. See *International Trade Organization* (Sec. II).

High Technology. Products that embody relatively intensive research and development (R&D) inputs, either directly at the final manufacturing stage or through the intermediate components used in their production. Numerous classification schemes have been proposed in academic studies and international discussions to designate high-technology industries, but all have shortcomings. For example, technologically "mature" products such as industrial chemicals and consumer electronics make up a significant proportion of high technology as delineated by some R&D-based definitions. As a rule of thumb, high-technology industries can be designated as those producing microelectronics, computers, telecommunications equipment, machine tools and robotics, aerospace equipment, scientific and precision instruments, medicine and biological compounds, and specialty chemicals including certain advanced materials.

Horizontal Reduction. Negotiated cuts in tariff rates by the same percentage for all parties to an agreement. Also known as equal-percentage of *linear reduction.*

Impairment. See nullification or impairment, import deposits, prior deposits.

Import Deposits. A requirement that importers deposit some amount of money in an account, usually with a central bank, before the goods are imported into a country and the transaction takes place. This deposit may be used to assure that import duties will be paid, if applicable, and is usually considered a nontariff barrier. See *prior deposit.*

Import Licensing. Procedures requiring the submission of an application or other documentation (other than those normally required for customs purposes) to an administrative body for approval as a prior condition for importation into the customs territory of a country. See also *prior deposits.*

Import Licensing Code. Formally known as the Agreement on Import Licensing Procedures. A *GATT Code* negotiated during the *Tokyo Round* to simplify and harmonize *import licensing* procedures of signatory governments to ensure that they do not in themselves restrict imports. Signatories are required to submit details of their licensing procedures and laws for examination by the Committee on Import Licensing. For more information, visit www.wto.org.

Import Quota. A means of restricting or controlling imports by specifying the quantity or value of a commodity that may be imported during a specified period. Such restrictions may take the form of "global" or "basket quotas" – limiting total imports from all sources without differentiating among originating countries – or of country-specific "allocated quotas" in which producing countries may be assigned a portion of the total quantity permitted to be imported. Some global quotas contain sub-quotas designating individual limits for various supplier countries. Import quotas result in protection that tends to be more predictable than with a *tariff* and can thus be "fine-tuned" by governments. As with a tariff, domestic producers protected by a quota are able to charge higher prices, and there are some efficiency losses, but these are not offset by the additional government revenue that a tariff provides, so that a greater deadweight loss results. See also *quantitative restriction* and *tariff quota.*

Import Quota Auctioning. The process of allocating the right to import a product subject to *quantitative restriction* by auctioning the quota among potential importers. Through the auction proceeds, the importing government can extract some of the revenue it might otherwise obtain by levying a tariff on the goods in question.

Import Relief. Governmental action to temporarily restrict imports in order to prevent or remedy *injury* to domestic workers or firms producing goods competitive with those being restricted. See *safeguards.*

Import Restrictions. Measures to limit or control the volume of imports by means of *tariffs* or *nontariff barriers*, including *import quotas, exchange controls, import licensing,* requirements for *prior deposits,* levies of *import surcharges,* or prohibitions of various categories of imports.

Import Sensitivity. The vulnerability of a domestic industry to *injury* from foreign competition. See also *sensitive products.*

Import Surcharge. A temporary tax on imports over and above established tariffs, usually enacted in times of economic crisis. The United States, for example, imposed a 10% import surcharge when the dollar-gold linkage was severed in 1971. The Tokyo Round *Framework Agreement* legitimized use of surcharges for balance-of- payments purposes, provided they do not give special protection for particular products and do not discriminate among individual exporting countries.

Import Surge. A substantial and usually unforeseen increase in imports above recent trends for a particular product or class of goods presenting serious adjustment costs for domestic workers and firms producing such goods. When an import surge is due to economic or commercial factors other than *unfair trade practices,* governments may resort to *safeguards* to provide temporary *import relief* to the domestic industry.

Indirect Tax. A tax levied on expenditures, such as a sales tax, excise tax, or value-added tax, rather than a *direct tax* on individual or corporate earnings. GA TT rules permit countries to rebate indirect taxes on goods destined for export, but not direct taxes.

Industrial Countries or Industrialized Countries. (Also known as developed countries) A term used to distinguish the more industrialized nations from *developing countries (LDCs)* as well as the *newly industrializing economies (NIEs)* and *countries in transition.* The International Monetary Fund categorizes the following as industrial countries: Australia, Germany, Luxembourg, Slovenia, Austria, Greece, Malta, South Korea, Belgium, Hong Kong, Netherlands, Spain, Canada, Iceland, New Zealand, Sweden, Cyprus, Ireland, Norway, Switzerland, Denmark, Israel, Portugal, Taiwan, Finland, Italy, San Marino, United Kingdom, France, Japan, Singapore, United States. The *industrial countries* are sometimes collectively designated as the "North" because most of them are in the Northern Hemisphere.

Industrial Property. Encompasses most forms of intellectual property with the exception of copyrights (e.g., *patent, trademark,* and *trade secret, intellectual property rights).*

Initial Negotiating Right (INR). A right held by a WTO member to be compensated by another member if a given bound tariff rate is raised by the latter. INRs stem from past negotiating concessions and allow the holder to seek compensation for an impairment of tariff concessions whether or not the country holds status as a *principal supplier* of the product in question.

Injury. In the GATT context, refers to economic damage sustained by workers or firms in an industry as a consequence of foreign competition or *unfair trade practices.* Under GATT rules and various *GATT Codes* as well as under U.S. law, mechanisms are established for determining whether injury has occurred or is threatened as a prerequisite for taking countermeasures (see *injury test).* Different gradations of injury are referred to in U.S. law and international discussions. The two most prominent are:

- ▶ **Material injury.** *Anti-dumping* and *countervailing duty* cases are based on findings of "material" injury (including the threat of material injury and the "material retardation" of a new, emerging industry). Rather than define material injury, the GATT *Subsidies Code* lists factors that may be taken into account in determining its existence, including an actual or potential decline in output, sales, market share, profits, prices, or employment, and in the case of agricultural subsidies whether there has been an increased burden on government support programs. Material injury is defined by the U.S. Trade Act of 1979 as "harm which is not inconsequential, immaterial, or unimportant."

- ▶ **Serious injury.** *Safeguard* or *escape clause* actions require a finding of "serious" injury to a domestic industry. GATT jurisprudence is ambiguous on the meaning of this term, but WTO legal experts assert that it is meant to be a higher standard than material injury --reasoning that the escape clause is designed to respond to situations that do not involve allegations of unfair action by foreign exporters so that its standard for establishing injury should be the most rigorous. Under U.S. trade law, factors mentioned in determinations of serious injury include the significant idling of productive facilities of an industry; the inability of a significant number of firms in the industry to operate at a reasonable level of profit; and significant unemployment or underemployment within the industry.

Injury Test. An administrative determination establishing that *injury* to a domestic industry has occurred as a result of an import surge or foreign *unfair trade practices.* Such a test is a prerequisite for imposition *of safeguards, countervailing duties,* or *anti-dumping duties.* By requiring an industry seeking trade relief to establish that it has been injured by foreign competition – a significant burden-of-proof threshold -- the injury test is intended to prevent abuse of unfair trade laws for protectionist purposes.

Intellectual Property Rights (IPRs). The right to possess and use intellectual property, conferred by means of *patents, trademarks*, and *copyrights.* Even though IPR laws are enacted and enforced on a strictly national basis, once a patent or copyright has been granted in one country and disclosure of an invention or creative work has been made, information technology makes it available throughout the world. As a result, cross-country differences in patent and copyright laws can result in inadequate IPR protection. Negotiated in the 1986-94 *Uruguay Round*, trade-related intellectual property rights (referred to as *TRIPs*) seek to balance goals of facilitating technology diffusion with the objective of promoting innovation through more effective IPR protection. (See *Agreement on Trade-related Aspects of Intellectual Property Rights.*)

International Atomic Energy List. See *COCOM List.*

International Commodity Organization. An organization of nations engaged in international trade involving a particular commodity. Principal motives for such an organization, such as price collaboration among producers, may be similar to those of a producer cartel, The organization may also establish buffer stocks to prevent wide swings in the market price of the commodity. Some international commodity organizations, established to implement a *commodity agreement,* include both producing and consuming nations. Examples of principal international commodity organizations (descriptive details of which may be found in Sec. II) include:

► Association of Natural Rubber Producing Countries

► Intergovernmental Council of Copper Exporting Countries

► International Bauxite Association

► International Cocoa Organization

► International Coffee Organization

► International Cotton Advisory Committee

► International Jute Organization

► International Lead and Zinc Study Group

► International Natural Rubber Organization

► International Olive Oil Council

► International Sugar Organization

► International Tropical Timber Organization

► International Wheat Council

► International Rice Commission

► International Tea Committee

► International Tin Council

► International Wool Secretariat

► Organization of Petroleum Exporting Countries

International Convention on the Simplification and Harmonization of Customs Procedures. See *Kyoto Convention.*

International Dairy Arrangement. A *Tokyo Round* agreement covering trade in dairy products, consisting of three protocols establishing minimum prices for milk powder, milk fats (including butter), and certain cheeses, which had been in effect since 1980. The arrangement was overseen by the *International Dairy Products Council* (Sec. II). One of four plurilateral agreements in the area of goods, this agreement was replaced by a successor agreement, The International Dairy Agreement, which entered into effect on January 1, 1995. However, in 1997, the agreement was terminated along with the *Bovine Meat Arrangement.*

International Import Certificate-Delivery Verification System. See *COCOM List.*

International Munitions List. *See COCOM List.*

Intervention Price. See Common Agricultural Policy.

Investment Performance Requirements. See *Performance Requirements.*

Item-by-Item Negotiations. A method of tariff negotiations in which the expected trade effects of each proposed tariff cut is evaluated separately. At the end of the negotiations, participants are expected to have achieved approximate balance in the total effect of tariff cuts offered and received. The first five *GATT Rounds* used the item-by-item approach, but by the mid-1960s it became too cumbersome for multilateral negotiations with increasing numbers of participating countries. See *formula approach.* Negotiation on trade in services are mostly carried out on an item-by-item basis through a request offer procedure.

J-List. A list originally established under the U.S. Tariff Act of 1930, indicating products that are exempted from requirements that imported goods be marked to show country of origin. Items on the list are difficult or impossible to mark. See *marks of origin.*

Judicial Review. In unfair trade cases (see *unfair trade practices)*, a mechanism for parties to a case to appeal a finding of subsidization, dumping, or injury to a court of law in the importing country.

Kennedy Round. The sixth *GATT Round* of multilateral trade negotiations, held in Geneva from June 1963 to June 1967 with 48 countries participating. Tariff reductions based for the first time on *a formula approach* covered $40 billion in trade and led to an average tariff reduction among the participating countries of about 35%. The Kennedy Round was the first GATT negotiation in which the member states of the European Community participated as a single entity. Moreover, developing countries for the first time played an important part in the negotiations, which resulted in the addition of

Part Four of the GATT. The Round was named for President John F. Kennedy, who first sounded the call for the negotiations.

Kyoto Convention. Formal name is the International Convention on the Simplification and Harmonization of Customs Procedures. An international agreement sponsored in 1973 by the *Customs Cooperation Council* (Sec.II) to harmonize the methods and procedures of national customs authorities. The convention consists of a set of principles that apply to all signatories, together with 30 individual annexes dealing with various aspects of *customs and administrative entry procedures, rules of origin, transshipment, duty drawback, and free trade zones.* A signatory may accept or reject any of the annexes but must adopt at least one of them and must endeavor to implement all of the annexes as soon as feasible.

Law of Similars. Regulations limiting importation of a product or altering its tariff treatment if a "similar" item is produced domestically. Also known as Market Reserve Policies.

LDCs. See *developing countries.*

Least Developed Countries (LLDCs). Refers to those *developing countries* experiencing no significant economic growth, very low per capita incomes, and low literacy rates. Today these countries are referred to in the WTO as LDCs. The WTO uses the UN definition for least developed countries: the world's poorest countries. The WTO refers to the UN list on http://www.un.org/special-ep/ohrlls/ldc/list. htm and the website http://www.ldcgroups.org. The UN General Assembly has designated 46 countries as LLDCs: Afghanistan, Angola, Bangladesh, Benin, Bhutan, Burkina Faso, Burundi, Cambodia, Central African Republic, Chad, Comoros, Congo (Kinshasa), Djibouti,Equitorial New Guinea, Eritrea, Ethiopia, Gambia, Guinea, Guinea-Bissau, Haiti, Kiribati, Laos, Lesotho, Liberia, Madagascar, Malawi, Maldives, Mali, Mauritania, Mozambique, Nepal, Niger, Rwanda, Samoa, Sao Tome and Principe, Sierra Leone, Solomon Islands, Somalia, Sudan, Tanzania, Timor-Leste, Togo, Tuvalu, Uganda, Vanuatu, Yemen, and Zambia**.**

Less-Developed Countries (LDCs). It used to be an alternative term for *developing countries*, but today it is used in the WTO to refer to *Least Developed Countries.*

Less Than Fair Value. See fair value and dumping.

Licensing. See import licensing, import licensing code, cross-licensing.

Linear Reduction. A tariff negotiating procedure based on reduction of tariffs by a specified percentage on an entire range of goods (also known as *horizontal reduction).* A linear reduction in tariff negotiations is the simplest form of a *formula approach* and is far broader than an item-by-item approach.

Liner Code. Formal name is the United Nations Code of Conduct for Liner Conferences. Adopted in 1974
and entered into force in 1983, the Code seeks to allocate international shipping among ship owners in industrial and developing countries. The United States is not a signatory.

Local Content Requirements. Government-imposed conditions on inward direct investments requiring that a minimum proportion of value added as of the resulting output be derived from host country goods or services. See *performance requirements.* Similar measures applying to imports are referred to as *domestic content requirements.*

Lome Convention. A series of preferential trade and economic assistance agreements, the first of which was signed in 1975 in Lome, Togo, between the European Community and 69 former colonies of the EC member states (the *ACP countries*). This Convention superseded the Yaounde Conventions of 1963 and 1969.

Madrid Agreement. Formal name is the Madrid Agreement Concerning the International Registration of Marks. An international agreement signed in 1891 establishing a system for standardized registration of and protection for trademarks and service marks (see *intellectual property rights).* The agreement is administered by the *World Intellectual Property Organization (WIPO)* (Sec. II) and is open to all states adhering to the *Paris Convention.*

Madrid Union. Formal name is the Madrid Agreement for the Repression of False or Deceptive Indications of Source on Goods. An international agreement, signed in 1891 and revised several times subsequently, concluded for the purpose of suppressing false or misleading origin markings on internationally traded goods. Signatories are obligated to seize and deny importation to merchandise bearing false markings indicating origin in any other signatory country. The agreement is administered by the *World Intellectual Property Organization WIPO)* (Sec. II) and is open to all states adhering to the *Paris Convention.* See also *commercial counterfeiting.*

Margin of Preference. The difference between the duty paid under a system of tariff preferences and the duty payable on a *most-favored-nation (MFN)* basis. Some LDCs have complained that as average tariff levels in the *industrial countries* have been lowered through successive *GATT Rounds,* the margin of preference enjoyed by beneficiaries of the *General System of Preferences (GSP)* has been eroded.

Market Access. The ability of foreign firms to compete in a country's markets for given products, reflecting the extent of formal trade barriers --including tariffs as well as nontariff barriers --and the government's willingness to tolerate unimpeded foreign competition with domestic firms (see *national treatment).*

Market Access Negotiations. In the context of the *Uruguay Round* as well as bilateral trade negotiations, refers broadly to efforts to lower tariffs and nontariff barriers on manufactured and agricultural goods.

Market Disruption. A situation arising when a surge of imports of a particular product causes sales of domestically produced goods to decline to such an extent that the domestic producers and their employees suffer major economic reversals. The existence of market disruption is the basis for *escape clause* actions providing temporary import relief. As specified in Section 406 of the Trade Act of 1974, market disruption is considered to exist within a U.S. industry whenever imports "are increasing rapidly, either absolutely or relatively, so as to be a significant cause of material *injury,* or threat thereof' to that industry."

Market Reserve Policies. See *Law of Similars.*

Marketing Orders. Official directives concerning the size and quality of fresh fruits and vegetables that may be marketed during specified periods within a given region. The effect of marketing orders is to maintain prices at high levels by restricting supply. In the United States, marketing orders are issued by regional boards established by the Department of Agriculture and include agricultural producers as members.

Marking Duties. A special charge on imported good, in addition to normal duties, imposed on merchandise not properly marked so as to indicate the country of origin. Under U.S. law marking duties are not considered to be penalty duties and are not eligible for *drawback* should the foreign article be re-exported.

Marks of Origin. Physical markings indicating where an article was produced, as required by most countries' customs regulations (see *rules of origin).*
Material Injury. See *injury.*

Material Retardation. See *injury.*

Mercantilism. A once-prominent economic philosophy that equated national wealth and prowess with the accumulation of gold and other international monetary assets, and hence with running a persistent trade surplus.

Minimum Import Price. See *variable levy.*

Minimum Valuation. A form of valuation for tariff purposes in which all items below a certain threshold value in an import category are valued as if they were of the minimum value.

Ministerial Declaration. A decision by trade ministers of GATT members to launch a *GATT Round* of multilateral trade negotiations, establishing the agenda for the negotiations, and setting out general objectives.

Mixed Credits. Exceptionally liberal financing terms for an export sale. Ostensibly provided for foreign aid purposes, mixed credits can have effects similar to *export subsidies.*

Mixed Tariff. See *compound tariff.*

Modifications. Alteration or withdrawal of trade concessions previously made within GATT. Contracting Parties are permitted by Article XXVIII to modify concessions in their tariff schedules every three years by renegotiating changes with those GATT members that would be primarily affected. By introducing some flexibility to the structure of GATT obligations, this provision allows members to adapt to changing conditions in world trade while proscribing frequent tariff changes that would create uncertainty and instability. See also *rectifications.*

Montreal Protocol. Full title is the Montreal Protocol on Substances That Deplete the Ozone Layer. Signed in 1987, the Montreal Protocol was the first major international agreement to establish *environmental trade measures.* Under the Protocol, trade with non-signatory countries of products containing chlorofluorocarbons (CFCs) – principally used in refrigerators and air conditioners – and fire-extinguishing halons are to be limited or banned. The Protocol also discouraged relocation of CFC plants to non-signatory countries. As of September 1993-94 *industrial countries* and LDCs were parties to the Protocol.

Moral Rights. An artist's ability to control use of creative works such as books and films, even after relinquishing economic rights to another copyright holder, such as a publisher or producer. Differences in countries' treatment of moral rights pose obstacles to international negotiations on protection of *intellectual property rights.*

Most-Favored-Nation (MFN). The principle according to which each signatory of a trade agreement will apply its trade restrictions or concessions equally among all other signatories. MFN is the fundamental principle of the GATT; all *Contracting Parties* agree to apply MFN treatment to one another, although exceptions exist, for example, in granting preferential treatment to developing countries or for members of a customs union or free trade area (see *waiver).* When a country agrees to reduce tariffs on a particular product imported from one country, the tariff reduction automatically applies to imports of that product from any other country eligible for MFN treatment. Because of this, MFN serves as a powerful inducement for countries to join GA TT as well as a facilitator of trade liberalization generally. MFN terminology dates from the sixteenth century when it was used in commercial agreements according the most advantageous customs treatment extended by a government to any trading partner (i.e., to the "most favored nation"), but in modern usage it refers to nondiscrimination in international trade relations. Despite occasional misinterpretation in press reports, MFN does not entail "favored" (i.e., preferential) treatment of a trading partner.

MTN Codes. See multilateral trade negotiations.

Multifiber Arrangement (MFA). Full name is the Multifiber Arrangement Regarding International Trade in Textiles. An international arrangement, the MFA was negotiated under GATT auspices even though its provisions for quantitative import restrictions were otherwise illegal under GATT. It went into effect in 1974, superseding the Long-term Agreement on International Trade in Cotton Textiles, which had been in effect since 1962, and remained in force through 2004. During the *Uruguay Round* (1986-94), it was decided to bring the textile trade under the jurisdiction of the World Trade Organization.

Under MFA, GATT members applied quantitative restrictions on imports of textiles and clothing when importing countries considered them necessary to prevent *market disruption.* The MFA, covering cotton, wool, and man-made fiber textiles and apparel products, established a framework for negotiating bilateral *voluntary export restraints (VERs)* or *orderly marketing agreements (OMAs)* among textile exporting and importing countries to prevent market disruption or to counter market-disruptive *import surges* originating from low-wage producing countries. It provided standards for determining market disruption, minimum levels of import restraints, and annual growth of imports. The MFA also provided that restrictions should not reduce imports to levels below those of the preceding year. Because of this, and the fact that an importing country may impose quotas unilaterally to restrict rapidly rising textile imports from countries with which it has no bilateral agreements, most important textile exporting countries considered it advantageous to negotiate bilateral agreements under the MFA with the principal textile importing countries.

Critics claim that the MFA amounted to a bureaucratically rigged market that distorts prices; proponents argue that it was the only realistic alternative to more draconian protection of a politically sensitive sector. Virtually all major textile importing countries and exporting countries were signatories to the Multi Fiber Arrangement. See also *Textile Surveillance Board* and *International Textiles and Clothing Bureau* (Sec. II).

Multilateral Acceptance of Test Data. Recognition by signatories of the GATT *Standards Code* of test data and certification markings from other signatories. The Code recognized that governments may require prior consultations with other signatories to arrive at a mutually acceptable understanding of testing methods and results. Negotiations during the *Uruguay Round* strengthened and expanded the provisions of the Code.

Multilateral Steel Agreement (MSA). A proposed agreement that would phase out tariffs, eliminate nontariff barriers, and end direct state subsidies to the steel sector. MSA negotiations collapsed in March 1992 and resumed in mid-1993 among 37 steel-producing nations. However, there was extreme opposition within the industry and the MSA was abandoned.

Multilateral Trade Negotiations. See *GATT Round.* The 1974-79 *Tokyo Round* was referred to formally as the Multilateral Trade Negotiations (MTN). As a result, the various *GATT Codes* negotiated during the Tokyo Round are sometimes referred to as "MTN Codes."

Multiple Exchange Rates (also known as Differential Exchange Rates). A system of officially prescribed rates of exchange for a country's currency that varies depending on the type of transaction involved. For example, a government may assign its currency a given value for capital transfers but provide for a less favorable rate of exchange for imports of luxury items, thereby increasing the price of the latter and discouraging their importation. As with other forms of *exchange controls,* multiple exchange rates can function as a disguised trade barrier, and their use is discouraged by the IMF.

National Trade Estimate (NTE) Report. A report on significant foreign trade barriers published in the spring of each year by the Office of the *United States Trade Representative (USTR)* see (Sec. II), with contributions from other Executive Branch departments and agencies and U.S. embassies overseas. The NTE Report is required by the *Trade Act of 1974,* as amended by the Trade and Tariff Act of 1984 and Trade Act of 1988, and inventories the most important barriers affecting U.S. exports of goods and services, U.S. direct investment in other countries, and foreign protection of *intellectual property rights.* The NTE Report covers barriers deemed to have a significant bearing on U.S. interests, whether or not they are consistent with international trading rules. Many countries are excluded from the NTE Report due either to the relatively small size of their markets or the lack of major complaints from U.S. industry and agriculture groups.

National Treatment. The principle that foreign goods, services, or investments are to be treated "no less favorably" within a nation's domestic markets than competing products or services produced locally, once import duties have been paid and applicable customs regulations are satisfied. National treatment is one of the fundamental principles of the *GATT.*

Natural Resource-Based Products. Designation for one of the negotiating groups in the *Uruguay Round* that focused on trade barriers affecting non-agricultural primary products, including forestry products, fishery products, and nonferrous metals and minerals.

Negotiating Group. A group of country delegates in a *GATT Round* charged with planning and managing multilateral negotiations concerning a particular issue or product sector. At the outset of the *Uruguay Round,* two major groups were established – the Group on Negotiations of Goods (GNG) and the Group on Negotiations of Services (GNS) – with 14 issue-oriented subgroups. In April 1991 these activities were consolidated into seven negotiating groups. Work in the final phase of the Round has been organized within four major issue clusters or *Tracks.*

Net Subsidy Test. A proposed modification of rules governing application of *countervailing duties,* whereby an importing country could impose duties on the margin by which export subsidies exceed subsidies provided to producers of competing goods in the importing country.

New Economic Partnership. See *Framework Initiative.*

New International Economic Order (NIEO). An agenda for discussions between industrial and developing countries that focused on restructuring of the world's economy to permit greater participation by and benefits to LDCs (also known as the "North-South Dialogue"). The term is derived from the Declaration for the Establishment of a New International Economic Order, adopted by the United Nations General Assembly in 1974, and referred to a wide range of trade, financial, commodity, and debt-related issues. While the term continues to have currency in academia, it has fallen into disuse in policy-related discussions.

Newly Industrialized Countries (NICs). Now a generally obsolete term; NICs has been superseded by *NIEs,* since inclusion of Taiwan and Hong Kong made use of the word "countries" inappropriate.

Newly Industrialized Economies (NIEs). A subgroup of *developing countries* that have experienced particularly rapid industrialization of their economies, with industrial production and exports expanding accordingly. Current NIEs include South Africa, Mexico, Brazil, China, India, Malaysia, Philippines, Thailand, and Turkey.

Newly Independent States (NIS). The successor states to the former Soviet Union (i.e., Armenia, Azerbaijan, Belarus, Estonia, Georgia, Kazakhstan, Kyrgyzstan, Latvia, Lithuania, Moldova, Russia, Tajikistan, Turkmenistan, Ukraine, and Uzbekistan.

Nomenclature. See customs classification.

Nondiscrimination. Equal application of tariffs, quotas, or other trade restrictions to products from different trading partners. The principle of nondiscrimination is enshrined in Article I of the GATT (see *most-favored-nation* and *national treatment.*

Nondumping Certificate. A document or notation on a shipper's invoice attesting that the merchandise described is being sold at a price no lower than that applying to sales of similar products in the country of origin.

Nonmarket Economy Country. A country in which economic activity is regulated by central planning, in contrast to a market economy that relies principally upon market-based prices to allocate productive resources. In such a country, tariffs have no meaningful impact on import decisions. In GATT contexts, the term applies to members that were not market economies at the time of their accession (e.g., Poland, Hungary, and Romania). These countries joined under special provisions designed to prevent disruption of other members' trade, together with arrangements to ensure steady expansion of the nonmarket economy country's imports from other GATT members. Poland, the first centrally planned economy to accede to the GATT in 1967, has since renegotiated its accession protocol in light of its abandonment of central planning. Countries acceding to the WTO in recent years with non-market economy status are Vietnam (2007) and China (2001). They, too, are now *CITs*. (See also *State Trading Nations*).

Non-Paper. In GATT/WTO parlance, a proposed agreement or negotiating text circulated informally among delegations for discussion without committing the originating delegation's country to the contents.

Nontariff Barriers (NTBs). Measures other than tariffs that burden or restrict international trade. NTBs may be financial (e.g., internal taxes and customs fees) or nonfinancial (e.g. quantitative restrictions and excessive documentation requirements). The term is sometimes used in reference to nongovernmental actions or impediments to trade, such as internal distribution systems that discourage imports, but in the WTO contexts the term refers to measures imposed by governments. Negotiations involving reduction of NTBs are generally more difficult than tariff negotiations since NTBs are almost always closely linked to other national policies or programs.

Nontariff Measures (NTMs). A broader term than *NTBs,* including not only import-restricting barriers but also measures that distort trade by stimulating exports. See *GATT Codes.*

Nonviolation Complaints. In GATT/WTO *dispute settlement* negotiations, refers to provisions allowing members to investigate and rule upon complaints concerning measures that are not in violation of GATT or are outside its scope, but which may affect the balance of a member's rights and benefits under the General Agreement. Because any country that considers itself harmed by such measures would claim the right to alter its GATT legal obligations in response, Article XXIII provides a way of adjudicating such situations in a multilateral forum. Nevertheless, GATT/WTO supervision of nonviolation complaints has proven difficult to implement since it implies altering legal relationships already consented to among members.

Norm Price. See Common Agricultural Policy.

Normal Value. An alternative term for *fair value.*

North-South Dialogue. See New International Economic Order (NIEO).

North-South Trade. In the parlance of the 1970s and 1980s, trade between the developed market economies (the North) and developing countries (the South).

Note Verbale. A formal diplomatic communication delivered orally to an official representative of another country. The written form is a *demarche.*

Notification. In the context of the WTO, refers to the procedure of informing the WTO Secretariat of a change in a country's trade policies, such as application of a new or revised trade-restrictive measure, and of subsequently informing other member countries of the change by the Secretariat.

Nullification or Impairment. The adverse effect on a WTO member's trade interests caused by changes in the trade regime of another member, or by another member's failure to carry out its obligations under the GATT Agreement. In GATT parlance, "nullification or impairment" is the basis for initiating formal action under the *dispute settlement* procedures.

Obligations. In the context of the WTO, the principal obligations of members are (a) to use only approved instruments of protection, primarily tariffs; (b) to use those instruments in a nondiscriminatory way, extending any opening of a market to all WTO trading partners; and (c) to submit all protection to a long-term process of non-reversible reductions through negotiations with other WTO members. For specific substantive obligations, see *disciplines.*

Observer. An observer to the WTO is a country or international organization that has been authorized by the *General Council* (Sec. II) to attend but not participate in sessions of the Council and various WTO committees and negotiating groups. Most *countries in transition* have been accepted as observers to the WTO, which allows officials from these countries to familiarize themselves with Western trade practices and consultation procedures. There are currently 30 countries with observer status, and most are pursuing accession. The *International Monetary Fund* and *UNCTAD* (Sec. II) are among the institutional observers to the WTO.

Offer List. Concessions offered by a country in trade negotiations or a list of selected commodities on which a country proposes to make concessions. An offer list may cover proposed exceptions if *a formula approach* is being used in a tariff negotiation, or it may offer to accept expanded coverage under a proposed *GATT Code.*

Offsets or Offset Requirements. Requirements imposed by governments on foreign exporters as a condition for approval of major sales agreements. Offsets can be intended either to reduce the adverse trade-balance impact of a major sale or to "leverage" specific industrial benefits for the importing country .In one type of offsets, an exporter may be required to purchase a specified amount of locally produced goods or services from the importing country. In a second form, the exporter may be required to establish manufacturing facilities in the importing country or to secure a specified percentage of the components used in manufacturing the product from producers based in the importing country.

Orderly Marketing Agreement (OMA). A contractual agreement between two or more governments to restrain the export growth of specific products. OMAs are supposed to ensure that export surges do not disrupt, threaten, or impair sensitive sectors in the importing country or countries. OMAs usually entail establishment of an export licensing system and export or import quotas for the goods in question. The economic effect of an OMA is similar to that of a *quota,* with the important difference that real income is also transferred from consumers in the importing country to established producers in the exporting country. See also *Voluntary Restraint Agreement.*

Packaging, Labeling, and Marking Regulations. National requirements that importers must package their goods in certain types of containers or identify the contents in a particular way. Such measures are normally intended to meet domestic policy objectives, such as consumer protection, but may be regarded as a *nontariff barrier* to the extent that they pose more problems for producers of imported goods than for domestic producers.

Panel of Experts. In the WTO *dispute settlement* process, an ad hoc group of impartial and knowledgeable trade experts – usually three to five serving in their personal capacity and not as representatives of governments – commissioned to hear opposing arguments and investigate the facts involved in a dispute, to issue findings, and make recommendations as appropriate.

Parallel Imports. Goods, which are authorized by the owner of *intellectual properly rights* for sale in one country, but which are then subsequently shipped to another country without the owner's permission. Traders who engage in such activities are known as parallel traders. Parallel imports are likely to occur when a trader can purchase a particular good in one country and resell the good in another country at a price which is sufficiently higher to cover the costs of the operation. Such activities take place at the expense of the rights owner and of authorized licensees. Many LDCs have laws that prevent intellectual property owners from enforcing restrictions on licensees' exports (see *compulsory licensing* and the *exhaustion* principle).

Paris Convention. Formally known as the Paris Convention for the Protection of Industrial Property. An international agreement on protection of *industrial property* such as *patents, trademarks,* and *appellations of origin,* concluded in 1883 and administered by the *World Intellectual Property Organization (WIPO)* (Sec. II). The Convention provides for *national treatment* (also known as "assimilation") in signatories' patent and trademark laws, and provides a means of determining priority between competing claims (see *right of priority).* LDC participants in the *Uruguay Round* negotiations on *intellectual property rights (IPR)* generally prefer the Paris Convention to the *Berne Convention* because the former permits exception from patent coverage for foods, drugs, and chemicals, and because it allows them autonomy in establishing national IPR systems in accordance with their development objectives and strategies.

Part IV of GATT. Articles XXXVI, XXXVII, and XXXVIII, added to the GATT in 1966 to address the needs of developing country members.

Patent. The grant of an exclusive right to manufacture and market an invention for a specified time, based on a novel idea that provides a solution to a specific technological problem. See *intellectual property rights).*

Patent Cooperation Treaty. An international agreement that permits nationals and residents of a signatory country to seek patent protection in any or all of the signatories by means of a single patent application. See *intellectual property rights.*

Performance Requirements. Government-imposed rules or conditions requiring foreign investors to serve particular national objectives. Trade-related performance requirements – such as commitments to export a specified amount of the output of a new plant or to incorporate a minimum share of local content in its production – can have the same effect as export-stimulating or import-restricting *nontariff measures,* but without being subject to GA TT rules. Nearly all major trading partners of the United States impose performance requirements on at least some local affiliates of foreign corporations. See *Trade-Related Investment Measures.*

Petition. A request to investigate alleged *dumping* by foreign companies or export subsidies by a foreign government. Petitions are usually filed with a designated governmental agency of the importing country by private firms or industry associations, although sometimes governments independently initiate unfair trade investigations (See *unfair trade practices*).

Phytosanitary Measures. See Sanitary and Phytosanitary Measures.

Plurilateral. In WTO parlance, refers to a consultation or negotiating session involving more than two countries (bilateral) but less than the full WTO membership (multilateral).

Preemption. The prerogative of customs authorities to seize and sell merchandise that an importer has deliberately undervalued to avoid payment of duties.

Preferences. Special trade advantages granted by an importing country to certain trading partners, in contrast to nondiscriminatory treatment conforming to the *most-favored-nation* principle. Most preferences are granted to LDCs by *industrial countries* to promote export growth and development (see *GSP*). In addition to preferential tariff rates, preferential application of other measures such as licensing practices, quotas, or taxes may also be granted. The term is not normally applied to special trade treatment granted by a country to its partners in *a free trade area, customs union,* or *common market.*

Preferential Arrangement. A group of countries that grant each other special trade advantages, such as preferential tariff rates, in order to promote member countries' export growth. Special licensing practices, quotas, or preferential application of taxes and other measures are sometimes granted. Many such arrangements are nonreciprocal, in which beneficiary members – usually LDCs – are accorded preferential access to markets of preference-granting countries without making similar market access commitments themselves. Because preferential arrangements violate the *most* *favored-nation* principle, a *waiver* is required for establishing any such arrangement in which WTO members participate.

Preliminary Duties. Duties imposed on a provisional basis during the course of an anti-dumping investigation (See *anti-dumping code)*, following a preliminary finding of *dumping* and *injury* to domestic industries.

Previously Centrally Planned Economies. See *countries in transition.*

Price Undertaking. An agreement by an exporting firm with the government of an importing country to raise the price of its products to a level sufficient to avoid *injury* to producers of similar goods in the importing country, in order to forestall imposition of anti-dumping duties. (See *anti-dumping code* and *suspension agreement.*

Principal Supplier. The country that accounts for the largest portion of total GATT trade in a product imported into a given country. In multilateral WTO negotiations, a country offering to reduce import duties or other barriers on a particular item will generally expect the principal supplier of that item to reciprocate by offering reductions of barriers on some other item. Any tariff concessions exchanged through such negotiations are extended automatically to all other countries that enjoy *most-favored-nation* status. The principal supplier – along with any country holding *initial negotiating rights* – has first claim to negotiate compensation in the event that an importing country raises a tariff above its bound rate (see *binding* and *modifications).* See also *substantial supplier.*

Prior Deposits. A requirement as a condition for importing that an importer deposit a specified sum of money, in domestic or foreign currency and usually a percentage of the value of the imported goods, in a commercial bank or central bank for a specified length of time. Prior deposits are usually administered in conjunction with *import licensing,* with deposits required at the time a license is granted. Since such funds are often held without interest from the time an order is placed until the import transaction has been completed, prior deposits are usually regarded as *nontariff barriers* to trade.

Procedural Protectionism. Abusive administration of import control procedures allowed under GATT (especially those related to *unfair trade practices)* so that domestic industries were protected in ways never intended by signatories to the GATT or the relevant *GATT Codes.*

Process and Production Methods (PPMs). In the context of *environmental trade measures,* refers to factors other than a commodity's physical characteristics – such as processes and methods used in its production – that have an impact on pollution levels or loss of endangered species, and that are regulated by national product *standards* or other restrictions in order to meet environmental objectives.

Producer Subsidy Equivalent (PSE). The share of a producer's total revenue that is attributable to direct or indirect government transfers.

Prohibitive Duty. A tariff rate that is sufficiently high that it effectively precludes most or all imports. Prohibitive duties are usually intended to protect infant or ailing industries from foreign competition or to retaliate against another country's trade practices.

Protection. Government measures – including tariffs and nontariff barriers – that raise the cost of imported goods or otherwise restrict their entry, and thus strengthen the competitive position of domestic producers vis-a-vis foreign producers. See *protectionism.*

Protective Tariff. See *tariff.*

Protectionism. Restriction of international trade by a government in order to shelter domestic producers from foreign competitive pressures. Fundamentally at odds with the principle of *comparative advantage.*

Protocol of Accession. A legal document that recognizes the rights and obligations agreed to as a consequence of a country's signing an international agreement or joining an organization, such as the *World Trade Organization (WTO)* (See Sec. II).

Protocol of Provisional Application (PPA). The legal device that enabled the original Contracting Parties of the GATT to accept general GATT obligations and benefits, despite the fact that some of their existing domestic legislation discriminated against imports in a manner that was inconsistent with certain GATT provisions (see *grandfather clause).* Although the protocol was intended to be temporary, it has remained in effect since 1947 (see *International Trade Organization,* Sec. II). Countries that acceded to the GATT after 1947 do not have recourse to the protocol.

Protocol Relating to Trade Negotiations Among Developing Countries. An agreement negotiated under GATT auspices in 1973 providing for reciprocal tariff and other trade concessions among developing countries.

Punta del Este Declaration. A declaration adopted by trade ministers of GATT member countries in September 1986 at Punta del Este, Uruguay, launching the *Uruguay Round* of multilateral trade negotiations.

Quadrilateral (Quad). In trade parlance, a meeting involving senior trade officials or ministers from the United States, Japan, the European Community, and Canada, which convened to discuss trade policy matters and review the status of multilateral negotiations.

Quantitative Restriction (QR). A term that applies to a *quota* or other administratively determined ceiling on imports or exports, usually expressed in volume terms, and sometimes specifying the amount that may be imported from each supplying country. QRs are distinguished from trade restrictions that operate through the price mechanism, such as a *tariff* or *surcharge*. GATT Article XI generally prohibits quantitative restrictions, although several exceptions are made.

Quota. See import quota.

Quota Auctioning. See *import quota auctioning*.

Rebalancing. A term used in GATT agriculture negotiations, referring to the ability to shift import protection from one product sector to another following an international agreement to cut overall subsidy levels. However, currently the term rebalancing has been used by the WTO in the context of rebalancing the rules of the Multilateral Trading System in favor of the poor.

Reciprocity. The principle traditionally underlying GATT/WTO negotiations, according to which trading partners exchange comparable concessions by negotiating mutually advantageous reductions in import barriers. GATT rules specify that LDC members are not expected to offer fully reciprocal concessions in negotiations with *industrial countries*. The term "relative reciprocity" is sometimes used to characterize the practice by industrial countries to seek less than full reciprocity from LDCs in trade negotiations. See also *sectoral reciprocity* and *selective reciprocity*.

Rectifications. Changes made in a country's schedule of WTO concessions, usually involving correction of errors but occasionally involving duty changes or withdrawal of items from a schedule as a result of the negotiated settlement of a dispute with another country .See also *modifications*.

Reference Price. See Common Agricultural Policy.

Regional Cooperation Organization. A group of countries that have established a mechanism for trade-related discussions and negotiations with outside countries and regional groupings, and for ongoing consultation and cooperation on economic and trade issues of mutual concern.

Regional Trade Arrangement. See *trade bloc.*

Related Specificity. A rule of customs law that when two or more tariff provisions might be applied to an imported item, the one that most specifically describes the article shall be applied.

Relative Reciprocity. See reciprocity, duty remission.

Request-Offer Approach. A tariff or services negotiating procedure whereby specific requests (e.g., cuts of a specified amount in the tariff on particular products or a particular modification of a restrictive regulation in services) are submitted to a trading partner identifying the concessions sought and those proposed to be given in return. Counter offers are exchanged and negotiated by the countries involved, and once the deal is struck results are extended to all other WTO members in accordance with the *MFN* principle. In contrast with the *formula approach,* the request-offer approach tends to concentrate negotiating efforts in areas of primary commercial interest to participating countries. A potential drawback is that it may forego opportunities to achieve broad, across-the-board trade liberalization.

Residual Restrictions. *Quantitative restrictions* maintained since before 1947 by governments that were original signatories of the GATT, and hence were permitted under the *grandfather clause.* Most residual restrictions were maintained by *industrial countries* against imports of agricultural products.

Retaliation. Punitive action taken to limit imports from a trading partner that has violated or reneged on a trade agreement. The Dispute Settlement Body may authorize retaliation if the *dispute settlement* process has been exhausted without success. In principle, the value of trade subjected to retaliation should approximately equal the value of trade affected by the offending action, but there are no accepted guidelines in WTO practice for determining the extent of trade damage suffered by an injured member. Although the threat of retaliation, especially by a major trading country, can have considerable persuasive force, actual imposition offers little economic remedy to the injured party. In some cases it can provoke counter-retaliation (see *trade war).* U.S. authority for taking retaliatory trade actions is provided by Section 301 of the Trade Act of 1974, as amended.

Revenue Tariff. See *tariff.*

Reverse Consensus. A modification of the GATT's *dispute settlement* procedures in the WTO under which the report and recommendations of a Dispute Resolution Body (DSB) panel are adopted by the DSB unless *consensus* exists to reject them. Reverse consensus thus removes a major weakness inherent in GATT consensus-based procedures, which allows a disputing party to block adoption of a panel report with which it disagreed.

Reverse Countertrade. See *Countertrade.*

Reverse Preferences. Tariff advantages once offered by LDCs to imports from certain *industrial countries* that have granted them preferences. Reverse preferences have largely been superseded by the *GSP* system.

Review. See administrative review and judicial review.

Right of Priority. The principle according to which an owner of *industrial property* applying for protection in any country adhering to the *Paris Convention* is permitted –

within a prescribed period of time (12 months for patents, six months for industrial designs and trademarks) – to apply for protection in any other signatory country and have that application treated as though it were filed at the time of the first application.

Road Taxes. Excise taxes imposed on the sale or operation of motor vehicles that have the effect of discriminating in favor of one type of vehicle over another.

Rollback. A commitment to phase out all trade restrictions or policies that distort trade or bring them into conformity with the GATT agreement or instruments negotiated within the framework of the GATT. Under the rollback commitment made at the outset of the *Uruguay Round,* participants were not to seek compensatory concessions for rollback measures.

Round (of trade negotiations). See *GATT Round.*

Rules of Origin. The laws, regulations, and administrative practices that are applied to ascribe a *country of origin* to goods in international trade. Rules of origin include those applicable for administering country-based quotas and for establishing eligibility for preferential tariff programs as well as for statistical reporting.

Safeguards. Import restrictions to prevent commercial injury to a domestic industry from a sudden surge in imports, providing temporary protection while workers and firms in the importing country adjust to the increased foreign competition. Safeguards can take the form of tariffs or quotas. Unlike *anti-dumping duties* or *countervailing duties,* safeguard measures are not based on a claim of unfair trade actions on the part of exporters; however, their economic effects are similar. Article XIX of the GATT sets important limits on the use of safeguards – especially that they must be temporary, degressive (see *degressivity*), and applied equally to imports from all sources – and they require the country imposing safeguard measures to extend compensatory trade benefits to exporting countries adversely affected by the action. Critics charge that excessive strictures of Article XIX have resulted in few countries applying GATT-sanctioned safeguards, resorting instead to more distortive *grey area measures.* Because safeguards usually involve imports from rapidly growing, export-oriented developing countries, however, efforts to reform or modify the provisions of GATT Article XIX have been among the most divisive areas of negotiation between *industrial countries* and LDCs. See *selectivity.*

Sanctions. Trade or financial restrictions imposed against an individual country for political purposes, in an effort to influence its conduct or policies. See *blockade* and *embargo.*

Sanitary and Phytosanitary Measures. Health and safety standards affecting imports ("sanitary" regulations apply to human and animal products; "phytosanitary" regulations apply to plants and plant products). Such standards are established to ensure that animals and plants and their products are safe for consumption and not damaging to the environment. See also *Codex Alimentarius.*

Sectoral Reciprocity. The objective of achieving a balanced set of trade liberalization measures through trade negotiations conducted on a sector-by-sector basis. Sectoral reciprocity contrasts with the customary across-the-board approach to negotiations aimed at achieving mutually beneficial agreements comprising concessions in one sector exchanged for gains in another. See also *selective reciprocity* and *zero-for-zero.*

Selective Reciprocity. (Also known as "contingent reciprocity.") The provision of market access to particular trading partners in particular industries, linked to the granting of comparable access to foreign markets. Examples include the WTO *Civil Aircraft Code, Government Procurement Code,* and *Subsidies Code,* in each of which reciprocity is accorded only to other signatories of the Code. In contrast, the WTO is based on the premise that members will grant comparable access across a broad range of goods and trading partners (sometimes called "broad-based" or "diffuse reciprocity.") Proponents argue that most major trade policy problems facing the *industrial countries* concern disputes in specific industries with specific trading partners, where current international trade rules are seen to be either inapplicable or unenforceable. Critics charge that selective reciprocity risks undermining incentives for multilateral trade-liberalizing efforts based on broad-based reciprocity via *MFN* treatment.

Selectivity. The application of *safeguards* in such a way as to restrict imports from a particular country or group of countries, in contrast with nondiscriminatory actions taken according to the *most-favored-nation* principle. Proponents of selectivity argue that the disruptive effects of safeguards should be minimized by applying restrictions only to exporting countries that are the source of disruption; opponents argue that selective safeguards effectively penalize "efficient but law-abiding" foreign producers.

Semiconductor Agreement. A bilateral agreement concluded in 1986 between the United States and Japan to open the Japanese market to U.S. integrated circuits and semiconductor devices, and to deter the *dumping* of Japanese semiconductors in the U.S. market.

Sensitive Products. Goods produced by a domestic industry employing large numbers of workers, for which the costs of production are such that any reduction in import protection would render the industry vulnerable to *injury.* Products deemed sensitive are most likely to be exempted from tariff reduction formulas in trade negotiations – or subjected to *export restraints* – since changes in the competitive position of such industries could cause major economic and social dislocations in the importing country.

Serious Injury. See *injury.*

Service Mark. A distinctive mark used in the sale or advising of services to distinguish them from the services of others. See also *trademark.*

Service Supply License. A validated export license issued by the U.S. government to a U.S. or foreign firm authorizing the export of spare and replacement parts to controlled purchasers abroad who originally purchased U.S. equipment under license. See *export controls.*

Seven-Plus-Seven. An informal meeting of GATT delegations from industrial and developing countries (originally seven of each) convened by the Director-General to clarify positions or resolve procedural issues. Sometimes as many as 17 delegations were invited, with care taken to ensure representation of countries with strongly held views on an issue. See also *Green Room Consultations.*

Sherpa. An official of sub-cabinet rank from each of the major *industrial countries* responsible for coordinating his/her government's preparatory work for the annual *G7 Economic Summit.* The term sherpa comes from the Nepalese and were typically guides who supported hikers to mountain summits.

Single-Column Tariff. A tariff schedule specifying only one rate of duty for each imported commodity.

Single Undertaking. See *free riders.*

Sluice-Gate Price. See Common Agricultural Policy.

Snapback. Provisions in a trade agreement that allow a signatory to temporarily rescind concessions under specified circumstances, such as an *import surge* or unanticipated balance-of-payments disequilibria.

Social Dumping. An unfair trade practice whereby an exporter achieves a cost advantage over its rivals in foreign markets through inadequate labor laws or lack of human rights protection in its home country. A similar concept, referring to inadequate environmental regulations, is known as *environmental dumping.*

Soft Loan. Refers to interest-free loans granted to developing countries by the *International Development Association* (Sec. II).

South-South Trade. In the parlance of the 1970s and 1980s, refers to trade among developing countries (the South).

Sovereign Compulsion. A legal doctrine in the United States, according to which antitrust liability may be avoided when concerted action by private companies is taken at the direction of a government agency, such as *price undertakings* or *voluntary restraint agreements.*

Special and Differential Treatment (S&D). Preferential treatment given to *industrial countries* in a trade agreement, such as providing better access to developed countries' markets, accelerating implementation of tariff cuts on products exported by LDCs, or allowing LDCs longer time periods to phase in trade reforms.

Special Economic Zone. See export processing zone, duty.

Specific Limitations on Trade. Measures that limit imports or exports of a product during a specified period to a specific volume or value, or that require specific authorization for each import or export transaction. See *import quota, quantitative restriction, exchange controls, licensing, residual restrictions, tariff quota, boycott,* and *embargo.*

Standards. See Technical Barriers to Trade.

Standards-Related Activity. An activity undertaken in conjunction with administration or enforcement of *technical barriers to trade,* including testing and certification of imports for conformity with officially-mandated product standards.

Standards Code. A *GATT Code* negotiated during the *Tokyo Round* to prevent technical requirements – including product standards and testing and certification procedures – from functioning as impediments to trade unless they are necessary for advancing a "legitimate domestic objective" such as health, safety, or environmental protection. The Code neither attempted to formulate standards themselves, nor to set up specific testing and certification systems. The Standards Code has been superseded by the WTO Agreement on *Technical Barriers to Trade.*

Standing Committees. See GATT Standing Committees.

Standstill. A commitment undertaken at the outset of a WTO negotiation to refrain from legislating or implementing new trade-restricting or distorting actions inconsistent with WTO rules or principles, or actions that would improve a participant's negotiating position.

State Trading Enterprises. Entities established by governments to import, export, or produce certain products. GATT Article XVII requires members to operate such entities on the basis of commercial considerations.

State Trading Nations. Countries that rely on government entities instead of private corporations to conduct their trade with other countries. See *nonmarket economy country.*

Stockholm Convention. See *European Free Trade Association* (Sec. II).

Structural Impediments Initiative (SII). A series of bilateral negotiations begun in 1989 by the United States and Japan to identify and attempt to reduce "structural" impediments to trade between the two countries.

Subsidies Code. Formally known as the Agreement on the Interpretation and Application of Articles VI, XVI, and XXIII of the GATT. A *Tokyo Round* agreement designed to strengthen GATT rules relating to *export subsidies* and *countervailing duties* and to reduce the distortive effects of subsidies on world trade (see *GATT Codes*). The Code prohibited industrial country signatories from using export subsidies for manufactured and semi-manufactured goods and attempts to regulate signatories' use of domestic subsidies that have adverse effects on the economies of trading partners. In addition, signatory countries were required to provide details of their countervailing duty legislation and of actions taken pursuant to that legislation to the GATT Committee on Subsidies and Countervailing Measures. The Code was superseded by the WTO Agreement on Subsidies and Countervailing Duties.

Subsidy. A payment or economic benefit conferred by a government on a specific industry or enterprise in order to advance an economic objective deemed to be in the public interest. Although escalating use of subsidies may be displacing tariffs as the principal distortion of international trade as some trade experts assert, there is still no precise definition of the term "subsidy" in the GATT; see *domestic subsidy* and *export subsidy*.

Substantial Supplier. An exporting country accounting for at least 10% of a country's imports of a given product. In WTO tariff negotiations, countries with substantial supplier status may take precedence over all other countries except *principal suppliers* and countries holding *initial negotiating rights* in claiming compensation for a change in a bound tariff.

Super Deductive. A *customs valuation* procedure (also known as the "further processing method") that permits a deduction from the value of imported merchandise to allow for further processing to be undertaken in the importing country prior to final sale. Under U.S. Customs regulations, the super deductive can be applied to goods sold between 90 and 180 days of importation but may not be applied if the processing destroys the identity of the product as imported. See also *deductive value*.

Supplementary Levy. An additional duty that may be imposed under the European Union's *Common Agricultural Policy* on imports of pork, poultry, or eggs when the purchase price falls below the established *gate price*. See also *variable levy*.

Supplier Credits. See *export credits*.

Supply Access. Assurances that importing countries will have fair and equitable access at reasonable prices to supplies of raw materials and other essential imports. Pursuit of supply access commitments usually includes seeking explicit constraints on the use of *export restrictions* as instruments of foreign policy. U.S. efforts to negotiate supply access commitments, such as during the 1973-79 *Tokyo Round,* have generally not met with success.

Surcharge. See Import Surcharge.

Surveillance. The monitoring of trade practices to help ensure that governments fulfill their obligations under trade agreements. See *Surveillance Body* and *Trade Policy Review Mechanism*.

Surveillance Body. A body created at the outset of the *Uruguay Round* to monitor participating countries' trade practices and implementation of their *standstill* and *rollback commitments.*

Suspension. See duty suspension.

Suspension Agreement. A legal agreement between an exporting firm and the government of an importing country restraining the volume of exports to avoid injury to producers of similar goods in the importing country. Suspension agreements are designed to forestall imposition of *anti-dumping duties* or *countervailing duties.* Under U.S. law, countervailing or anti-dumping proceedings may be suspended when the exporters involved agree to change offending practices, offset subsidies, raise prices, or cease shipments. See also *price undertaking.*

Swap Schemes. See *Countertrade.*

Swing. In international textile agreements, referred to the shift of allowable imports from a filled quota to an under-filled quota. Swing provisions usually permitted 5-10% of specified quota levels to be shifted to another product heading.

Switch Trading. See *Countertrade.*

Target Price. See Common Agricultural Policy.

Tariff. A tax or duty levied upon goods imported into a country or customs area. (The term also refers to a list or "schedule" of articles of merchandise specifying the rate of duty to be paid to the government of the importing country.) A "protective tariff" is one which is designed to discourage foreign import competition; a "revenue tariff" is primarily intended to raise money for the government of the importing country .Tariffs increase prices paid by domestic purchasers while reducing the total amount imported. Domestic producers of the product and the importing country's government gain but not by as much as domestic purchasers lose. See also *export duty.*

Tariff Anomaly. A situation in which the tariff on raw materials or semi-manufactured goods is higher than the tariff on the finished product. The opposite of *tariff escalation.*

Tariff Binding. See *binding.*

Tariff Escalation. The application of tariff rates on raw materials that are lower than on processed versions of the same or derivative products. Exporters of primary commodities argue that tariff escalation in importing countries impedes their efforts to move "upstream" to higher value-added processing and manufacturing activities.

Tariff Peaks. See *harmonization.*

Tariff Quota. A two-stage tariff providing a base tariff rate that applies to goods up to a specified quantity imported during a certain period – usually a calendar year – and a higher tariff rate that "kicks in " once the quota threshold is reached. Because tariff quotas focus their protective effects on import surges, they tend to provide selective protection against highly competitive suppliers.

Tariff Rate Quota (TRQ). Alternative term for *tariff quota.*

Tariff Schedule. A comprehensive list of the goods that a country imports and the import duties applicable to each product. See *tariff.*

Tariff Surcharge. See *import surcharge.*

Tariffication. Conversion of a *quota* or other *nontariff barrier (NTB)* to a tariff providing an equivalent amount of protection to domestic producers of the product in question. In principle, conversion of NTBs to a tariff basis enhances *transparency,* minimizes economic distortions, and facilitates future negotiations aimed at reducing levels of protection.

Technical Barriers to Trade (also referred to as Standards). Government-established specifications of product characteristics, such as levels of quality or purity, performance, safety, environmental impact, or physical dimensions that must be met in order to receive permission to import the product. The specifications may cover testing and test methods, terminology, symbols, packaging, marking, or labeling requirements. Standards normally reflect policy criteria not purposely established to impede imports, but some standards systems clearly function as disguised trade barriers. The WTO Agreement on Technical Barriers to Trade tries to ensure that regulations, standards, testing, and certification procedures do not create unnecessary obstacles, while providing members with the right to implement measures to achieve legitimate policy objectives, such as the protection of human health and safety or the environment. See *standards code* and *sanitary and phytosanitary measures.*

Third World. See *developing countries.* The term originated during the Cold War when it was applied to countries that belonged neither to the Western industrialized countries (the "First World") nor to the Communist bloc (the "Second World").

Threshold Price. See Common Agricultural Policy.

Threshold Value. The monetary value of contracts above which government entities are covered by the *Government Procurement Code.*

Tied Aid. Foreign assistance that is linked to procurement of goods and services from the donor country.

Tied Loan. A loan made by a government agency that requires a foreign borrower to spend the proceeds in the lender's country.

TIR Convention. An international agreement designed to facilitate international cargo movements across third countries en route to a final destination. Originally established in 1949 as a means of facilitating West European road transportation ("TIR" is a French acronym for Transports Internationaux Routiers, or international long-haul trucking), the convention now applies to other countries and other modes of transport as well.

Tokyo Declaration. The statement signed in September 1973 in Tokyo initiating the *Tokyo Round* of trade negotiations.

Tokyo Round. The seventh *GATT Round* of multilateral trade negotiations, held from September 1973 to April 1979 with 99 countries participating. The Tokyo Round achieved substantial tariff cuts covering $300 billion of trade, and reduced the *industrial countries'* average tariff on manufactured goods from 7% to 4.7%. For the first time, the Round also focused on *nontariff measures*, and a series of agreements regulating their use, called the *GATT Codes,* were negotiated. In addition, the *Framework Agreement* reforming certain aspects of the GATT system was adopted. Through the various codes and agreements, the Tokyo Round completed a major overhaul of the global trading system; however, the Round did not settle controversial issues of international trade policy so much as it provided ground rules and a mechanism for resolving such issues. The Round derived its name from the site of the ministerial meeting at which it was launched, but negotiations took place in Geneva.

Torquay Round. The third *GATT Round* of multilateral trade negotiations, held in Torquay, England, from September 1950 to April 1959. The Round dealt with institutional matters and the accession of new members but did not make significant progress in reducing tariffs.

TPM. See trigger price mechanism.

Trade and Investment Framework Agreement (TIFA). See *Framework Agreement* (2).

Trade Bloc. A general term referring to regional arrangements among countries that have established formal mechanisms for cooperation on trade issues. The term does not necessarily imply a protectionist stance with respect to nonmember countries, although it is sometimes used in this way. No widely accepted definition of "trade bloc" exists, but it is commonly understood to include six types of arrangements. In descending order of political-economic integration, these categories are *economic union, common market, customs union, free trade area, preferential arrangement,* and *regional cooperation organization.*

Trade Opportunities Program. An export promotion service of the U.S. Department of Commerce.

Trade Policy Review Mechanism (TPRM). A process of examination by the Trade Policy Review Body to provide information on and discuss the trade policy regimes of individual members. The TPRM is an integral part of the WTO. The frequency of reviews of a WTO member's trade regimes takes place based on its weight in the multilateral trading system and its share of world trade in goods and services

Trade-Related Aspects of Intellectual Property Rights (TRIPS). Covers *copyrights* and related rights; *trademarks*, including service marks; geographical indications including appellations of origin; industrial designs; *patents* including the protection of new varieties of plants; layout-designs of integrated circuits; and undisclosed information *including trade secrets* and test data. The three main features of the Agreement include *standards* – the Agreement sets out minimum standards protection to be provided by members; enforcement – provisions on domestic procedures and remedies for the enforcement of intellectual property rights; and *dispute settlement* – disputes between WTO Members about the respect of the TRIPS obligations. The Council for Trade-Related Aspects of Intellectual Property Rights (TRIPS Council) monitors implementation of the Agreement and reports to the General Council.

Trade-Related Investment Measures (TRIMs). Negotiated during the *Uruguay Round*, TRIMS prohibits trade-related investment measures such as *local content requirements* and *export performance requirements* that are inconsistent with basic provisions of GATT 1994 and restrict or distort trade. TRIMS only applies to trade in goods. The Agreement on Trade-Related Investment Measures (TRIMS Agreement) resulted from this negotiation, and a Committee on TRIMs was established to monitor the operation and implementation of these commitments.

Trade Secret. A form of *industrial property.* Refers to a non-patented process, mechanism, or formula, known only to its owner, that is used in producing something of commercial value.

Trade War. An "unwinding" of the liberalization process in which countries impose trade restrictions for punitive purposes and others retaliate in kind.

Trademark. A name or symbol used by a manufacturer or merchant to distinguish goods from those made or sold by others. See *intellectual property rights.*

Transaction Value. The cornerstone of the GATT *Customs Valuation Code,* which obligates signatory governments to use transaction value or the price actually paid or payable for goods when sold for export (subject to certain adjustments for costs or charges not reflected in the price), as the principal basis for valuing goods for customs purposes. In cases where the transaction value cannot be used – for example, shipments between corporate affiliates or related entities – the primary alternative method is the transaction value of identical merchandise shipped from the same country of origin. A secondary alternative is the transaction value of similar goods sold from the country of origin. If none of the foregoing methods can be used, the *deductive value* or the *computed value* may be employed.

Transition. A term referring to the period of time during which provisions of a trade agreement will be implemented (including, in some cases, phasing out existing trade restrictions) by signatories.

Transit Zone. A port of entry in a coastal country that is established as a storage and distribution center for a neighboring country lacking adequate port facilities or access to the sea. Goods in transit to and from the neighboring country are exempt from customs duties, import controls, and many of the entry and exit formalities of the host country. A transit zone is a more limited type of facility than *a free trade zone.*

Transitional Protection. See *pipeline protection.*

Transshipment. Shipping goods through one country to another country in order to conceal the true country of origin. Transshipment may occur for *circumvention* purposes or to take advantage of preferential tariff rates applied to imports from the intermediary country.

Transparency. Openness, clarity, and predictability of a country's trade laws and regulations. Transparency, especially as it connotes freedom from capricious bureaucratic action or manipulation of rules for protectionist purposes, is one of the fundamental tenets of the GATT. *Tariffication* is regarded by many GATT members as a key to promoting transparency.

Treaty of Rome. The agreement, signed in Rome in 1957 by Belgium, France, Germany, Italy, Luxembourg, and the Netherlands, by which the European Economic Community – the forerunner to the present *European Union* – was established. The Treaty took effect January 1, 1958.

Trigger Price Mechanism (TPM). Refers to a mechanism for controlling imports of sensitive products by establishing a minimum "fair price" for the imported goods. Under the TPM established by the United States in 1978 for steel imports, the trigger price (or reference price) was pegged to within 5% of the cost of production of the most efficient international steel supplier, Japan, plus 8% nominal profit plus transportation costs. Imported steel sold below the reference price would automatically "trigger" an investigation of presumed *dumping.*

TRIMS. See Trade-Related Investment Measures.

TRIPS. See Trade-Related Aspects of Intellectual Property Rights.

Tropical Products. Agricultural and other products of export interest to countries in tropical regions of Latin America, Africa, Asia, and Oceania. Examples include coffee, tea, cocoa, bananas, spices, rubber, and tropical timber. Liberalizing trade in these products is a high priority for many developing countries, and was a subject addressed at both the *Tokyo Round* and *Uruguay Round*.

Unfair Competition. See unfair trade practices.

Unfair Trade Practices. International usage tends to mirror terminology in U.S. legislation that applies the term to export-related practices that may be subject to *countervailing duties* (i.e., export subsidies by foreign governments) and *anti-dumping duties* (i.e., dumping by foreign firm), as well as certain anticompetitive practices such as discriminatory shipping arrangements. The term is not normally applied to the range of import-related *nontariff barriers* even though discriminatory elements may be involved. Determination of "unfairness" is left to administrative proceedings in the importing country, subject to procedural requirements of the relevant *GATT Codes.* See *competitive policies and practices*).

Universal Copyright Convention (UCC). One of two international conventions on *intellectual property rights.* UCC was negotiated under United Nations auspices in 1952 and revised in 1971. UCC member states agreed to provide "adequate and effective" copyright protection and to accord *national treatment* to the works of nationals of other UCC signatories. Most countries are now part of the *Berne Convention* (1986).

Upstream Subsidization. An "indirect export subsidy," whereby a producer benefiting from a government subsidy sells a subsidized product to an unrelated company, which in turn performs further processing and then exports the product.

Uruguay Round. The eighth *GATT Round,* launched in 1986 with 105 countries participating, and extended in December 1990 after failure to reach agreement by the original target completion date. In the Uruguay Round, efforts focused on expanding GA TT disciplines to new areas such as agriculture, intellectual property rights, investment, and services, as well as reducing barriers and strengthening international rules affecting *market access, dispute settlement, safeguards,* and enforcement measures under the GA TT. The Round derived its name from Punta del Este, Uruguay, the site of the Ministerial Meeting at which it was launched, but negotiations took place in Geneva.

User Fee. A fee for a service, such as the provision of customs operations by the government of the importing country, assessed on imported goods. GATT Article VIII requires user fees to be assessed on the basis of the estimated or computed cost of the service.

Valuation. See customs valuation.

Variable Levy. An import duty that is subject to alteration as world market prices change, designed to ensure that the imported product's price after payment of the duty will be no less than a predetermined minimum import price. As applied to imported farm products under the European Union's *Common Agricultural Policy,* the variable levy amounts to the difference between the EU target price for domestic producers and the lowest available prices on world markets. For imports of cattle, beef, and veal, the variable levy is applied in addition to normal customs duties. The amount of EU variable levies are adjusted for changes in world market conditions on a daily basis for sugar and grains; weekly for dairy products, beef, live cattle, veal, and rice; monthly for olive oil; and quarterly for pork, poultry , and eggs. See also *supplementary levy.*

Voluntary Export Restraints (VERs). A trade restriction on the quantity of goods an exporting country is allowed to export to another country. The *Multifiber Arrangement* was one of the most well known VERs, which discriminated against textile and clothing exports from developing countries

Waiver. A legal exception whereby WTO members agree to allow another WTO member not to comply with normal commitments to maintain a specific practice that would otherwise violate the *MFN* principle or other WTO obligation.

Working Party. An ad hoc subgroup established by the WTO General Council to address a specific trade policy issue, such as a country's application for *accession* or a dispute between two members. Members of a working party function as representatives of their governments.

Working Requirement. A term associated with the lapse of *intellectual property* protection or the granting of *compulsory licenses* if a patented invention, trademarked good, or copyrighted work is not produced or sold within a specified period of time.

World Economic Conference of 1927. The first attempt to negotiate a cooperative multilateral approach to problems facing the world trading system. Along with its subsidiary Conference on Import and Export Prohibitions and Restrictions, the Conference sought to counter the trend toward increased protectionism that had begun in Europe in the 1870s; by the 1920s this was intensified in all major countries. A code negotiated at the Conference regulating use of *quantitative restrictions* and other trade barriers fell short of necessary ratification by one country, while a tariff truce agreed at the Conference was effectively ended upon adoption of the Smoot-Hawley Act by the United States in 1930. Although unsuccessful, the Conference served ultimately as a progenitor of the GATT.

World Economic Conference of 1933. The second multilateral effort to deal with the global economic crisis of the interwar period. The Conference focused on European efforts to secure an international currency stabilization plan. Following the collapse of the Conference, nations engaged in a period of competitive currency devaluations through the mid-1930s, further exacerbating trade tensions. The experience of both Conferences weighed heavily on the minds of the architects of the *Bretton Woods System* a decade later.

Yaounde Convention. See *Lome Convention.*

Zero-For-Zero. A term used in the *market access* negotiations in the *Uruguay Round* to denote a sectoral free trade initiative that would essentially eliminate tariffs on an entire category of goods. Meeting in Tokyo in July 1993, the *Quad* trade ministers announced plans to negotiate zero-for-zero agreements in eight industrial areas including pharmaceuticals, medical equipment, steel, construction equipment, farm equipment, furniture, beer, and distilled spirits.

GLOSSARY

SECTION 2

TRADE-RELATED ORGANIZATIONS

This Section introduces the reader to a variety of trade-related organizations that are either currently engaged in trade activities or have played a critical role in past trade-related decisions.

ACP (African, Caribbean, and Pacific) Countries. A group of developing countries with preferential trade and financial ties to the European Union (see Sec. I). Includes Angola, Antigua and Barbuda, Bahamas, Barbados, Belize, Benin, Botswana, Burkina Faso, Burundi, Cameroon, Cape Verde, Central African Republic, Chad, Comoros, Democratic Republic of Congo, Cook Islands, Cote d'Ivoire, Cuba, Djibouti, Dominica, Dominican Republic, East Timor, Equatorial Guinea, Eritrea, Ethiopia, Fiji, Gabon, The Gambia, Ghana, Grenada, Guinea, Guinea-Bissau, Guyana, Haiti, Jamaica, Kenya, Kiribati, Lesotho, Liberia, Madagascar, Malawi, Mali, Marshall Islands, Mauritania, Mauritius, Federal States of Micronesia, Mozambique, Namibia, Nauru, Niger, Nigeria, Niue, Palau, Papua New Guinea, Rwanda, St Kitts and Nevis, St Lucia, St Vincent and the Grenadines, Samoa, Sao Tome and Principe, Senegal, Seychelles, Sierra Leone, Solomon Islands, Somalia, South Africa, Sudan, Suriname, Swaziland, Tanzania, Togo, Tonga, Trinidad and Tobago, Tuvalu, Uganda, Vanuatu, Zambia, and Zimbabwe.

Advisory Committee on Trade Policy and Negotiations (ACTPN). The highest-level group in the private sector advisory system established by the U.S. Congress to ensure that U.S. trade policy and negotiating objectives reflect U.S. commercial and economic interests. Appointed by the President to two-year terms, there are currently 34 ACTPN members responsible for considering trade policy issues in the context of the overall national interest.

Agency of Industrial Science and Technology (AIST). A newly formed research organization (2001), funded primarily by the Japanese government. The new AIST is the result of combining 15 research institutes previously under the Ministry of International Trade and Industry (MITI) and the Weights and Measures Training Institute. AIST is responsible for promoting a range of technologies and has over 40 research units that conduct in-house research and sponsor research programs to encourage private-sector technology development.

Agriculture Policy Advisory Committee (APAC). A policy-level committee that forms part of the private sector advisory system established by the U.S. Congress to ensure that trade policy and negotiating objectives reflect U.S. commercial and economic interests. The APAC and the individual *agriculture technical advisory committees (ATACs)* provide policy advice and technical expertise on bilateral and multilateral agriculture negotiations. Members are appointed by the *United States Trade Representative (USTR)* in conjunction with the Secretary of Agriculture. The counterpart committee in the industrial sector is the *Industry Policy Advisory Committee (IPAC)*. See also *ACTPN*.

Agriculture Technical Advisory Committee (ATAC). One of more than 30 technical, sectoral, and functional committees forming part of the private sector advisory system established by the U.S. Congress to ensure that trade policy and negotiating objectives reflect U.S. commercial and economic interests. ATACs are subordinate to the *APAC* and represent individual farm commodity groups, providing specific, often highly technical advice concerning the likely effects of trade policy decisions or negotiating concessions on the sector. ATAC members are appointed jointly by the *United States Trade Representative (USTR)* and the Secretary. ATACs for trade consists of six commodity groups: 1) animals and animal products; 2) fruits and vegetables; 3) grains, feed and oilseeds; 4) sweeteners and sweetener products; 5) tobacco, cotton, peanuts, and planting seeds; and 6) processed foods.

American Enterprise Institute for Public Policy Research. A research and educational organization, based in Washington, DC, specializing in monetary, tax, trade, and regulatory policy issues.

Andean Pact (Andean Subregional Integration Agreement). One of the world's oldest free trade arrangements, a *regional cooperation organization* (Sec. 1) including Bolivia, Colombia, Ecuador, Peru, and Venezuela. Chile was a founding member, but withdrew in 1976. Members began serious efforts to reduce intra-regional trade barriers only in 1991. Colombia and Venezuela liberalized bilateral trade and adopted a *common external tariff* (Sec. I) in January 1992, creating the Colombia-Venezuela Customs Union. An agreement was signed in March 1993 among all members except Peru to establish a customs union by January 1994, with special treatment for Bolivia and Ecuador in implementing a common external tariff. The four *MERCOSUR* members gained associate membership in 2005 (Argentina, Brazil, Paraguay and Uruguay). Venezuela withdrew in 2006.

Arab Common Market (ACM). A moribund common market including Egypt, Iraq, Jordan, Libya, Mauritania, Syria, and Yemen established in 1964. The long-term goal was to establish a full customs union to abolish trade restrictions and quotas, and restrictions on employment, labor, residence, and transportation among members. The ACM trade provisions have been largely unimplemented.

Arab Mahgreb Union (AMU). A moribund common market between Algeria, Libya, Mauritania, Morocco, and Tunisia established in 1989. Goals of the AMU included the adoption of common customs and financial legislation and coordinated economic planning. Negligible progress toward AMU trade integration has been achieved.

Asia Pacific Economic Cooperation (APEC). A regional cooperation organization that began in 1989, with objectives including consulting and cooperating on a broad range of economic and trade-related policies and promotion of trade liberalization among members in a GATT-consistent manner. Founding members were Australia, Brunei Darussalam, Canada, Indonesia, Japan, Korea, Malaysia, New Zealand, the Philippines, Singapore, Thailand, and the United States. China, Hong Kong, and Taipei joined in 1991; Mexico and Papua New Guinea followed in 1993; Chile joined in 1994; and Peru, Russia, and Vietnam joined in 1998. APEC ministerial meetings have been held since November 1989.

Association Francaise de Normalisation (AFNOR). France's industrial standards authority.

Association of Coffee Producing Countries (ACPC) or Asociacion Mundial de Paises Productores de Cafe (AMPC). An *international commodity organization* (Sec. I). Following collapse of the export quota system of the *International Coffee Organization* and faltering efforts to negotiate a new International Coffee Agreement with consuming countries, the major coffee producing countries in Latin America, Africa, and Asia, representing about 70% of world production, agreed in September 1993 to form the ACPC, a producer cartel that would withhold 20% of production from the world market in order to buoy prices. However, because of the rapid fall in coffee bean prices between 1993-2001, ACPC dissolved in January 2002.

Association of Natural Rubber Producing Countries (ANRPC). An *international commodity organization* (Sec. I) established in 1970 to coordinate production and marketing of natural rubber. The International Natural Rubber Agreement on Price Stabilization was signed in 1976 by five member countries. Membership is open to all countries producing natural rubber. Current ANRPC members include Cambodia, China, India, Indonesia, Malaysia, Papua New Guinea, Philippines, Singapore, Sri Lanka, Thailand and Vietnam, which account for approximately 92% of the global production of natural rubber. The organization is based in Kuala Lumpur, Malaysia. See also *International Natural Rubber Organization.*

Association of South East Asian Nations (ASEAN). A regional cooperation organization and free trade area consisting of Brunei, Cambodia, Indonesia, Laos, Malaysia, Myanmar, Philippines, Singapore, and Thailand. Founded in 1967, ASEAN objectives

include regional economic integration and policy coordination and industrial cooperation and promotion. Negotiations were launched in 1992 on liberalizing trade among
members within 15 years under the rubric of the ASEAN Free Trade Area (AFTA).
ASEAN Ministers also established a seven- to ten-year timetable for cutting tariffs on
15 product groups, with initial cuts to go into effect during 1993. Previous ASEAN free
trade agreements were repeatedly postponed. The ASEAN Charter entered into force
in December 2008 to operate under a legal and institutional framework. Comprised of
three pillars, (i.e., the ASEAN Political-Security, Economic, and Socio-Cultural Communities), ASEAN members are now committed to accelerate the Initiative for ASEAN
Integration (IAI) Strategic Framework and IAI Work Plan Phase II by 2015.

Atlantic Council. A private, nonprofit organization that conducts studies and makes
recommendations on international economic issues in the Atlantic and Pacific communities. The Council is based in Washington, DC.

Auswartiges Amt. Germany's foreign ministry.

Balance of Payments Committee. See Committee on Balance of Payments Restrictions.

Baltic Free Trade Area (BAFTA). A free trade area linking Estonia, Latvia, and Lithuania. Objectives included elimination of customs duties and quotas on intra-regional
trade; a moratorium on introduction of new export restrictions; and cessation of state
aid or other actions that distort competition among enterprises in the Baltic republics.

Berne Union. Formal name is the Union d' Assureurs des Credits Internationaux, or
International Union of Credit and Investment Insurers. The leading association for
export credit and investment insurance worldwide. Established in 1934, The Berne
Union establishes uniform criteria and standards for export credit insurance. See
export credits and *Export Credits Arrangement* (Sec. I).

Black Sea Economic Cooperation (BSEC). A regional *cooperation organization* (Sec.
1) originally consisting of Albania, Armenia, Azerbaijan, Bulgaria, Georgia, Greece,
Moldova, Romania, Russia, Turkey, and Ukraine. Objectives included expansion of
mutual trade through gradual removal of trade barriers; sectoral cooperation in
several areas including agriculture, transportation, and product standardization
and certification; and eventual creation of a foreign trade and investment bank. The
BSEC Declaration was signed by heads of state in June 1992 and the Charter entered
into force in May 1999, whereby BSEC acquired an international legal identity and
became a regional economic organization known as the *Organization of the Black Sea
Economic Cooperation*. The State Union of Serbia and Montenegro became a member
in 2004, bringing membership to 12. The Secretariat (BSEC-PERMIS) is located in
Istanbul, Turkey.

BOP Committee. See Committee on Balance of Payments Restrictions.

Brookings Institution. An independent research organization founded in 1927, specializing in economics, government, foreign policy, and the social sciences and based in Washington, DC.

Bundesamt fur Wirtschaft (BAW). Germany's federal office of economics and export control.

Bundesverband der Deutschen Industrie (BDI). German employers' council, roughly equivalent to the U.S. National Association of Manufacturers. Along with the *Deutscher Industrie- und Handelstag (DIHT)*, BDI leaders confer with German officials on trade policy issues, and the association's staff members conducts economic and business research.

Bundesministerium fur Finanzen (BMF). Germany's finance ministry, sometimes referred to as Bundestinanzministerium (BFM).

Bundesministerium fur Wirtschaft (BMWi). Germany's economics ministry.

Business Roundtable (BR). Headquartered in New York City, an association of chief executives of leading U.S. corporations with nearly $6 trillion in annual revenues and more than 13 million employees. The Business Roundtable sponsors conferences and reports on issues of concern to business, including taxation, antitrust, international trade, employment policy, and the federal budget.

Cairns Group. A negotiating group of agricultural exporting countries formed to support agricultural trade reform in GATT. The group advocates the systematic reduction of farm subsidies and import barriers. Formed in 1986, the Cairns Group continues to play a key role in pushing the WTO membership to meet the full mandate set in Doha. Members include Argentina, Australia, Bolivia, Brazil, Canada, Chile, Colombia, Costa Rica, Guatemala, Indonesia, Malaysia, New Zealand, Pakistan, Paraguay, Peru, Philippines, South Africa, Thailand, and Uruguay. The Australian government led the formation of the group, which takes its name from the site of early meetings in the Australian resort town of Cairns.

Caribbean Community and Common Market (CARICOM). A customs union founded in 1973, making it a

free trade area, superseding the Caribbean Free Trade Agreement (CARIFTA). The objectives of CARICOM were to improve standards of living, full employment and other factors of production, covering areas such as accelerating and sustaining economic development, expanding trade and economic relations, enhancing levels of international competitiveness through increased production and productivity, as well as enhancing coordination of member states' foreign and economic policies. Member states include Antigua and Barbuda, Bahamas, Barbados, Belize, Dominica, Grenada, Guyana, Haiti, Jamaica, Montserrat, Saint Lucia, St. Kitts and Nevis, St Vincent and the

Grenadines, Suriname, and Trinidad and Tobago. Associate members include Anguilla, Bermuda, British Virgin Islands, Cayman Islands, and Turks and Caicos Islands.

Carpathian Euro region. A *regional cooperation organization* (Sec. 1) established in February 1993 among Hungary , Poland, Slovakia, and Ukraine to facilitate trade and promote infrastructure development in the Carpathian region.

Center for Strategic and International Studies (CSIS). A nonprofit research organization founded in 1962 to conduct analyses of international issues on an interdisciplinary basis. CSIS was originally affiliated with Georgetown University and is based in Washington, DC.

Center for the Study of Public Choice. A research institution at George Mason University that promotes research in public choice, an interdisciplinary approach to the study of the relationship between economic and political institutions. Its interests include trade protection and regulation, in addition to public finance, constitutional economics, federalism and local government, and econometrics. The Center is located in Fairfax, Virginia.

Central African Customs and Economic Union or Union Douaniere et Economique de l' Afrique Centrale (UDEAC). A customs union including Cameroon, Central African Republic, Chad, Congo, Equatorial Guinea, and Gabon. It was founded in 1963, superseding the Equatorial Customs Union. Objectives included intra-regional trade liberalization; adoption of a *common external tariff* (Sec. I); creation of a common investment code; and economic policy harmonization and factor mobility cooperation. UDEAC signed a treaty to establish the Economic and Monetary Community of Central Africa (CEMAC) in 1999, which replaced UDEAC. However, liberalization objectives have not been met.

Central American Common Market (CACM) or Mercado Comun Centroamericana (MCCA). A customs union including Costa Rica, El Salvador, Guatemala, Honduras, and Nicaragua; Belize and Panama participate in CACM summits, but do not participate fully in regional trade integration. CACM was founded in 1960 and revised June 1991; a *common external tariff* (Sec. I) established in 1986 was not effective in all members.

Central European Free Trade Agreement (CEFTA). A *regional cooperation organization* (Sec. 1) and prospective free trade area consisting of the Czech Republic, Hungary , Poland, and Slovakia. Objectives included regional coordination and cooperation following the collapse of *CEMA,* to help offset members' current difficulties competing in Western markets and to help pave the way for eventual EC accession. Elimination of barriers to trade among participants in industrial products were to be phased over an eight-year transition period. The CEFTA agreement signed in December 1992 covered 25% of intra-group trade initially, with the intention of increasing to 85%. Under the rubric of the Visegrad Group or Trojkat, the group functioned principally as a mechanism for cooperation on security and other non-trade issues and for promoting integration into Western political and economic structures. Amendments to the agreement took place in 1995 and 2003. Slovenia joined CEFTA in 1996, Romania in 1997, Bulgaria in 1999, Croatia in 2003, and Macedonia in 2006. The original signatories left CEFTA and joined the EU and therefore CEFTA 2006 extended inclusion to the rest of the Balkan states. Current members include Albania, Bosnia and Herzegovina, Croatia, Macedonia, Moldova, Montenegro, Serbia, and UNMIK-Kosovo. CEFTA fully conforms to WTO rules and EU regulations.

Central European Initiative (CEI). A regional cooperation founded by Italy, Austria, Hungary, and Yugoslavia known as the Quadrangolare, and when Czechoslovakia joined, changed its name to Pentagonale. With the admission of Poland in 1991, it once again changed its name to Hexagonale. Current members include Albania, Austria, Belarus, Bosnia and Herzegovina, Bulgaria, Croatia, Czech Republic, Hungary, Italy, Macedonia, Moldova, Montenegro, Poland, Romania, Serbia, Slovakia, Slovenia, and Ukraine. CEI is now the largest forum of economic cooperation among the member states of Central, Eastern, and South Eastern Europe.

Centre d'Etudes Prospectives et d'Informations Internationales (CEPII). France's center for forecasting and international information, a government-staffed research organization affiliated with the Planning Commission. CEPII conducts studies on global economic and financial issues and publishes data on industrial structures.

Centre for Economic Performance (CEP). CEP is research institute at the London School of Economics (LSE) Research Laboratory. It was established by the Economic and Social Research Council (ESRC) in 1990 and is now one of the leading economic research groups in Europe. CEP prepares economic studies for the general business community as well as government.

Centre for Economic Policy Research (CEPR). A British research institute specializing in international trade and macroeconomics.

Centre Francais du Commerce Exterieur (CFCE). France's Board of Foreign Trade.

Chaebols. South Korea's industrial conglomerates. The four largest chaebols are Hyundai, Samsung, Lucky-Goldstar, and Daewoo.

Chancellery. The office of Germany's Chancellor (prime minister).

CIS Economic Union. A customs union among most members of the *Commonwealth of Independent States,* intended to restore economic ties that were broken following the demise of the Soviet Union in 1991. Armenia, Azerbaijan, Belarus, Kazakhstan, Kyrgyzstan, Moldova, Russia, Tajikistan, Turkmenistan, and Uzbekistan signed a framework accord in December 1991, pledging to establish a customs union and to coordinate monetary and credit policies. Georgia joined in December 1993, but due to conflict with Russia withdrew in 2009. In 2007 the effectiveness of the CIS was in question. In 2009 six countries (Armenia, Azerbaijan, Belarus, Georgia, Moldova and Ukraine) joined the Eastern Partnership, a project initiated by the European Union.

Codex Alimentarius Commission. An organization established in 1963 by the *Food and Agriculture Organization* in conjunction with the World Health Organization to establish international standards for raw and processed food products. See *Codex ~ Alimentarius* and *sanitary and phytosanitary standards* (Sec. I).

Colombia-Venezuela Customs Union. See *Andean Pact.*

Commission on International Commodity Trade. A UN specialized agency established in 1954 to monitor activities in primary commodity markets.

Committee on Balance of Payments Restrictions (BOP Committee). A WTO standing committee responsible for authorizing and monitoring temporary import restrictions imposed by WTO members to deal with balance-of-payments problems.

Committee on Foreign Investment in the United States (CFIUS). A U.S. government inter-agency committee established in 1975 to monitor the impact of foreign investment in the United States. With the passage of the Exon-Florio Amendment in 1988, CFIUS was given authority to review and recommend action against mergers, acquisitions, and takeovers that place U.S. assets under foreign control. CFIUS is chaired by the Treasury Department and is represented at the Assistant Secretary level by the Departments of Commerce, State, Defense, and Justice, and by the Office of the Management and Budget, the Council of Economic Advisers, the Office of the U.S. Trade Representative, the Office of Science and Technology Policy, the National Security Advisor, and the Assistant to the President for Economic Policy.

Committee of Permanent Representatives (COREPER). A key group in the decision-making process of the *European Union,* comprising ambassadors and representatives from EU member states. COREPER is responsible for preparing for the ministerials of the Council of the European Union Meetings. COREPER serves as liaison between member-state governments and EU institutions and works to resolve policy differences between the Council and the European Commission. The Committee operates at two levels: COREPER 1 consists of deputies permanent representatives, dealing with technical matters and COREPER 2 comprises ambassadors who deal with more sensitive political, commercial, economic, or institutional questions.

Committee on Tariff Concessions. A standing committee adopted in 1991 under GATT to review the results of tariff negotiations and oversee implementation of the agreements

Committee on Trade and Development (CTD). A WTO committee that coordinates technical assistance and development-related activities to improve the integration of LDC members into the multilateral trading system.

Commodity Credit Corporation (CCC). A federally chartered corporation administered as part of the U.S. Department of Agriculture. CCC administers price support,
storage, and reserve programs that focus on stabilizing, supporting, and protecting
farm income and prices; assisting in the maintenance of adequate supplies of foodstuffs, feeds, and fibers; and facilitating orderly distribution of agricultural commodities. CCC is managed by a Board of Directors and supervised and directed by Secretary
of Agriculture, who is an ex-officio director and chairperson of the Board.

Commonwealth of Independent States (CIS). An organization of II countries, including all former Soviet republics except Georgia and the Baltic states, established by the
Alma-Ata Declaration of December 1991 to coordinate inter-commonwealth relations
and to provide a mechanism for the orderly dissolution of the USSR. The agreement
pledged cooperation in forming and developing a united economic area and a common
customs policy, and established the city of Minsk as the official location of the CIS
coordinating bodies. Members include Armenia, Azerbaijan, Belarus, Kazakhstan, Kyrgyzstan, Moldova, Russia, Tajikistan, Turkmenistan, Ukraine, and Uzbekistan. Georgia
joined two years later, but following an escalation of hostilities between Georgia and
Russia in 2008, withdrew from CIS in August 2009. See also *CIS Economic Union.*

Compagnie Francaise d' Assurance pour le Commerce (COFACE). France's export
credit guarantee

agency.

The Conference Board. An organization of senior executives from various industries
worldwide that sponsors conferences and reports on national and international economic issues and business management. It is based in New York City.

Conseil National du Patronat Francais (CNPF). An employers union formed in
France in 1945. CNPF became *Mouvement des Entreprises de France* in 1998.

Confederation of British Industry (CBI). The premier lobbying organization and
employers' council in the United Kingdom, roughly equivalent to the U.S. National
Association of Manufacturers.

Coordinating Committee for Multilateral Export Controls (COCOM). A working
group of 17 nations established to monitor exports of strategic goods – especially
high-technology products – to potentially hostile countries. The members were Australia, Belgium, Canada, Denmark, France, Germany, Greece, Italy, Japan, Luxembourg,
Netherlands, Norway, Portugal, Spain, Turkey, the United Kingdom, and the United
States. See *COCOM List* (Sec. I). Due, in part, by a lack of enforcement as well as the fall
of Communism, COCOM was dissolved in March 1994.

Council of Baltic Sea States (CBSS). A regional cooperation between Denmark, the
European Commission, Estonia, Finland, Germany, Latvia, Lithuania, Norway, Poland,

Russia. Objectives included economic assistance and cooperation; assistance to new democratic institutions; environmental protection; energy cooperation; humanitarian matters and health; and cooperation on transport and communication, culture, education, tourism, and information. Ten additional countries – Belarus, France, Italy, the Netherlands, Romania, Slovakia, Spain, the Ukraine, the United Kingdom, and the United States of America – currently have observer status. The Council also cooperates with 16 strategic partners to further extend regional cooperation in and with the Baltic Sea area. The CBSS Declaration was signed by members' foreign ministers in March 1992.

Council of Europe. An association of 47 member countries, formed in 1949 by ten countries – Belgium, Denmark, France, Ireland, Italy, Luxenbourg, the Netherlands, Norway, Sweden, and the United Kingdom. The primary aim was to identify areas of common interest and provide a forum for the articulation of European unity. The Council's headquarters is Strasbourg, France.

Council on Foreign Relations. A privately funded nonprofit, nonpartisan membership organization devoted to promoting improved understanding of international affairs through research, conferences, and publications. The Council has offices in New York City and Washington, D.C.

Council on Mutual Economic Assistance (CEMA, CMEA or COMECON). Formed in 1949, CEMA was a Soviet-led economic association of Communist nations. Members included the Soviet Union, Poland, East Germany, Czechoslovakia, Hungary, Romania, Bulgaria, Mongolia, Vietnam, and Cuba. CEMA trade patterns were based on long-term state agreements primarily involving barter exchanges of East European industrial and consumer products for Soviet energy and raw materials that fixed prices far in advance and recorded payments in nonconvertible transferable rubles. CEMA members decided in March 1991 to disband the organization.

Court of International Trade. A U.S. Federal Court (formerly the Court of Tariff Appeals) that hears appeals from proceedings under U.S. trade laws.

Customs Cooperation Council (CCC). Now called the *World Customs Organization (WCO),* headquartered in Brussels. The CCC/WCO is multilateral organization in which customs officials from participating countries meet to simplify and standardize customs procedures and techniques of member countries. The organization is concerned with the mechanics of customs administration and is not involved in matters relating to tariff levels or questions of trade policy. The CCC/WCO and the WTO cooperate regularly on the classification of goods to ensure uniformity in the application of GATT Article VII and other rules concerning *customs valuation* (Sec. I). The *Harmonized System* (Sec. I) was negotiated in the CCC. See also *Kyoto Convention* (Sec. I).

Defense Policy Advisory Committee on Trade (DPACT). A policy-level committee that funds part of the private sector advisory system established by Congress to ensure that U.S. trade policy and negotiating objectives reflect U.S. commercial and economic interests. The DPACT provides advice on defense trade issues, including defense export policies and the defense industrial base related to bilateral and multi-lateral trade negotiations. DPACT members are appointed by the United States Trade Representative in conjunction with the Secretary of Defense.

Deutscher Industrie und Handelskammertag (DIHK). Formerly Deutscher Indus-trie-und Handelstag (DIHT), Germany's industry and trade council, an umbrella organization for over 80 local chambers of commerce and industry. Along with the *Bundesverband der Deutschen Industrie,* DIHK leaders confer with German officials on trade policy issues. The association's staffs conduct economic and business research.

Direction des Relations Economiques Exterieures (DREE). France's foreign eco-nomic relations directorate. Formally subordinate to the Ministry of Industry and Foreign Trade, DREE has traditionally had the lead in developing French trade policy. It is also responsible for export promotion.

Directorates-General (DGs). Functional departments and services of the *European Commission.* Currently there are 33 departments and 11 services managed by the DG.

Directorate-General des Strategies Industrielles (DGSI). France's directorate of industrial strategies, part of the Ministry of Industry and International Trade.

Downing Street (No.10). The office of Britain's Prime Minister.

East Asia Economic Caucus (EAEC). A Malaysian-proposed consultative group, including the *ASEAN* members, China, Hong Kong, Japan, South Korea, Taiwan, and Vietnam, intended to serve as a forum for coordinating positions in trade relations and negotiations with countries outside the region. Apart from Malaysia, the interest of other East Asian countries in EAEC was unclear; ASEAN foreign ministers decided in July 1993 that the caucus could be a sub-group within *APEC,* but stopped short of formally endorsing EAEC.

Economic Community of Central African States or Communaute Economique des Etats de I' Afrique Centrale (CEEAC). A customs union including Burundi, Cameroon, Central African Republic, Chad, Congo, Equatorial Guinea, Gabon, Rwanda, Sao Tome and Principe, and Zaire, founded in 1983. The objectives were to expand intra-regional trade; adopt of a *common external tariff* (Sec. I); and establish a regional common market by 2000. Only limited progress has been achieved, as trade among members is hindered by poorly developed trade financing and by the existence of five separate, mostly non-convertible currencies within the region.

Economic Community of Great Lakes Countries or Communaute Economique des Pays des Grands Lacs (CEPGL). A free trade area including Burundi, Rwanda, and the Democratic Republic of Congo (formerly Zaire), founded in 1976. Objectives include promotion of economic cooperation and development; reduction of tariffs on intra-group trade; free factor mobility; and joint industrial projects. An accord on customs and preferential tariffs was signed but not implemented. Some progress in cooperation on power generation has been achieved.

Economic Community of West African States (ECOWAS) or Communaute Economique des Etats de l' Afrique de l'Ouest (CEDEAO). A regional group of 15 countries currently consisting of Benin, Burkina Faso, Cape Verde, Cote-D'Ivoire, Gambia, Ghana, Guinea, Guinea-Bissau, Liberia, Mali, Niger, Nigeria, Senegal, Sierra Leone, and Togo. Founded in 1975, objectives include phased elimination of tariffs and nontariff restrictions on intra-regional trade in manufactured goods; liberalization of intra-regional trade in agriculture; establishment of a *common external tariff* (Sec. I); removal of restrictions on the movement of capital, services, and labor; harmonization of agricultural and industrial policies; and creation of a monetary union. ECOWAS and the ECOWAS Bank for Investment and Development are its two main institutions designed to implement policies and programs.

Economic Cooperation Organization (ECO). A *regional cooperation organization* (Sec. 1) including Afghanistan, Azerbaijan, Iran, Kazakhstan, Kyrgyzstan, Pakistan, Tajikistan, Turkey, Turkmenistan, and Uzbekistan. Objectives include bilateral trade promotion and cooperation in industrial planning; the February 1992 ECO Summit referred to the goal of eventual creation of an Islamic Common Market. It was founded in 1964 as the Regional Cooperation for Development (RCD) linking Iran, Pakistan, and Turkey; it came to a standstill after the Iranian revolution in 1979 but was not formally dissolved. Following Iranian initiatives in 1984, some cooperative projects were discussed under the heading of the ECO. Five Central Asian CIS republics joined the ECO at the Tehran Summit in February 1992; Kazakhstan and Afghanistan joined in November 1992. Currently member states are working to accelerate the pace of regional development, which was addressed at the 10th ECO Summit in Istanbul, Turkey, in December 2010.

Economic Strategy Institute. A private organization based in Washington, DC, that conducts studies and makes policy recommendations on domestic and international economic issues, industrial and technological developments, and global security issues.

Elysee. The office of the French Presidency.

European Community (EC) 1973-1993. (Previously the European Economic Community, or EEC; the term "European Communities" referred to the collectivity of the EEC, the European Coal and Steel Community, and Euratom.) A common market established in 1958 by the *Treaty of Rome* (Sec. I) that linked France, West Germany, Italy, Belgium, the Netherlands, and Luxembourg. Subsequently the United Kingdom, Ireland, Denmark, Greece, Spain, and Portugal became member states, bringing the membership to 12. Some of the purposes of the EC were the elimination of tariffs and other restrictions on trade between member states; maintenance of a *common external tariff* (Sec. I) toward other countries; free movement of labor and capital among member states; and establishment of a *common agricultural policy* (Sec. I). In accordance with Article 113 of the Treaty of Rome, the EC acted for the member states on matters of trade policy and represents them in GATT discussions and negotiations. The EC was superceded by the *European Union* in 1993.

European Council. Defines the development and general political direction and priorities of the EU, but is not responsible for any legislative functions. It is distinct from the *EU Council of Ministers,* which prepares its agenda.

European Court of Justice. As the" judicial branch" of the *European Union*, the Court is responsible for interpreting the scope of EU jurisdiction and settles disputes between EU governments and EU institutions. Companies, organizations, and individuals can also bring cases before the Court if they feel their rights have been infringed by an EU institution. The Court, which is located in Luxenbourg, has one judge per EU country and eight 'advocates-general' who present, publicly and impartially, opinions on the cases brought before the Court.

European Economic Area (EEA). A free trade area established in 1994 consisting of Austria, Belgium, Denmark, Finland, France, Germany, Greece, Iceland, Ireland, Italy, Liechtenstein, Luxembourg, Netherlands, Norway, Portugal, Spain, Sweden, and the United Kingdom. Objectives included establishment of a homogeneous economic area with free movement of goods, services, capital, and labor under equal competitive conditions; extension of the provisions of the EC Single Market program (EC-92) to *EFTA* members; and harmonization of technical standards. To date, Switzerland has not joined the EEA.

European Free Trade Association (EFTA). EFTA was founded by Austria, Finland, Iceland, Liechtenstein, Norway, Sweden, and Switzerland at the Stockholm Convention of 1960. In 1986 Portugal joined, followed by Austria, Finland and Sweden in 1995. The purpose of EFTA was to liberalize trade in industrial products without the political implications of a customs union; free trade in most industrial products has existed among EFTA members since 1977. All EFTA members signed individual free trade agreements with the *European Community* in 1972-73. With the accession of Sweden, Austria, Finland, and Portugal to the European Union, they ceased their membership in EFTA. The members of EFTA today consist of Iceland, Liechtenstein, Norway and Switzerland.

European Parliament. One of the EU's main lawmaking institutions along with the *European Council*

having authority to review policy proposals of the *European Commission* and the *European Council of Ministers.* While the Parliament shares budgetary authority with the Council of Ministers, it does not have full budgetary oversight powers, nor does it have the right to initiate legislation. Parliament is elected by EU voters every five years. Members of European Parliament (MEPs) are based on proportion to population. No country can have fewer than six or more than 96 MEPs. The European Parliament has three locations: Brussels, Luxembourg, and Strasbourg. Luxembourg is the administrative office for the General Secretariat; Parliamentary meetings take place in Strasbourg and in Brussels; and Committee meetings are held in Brussels.

European Union (EU) 1993-present. The European Union (EU) is an economic and political arrangement between 27 European nations. The EU promotes human rights and democracy and has abolished border controls between member countries. The EU has merged into a single market with a common currency – the euro – among some of its members. Current members are Austria, Belgium, Bulgaria, Cyprus, the Czech Republic, Denmark, Estonia, Finland, France, Germany, Great Britain, Greece, Hungary, Ireland, Italy, Latvia, Lithuania, Malta, Luxembourg, the Netherlands, Poland, Portugal, Romania, Slovakia, Slovenia, Spain, and Sweden. *(see European Community).*

EU Council of Ministers. The primary decision-making body of the European Union in which member states are directly represented. Although the Council is a single legal entity, it takes different forms comprising different individuals as members.

Export Credit Group (ECG). A subgroup of the *OECD Trade Committee* comprising all OECD member countries, except Chile and Iceland, that participate in the *Export Credits Arrangement* (Sec. I).

Export-Import Bank of the United States (Ex-Im Bank). The official export credit agency of the United States, created by executive order of the President in 1934. A public corporation, Ex-Im Bank makes guarantees and insures loans to help finance U.S. exports, particularly for equipment to be used in capital improvement projects. Ex-Im Bank also provides short-term insurance against both commercial and political risk, either directly or in conjunction with U.S. commercial banks.

Food and Agricultural Organization (FAO). A specialized agency of the United Nations created in 1945 to increase the production and improve the distribution of agricultural products and improve the conditions of rural populations. The FAO is headquartered in Rome and has liaison offices where many UN organizations are working with other international, intergovernmental, or nongovernmental organizations.

Foreign Credit Insurance Association (FCIA). A U.S. federal agency established in 1961 and part of the *Ex-Im Bank*; became a public company in 1990. FCIA offers insurance to U.S. exporters against commercial risk and political risk. FCIA policies are administered by the FCIA Management Co. and most policies are underwritten by the Great American Insurance Company of Cincinnati, Ohio. Ex-Im Bank still handles sovereign risks for the FCIA, and Great American and other insurance companies handle bankruptcy risks.

General Agreement on Tariffs and Trade (GATT). The GATT contains the rules for world trade in goods, and until the creation of the WTO at the end of the *Uruguay Round* (Sec. 1), it also served as the de facto institutional framework for world trade. The GATT was meant to be an interim arrangement pending establishment of the projected *International Trade Organization* (*ITO*) and was envisaged primarily as a code of conduct for commercial policy among a fairly small group of countries. After the U.S. Congress failed to ratify the ITO charter, the articles of the GATT and related agreements served as the de facto legal framework for world trade (see full text of the agreement at http://www.wto.org/english/docs_e/legal_e/gatt47_e.pdf).

The GATT provided also provided a framework for multilateral negotiations to reduce trade barriers (see *GATT Round,* Sec. I); for *dispute settlement* (Sec. I); and for negotiating new trade rules and improving existing rules). Since the GATT had no formal legal basis as a self-standing international organization, and since the Uruguay Round extended the rules of trade into new areas not covered by the GATT, countries participating in the Uruguay Round decided to create the World Trade Organization as the formal legal institutional framework for world trade. With the creation of the WTO, the GATT was absorbed by the WTO.

General Agreement on Trade in Services (GATS). An agreement negotiated during the *Uruguay Round* (Sec. 1) for the liberalization of trade in services. GATS contains a set of rules similar to the GATT and a framework for the negotiation of the further liberalization of barriers to trade in services. The GATS, like the GATT, is an integral part of the WTO, which serves as the umbrella organization and provides for a common institutional framework for implementing and administering the agreements, settling disputes, and monitoring the trade policies of member countries. All of the current WTO member countries have assumed commitments in various services sectors.

GATT Council. Formerly known as the Council of Representatives, the GATT Council was the principal decision-making body of the GATT on a day-to-day basis. The Council was established in 1960 to conduct GATT business between the annual sessions of the Contracting Parties and met seven to nine times a year. While the GATT Contracting cold vote for or adopt measures as provided for in the General Agreement, the Council acted on a basis of consensus, and its rulings were subsequently approved formally by the Contracting Parties at their annual sessions. With the creation of the WTO, the GATT Council has been replaced by the Council for Trade in Goods and the General Council of the WTO.

General Council. The WTO has a General Council that governs the WTO, along with a Ministerial Conference that meets every two years. The General Council is the WTO's highest-level decision-making body in Geneva and acts on behalf of the Ministerial Conference on all WTO matters. Through a number of governing bodies and committees, the General Council oversees the Council for Trade in Goods, Council for Trade-Related Aspects of Intellectual Property Rights, Council for Trade in Services, and Trade Negotiations Committee. A country seeking accession to the WTO must submit an application to the General Council. Countries seeking observer status to the WTO must also be granted that status through the General Council.

Goods Council. Responsible for the operation of the GATT agreement. Made up of representatives from all WTO member countries, the Goods Council has ten committees (i.e., agriculture, anti-dumping, customs valuation, import licensing, information technology agreement, investment, market access for goods, rules of origin, safeguards, sanitary phyto-sanitary measures, state trading enterprises, subsidies and countervailing measure). Each committee consists of all member countries.

Group of Fifteen (G-15). A group of developing countries seeking recognition as interlocutor for developing countries in discussions of international economic issues with *industrial countries.* Established in 1989 among Algeria, Argentina, Brazil, Egypt, India, Indonesia, Jamaica, Malaysia, Mexico, Nigeria, Peru, Senegal, Venezuela, the former Yugoslavia, and Zimbabwe. Three countries have since been added to the G-15 (i.e., Chile, Iran, and Kenya), and Yugoslavia has left the group, but the name remains the same.

Group of Seven (G- 7). The seven leading *industrial countries* (Sec. I) of the world: the United States, Japan, Germany, France, the United Kingdom, Italy, and Canada. In 1975, the leaders of the G- 7 countries held a summit meeting in Rambouillet, France, to discuss global economic problems in the wake of the OPEC crisis. G- 7 "Economic Summits" have been held annually since then, usually in late June or early July, with the venue rotating among the members.

Group of Eight (G-8). The above countries plus Russia, created by France in 1975. Formerly the Group of 6 (United States, Japan, France, the United Kingdom, Germany, and Italy), Canada joined in 1976 and Russia joined in 1997. Because of the growing number of *industrial countries* (Sec. I), It was announced in September 2009 at the annual summit in Pittsburgh that the Group of 20 (G-20) major economies will replace the G-8.

Group of Seventy-Seven (G- 77). A caucus for the developing countries on economic matters in the United Nations and subsidiary organizations. The group had its origins in the "Joint Declaration of the 77 Developing Countries" appraising the work of the first *UNCTAD* in 1964. During the first Ministerial Meeting in Algiers, Algeria in October 1967, the G-77 adopted the Charter of Algiers, a permanent institutional structure for the group. Membership has grown to 131 countries plus Palestine.

Group of Twenty (G-20). Established in 1999 as a result of the 1997 Asian Financial Crisis to bring together major advanced and emerging economies to regain global financial stability and achieve economic growth and development. The first G-20 meeting was held in December 1999 in Berlin, Germany, and since then the group holds annual meetings at both a ministerial and summit (heads of government) level to promote financial stability and achieve sustainable economic growth and development. Member countries include Argentina, Australia, Brazil, Canada, China, European

Union, France, Germany, India, Indonesia, Italy, Japan, Korea, Mexico, Russia, Saudi Arabia, South Africa, Turkey, United Kingdom, and the United States.

Group on Environmental Measures and International Trade (EMIT). A standing GATT committee for discussions and negotiations concerning *environmental trade measures* (Sec. I). It has been superseded by the WTO Committee on Trade and Environment.

Gulf Cooperation Council (GCC). An alliance formed between Bahrain, Kuwait, Oman, Qatar, Saudi Arabia, and the United Arab Emirates, founded in 1981. Objectives included political coordination and harmonization of economic, financial, commercial, and customs policies; and establishment of a *common external tariff* (Sec. I). Most internal tariffs were eliminated by 1982 with significant unification of tariff schedules and liberalization of trade in services was achieved by 1983. The GCC created a common market in 2008 with plans to adopt a single currency, but attempts were suspended. A customs union was set up in 2003 but it will take many years for it to be fully implemented. The GCC structure includes a Supreme Council, Ministerial Council, Secretariat-General, Consultative Commission, Commission for the Settlement of Disputes, and a Secretary-General. The GCC is headquartered in Riyadh, Saudi Arabia.

Hamburgisches Weltwirtschaftsarchiv (HWWA). Germany's institute for international economic research, based in Hamburg.

Hexagonal Group. See *Central European Initiative.*

Indian Ocean Commission (Commission de l'Ocean Indien [COI]). A *regional cooperation organization* (Sec. 1) including Comoros, Madagascar, Mauritius, Reunion (France), and Seychelles, founded in 1982. Objectives include policy coordination and trade integration. Establishment of a preferential trade regime has been blocked by membership of Mauritius and Comoros in the *PTA*, while Reunion has no autonomy in setting its trade policy. Limited transport links inhibit intra-regional trade.

Industry Functional Advisory Committee (IFAC). One of more than 30 technical, sectoral, and functional committees forming part of the private sector advisory system established by the U.S. Congress to ensure that U.S. trade policy and negotiating objectives reflect U.S. commercial and economic interests. The four IFACs provide cross-sectoral technical advice on standards, customs, and intellectual property and electronic commerce issues. IFAC members are appointed jointly by the USTR and the Secretary of Commerce. See also *ATACs* and *IFACs.*

Industry Policy Advisory Committee (IPAC). A policy-level committee that forms part of the private sector advisory system established by Congress to ensure that U.S. trade policy and negotiating objectives reflect U.S. commercial and economic interests. The IPAC and the individual industry sector advisory committees *(ISACs)* are the source of policy advice and technical expertise on industrial sector issues related to bilateral and multilateral trade negotiations. IPAC members are appointed jointly by the USTR and the Secretary of Commerce. The counterpart committee in the agriculture sector is the *APAC*. See *also ACTPN*.

Industry Sector Advisory Committee (ISAC). One of more than 30 technical, sectoral, and functional committees forming part of the private sector advisory system established by U.S. Congress to ensure that U.S. trade policy and negotiating objectives reflect US commercial and economic interests. Each ISAC represents an individual industrial sector and provides specific, often highly technical advice concerning the likely effects of trade, policy decisions, and negotiating concessions on the sector. ISAC members are appointed jointly by the USTR and the Secretary of Commerce. Counterpart committees in the agricultural sector are known as *ATACs*. See also *IFACs*.

Institut fur Weltwirtschaft (IfW). Germany's institute of world economics based in Kiel.

Institut fur Wirtschaftsforschung (IfO). Germany's economic research institute, based in Munich. The IfO receives funding from the federal and state governments and specializes in research concerning international imbalances.

Institut fur Wirtschaft und Gesellschaft (IWG). Germany's institute for industry and commerce based in Bonn. IWG is privately funded by German companies and associations.

Institut National de la Statistique et des Etudes Economiques (INSEE). France's institute for economic studies and statistics, a government agency roughly equivalent to the U.S. Bureau of Economic Analysis and Bureau of Labor Statistics.

Institute for International Economics (IIE). A private, nonprofit research institution for the study and discussion of international economic issues. IIE was created in 1981 through a grant from the German Marshall Fund of the United States, and receives funding from private corporations and foundations. It is based in Washington, DC. The IIE has subsequently been renamed as the Peterson Institute for International Economics (PIIE) following a substantial grant from Peter Peterson.

Intergovernmental Council of Copper Exporting Countries (CIPEC). An *international commodity organization* (Sec. I) established in 1968 to coordinate members' production and marketing decisions. Chile, Peru, Zambia, and Zaire were CIPEC's initial members with four countries added in 1975, including Australia, Indonesia, Papua New Guinea, and Yugoslavia. Efforts by the group to increase prices by withholding supply were unsuccessful, as were attempts in 1979 to establish a *commodity agreement* (Sec. I) with consuming countries. CIPEC was dissolved in 1988.

Intergovernmental Organizations (IGOs). A term designating international organizations outside the United Nations system through which nations cooperate on a governmental level.

Intergovernmental Policy Advisory Committee (IGPAC). A policy-level committee that forms part of the private sector advisory system established by the U.S. Congress to ensure that U.S. trade policy and negotiating objectives reflect U.S. commercial and economic interests. There are currently 27 IGPAC advisory committee members consisting of representatives from state and local government bodies with an interest in or responsibility for trade. Members are appointed by the USTR.

International Bank for Reconstruction and Development (IBRD). See *World Bank.*

International Bauxite Association (IBA). An *international commodity organization* (Sec. I) established in 1975 and based in Kingston, Jamaica, IBA promoted orderly development of the bauxite industry. Members included Australia, Ghana. Guinea. Guyana, India, Indonesia, Jamaica, Sierra Leone, and Suriname. IBA was dissolved in 1997.

International Center for Settlement of Investment Disputes (ICSID). An international agency affiliated with the *World Bank* that serves as a forum for resolution of international investment disputes. The Center was established by the *Convention on Settlement of I investment Disputes Between States and Nationals of Other States* (Sec. I), signed in 1965. The Center provides impartial panels of conciliators and arbitrators to assist parties in reconciling differences. Failing such conciliation, binding arbitration may be enforced.

International Cocoa Organization (ICCO). An *international commodity organization* (Sec. I) established in 1973 to implement the International Cocoa Agreement of 1972. The Organization is based in London. Exporting members as of October 2011 are Costa Rica, Cote d'Ivoire, Ghana, Indonesia, and Togo. Importing member countries include Austria, Belgium, Bulgaria, Cypress, Czech Republic, Denmark, Estonia, Finland, France, Germany, Greece, Hungary, Ireland, Italy, Latvia, Lithuania, Luxembourg, Malta, the Netherlands, Poland, Portugal, Romania, Slovakia, Slovenia, Spain, Sweden, Switzerland, and the United Kingdom. ICCO has negotiated six agreements since 1973, the last of which was negotiated in Geneva in 2001 and came into effect in October 2003. One of ICCO's main accomplishments has been the founding of the Consultative Board on the World Cocoa Economy.

International Coffee Organization (ICO). An *international commodity organization* (Sec. I) founded in 1963 and based in London. The ICO became the administrative agency of the International Coffee Agreement (ICA) of 1976, a *commodity agreement* (Sec. I) among coffee-producing and consuming countries designed to control the amount of coffee produced and sold internationally. The ICO functions through the International Coffee Council, which consists of all members and meets twice a year. As of August 1011, exporting members are Angola, Brazil, Burundi, Central African Republic, Colombia, Costa Rica, Cote d'Ivoire, Cuba, Ecuador, El Salvador, Ethiopia, Gabon, Ghana, Guatemala, Honduras, India, Indonesia, Jamaica, Kenya, Liberia, Mexico, Nicaragua, Panama, Papua New Guinea, Philippines, Sierra Leone, Tanzania, Thailand, Timor-Leste, Togo, Uganda, Vietnam, Yemen, and Zambia. Importing members are Austria, Belgium, Bulgaria, Cyprus, Czech Republic, Denmark, Estonia, Finland, France, Germany, Greece, Ireland, Italy, Latvia, Lithuania, Luxembourg, Malta, the Netherlands, Norway, Poland, Portugal, Romania, Slovakia, Slovenia, Spain, Sweden, Switzerland, Tunisia, Turkey, the United Kingdom, and the United States. The ICA's rigid export quota system was abandoned in 1989 after widespread discounting to nonmembers. Seven agreements have been adopted, the last of which entered into force in 2007, which strengthened its role as a forum for inter-governmental consultations to facilitate international trade through increased transparency and promote a sustainable coffee economy.

International Cotton Advisory Committee (ICAC). An *international commodity organization* (Sec. I) established in 1939 among ten cotton-producing countries to improve technology and engage in market promotion, and subsequently opened to interested importing and exporting countries. Members as of 2010 include Argentina, Australia, Belgium, Brazil, Burkina Faso, Cameroon, Chad, China, Colombia, Cote d'Ivoire, Egypt, Finland, France, Germany, Greece, India, Iran, Israel, Italy, Kazakhstan, Kenya, Korea, Mali, Mexico, Mozambique, the Netherlands, Nigeria, Pakistan, Poland, Russia, South Africa, Spain, Sudan, Switzerland, Syria, Tanzania, Togo, Turkey, Uganda, the United States, Uzbekistan, Zambia, and Zimbabwe. ICAC is based in Washington, DC.

International Dairy Products Council. A group established within the GATT framework to oversee the *International Dairy Arrangement* (Sec. I), charged with improving international cooperation and promoting stability of trade in the dairy sector. Members were Argentina, Australia, Botswana, Bulgaria, Egypt, the European Community, Finland, Hungary, Japan, New Zealand, Norway, Poland, Romania, South Africa, Sweden, Switzerland, and Uruguay. This agreement was subsequently discontinued.

International Development Association (IDA). A component of the *World Bank* that lends to the poorest developing countries on lenient terms.

International Finance Corporation (IFC). Established in 1956 as part of the *World Bank* to facilitate the financing of privately owned enterprises in developing countries.

International Fund for Agricultural Development (IFAD). A specialized agency of the United Nations created in 1976 to help developing countries increase their food production with low-interest loans and direct assistance to raise productivity and improve livelihoods.

International Grains Council (IGC). A multilateral cooperation organization that superseded the *International Wheat Council (IWC)* in 1995, which responded to the changing trading environment and the formation of the WTO. Current IGC members consists of Algeria, Argentina, Australia, Canada, Cote d'Ivoire, Cuba, Egypt, the European Union, India, Iran, Japan, Kazakhstan, Kenya, Korea, Morocco, Norway, Pakistan, Russia, Saudi Arabia, South Africa, Switzerland, Tunisia, Turkey, Ukraine, the United

States, and Vatican City. The IGC Secretariat is located in London and provides administrative services for both the IGC and the Food Aid Committee, as well as monitors operations of the Food Aid Convention (FAC).

International Jute Organization (IJO). See *International Jute Study Group (IJSG).*

International Jute Study Group (IJSG). An *international commodity organization* (Sec. I) and the legal successor of the *International Jute Organization* (1984) to administer the International Agreement on Jute and Jute Products. IJSG entered into force in 2002 and was the outcome of a series of meetings and conferences held by UNCTAD in 2000-2001. Present members include Bangladesh, India, Switzerland, and the EU member states (27 countries). The Organization is based in Dhaka, Bangladesh.

International Lead and Zinc Study Group (ILZSG). An *international commodity organization* (Sec. I) established in 1958 to provide for intergovernmental consultations on international trade in lead and zinc. Members are Australia, Belgium, Brazil, Bulgaria, Canada, China, Finland, France, Germany, India, Iran, Ireland, Italy, Japan, Korea, Morocco, the Netherlands, Norway, Peru, Poland, Portugal, Russia, Serbia, South Africa, Spain, Sweden, Thailand, Tunisia, and the United States, and currently account for over 85% of the world's production and usage of lead and zinc. The Group is based in Portugal.

International Meat Council. A group established within the GATT framework to oversee the *Bovine Meat Arrangement* (Sec. I). In addition, the Council conducted studies on trade in bovine meat and organizes consultations among signatory countries, which together account for about 90% of world exports of beef and veal (excluding intra-EC trade), and about 60% of world consumption and production. Members were Argentina, Australia, Austria, Brazil, Bulgaria, Canada, Colombia, and Egypt. the European Community, Finland, Guatemala, Hungary, Japan, New Zealand, Nigeria, Norway, Poland, Romania, South Africa, Sweden, Switzerland, Tunisia, the United States, and Uruguay. The Council has been dissolved.

International Monetary Fund (IMF). The central international monetary institution, the IMP was established after World War II as part of the *Bretton Woods system* (Sec. I) to ensure exchange-rate stability and facilitate resolution of payments imbalances among members. Its original purpose was to contribute to the expansion and growth of international trade by working toward making currencies freely convertible and with relatively stable values. Since the advent of flexible and managed exchange rates in the years since 1971, the IMF has assumed responsibility for monitoring members' compliance with guidelines proscribing exchange-rate manipulation to gain unfair competitive advantage over other members. Through its ability to provide funds for countries to ease temporary balance-of-payments difficulties, the IMF can exert considerable influence over their economic policies. The IMF is headquartered in Washington, DC.

International Natural Rubber Organization (INRO). An *international commodity organization* (Sec.l) formed in 1980 to implement the International Natural Rubber Agreement of 1979. As of September 1999, the participating nations agreed to terminate the Agreement. (See *International Rubber Research and Development Board.*

International Olive Council (IOC). An *international commodity organization* (Sec. l) formed in 1959 to administer the International Olive Oil Agreement. The IOC contributes to sustainable development of olive growing and provides a forum for discussions on policy making. Members as of December 2010 include Albania, Algeria, Argentina, the European Union, Croatia, Egypt, Iran, Iraq, Israel, Jordan, Lebanon, Libya, Montenegro, Morocco, Syria, Tunisia, and Turkey. The Council is based in Madrid.

International Organization for Standardization (also referred to as the International Standards Organization [ISO]). A specialized international agency promoting the development of worldwide standardization and other activities related to *technical barriers to trade* (Sec. l). Founded in 1946, the ISO as of 2011 is comprised of the national standards bodies of 162 countries. ISO management and leadership standards include ISO 26000, social responsibility; ISO 31000, risk management; ISO 50001, energy management; and ISO 9000 quality management; and ISO 14000, environmental management. The ISO Secretariat is located in Geneva, Switzerland.

International Rice Commission (IRC). An international organization established in 1948 in Rome to promote national and international action concerning rice production, conservation, and distribution, but excluding matters relating to international trade. Membership is open to all member states of the *Food and Agricultural Organization (FAO).* Currently, there are 62 member countries of the IRC, which comprise approximately 98% of the global rice harvest.

International Rubber Research and Development Board (IRRDB). A research and development network that brings together natural rubber research institutes in most of the rubber producing countries. With origins that date back to 1934, IRRDB addresses all aspects of natural rubber, from cultivation to the development of new products. IRRDB is based in Kuala Lumpur, Malaysia. Members include Brazil, Cameroon, China, Vietnam, Cote d'Ivoire, France, Gabon, India, Indonesia, Malaysia, Mexico, Philippines, Sri Lanka, Thailand, Nigeria, Cambodia, Ethiopia, Guatemala, and Myanmar. See also *Association of Natural Rubber Producing Countries* and *International Natural Rubber Organization.*

International Sugar Organization (ISO). An *international commodity organization* (Sec. l) established in 1968 to administer the International Sugar Agreement; it succeeded the International Sugar Council, which functioned from 1937 to 1958. The ISO is based in London. In 1992 ISO members adopted a resolution establishing the text of a new, permanent International Sugar Agreement, which came into force provisionally as of January 1993. The new Agreement contains market-transparency provisions, but does not contain economic provisions. The United States was not able to agree to certain provisions of the new Agreement, and accordingly left the ISO at the end of 1992. Membership of the 1992 International Sugar Agreement include Argentina, Australia, Barbados, Belize, Brazil, Cameroon, Chad, Colombia, Congo, Costa Rica, Cote d'Ivoire, Croatia, Cuba, Dominican Republic, Equador, European Union (27 member states), Egypt, El Salvadore, Ethiopia, Fiji, Ghana, Guatemala, Guyana, Honduras, India, Indonesia, Iran, Jamaica, Kenya, Korea, Malawi, Mauritius, Mexico, Moldova, Morocco, Nicaragua, Pakistan, Panama, Paraguay, Philippines, Russia, Serbia, South Africa, Sudan, Swaziland, Switzerland, Tanzania, Thailand, Trinidad & Tobago, Tunisia, Uganda, Ukraine, United Arab Emirates, Vietnam, Zambia, and Zimbabwe.

International Tea Committee. An international organization established in London in 1933 to administer the International Tea Agreement, which was signed by representatives of the tea industries in Ceylon, India, and the Netherlands East Indies, and was in force from 1933 through 1955. Since 1979, the Committee has functioned as a statistical and information center. Membership is broken down into three categories: full membership, which comprise organizations that represent interests of tea in their country; associate membership, which includes organizations to receive selected publications and information; and corporate membership, which is open to private sector companies involved in tea trade. Active participating organizations are from Bangladesh, India, Indonesia, Kenya, Malawi, Sri Lanka, and Zimbabwe; consumers in Canada and the United States; and the European Tea Committee.

International Textiles and Clothing Bureau (ITCB). Founded in 1984 by 18 developing countries to coordinate the negotiating positions of developing country textile exporters in the *Uruguay Round* (Sec. I). Founding member countries included Argentina, Bangladesh, Brazil, Colombia, China, Egypt, Hong Kong, India, Indonesia, Jamaica, Korea, Macau, Mexico, Pakistan, Peru, Sri Lanka, Turkey, and Uruguay. See *Multifiber Arrangement* (Sec. I).

International Tin Council. An international organization originally established in 1956 in London to administer the International Tin Agreement, a *commodity agreement* (Sec. I) among 27 countries that was intended to foster price stability in international tin markets. Divergent views among consuming countries led to collapse of the Agreement in 1985, and the Council is now defunct.

International Trade Administration (ITA). Part of the U.S. Department of Commerce that administers portions of U.S. trade laws, including aspects of anti-dumping duties and countervailing duties.

International Trade Centre (ITC). A joint agency of the *World Trade Organization* and *UNCTAD*, based in Geneva, Switzerland. The ITC provides technical assistance to help developing countries become more competitive in global markets through programs focused on economic, social, and environmental sustainability.

International Trade Commission (ITC). See *U.S. International Trade Commission.*

International Trade Organization (ITO). (Not to be confused with *Multilateral Trade Organization,* Sec. I). An international organization envisaged as part of a triad along with the *International Monetary Fund* and the *World Bank* that was to govern the international economy under the *Bretton Woods System* (Sec. I). The ITO never came into being; see *Havana Charter* (Sec. I).

International Tropical Timber Organization (ITTO). An *international commodity organization* (Sec. I) established in 1985 under the auspices of the United Nations to implement the International Tropical Timber Agreement (ITTA) of 1983, which governed ITTO until December 1996. Negotiations for a successor agreement concluded in 2006 under UNCTAD. ITO producing members include Bolivia, Brazil, Cambodia, Cameroon, Central African Republic, Colombia, Congo, Cote d'Ivoire, Democratic Republic of Congo, Ecuador, Figi, Gabon, Ghana, Guatemala, Guyana, Honduras, India, Indonesia, Liberia, Malaysia, Mexico, Myanmar, Nigeria, Panama, Papua New Guinea, Peru, Philippines, Thailand, Togo, Suriname, Trinidad and Tobago, Vanutu, and Venezuela.

Consumer members are Austria, Australia, Belgium/Luxembourg, Canada, China, Denmark, Egypt, Finland, France, Germany, Greece, Ireland, Italy, Japan, Korea, Nepal, Netherlands, New Zealand, Norway, Poland, Portugal, Spain, Sweden, Switzerland, the United Kingdom, and the United States. The organization is based in Yokohama. Japan.

International Whaling Commission (IWC). An organization established in 1946 in Washington, DC, under the International Convention for the Regulation of Whaling. Today the IWC has a full-time Secretariat located in Cambridge, England. Members include Antigua and Barbuda, Argentina, Australia, Austria, Belgium, Belize, Benin, Brazil, Bulgaria, Cambodia, Cameroon, Chile, China, Colombia, Republic of the Congo, Costa Rica, Cote d'Ivoire, Croatia, Cypress, Czech Republic, Denmark, Dominica, Dominican Republic, Equador, Eritrea, Estonia, Finland, France, Germany, Ghana, Greece, Grenada, Guatamala, Guinea-Bissau, Republic of Guinea, Hungary, Iceland, India, Ireland, Israel, Italy, Japan, Kenya, Kiribati, Korea, Laos, Lithuania, Luxenbourg, Mali, Marshall Islands, Mauritania, Mexico, Monaco, Mongolia, Morocco, Nauru, the Netherlands, New Zealand, Nicaragua, Norway. Oman. Palau, Panama, Peru, Poland, Portugal, Romania, Russia, San Marino, St. Kitts & Nevis, St. Lucia, St. Vincent and the Grenadines, Senegal, Slovak Republic, Slovenia, Solomon Islands, South Africa, Spain, Suriname, Sweden, Switzerland,Tanzania, Togo, Tuvalu, the United Kingdom, the United States, and Uruguay. Beginning in 1986. the IWC set all catch limits for commercial whaling at zero, pending assessment of whale stocks and development of new whale management procedures.

International Wheat Council. Established in 1949 to stabilize international trade in wheat and flour. Various wheat agreements (1949, 1953, 1956, 1967, 1971, and 1986) were implemented by the IWC. The IWC was superseded by the *International Grains Council* in 1995.

International Wool Secretariat (IWS). An organization established in 1937 by representatives of the Australian, South African, and New Zealand Wool Boards. The

Uruguayan Wool Secretariat joined in 1970. The organization engaged in research, developed test methods and standards, and conducted product certification programs. In 1994 the IWS merged with the Australian Wool Research and Promotion Organisation (AWRAP), and as of 1997 changed its name to the Woolmark Company.

Investment Policy Advisory Committee (INPAC). A policy-level committee that formed part of the private sector advisory system established by Congress to ensure that U.S. trade policy and negotiating objectives reflected U.S. commercial and economic interests. The INPAC was the primary committee for private sector advice on investment-related negotiations in the *Uruguay Round* (Sec. 1) and NAFTA as well as on *Bilateral Investment Treaties* (Sec. I). Members were appointed by the USTR.

Islamic Common Market. See *Economic Cooperation Organization.*

Itamaraty. Brazil's Ministry of External Relations.

Japan Center for Economic Research (JCER). A nongovernmental economic forecasting organization funded primarily by Japanese corporations. JCER conducts seminars and lectures, sponsors international conferences, undertakes research projects, and publishes reports as well as a monthly bulletin.

Japan Economic Research Institute (JERI). A nongovernmental economic research institute funded by Japanese corporations. JERI provides research and advisory services to government and business leaders and academia.

Japan External Trade Organization (JETRO). A government-related organization charged with gathering commercial intelligence, conducting market research, and performing public relations services for Japanese industry worldwide. JETRO was originally established in 1958 to promote Japanese exports abroad. Today JETRO also focuses on increasing foreign direct investment into Japan and puts special emphasis on supporting small-medium size firms in order to maximize their export potential. While it nominally remains an independent public corporation, JETRO is effectively controlled by *METI,* and its overseas offices are staffed almost exclusively with METI personnel.

Keidanren. A federation of Japanese economic organizations, Keidanren is Japan's premier organization representing big business. Keidanren leaders often confer with Japanese government officials in developing and implementing policy. See also *Nikkeiren.*

Keiretsu. Major industrial groups or combines in Japan. "Horizontal" keiretsu – some descended from pre-World War II zaibatsu – consist of affiliated companies in diverse fields. The six principal horizontal keiretsu are Mitsubishi, Sumitomo, Mitsui, Sanwa, Fuyo, and Dai Ichi Kangyo. Most of Japan's largest corporations are linked to one or another of these groups. "Vertical " keiretsu consist of a network of suppliers and distributors centered around a single, large firm. See also *sogo shasha.*

Labor Advisory Committee (LAC). A policy-level committee that forms part of the private sector advisory system established by Congress to ensure that U.S.trade policy and negotiating objectives reflect U.S. commercial and economic interests. The LAC provides advice on labor issues related to bilateral and multilateral trade negotiations. The roughly 100 LAC members, representing the range of organized labor in the United States, are appointed by the USTR in conjunction with the Secretary of Labor.

Latin American Integration Association (LAIA) or Asociacion Latino Americana de Integracion (ALADI). A *regional cooperation organization* (Sec. 1) and preferential arrangement including Argentina, Bolivia, Brazil, Chile, Colombia, Ecuador, Mexico, Paraguay, Peru, Uruguay, and Venezuela. LAIA was established by the Montevideo Treaty of 1980 and it superseded the Latin American Free Trade Area (LAFTA), which was abandoned largely because of inflexible rules governing the integration process.

Mano River Union (MRU). A customs union founded in 1973 as a bilateral agreement between Liberia and Sierra Leone; Guinea joined in 1980. Objectives included trade expansion through elimination of tariffs on intra-group trade and economic integration and sectoral cooperative programs, but little progress was made in reducing nontariff barriers. Policy coordination was suspended due to the civil war in Liberia; however, the Union was reactivated at a summit between the countries' leaders in 2004. In 2008 Cote d'Ivoire also agreed to join the Union. While trade is taking place beween the countries, very little is documented.

Matignon or Hotel Matignon. The official residence e of France's Prime Minister.

Mouvement des Entreprises de France: The largest employers union in France, with over 700,000 member firms. (See *Conseil National du Patronat Francais [CNPF]*)

MERCOSUR. See *Southern Common Market.*

METI. Japan's Ministry of Economy, Trade, and Industry, responsible for international trade policy (including trade finance and export insurance) as well as various industrial policies of Japan (See *MITI).*

MITI. Japan's Ministry of International Trade and Industry, responsible for international trade policy – the role of which was assumed by *METI*, the Ministry of Economy, Trade, and Industry, in 2001.

MOF. Ministry of Finance (various countries).

MOFA. Ministry of Foreign Affairs (various countries).

MOFERT. China's Ministry of Foreign Economy Relations and Trade.

Multilateral Investment Guarantee Agency (MIGA). An independent agency of the *World Bank Group* established in 1988 to guarantee eligible investments against noncommercial losses.

Multilateral Trade Organization (MTO). An organizational arrangement proposed during the *Uruguay Round* (Sec. 1) to implement the results of the Round, including agreements in areas such as *services* and *intellectual property rights.* In place of an MTO the negotiators decided to create the *World Trade Organization* as the overall umbrella organization for the implementation of the agreements resulting from the Uruguay Round.

National Association of Manufacturers (NAM). An organization representing U.S. industry views on national and international economic issues, including trade, international finance and investment, and multinational corporations. NAM also reviews and responds on legislation, administrative rulings, and judicial decisions affecting U.S. industry. It is based in Washington, DC.

National Bureau of Economic Research (NBER). Founded in 1920, a private, nonprofit, nonpartisan organization engaged in quantitative analysis of U.S. domestic and international economic issues. NBER-sponsored studies and conferences generally involve leading economists from U.S. universities. It is based in Cambridge, Massachusetts.

National Economic Council (NEC). The NEC was established at the outset of the Clinton Administration to coordinate U.S. domestic and international economic policies. Chaired by the President, the NEC is composed of the Vice President, the Secretaries of State, Treasury, Commerce, Agriculture, Labor, Housing and Urban Development, Transportation, and Energy , as well as the Administrator of the Environmental Protection Agency, the Chair of the Council of Economic Advisors, the Director of the Office of Management and Budget, the U.S. Trade Representative, the National Security Advisor, and the Assistants to the President for Economic Policy, Domestic Policy, and Science and Technology Policy. All executive departments and agencies, whether or not represented on the NEC, coordinate economic policy through the Council. The NEC Deputies Committee considers decision memoranda from the *TPRG* as well as particularly important or controversial trade-related issues and thus serves as the highest level group in the interagency mechanism for developing and coordinating U.S. policies on international trade and trade-related investment issues.

National Foreign Trade Council (NTFC). An organization of U.S. companies engaged in international trade and investment, based in Washington, DC. The Council advocates open international trade, export expansion, and policies to assist U.S. companies competing in world markets.

National Institute of Economic and Social Research (NIESR). A privately funded British research institute specializing in macroeconomic issues, industrial productivity, and the international economy.

Nikkeiren. Japan's employers' federation, roughly equivalent to the U.S. National Association of Manufacturers. See also *Keidanren.*

Nongovernmental Organizations (NGOs). In general parlance, the term NGO refers to organizations representing various private economic, social, or policy interests. In international governmental parlance, the term originated from the UN as early as 1945. It referred to transnational organizations of private parties, including professional associations, foundations, multinational businesses, or other groups with a common interest in a particular policy issue. Many NGOs are funded or partially funded by governments but maintain nongovernmental status usually by excluding government representatives from membership in the organization. Sometimes they are referred to as civil society organizations (CSOs).

Nordic Regional Cooperation (Nordic Group). A regional cooperation established by the Helsinki Convention in 1962 between Denmark, Finland, Iceland, Norway, and Sweden. These countries coordinated and covered various activities pertaining to GATT/ WTO, including economic, trade, environmental, and social policies as well as relations with outside countries and multilateral organizations. An inter-parliamentary group functioned as the Nordic Council, headquartered in Stockholm. Prime Ministers of the Nordic countries decided in October 1992 to establish a rotating presidency on the EC model in an effort to increase Nordic influence within the *EEA.* Institutional mechanisms for trade policy coordination among members were well established members that had generally been successful in harmonizing policies and establishing cohesion for participation as a group in GATT/WTO consultations and negotiations. The Nordic Group ceased to function when Finland and Sweden joined the EU.

One-Thirteen Committee (113 Committee). The central organization in the trade policy-making structure of the *European Community.* The Committee was comprised of 12 member-state delegates and one from the *EU Commission* and was the primary link between the Commission and member states on trade issues. The 113 Committee assisted the Commission in defining and implementing the Community's commercial policy, including tariff rates, export policies, and measures to liberalize trade or protect EC industries. While the Commission usually acted as the policy initiator and primary trade negotiator with non-EC countries, it worked closely with the 113 Committee -- taking into account various national interests -- in order to ensure eventual approval of its draft agreements. It was subsumed in 1993 into the institutional structure of the European Union.

Organization for Economic Cooperation and Development (OECD). An international organization headquartered in Paris that serves as a forum for discussion of trade and other economic and social issues confronting the industrial market economies. The OECD was established in 1960 as successor to the OEEC, the organization originally set up to assist European postwar economic recovery under the Marshall Plan. OECD periodically publishes surveys of member countries' economic performance and prospects as well as the semi-annual Economic Outlook covering the entire industrialized world and is the principal source of comparative data on the industrial economies. OECD publications cover a wide range of issues including trade, banking and financial markets, employment, social policies, the environment, agriculture, energy, industry, development aid, science and technology, R&D, nation, education, and transportation. The member countries use the OECD and its various committees and working groups to conduct both studies and negotiations on particular economic, financial, and trade issues.

The OECD Secretariat consists of economists, statisticians, and analysts together that work alongside OECD personnel to support meetings and conferences and prepare documentation and publications. The Secretariat also calls on established scholars in various fields to participate as consultants in the work of the Organization. The Secretariat is divided into specialized Directorates, corresponding roughly to the principal Committees. Several autonomous and semi-autonomous bodies have also been set up within the OECD framework, each with its own governing committee.

Each of the member countries maintains a permanent delegation to OECD, headed by an ambassador who attends weekly meetings of the OECD Council, chaired by the Secretary-General. Every year in late Mayor early June, the Council meets at the Ministerial level, under the chairmanship of one or more ministers from the member country elected annually to this function. There are currently 34 member countries Australia, Austria, Belgium, Canada, Chili, Czech Republic, Denmark, Finland, France, Germany, Greece, Hungary, Iceland, Ireland, Israel, Italy, Japan, Korea, Luxembourg, Mexico, the Netherlands, New Zealand, Norway, Poland, Portugal, Slovakia, Slovenia, Spain, Sweden, Switzerland, Turkey, the United Kingdom, and the United States. The *EU Commission* participates in OECD activities alongside the EU member countries.

Organization of East Caribbean States (OECS). A customs union formed in 1981 as a subregional group of *CARICOM*, including Antigua and Barbuda, Dominica, Grenada, Montserrat, St. Kitts and Nevis, St. Lucia, and St. Vincent and the Grenadines. Associate members are Anguilla and the British Virgin Islands. Only Dominica and St. Vincent have implemented the OECS common external tariff.

Organization of Petroleum Exporting Countries (OPEC). A producer cartel comprising the leading oil-producing countries that seek to coordinate oil production and pricing policies. Members include Algeria, Angola, Ecuador, Iran, Iraq, Kuwait, Libya, Nigeria, Qatar, Saudi Arabia, the United Arab Emirates, and Venezuela. OPEC was established in September 1960 and is headquartered in Vienna, Austria.

Organization of Black Sea Economic Cooperation. See *Black Sea Economic Cooperation (BSEC)*.

Overseas Development Council (ODC). A research and educational organization that encourages review of U.S. policies toward developing countries by the business community, educators, policymakers, and journalists. It is based in Washington, DC.

Overseas Private Investment Corporation (OPIC). An agency of the U.S. government established in 1971 to promote private investment in overseas projects, especially in developing countries. OPIC provides start-up assistance as well as direct loans and loan guarantees for equity participation in foreign ventures, but its primary activity is insuring against losses sustained by U.S. investors in foreign equity ventures as the result of political risks. OPIC services are available only to U.S. citizens and U.S.-controlled corporations.

Pacific Basic Economic Council (PBEC). PBEC's multinational membership includes senior executives from Australia; Brunei; Darussalam; Canada; Chili; People's Republic of China; Colombia; Ecuador; Hong Kong, China; Indonesia; Japan; Korea; Malaysia; Mexico; New Zealand; Peru; The Philippines; Russian Federation; Singapore; Chinese Taipei; Thailand; and the United States. To best serve members' interests, PBEC has identified cross-sector issues and developed policy recommendations in trade, finance, economic development, human capital development, environment and sustainable development, and infrastructure development and maintenance. PBEC holds annual conferences and periodic meetings of working groups and is headquartered in Hong Kong.

Paris Club (Club de Paris). An informal designation for meetings between representatives of a developing country that wish to renegotiate its official debt (normally excluding debts owned by and to the private sector without official guarantees) and representatives of the relevant creditor governments and international institutions. The meetings are traditionally chaired by a senior official of the French Treasury.

Paris Union. The organization of signatory states to the *Paris Convention* for the Protection of Industrial Property *(*Sec. I*)*.

Pentagonal Group. See *Central European Initiative.*

Preferential Trade Area for Eastern and Southern Africa (PTA). A treaty signed in 1981 toward an eventual common market including Angola, Burundi, Comoros, Djibouti, Ethiopia, Kenya, Lesotho, Madagascar, Malawi, Mauritius, Mozambique, Nambia, Rwanda, Seychelles, Somalia, Sudan, Swaziland, Tanzania, Uganda, Zambia, and Zimbabwe. Objectives included commercial and economic cooperation, harmonization of policies; elimination of tariffs on all goods traded within region by 2000, and reduction of nontariff barriers; removal of foreign exchange constraints in intra-regional trade; and cooperation in agriculture. Some tariffs have been reduced on a limited range of products; a common list of goods receiving preferential rates is in effect. Restrictive rules of origin and value-added criteria have reduced coverage of intra-group trade liberalization. The PTA was replaced with COMESA in 1994.

Quai d'Orsay. France's Ministry of Foreign Affairs.

Regional Cooperation for Development (RCD). See *Economic Cooperation Organization.*

Rio Group. A *regional cooperation organization* (Sec. 1) created in December 1986. Current members include Argentina, Belize, Bolivia, Brazil, Chile, Colombia, Costa Rica, Cuba, Dominican Republic, Ecuador, El Salvadore, Guatemala, Guyana, Haiti, Honduras, Jamaica, Mexico, Nicaragua, Panama, Paraguay, Peru, Uruguay, and Venezuela.

SECOFI. Mexico's Secretariat of Commerce and Industrial Development.

Services Policy Advisory Committee (SPAC). A policy-level committee that forms part of the private sector advisory system established by Congress to ensure that U.S. trade policy and negotiating objectives reflect U.S. commercial and economic interests. Members are appointed by the USTR and are broadly representative of the spectrum of service industries in the United States.

Shoko Kaigisho. A Japanese organization roughly equivalent to the U.S. Chamber of Commerce. See also *Keidanren.*

South Asian Association for Regional Cooperation (SAARC). A *regional cooperation organization* (Sec. 1) founded in 1985. Originally, Bangladesh, Bhutan, India, Maldives, Nepal, Pakistan, and Sri Lanka made up the SAARC. Afghanistan joined in 2005. Objectives include promoting and improving the welfare and quality of life of the people of South Asia as well as to increase economic, social, and cultural development. SAARC countries also aim to cooperate with regional and international organizations to strengthen trade relations.

South Pacific Regional Trade and Economic Cooperation Agreement (SPARTECA). A non-reciprocal preferential arrangement including Australia, Cook Islands, Federated States of Micronesia, Fiji, Kiribati, Marshall Islands, Nauru, New Zealand, Niue, Papua New Guinea, Solomon Islands, Tonga, Tuvalu, Vanuatu, and Western Samoa, founded in 1981. Objectives include trade, investment, and industrial cooperation, aimed at redressing the unequal trade relationship of Australia and New Zealand with the small island economies in the Pacific region. Beneficiaries have been granted duty-free access to Australia and New Zealand for all products except sugar, textiles, clothing, footwear, steel, and passenger motor vehicles.

Southern African Customs Union (SACU). A customs union founded in 1969, including Botswana, Lesotho, Namibia, South Africa, and Swaziland. SACU superseded a customs union among the participants dating from the colonial era. In October 1992 Pretoria called for replacing SACU with a new regional trade arrangement, indicating that financial transfers to its SACU partners under a common income pool arrangement had become unacceptably high. A common external tariff is still in effect. SACU has been generally successful in liberalizing intra-regional trade, albeit behind high external trade barriers.

Southern African Development Community (SADC). A *regional cooperation organization* (Sec. 1) including Angola, Botswana, Democratic Republic of Congo, Lesotho,

Madagascar, Malawi, Mauritius, Mozambique, Namibia, Seychelles, South Africa, Swaziland, Tanzania, Zambia, and Zimbabwe. SADC was signed August 1992, superseding the Southern African Development Coordinating Conference established by the Lusaka Declaration of 1980. Objectives include economic integration through free movement of trade, capital, and labor and policy harmonization and project coordination to enable the region to compete effectively in the global marketplace.

Southern Common Market (Mercado Common del Sur [MERCOSUR] or Mercado Comum do Sul [MERCOSUL]). An agreement between Argentina, Brazil, Paraguay, and Uruguay, signed in March 1991 for the purpose of promoting free trade. It has been amended many times over the years and is now a customs union.

Tariff Commission. See *U.S. International Trade Commission.*

Textile Surveillance Board (TSB). A GATT standing committee that was responsible for oversight of the bilateral agreements between developed and developing countries under the *Multifiber Arrangement* (Sec. I).

Trade and Investment Council. A forum for bilateral consultations between the United States and various countries which have signed a *Trade and Investment Framework Agreement* (Sec. I) with Washington.

Trade Negotiations Committee (TNC). The steering group established at the outset of the GATT *Uruguay Round* (Sec. I) to oversee the negotiations. Also established were a Group of Negotiations on Goods, a Group of Negotiations on Services, and a Surveillance Body, all of which were subordinate to the TNC.

Trade Policy Research Centre. A London-based organization established in 1968 to promote independent research and discussion of international economic policy issues.

Trade Policy Review Group (TPRG). A senior level interagency group responsible for developing and coordinating U.S. policies on international trade and trade-related investment issues. The TPRG addresses particularly significant trade policy questions as well all issues on which agreement is not reached in the *TPSC.* The TPRG is administered by USTR and chaired by the Deputy U.S. Trade Representative. Member agencies, represented on the TPRG at the Under Secretary level, include the Departments of Commerce, Agriculture, State, Treasury, Labor, Justice, Defense, Interior, Transportation, and Energy, the Office of Management and Budget, the Council of Economic Advisors, and the International Development Cooperation Agency. The *National Economic Council* and the National Security Council have a joint representative. The *U.S. International Trade Commission* is an observer. Representatives of other agencies also may be invited to specific meetings.

Trade Policy Staff Committee (TPSC). The first-line operating group in the interagency mechanism for developing and coordinating U.S. policies on international trade and trade-related investment issues. The TPSC is administered and chaired by USTR. Member agencies, represented on the TPSC at the senior civil servant level, include the Departments of Commerce, Agriculture, State, Treasury, Labor, Justice, Defense, Interior, Transportation, and Energy, the Office of Management and Budget, the Council of Economic Advisors, and the International Development Cooperation Agency; the National Economic Council and the National Security Council have a joint representative. The *U.S. International Trade Commission* is a non-voting member. Representatives of other agencies also may be invited to specific meetings. Supporting the TPSC are more than 60 subcommittees and task forces focusing on specific topics to which USTR assigns responsibilities for economic analysis through the interagency process. Conclusions and recommendations are then presented to the full TPSC as the basis for reaching interagency policy consensus. See also *TPRG*.

United Nations Commission on International Trade Law (UNCTRAL). A specialized body of the United Nations established in 1966 to promote harmonization of international trade law. The Commission's functions include coordination of the work of various international organizations active in trade.

United Nations Conference on Trade and Development (UNCT AD). An organ of the UN General Assembly that has convened quadrenially since 1964 to discuss international economic and trade relations and measures that might be taken by *industrial countries* to accelerate the pace of economic development in LDCs. All members of the United Nations are members of *UNCTAD*; the Trade and Development Board handles day-to-day issues between *UNCTAD* sessions.

United Nations Conference on Trade and Development (UNCTAD). A permanent, intergovernmental body established in 1964 as the principal organ of the United Nations General Assembly dealing with trade, investment, and development issues.

United Nations Industrial Development Organization (UNIDO). A UN specialized agency established in 1966 to promote and accelerate the industrialization of LDCs. It provides a forum for consultations between industrial and developing countries concerning industrial development and provides technical assistance to LDCs. UNIDO is headquartered in Vienna, Austria.

U.S. Chamber of Commerce. A federation of business, trade, and professional associations; state and local chambers of commerce; and American chambers of commerce abroad. The Chamber represents the business community's views on domestic and international economic policy issues; among its activities is maintenance of a trade negotiations information service. It is based in Washington, DC.

U.S. Customs Service. An agency within the U.S. Department of the Treasury charged with enforcement of the tariff acts and other laws relating to the importation of goods into the United States.

U.S. International Trade Commission (ITC or USITC). An independent regulatory and fact-finding agency of the U.S. government whose members and staff make determinations of *injury* (Sec. I) and recommendations concerning industries or workers seeking relief from increasing import competition. In addition, upon the request of Congress or the President, the USITC conducts comprehensive studies of specific industries and trade problems and the probable impact on specific U.S. industries of proposed reductions in U.S. tariffs and nontariff barriers. The Commission may also undertake such studies on its own initiative. The USITC was established by the Trade Act of 1974 as the successor agency to the U.S. Tariff Commission. Its six members are appointed to nine-year terms by the President with the advice and consent of the Senate.

United States Trade Representative (USTR). An official in the Executive Office of the President with the rank of Ambassador responsible for the formulation and implementation of U.S. trade policy and for working with Congress accordingly. The USTR has lead responsibility for coordinating U.S. government positions in and conducting international trade negotiations. USTR is also the designation for the White House office headed by the U.S. Trade Representative. Prior to the Trade Act of 1979, which established the Office of the USTR, the comparable official was known as the President's Special Representative for Trade Negotiations (STR), a position first established in the Trade Act of 1962.

Visegrad Group. See *Central European Free Trade Agreement.*

West African Economic Community or Communaute Economique de l' Afrique de l'Ouest (CEAO). A customs union including Benin, Burkina Faso, Ivory Coast, Mali, Mauritania, Niger, and Senegal. It was founded in 1973, superseding the Customs Union of West African States. Objectives include elimination of internal tariffs and nontariff barriers to intra-regional trade; establishment of a common external tariff; freer labor mobility within the region; development of transportation and communications linkages; and harmonization of investment rules. Intra-regional trade in raw materials is largely duty-free. However, tariff-cutting procedures give members wide latitude to exclude sensitive products from liberalization, limiting coverage of manufactures and processed goods to products with little potential for intra-regional trade. Fewer than 500 products receive regional preferences. A community convention permitting free flow of migrant workers is in place.

West African Economic and Monetary Union or Union Economique et Monetaire Ouest Africaine (UEMOA). An organization of eight countries, including Benin, Burkina Faso, Cote D'Ivoire, Guinea-Bissau, Mali, Niger, Senegal, and Togo. It was approved by heads of state at the July 1992 summit of the West African Monetary Union. UEMOA was established to promote economic integration among countries that share the CFA franc as a common currency, as well as to harmonize tax policies and the legal environment.

Whitehall. Britain's Foreign Ministry.

World Bank. The International Bank for Reconstruction and Development (IBRD), commonly referred to as the World Bank, is an intergovernmental financial institution headquartered in Washington, D.C. Established in 1945 as part of the *Bretton Woods system* (Sec. I), its primary function is to make long-term, low-interest loans to developing countries.

World Customs Organization (WCO). See *Customs Cooperation Council (CCC).*

World Intellectual Property Organization (WIPO). A specialized agency of the United Nations dealing with legal and administrative aspects of intellectual property – such as copyrights, patents, and trademarks – and seeking to promote international cooperation in the protection of *intellectual property rights* (Sec. I). Among its treaties and agreements, WIPO administers the International Union for the Protection of Industrial Property (the *Paris Union)* formed to reduce discrimination in national patent practices, and the International Union for the Protection of Literary and Artistic Works (the *Berne Union)* formed to reduce discrimination in national copyright laws. WIPO is headquartered in Geneva, Switzerland.

The World Trade Organization (WTO). The organization officially commenced on January 1, 1995, under the Marrakesh Agreement, replacing the *General Agreement on Tariffs and Trade (GATT),* which commenced in 1948. The organization establishes global rules of trade between nations and deals with regulation of trade between participating countries. The WTO provides a framework for negotiating and formalizing trade agreements and a dispute resolution process aimed at enforcing participants' adherence to WTO agreements that are signed by representatives of member governments and ratified by their parliaments. Most of the issues that the WTO focuses on derive from previous trade negotiations, especially from the *Uruguay Round* (Sec. 1) (1986–1994). The WTO has 153 members, representing more than 97% of the world's population, and 30 observers, most seeking membership. The WTO is governed by a ministerial conference, meeting every two years; a general council, which implements the conference's policy decisions and is responsible for day-to-day administration; and a director-general, who is appointed by the ministerial conference. The WTO's headquarters is at the *Centre William Rappard* (Sec. 1), Geneva.

28622134R00239

Made in the USA
Lexington, KY
24 December 2013